Statistical Analysis with Python®

by Joseph Schmuller

for
dummies®
A Wiley Brand

Statistical Analysis with Python® For Dummies®

Published by: **John Wiley & Sons, Inc.**, 111 River Street, Hoboken, NJ 07030-5774, www.wiley.com

For general information on our other products and services, please contact our Customer Care Department within the U.S. at 877-762-2974, outside the U.S. at 317-572-3993, or fax 317-572-4002. For technical support, please visit https://hub.wiley.com/community/support/dummies.

Wiley publishes in a variety of print and electronic formats and by print-on-demand. Some material included with standard print versions of this book may not be included in e-books or in print-on-demand. If this book refers to media such as a CD or DVD that is not included in the version you purchased, you may download this material at http://booksupport.wiley.com. For more information about Wiley products, visit www.wiley.com.

Library of Congress Control Number is available from the publisher.

ISBN: 978-1-394-37032-0 (pbk); ISBN: 978-1-394-37033-7 (ebk); ISBN: 978-1-394-37034-4 (ebk)

Printed and bound by CPI Group (UK) Ltd, Croydon, CR0 4YY

C9781394370320_101125

Contents at a Glance

Introduction 1

**Part 1: Getting Started with Statistical
Analysis with Python** 7
CHAPTER 1: Data, Statistics, and Decisions 9
CHAPTER 2: Python: What It Does and How It Does It 17

Part 2: Describing Data 45
CHAPTER 3: Getting Graphic 47
CHAPTER 4: Finding Your Center 61
CHAPTER 5: Deviating from the Average 73
CHAPTER 6: Meeting Standards and Standings. 83
CHAPTER 7: Summarizing It All 93
CHAPTER 8: What's Normal? 105

Part 3: Drawing Conclusions from Data 121
CHAPTER 9: The Confidence Game: Estimation 123
CHAPTER 10: One-Sample Hypothesis Testing 137
CHAPTER 11: Two-Sample Hypothesis Testing 159
CHAPTER 12: Testing More than Two Samples 181
CHAPTER 13: More Complicated Testing 211
CHAPTER 14: Regression: Linear, Multiple, and the General Linear Model 233
CHAPTER 15: Correlation: The Rise and Fall of Relationships 273
CHAPTER 16: Curvilinear Regression: When Relationships Get Complicated 289

Part 4: Working with Probability 317
CHAPTER 17: Introducing Probability 319
CHAPTER 18: Introducing Modeling. 341
CHAPTER 19: Probability Meets Regression: Logistic Regression. 363

Part 5: The Part of Tens 373
CHAPTER 20: Ten Tips for R Veterans 375
CHAPTER 21: Ten Valuable Python Resources. 383

Index 387

Table of Contents

INTRODUCTION 1

About This Book... 1
Similarity with These Other For Dummies Books.................. 2
What You Can Safely Skip...................................... 2
Foolish Assumptions... 3
How This Book Is Organized 3
   Part 1: Getting Started with Statistical Analysis
   with Python... 3
   Part 2: Describing Data................................... 3
   Part 3: Drawing Conclusions from Data..................... 3
   Part 4: Working with Probability 4
   Part 5: The Part of Tens 4
Icons Used in This Book 4
Where to Go from Here 5

**PART 1: GETTING STARTED WITH STATISTICAL
ANALYSIS WITH PYTHON** 7

CHAPTER 1: **Data, Statistics, and Decisions** 9
The Statistical (and Related) Notions You Just Have to Know........10
   Samples and populations.................................10
   Variables: Dependent and independent 11
   Types of data 12
   A little probability 13
Inferential Statistics: Testing Hypotheses 14
   Null and alternative hypotheses 15
   Two types of error.....................................16

CHAPTER 2: **Python: What It Does and How It Does It**............ 17
Introducing Colab 18
Exploring the Colab Environment............................20
   Cells 20
   The left panel 22
   The Menu bar..23
   Gemini..24
Introducing Python 26
   Printing 26
   Variable names 28
   Variable types..28
   Lists 31
   Strings 32

Tuples 32
Sets 32
Dictionaries. 33
Working with Python Functions. 34
Checking Out Python Libraries 34
Creating an array. 35
Creating a DataFrame. 36
Installing a library 37
Going Round and Round with Looping 38
Considering Conditionals. 40
Comprehending List Comprehension 41
Defining Your Own Functions 42
Wrapping Up 44

PART 2: DESCRIBING DATA 45

CHAPTER 3: **Getting Graphic** 47
Getting the Data 47
Creating a Histogram 49
Barhopping. 50
Slicing the Pie 53
The Plot of Scatter 55
Of Boxes and Whiskers. 56
Continuous Variables 58
Wrapping Up 60

CHAPTER 4: **Finding Your Center** 61
Means: The Lure of Averages 61
The Average in Python 63
What's your condition?. 63
Exploring the data. 65
Outliers: The flaw of averages. 67
Other means to an end. 67
Medians: Caught in the Middle 69
The Median in Python. 70
Statistics à la Mode 71
The Mode in Python 72

CHAPTER 5: **Deviating from the Average** 73
Measuring Variation 74
Averaging squared deviations: Variance and how
to calculate it 74
Sample variance. 77
Variance in Python 78

Back to the Roots: Standard Deviation. 79
    Population standard deviation 79
    Sample standard deviation 80
Standard Deviation in Python 80
Conditions, Conditions, Conditions 80

CHAPTER 6: **Meeting Standards and Standings**. 83
Catching Some Z's 84
    Characteristics of z-scores 84
    Bonds versus the Bambino 85
    Exam scores 86
z-Scores in Python. 86
Where Do You Stand?. 89
    Ranking in Python 89
    Tied scores 89
    Percentiles 90

CHAPTER 7: **Summarizing It All**. 93
How Many?. 93
The High and the Low. 94
Living in the Moments 95
    A teachable moment. 95
    Back to descriptives. 96
    Skewness 96
    Kurtosis. 99
Tuning in the Frequency. 100
    Nominal variables 101
    Numerical variables 101
    Numerical and nominal together 102
Summarizing a DataFrame. 103

CHAPTER 8: **What's Normal?**. 105
Hitting the Curve 105
    Digging deeper. 106
    Parameters of a normal distribution 107
Working with Normal Distributions 109
    Distributions in Python. 109
    Normal density function in Python. 110
    Plotting a normal curve 110
    Calculating cumulative density 113
    Percentiles and cumulative density 114
    Random sampling 115
A Distinguished Member of the Family 116

PART 3: DRAWING CONCLUSIONS FROM DATA..........121

CHAPTER 9: **The Confidence Game: Estimation** 123
Understanding Sampling Distributions 124
An EXTREMELY Important Idea: The Central Limit Theorem 125
(Approximately) Simulating the central limit theorem.........127
Predictions of the central limit theorem 130
Confidence: It Has Its Limits! 131
Finding Confidence Limits for a Mean 132
Fit to a t..134

CHAPTER 10: **One-Sample Hypothesis Testing**....................137
Hypotheses, Tests, and Errors................................137
Hypothesis Tests and Sampling Distributions..................139
Catching Some Z's Again......................................141
z-Testing in Python 144
t for One 146
t Testing in Python..147
Working with *t*-Distributions 148
Visualizing *t*-Distributions................................149
Testing a Variance 150
Testing a Variance in Python 152
Working with Chi-Square Distributions 155
Visualizing Chi-Square Distributions.........................156

CHAPTER 11: **Two-Sample Hypothesis Testing**...................159
Hypotheses Built for Two.....................................159
Sampling Distributions Revisited 160
Applying the central limit theorem...........................161
Z's once more..163
z-testing for two samples in Python 164
t for Two 166
Estimating population variance...............................166
t-Testing in Python..168
Visualizing the results......................................169
A Matched Set: Hypothesis Testing for Paired Samples 171
Paired Sample *t*-Testing in Python 172
Testing Two Variances 173
F-testing in Python..175
F in conjunction with t......................................176
Working with F-Distributions.................................176
Visualizing F-Distributions 178

CHAPTER 12: Testing More than Two Samples 181

Testing More than Two 181
A thorny problem 182
A solution 183
Meaningful relationships 187
ANOVA in Python 187
Quick and dirty 188
Slower and more involved 188
Visualizing the results 190
After the ANOVA 192
Contrasts in Python 195
Another Kind of Hypothesis, Another Kind of Test 199
Working with repeated measures ANOVA 200
Repeated measures ANOVA in Python 202
Visualizing the results 205
Getting Trendy 206
Trend Analysis in Python 210

CHAPTER 13: More Complicated Testing 211

Cracking the Combinations 211
Interactions 213
The analysis 213
Two-Way ANOVA in Python 215
Visualizing the Two-Way Results 216
Two Kinds of Variables . . . at Once 219
Mixed ANOVA in Python 221
Visualizing the mixed ANOVA results 224
After the Analysis 225
Multivariate Analysis of Variance 226
MANOVA in Python 228
Visualizing the MANOVA results 230
After the analysis 232

CHAPTER 14: Regression: Linear, Multiple, and the General Linear Model 233

The Plot of Scatter 234
Graphing Lines 235
Regression: What a Line! 237
Using regression for forecasting 239
Variation around the regression line 239
Testing hypotheses about regression 241
Linear Regression in Python 246
Regression and ANOVA 249
Making predictions using Python 250

Juggling Many Relationships at Once: Multiple Regression 253
    Multiple regression in Python 255
    Making predictions 256
    Visualizing the 3D scatterplot and regression plane 257
ANOVA: Another Look. 259
Analysis of Covariance: The Final Component of the GLM 264
But Wait — There's More 270

CHAPTER 15: **Correlation: The Rise and Fall of**
Relationships 273
Scatterplots, Again. 273
Understanding Correlation 274
Correlation and Regression 276
Testing Hypotheses About Correlation 279
Correlation in Python 280
    Calculating a correlation matrix 281
    Visualizing a correlation matrix. 282
Multiple Correlation 284
    Multiple correlation in Python. 284
    Adjusting R-squared 285
Partial Correlation 285
Partial Correlation in Python 286
Semipartial Correlation 287
Semipartial Correlation in Python. 288

CHAPTER 16: **Curvilinear Regression: When**
Relationships Get Complicated 289
What Is a Logarithm? 290
What Is e? 292
Power Regression 295
Exponential Regression 301
Logarithmic Regression 306
Polynomial Regression: A Higher Power 310
Which Model Should You Use? 315

PART 4: WORKING WITH PROBABILITY 317

CHAPTER 17: **Introducing Probability**. 319
What Is Probability?. 319
    Experiments, trials, events, and sample spaces 320
    Sample spaces and probability 320
Compound Events. 321
    Union and intersection. 321
    Intersection again 322

Conditional Probability...323
    Working with the probabilities 324
    The foundation of hypothesis testing......................324
Large Sample Spaces 325
    Permutations 326
    Combinations..326
Python Functions for Counting Rules............................327
Random Variables: Discrete and Continuous 328
Probability Distributions and Density Functions 329
The Binomial Distribution 331
The Binomial and Negative Binomial in Python 332
    Binomial distribution 333
    Negative binomial distribution 335
Hypothesis Testing with the Binomial Distribution 336
More on Hypothesis Testing: Python versus Tradition 338

CHAPTER 18: **Introducing Modeling**...............................341
Modeling a Distribution 341
    Plunging into the Poisson distribution......................342
    Modeling with the Poisson distribution 343
    Testing the model's fit....................................347
    Playing ball with a model 349
A Simulating Discussion 353
    Taking a chance: The Monte Carlo method.................353
    Loading the dice 354
    Simulating the central limit theorem 359

CHAPTER 19: **Probability Meets Regression: Logistic Regression** 363
Getting the Data 366
Doing the Analysis..366
    Coding the models 370

PART 5: THE PART OF TENS..................................373

CHAPTER 20: **Ten Tips for R Veterans** 375
Python Libraries Are (Somewhat) Different from R Libraries.......375
Python's Statistics Functions Live in Libraries....................376
In Python, Distributions Also Live in Libraries....................376
Dot Notation in Python Is Important 377
Dot in Python is Much Like $ in R 377
Two Important Libraries: NumPy and Pandas 377
Use the Dictionary..378
Learn the `statsmodels` Library 378

Where Are the Vectors? 379
A Python Grammar of Graphics 380

CHAPTER 21: **Ten Valuable Python Resources** .383
Python.org 383
Python Library Websites. 383
W3 Schools 384
Pythonbooks 384
The Python Papers 384
Python for Everybody 384
KDNuggets 385
Geeks for Geeks. 385
Real Python 385
The Zen of Python 385

INDEX 387

Introduction

S o, you're holding a statistics book. In my humble (and absolutely biased) opinion, it's not just another statistics book. Nor is it just another Python book. I say this for two reasons.

First, many statistics books teach you the concepts but give you no easy way to apply them. That often leads to a lack of understanding. Because Python has a wealth of features and wide-ranging applicability, it's a good tool for applying (and learning) statistics concepts.

Second, let's look at it from the opposite direction: Before I tell you about one of Python's statistics-related features, I give you the statistical foundation it's based on. That way, you understand that feature when you use it — and you use it more effectively.

I didn't want to write a book that only covers the details of Python and introduces some clever coding techniques. Some of that is necessary, of course, in any book that shows you how to use a language like Python. My goal was to venture far beyond that.

Neither did I want to write a statistics "cookbook" — when-faced-with-problem-category-#431-use-statistical-procedure-#763. My goal was to venture far beyond that, too.

Bottom line: This book isn't just about statistics or just about Python — it's firmly at the intersection of the two. In the proper context, Python can be a useful tool for teaching and learning statistics, and I've tried to supply the proper context.

About This Book

Although the field of statistics proceeds in a logical way, I've organized this book so that you can open it in any chapter and start reading. The idea is for you to find the information you're looking for in a hurry and use it immediately — whether it's a statistical concept or a Python-related one.

On the other hand, reading from cover to cover is okay if you're so inclined. If you're a statistics newbie and you have to use Python to analyze data, I recommend that you begin at the beginning.

Similarity with These Other For Dummies Books

You might be aware that I've written two other books: *Statistical Analysis with Excel For Dummies* and *Statistical Analysis with R For Dummies* (both from Wiley). This is not a shameless plug for those books. (Shameless plugs appear elsewhere.)

I'm just letting you know that the sections in this book that explain statistical concepts are much like the corresponding sections in the other books. I use (mostly) the same examples and, in many cases, the same words. I've developed that material during decades of teaching statistics and found it to be quite effective. (Reviewers seem to like it, too.) Also, if you happen to have read either or both of the other books and you're transitioning to Python, the common material might just help you make the switch.

And, you know: If it ain't broke. . . .

What You Can Safely Skip

Any reference book throws lots of information at you, and this one is no exception. I intended for it all to be useful, but I didn't aim it all at the same level. So if you're not deeply into the subject matter, you can avoid paragraphs marked with the Technical Stuff icon.

As you read, you'll run into sidebars. They provide information that elaborates on a topic, but they're not part of the main path. If you're in a hurry, you can breeze past them.

Foolish Assumptions

I'm assuming this much about you:

>> **You know how to work with Windows or the Mac.** I don't describe the details of pointing, clicking, selecting, and other actions.

>> **You're able to install Google Colaboratory (I show you how in Chapter 2) and follow along with the examples.** I work in Windows, but you should have no problem if you're working on a Mac.

How This Book Is Organized

I've organized this book into five parts.

Part 1: Getting Started with Statistical Analysis with Python

In Part 1, I provide a general introduction to statistics and to Python. I discuss important statistical concepts and describe useful Python techniques. If it's been a long time since your last course in statistics or if you've never even had a statistics course, start with Part 1. If you have never worked with Python, *definitely* start with Part 1.

Part 2: Describing Data

Part of working with statistics is to summarize data in meaningful ways. In Part 2, you find out how to do that. Most people know about averages and how to compute them. But that's not the whole story. In Part 2, I tell you about additional statistics that fill in the gaps, and I show you how to use Python to work with those statistics. I also introduce Python graphics in this part.

Part 3: Drawing Conclusions from Data

Part 3 addresses the fundamental aim of statistical analysis: to go beyond the data and help you make decisions. Usually, the data are measurements of a sample taken from a large population. The goal is to use these data to figure out what's going on in the population.

This opens a wide range of questions: What does an average mean? What does the difference between two averages mean? Are two things associated? These are only a few of the questions I address in Part 3, and I discuss the Python capabilities that help you answer them.

Part 4: Working with Probability

Probability is the basis for statistical analysis and decision-making. In Part 4, I tell you all about it. I show you how to apply probability, particularly in the area of modeling. Part 4 also includes a chapter on a statistical technique, called *logistic regression*, that marries a method from Part 3 with probability. Python provides a rich set of capabilities that deal with probability, and here's where you find them.

Part 5: The Part of Tens

Part 5 has two chapters. In the first, I give R users ten tips for moving to Python. In the second, I cover ten valuable Python-related resources you can find online.

Icons Used in This Book

Icons appear all over *For Dummies* books, and this one is no exception. Each one is a little picture in the margin that lets you know something special about the paragraph it sits next to.

TIP

This icon points out a hint or a shortcut that can help you in your work (and perhaps make you a finer, kinder, and more insightful human being).

REMEMBER

This one points out timeless wisdom to take with you on your continuing quest for statistics knowledge.

WARNING

Pay attention to the information accompanied by this icon. It's a reminder to avoid an action that might gum up the works for you.

TECHNICAL STUFF

As I mention in the earlier section "What You Can Safely Skip," this icon indicates material you can blow past if it's just too technical. (I've kept this to a minimum.)

Where to Go from Here

You can start reading this book anywhere, but here are a couple of hints. Want to learn the foundations of statistics? Turn the page. Introduce yourself to Python? That's Chapter 2. Want to start with Python graphics? Hit Chapter 3. For anything else, find it in the table of contents or the index and go for it.

In addition to what you're reading right now, this product comes with a free, access-anywhere cheat sheet that presents a selected list of Python capabilities and describes what they do. To get this cheat sheet, visit www.dummies.com and type **Statistical Analysis with Python For Dummies Cheat Sheet** in the search box. Also, be sure to check out this book's companion website at www.dummies.com/go/statisticalanalysiswithpythonfd, where you will find all the sample code I use in this book in a downloadable format.

1

Getting Started with Statistical Analysis with Python

IN THIS CHAPTER

» **Introducing statistical concepts**

» **Generalizing from samples to populations**

» **Getting into probability**

» **Testing hypotheses**

» **Two types of error**

Chapter **1**

Data, Statistics, and Decisions

S tatistics? That's all about crunching numbers into arcane-looking formulas, right? Not really. Statistics, first and foremost, is about decision-making. Some number-crunching is involved, of course, but the primary goal is to use numbers to make decisions. Statisticians look at data and wonder what the numbers are saying. What kinds of trends are in the data? What kinds of predictions are possible? What conclusions can you make?

To make sense of data and answer these questions, statisticians have developed a wide variety of analytical tools.

About the number-crunching part: If you had to do it via pencil-and-paper (or with the aid of a pocket calculator), you'd soon grow discouraged with the amount of computation involved and the errors that might creep in. Software like Python helps you crunch the data and compute the numbers. As a bonus, working with Python can also help you comprehend statistical concepts.

Although Python is an all-purpose computing language, many of its libraries make it ideal for statistical work. I wrote this book to show you how to use these libraries and the statistical tools they make available.

The Statistical (and Related) Notions You Just Have to Know

The analytical tools you find in Python are based on statistical concepts I help you explore in the remainder of this chapter. As you'll see, these concepts are based on common sense.

Samples and populations

If you watch TV on election night, you know that one exciting occurrence that takes place before the main event is the prediction of the outcome immediately after the polls close (and before all the votes are counted). How is it that pundits almost always get it right?

The idea is to talk to a *sample* of voters right after they vote. If they're truthful about how they marked their ballots, and if the sample is representative of the *population* of voters, analysts can use the sample data to draw conclusions about the population.

That, in a nutshell, is what statistics is all about — using the data from samples to draw conclusions about populations.

Here's another example. Imagine that your job is to find the average height of 10-year-old children in the United States. Because you probably wouldn't have the time or the resources to measure every child, you'd measure the heights of a representative sample. Then you'd average those heights and use that average as the estimate of the population average.

Estimating the population average is one kind of *inference* that statisticians make from sample data. I discuss inference in more detail in the later section "Inferential Statistics: Testing Hypotheses."

REMEMBER

Here's some important terminology: Properties of a population (like the population average) are called *parameters,* and properties of a sample (like the sample average) are called *statistics.* If your only concern is the sample properties (like the heights of the children in your sample), the statistics you calculate are *descriptive.* If you're concerned about estimating the population properties, your statistics are *inferential.*

Now for an important convention about notation: Statisticians use Greek letters (μ, σ. ρ) to stand for parameters, and English letters ($\bar{X}$, s, r) to stand for statistics. Figure 1-1 summarizes the relationship between populations and samples, and between parameters and statistics.

FIGURE 1-1:
The relationship
between
populations,
samples,
parameters, and
statistics.

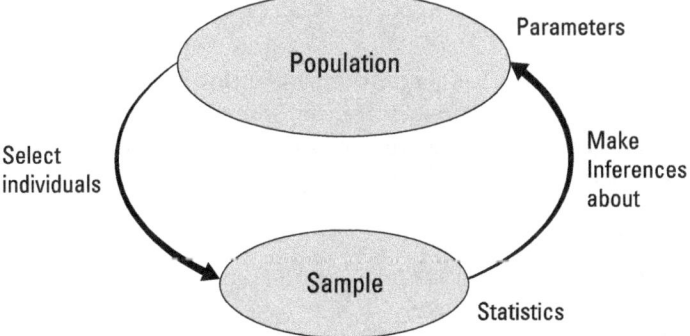

Variables: Dependent and independent

A *variable* is something that can take on different values at different times — like your age, the value of the dollar against other currencies, or the number of games your favorite sports team wins. Something that can have only one value is a *constant*. Scientists tell us that the speed of light is a constant, and we use the constant π to calculate the area of a circle.

Statisticians work with *independent* variables and *dependent* variables. In any study or experiment, you'll find both kinds. Statisticians assess the relationship between them.

Imagine a computerized training method designed to increase a person's IQ. How would a researcher find out whether this method does what it's supposed to do? First, that person would randomly assign a sample of people to one of two groups. One group would receive the training method, and the other would complete another kind of computer-based activity — like reading text on a website. Before and after each group completes its activities, the researcher measures each person's IQ. What happens next? I discuss that topic in the later section "Inferential Statistics: Testing Hypotheses."

For now, understand that the independent variable here is Type of Activity. The two possible values of this variable are IQ Training and Reading Text. The dependent variable is the change in IQ from Before to After.

A dependent variable is what a researcher *measures*. In an experiment, an independent variable is what a researcher *manipulates*. In other contexts, a researcher can't manipulate an independent variable. Instead, they note naturally occurring values of the independent variable and how they affect a dependent variable.

In general, the objective is to find out whether changes in an independent variable are associated with changes in a dependent variable.

In the examples that appear throughout this book, I show you how to use Python to calculate characteristics of groups of scores or to compare groups of scores. Whenever I show you a group of scores, I'm talking about the values of a dependent variable.

Types of data

When you do statistical work, you can run into four kinds of data. And when you work with a variable, the way you work with it depends on what kind of data it is. The first kind is *nominal* data. If a set of numbers happens to be nominal data, the numbers are labels — their values don't signify anything. On a sports team, the jersey numbers are nominal. They just identify the players.

The next kind is *ordinal* data. In this data type, the numbers are more than just labels. As the name *ordinal* might tell you, the order of the numbers is important. If I were to ask you to rank ten foods from the one you like best (1) to the one you like least (10), we'd have a set of ordinal data.

But the difference between your third-favorite food and your fourth-favorite food might not be the same as the difference between your ninth-favorite and your tenth-favorite. So this type of data lacks equal intervals and equal differences.

Interval data gives us equal differences. The Fahrenheit scale of temperature is a good example. The difference between 30° and 40° is the same as the difference between 90° and 100°. So each degree is an interval.

People are sometimes surprised to find out that on the Fahrenheit scale, a temperature of 80° is not twice as hot as 40°. For ratio statements ("twice as much as," "half as much as") to make sense, *zero* has to mean the complete absence of the thing you're measuring. A temperature of 0° F doesn't mean the complete absence of heat — it's just an arbitrary point on the Fahrenheit scale. (The same holds true for Celsius.)

The fourth kind of data, *ratio*, provides a meaningful zero point. On the Kelvin scale of temperature, zero means "absolute zero," where all molecular motion (the basis of heat) stops. So 200° Kelvin is twice as hot as 100° Kelvin. Another example is length. Eight inches is twice as long as 4 inches. *Zero inches* means "a complete absence of length."

An independent variable or a dependent variable can be either nominal, ordinal, interval, or ratio. The analytical tools you use depend on the type of data you work with.

A little probability

When statisticians make decisions, they use probability to express their confidence about those decisions. They can never be absolutely certain about what they decide. They can only tell you how probable their conclusions are.

What do I mean by *probability?* Mathematicians and philosophers might give you complex definitions. In my experience, however, the best way to understand probability is in terms of examples.

Here's a simple example: If you toss a coin, what's the probability that it turns up heads? If the coin is fair, you might figure that you have a 50-50 chance of heads and a 50-50 chance of tails. And you'd be right. In terms of the kinds of numbers associated with probability, that's ½.

Think about rolling a fair die (one member of a pair of dice). What's the probability that you roll a 4? Well, a die has six faces and one of them is 4, so that's ⅙. Still another example: Select 1 card at random from a standard deck of 52 cards. What's the probability that it's a diamond? A deck of cards has four suits, so that's ¼.

These examples tell you that if you want to know the probability that an event occurs, count how many ways that event can happen and divide by the total number of events that can happen. In the first two examples (heads, 4), the event you're interested in happens in only one way. For the coin, you divide 1 by 2. For the die, you divide 1 by 6. In the third example (diamond), the event can happen in 1 of 13 ways (ace through king), so you divide 13 by 52 (to get ¼).

Now for a slightly more complicated example. Toss a coin and roll a die at the same time. What's the probability of tails and a 4? Think about all the possible events that can happen when you toss a coin and roll a die at the same time. You could have tails and 1 through 6, or heads and 1 through 6. That adds up to 12 possibilities. The tails-and-4 combination can happen only one way. So the probability is $\frac{1}{12}$.

In general, the formula for the probability that a particular event occurs is

$$Pr(event) = \frac{\text{Number of ways the event can occur}}{\text{Total number of possible events}}$$

At the beginning of this section, I say that statisticians express their confidence about their conclusions in terms of probability, which is why I brought all this up in the first place. This line of thinking leads to *conditional* probability — the probability that an event occurs given that some other event occurs. Suppose that I roll a die, look at it (so that you don't see it), and tell you that I rolled an odd number. What's the probability that I've rolled a 5? Ordinarily, the probability of a 5 is ⅙, but "I rolled an odd number" narrows it down. That piece of information eliminates the three even numbers (2, 4, 6) as possibilities. Only the three odd numbers (1, 3, 5) are possible, so the probability is ⅓.

What's the big deal about conditional probability? What role does it play in statistical analysis? Read on.

Inferential Statistics: Testing Hypotheses

Before any statistician begins a study, they draw up a tentative explanation — a *hypothesis* that tells why the data might come out a certain way. After gathering all the data, the statistician has to decide whether to reject the hypothesis.

That decision is the answer to a conditional probability question — what's the probability of obtaining the data, given that this hypothesis is correct? Statisticians have tools that calculate the probability. If the probability turns out to be low, the statistician rejects the hypothesis.

Back to coin-tossing for an example: Imagine that you're interested in whether a particular coin is fair — whether it has an equal chance of heads or tails on any toss. Let's start with "The coin is fair" as the hypothesis.

To test the hypothesis, you'd toss the coin a number of times — let's say 100. These 100 tosses are the sample data. If the coin is fair (as per the hypothesis), you'd expect 50 heads and 50 tails.

If it's 99 heads and 1 tail, you'd surely reject the fair-coin hypothesis: The conditional probability of 99 heads and 1 tail given a fair coin is very low. Of course, the coin could still be fair and you could, quite by chance, get a 99–1 split, right? Sure. You never really know. You have to gather the sample data (the 100-toss results) and then decide. Your decision might be right, or it might not.

Juries make these types of decisions. In the United States, the starting hypothesis is that the defendant is not guilty ("innocent until proven guilty"). Think of the evidence as data. Jury members consider the evidence and answer a conditional probability question: What's the probability of the evidence, given that the defendant is not guilty? Their answer determines the verdict.

Null and alternative hypotheses

Think again about that coin-tossing study I just mentioned. The sample data are the results from the 100 tosses. I said that we can start with the hypothesis that the coin is fair. This starting point is called the *null hypothesis*. The statistical notation for the null hypothesis is H_o. According to this hypothesis, any heads-tails split in the data is consistent with a fair coin. Think of it as the idea that nothing in the sample data is out of the ordinary.

An alternative hypothesis is possible — that the coin isn't a fair one and it's loaded to produce an unequal number of heads and tails. This hypothesis says that any heads-tails split is consistent with an unfair coin. This alternative hypothesis is called, believe it or not, the *alternative hypothesis.* The statistical notation for the alternative hypothesis is H_1.

Now toss the coin 100 times and note the number of heads and tails. If the results are something like 90 heads and 10 tails, it's a good idea to reject H_o. If the results are around 50 heads and 50 tails, don't reject H_o.

Similar ideas apply to the IQ example I gave earlier. One sample receives the computer-based IQ training method, and the other participates in a different computer-based activity — like reading text on a website. Before and after each group completes its activities, the researcher measures each person's IQ. The null hypothesis, H_o, is that one group's improvement isn't different from the other. If the improvements are greater with the IQ training than with the other activity — so much greater that it's unlikely that the two aren't different from one another — reject H_o. If they're not, don't reject H_o.

REMEMBER

Notice that I did *not* say "accept H_o." The way the logic works, you *never* accept a hypothesis. You either reject H_o or don't reject H_o. In a jury trial, the verdict is either "guilty" (reject the null hypothesis of "not guilty") or "not guilty" (don't reject H_o). "Innocent" (acceptance of the null hypothesis) is not a possible verdict.

Notice also that in the coin-tossing example, I said "around 50 heads and 50 tails." What does *around* mean? Also, I said that if it's 90-10, reject H_o. What about 85-15? 80-20? 70-30? Exactly how much different from 50-50 does the split have to be for you to reject H_o? In the IQ training example, how much greater does the IQ improvement have to be to reject H_o?

I won't answer these questions now. Statisticians have formulated decision rules for situations like this, and I'll help you explore those rules throughout this book.

Two types of error

Whenever you evaluate data and decide to reject H_0 or not reject H_0, you can never be absolutely sure. You never really know the "true" state of the world. In the coin-tossing example, that means you can't be certain whether the coin is fair. All you can do is make a decision based on the sample data. If you want to know for sure about the coin, you have to have the data for the entire population of tosses — which means you have to keep tossing the coin until the end of time.

Because you're never certain about your decisions, you can make an error either way you decide. As I mention earlier, the coin could be fair, and you just happen to get 99 heads in 100 tosses. That's not likely, and that's why you reject H_0 if that happens. It's also possible that the coin is biased, yet you just happen to toss 50 heads in 100 tosses. Again, that's not likely, and you don't reject H_0 in that case.

Although those errors aren't likely, they're possible. They lurk in every study that involves inferential statistics. Statisticians have named them Type I errors and Type II errors.

If you reject H_0 and you shouldn't, that's a Type I error. In the coin example, that's rejecting the hypothesis that the coin is fair when in reality it's a fair coin.

If you don't reject H_0 and you should have, that's a Type II error. It happens when you don't reject the hypothesis that the coin is fair, and in reality, it's biased.

How do you know whether you've made either type of error? You don't — at least not right after you make the decision to reject or not reject H_0. (If it's possible to know, you wouldn't make the error in the first place!) All you can do is gather more data and see whether the additional data is consistent with your decision.

If you think of H_0 as a tendency to maintain the status quo and not interpret anything as being out of the ordinary (no matter how it looks), a Type II error means you've missed out on something big. In fact, some iconic mistakes are Type II errors.

Here's what I mean. On New Year's Day in 1962, a rock group consisting of three guitarists and a drummer auditioned in the London studio of a major recording company. Legend has it that the recording executives didn't like what they heard, didn't like what they saw, and believed that guitar groups were on their way out. Although the musicians played their hearts out, the group failed the audition.

Who was that group? The Beatles!

And *that's* a Type II error.

Chapter **2**

Python: What It Does and How It Does It

P ython is a computer language. You can use it for doing the kinds of computation and number-crunching that can set the stage for effective statistical
analysis and decision-making. An important aspect of statistical analysis is
to present the results in a comprehensible way. For this reason, I explore Python's
extensive graphics capabilities (in Chapter 3).

The brainchild of Guido van Rossum, Python is named after the long-running
BBC hit comedy series "Monty Python's Flying Circus." He intended Python to be
easy and intuitive to use, open source, and suitable for everyday tasks, from
website creation to more involved efforts like machine learning and data science.
He also wanted humans to be able to easily understand Python code.

To say that van Rossum succeeded is putting it mildly. In 2024, Python became
the most-often-used language on GitHub (the world's largest code management
website), and it's been one of the ten most popular languages since 2004.

TIP

To read more about how Python began, check out *Python: The Documentary* on
YouTube (www.youtube.com/watch?v=GfH4QL4VqJ0). It's a bit technically ori-
ented, but it's fun to watch Guido and his colleagues reminisce.

Introducing Colab

At this point, it might seem logical to tell you how to download Python and install it on your computer.

Instead, I move in a different direction. Why? In this book, I don't use Python on a local machine. Instead, I show you how to do your computing in the cloud. That way, you don't have to worry about installation issues or local hardware limitations. You don't fuss with command lines or path names. All you need is a Gmail account and a working Internet connection — and of course, the faster, the better.

What makes all this possible is the Google Colaboratory, dubbed Colab by its users. Google hosts Colab as a platform for learning, exploration, and experimentation. Because Google hosts it online, you work with Google hardware rather than your own. If you're an aspiring data scientist or machine learning engineer, or if you just want to learn Python, it's a good idea to get into Colab.

Colab is a browser-based version of a locally installable app known as the Jupyter Notebook, so named because of the languages it accommodates (Julia, Python, and R). It's pronounced "Jupiter," like the planet. (To be consistent with its spelling, I think it should be pronounced "JuPYter," but as usual, nobody asked me.)

REMEMBER

To make the going as easy as possible, I use the Chrome browser and store my work on Google Drive. That way, everything stays in the Google family.

TIP

The most user-friendly installable version of Jupyter, in my view, is Jupyter Lab Desktop (`https://github.com/jupyterlab/jupyterlab-desktop`). You can try it if you like, but I have nothing more to say about it in this book.

Time to dive into Colab:

1. **After registering your free Gmail account, open Colab by navigating to** `https://colab.research.google.com`.

   Doing so opens a page with an Open Notebook dialog box that resembles Figure 2-1. (I say "resembles" because yours won't look exactly like mine. I've been working with Colab for a while, so I have some files saved.)

2. **Click the blue New Notebook button to get started.**

   Figure 2-2 shows the page that opens.

   First things first — let's give this notebook a name.

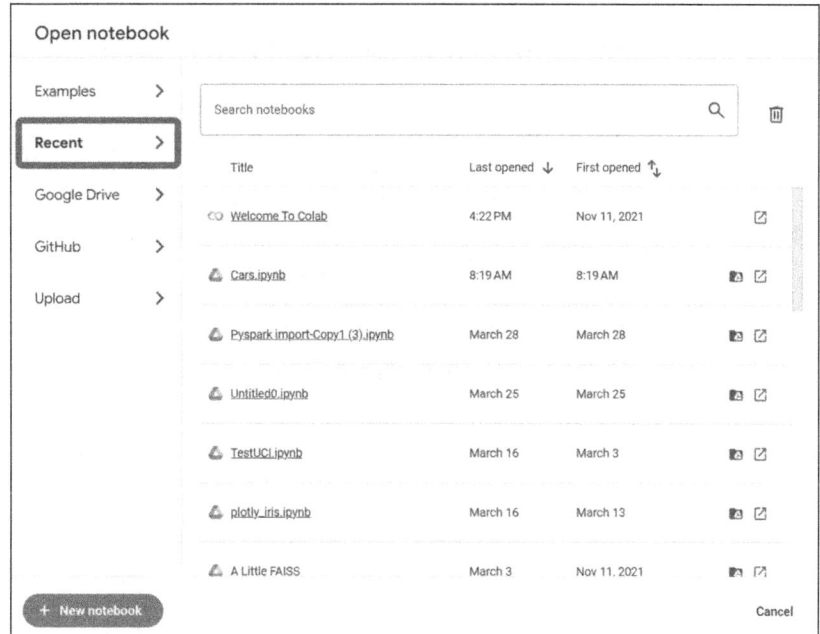

FIGURE 2-1:
The Open Notebook dialog box on the Colab welcome page.

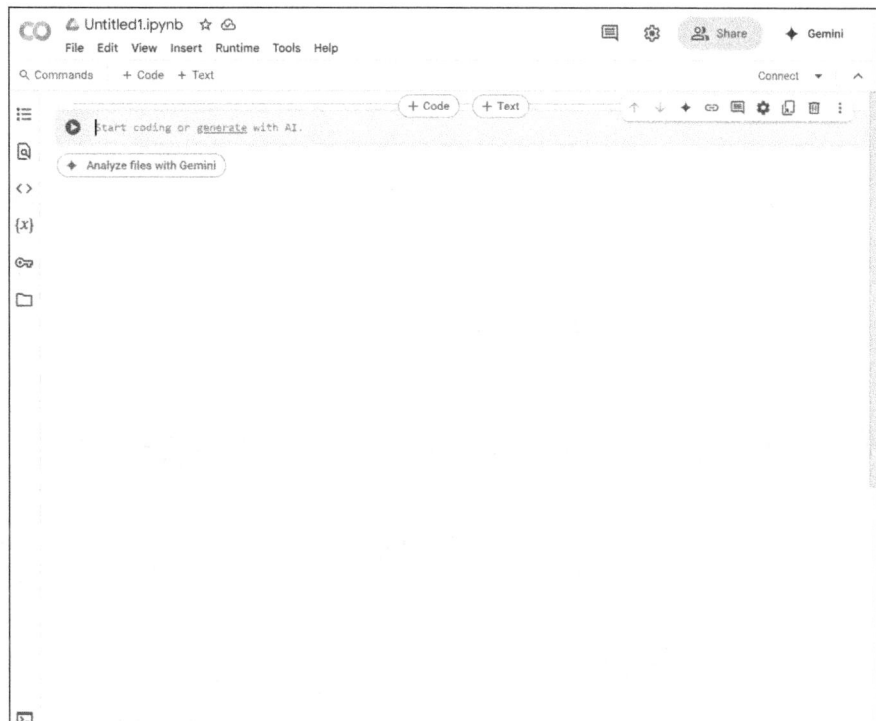

FIGURE 2-2:
The page that opens when you click the New Notebook button.

3. **Double-click on** Untitled **and type** My First Notebook**.**

4. **Press Enter to apply the name change.**

   Next, you know what you want to do — so let's just go ahead and do it.

5. **Locate the box with the right-pointing arrow on its left. (It's called a "cell.")**

   It says, "Start coding or generate with AI."

6. **In that cell, type** print("Hello world!")

7. **Click that right-pointing arrow on the left (I call it the *run arrow*) to run the code.**

   After Colab does its thing, the result looks like Figure 2-3.

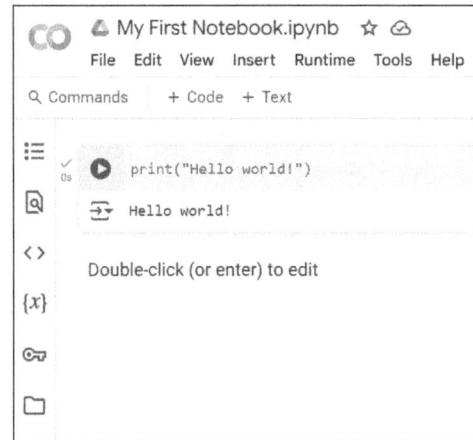

FIGURE 2-3:
The result of
running
print("Hello
world!")
in Colab.

Welcome to Python!

Exploring the Colab Environment

Colab has an extensive array of features. In this section, I examine the ones I think are the most helpful.

Cells

First and foremost, as I mention earlier, that little compartment where you enter and run Python code is called a *cell*. Cells make up a *notebook*, like the one you just named My First Notebook. The extension .ipynb stands for *interactive Python notebook.*

Each cell can contain either code (like the line in Python I tell you how to write in the previous section) or text. When you write text, it's in a language called Markdown. Considering its name, it's somewhat paradoxical that Markdown is a *markup* language — you format text by adding syntactic elements.

In the next exercise, you'll add a text cell:

1. **Begin by hovering the mouse pointer near the bottom of the first cell.**

Doing so opens the option to open the next cell for either code or text. Figure 2-4 shows what I mean.

TIP

If you hover the mouse pointer near the top of a cell, you can open a Code cell or Text cell above the current cell.

FIGURE 2-4:
Hovering the
mouse pointer
near the bottom
of a cell gives you
the option to
open the next cell
for either
code or text.

2. **Click Text to open a text cell.**

3. **To illustrate how Markdown works, type the following lines:**

```
# Heading 1
## Heading 2
### Heading 3

This is normal text

*This text is italic*

**This text is bold**
```

As you type, a Preview window in the right half of the cell shows how the text looks when it's rendered. Figure 2-5 shows the text cell after all the typing is complete.

FIGURE 2-5:
The text cell
after typing
some Markdown.

4. **To render the text, click the Pencil icon with the line through it in the panel in the upper right corner.**

   The cell now looks like Figure 2-6.

FIGURE 2-6:
The text cell
after rendering
the Markdown.

5. **To edit the cell, click the Pencil icon again (which, you'll notice, no longer has the line through it).**

   You can click the up arrow and the down arrow in the upper right panel to relocate the cell within the notebook.

TIP

Markdown has numerous features. This isn't a book about Markdown, however, so I don't cover them.

TIP

To get the complete lowdown on Markdown, check out www.markdownguide.org.

Most people use text cells to provide explanations for notebook consumers to understand the Python code in the code cells. Many online Python tutorials are Jupyter Notebook notebooks that follow that structure.

I, however, see another use for text cells. After many years of teaching and learning, I feel that the best way to learn a new subject is to take notes as you read the material (just as you would during a typical lecture). Accordingly, I recommend that you type notes in a text cell as you read this book and as you enter code in a code cell. I believe that note-taking will accelerate your understanding of Python.

The left panel

In the panel on the left side of the screen, clicking the Folder icon in the lower left corner opens File Explorer view, as shown in Figure 2-7.

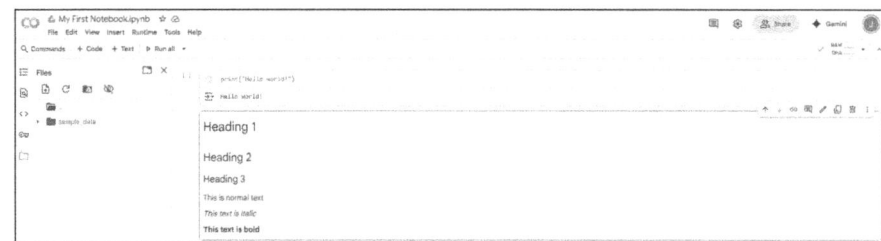

FIGURE 2-7:
The view that
opens when
you click the
Folder icon.

In addition to the various folder icons that now appear in the left panel, smaller icons appear at the top of the panel. The File icon with the up arrow on it enables you to upload files from your local drive into the notebook. This is helpful when you've downloaded a data file and you want to analyse it. (I use this capability in Chapter 18, in the section about baseball.)

The Menu bar

The Menu bar across the top of the screen has seven distinct menus. Each one has quite a few choices, so I won't tell you about all of them.

In my experience, the most useful one is the Runtime menu, shown in Figure 2-8.

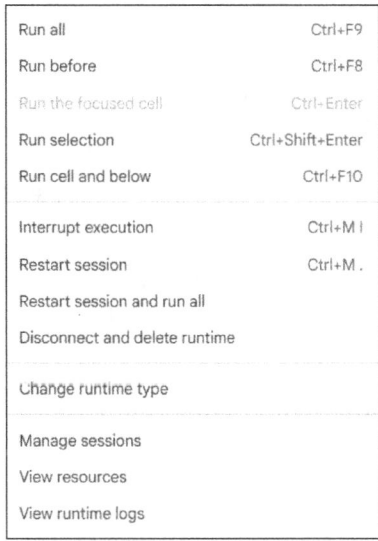

FIGURE 2-8:
The Colab
Runtime menu.

You put this menu to work after you leave a notebook open and unattended for an extended period. When that happens, Google disconnects Colab from the Google servers and opens a dialog box to that effect, as shown in Figure 2-9.

FIGURE 2-9:
The dialog box that opens when Google disconnects your notebook from its servers due to inactivity.

Click Reconnect to close the dialog box and reconnect to Google servers. Because your notebook is browser-based (and not in your computer), the results of any code you've run have disappeared. Thus, you must rerun your code. To do that, click Runtime on the menu bar and select the first choice, Run All.

The File menu is important, too. Use it for typical file tasks:

>> To save your notebook, choose File ⇨ Save.

>> To open an existing notebook, choose File ⇨ Open Notebook.

>> To create a new notebook, pick File ⇨ New Notebook in Drive.

Gemini

Gemini is Google's AI tool and is one of Colab's major selling points. It's like having an all-knowing assistant at your beck and call. Sometimes it's downright eerie — filling in code before you type it (although not always accurately). It's invaluable when you need an explanation of a code snippet, a correction of a coding error, or an answer to a question.

To activate Gemini, click its icon in the middle of the bottom of the notebook. It's something like a 4-pointed star and is shown in Figure 2-10.

FIGURE 2-10:
The Gemini icon.

Clicking the Gemini icon opens the box shown in Figure 2-11. I refer to this as the Gemini box.

FIGURE 2-11:
The Gemini box
opens when
you click the
Gemini icon.

My favorite way to use Gemini is to click the Move to Panel icon to the immediate right of the box. This opens a panel on the right half of the notebook, as shown in Figure 2-12. That right-side panel supports multiple tabs. In this case, it opens a tab where I ask questions and where Gemini answers them. I call it the Gemini tab.

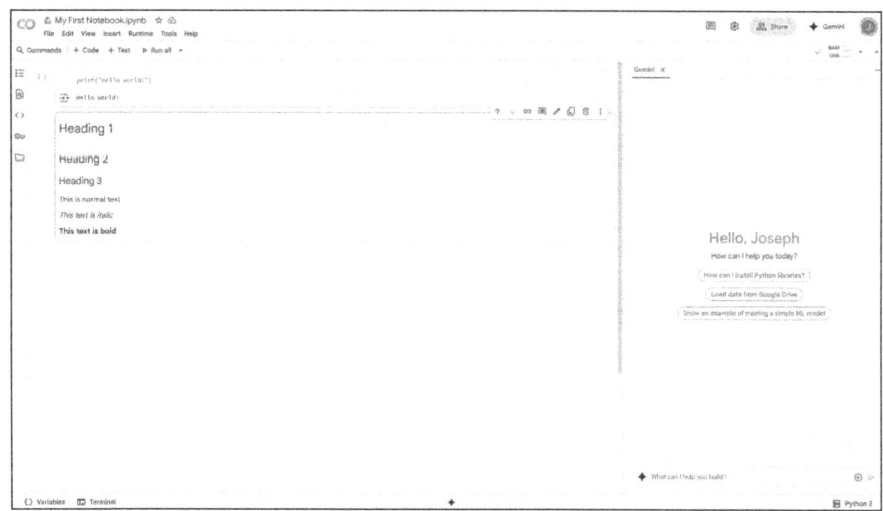

FIGURE 2-12:
The Gemini tab
on the right half
of the notebook.

To give you a glimpse of Gemini's capabilities, I type **Explain print("Hello world")** into the Gemini box. To send the request (AI honchos call it a *prompt*) to Gemini, I click the right-pointing arrowhead in the Gemini box. The prompt appears at the top of the Gemini tab, and after a couple of seconds of cogitation (Gemination?), the answer appears, as shown in Figure 2-13.

Okay, this was a simple answer to a simple question. When you're stuck on a more complex issue, feel free to ask (excuse mc, *prompt*) Gemini. I can almost guarantee you'll get a helpful response. If you don't understand the response, you can prompt Gemini for further explanation.

TIP

Using Gemini along with taking notes in text cells is a powerful combination for learning Python.

Did I use Gemini while writing this book?

Of course!

Introducing Python

Python comprises a huge set of concepts, and it's not possible to expound on all of them in just part of a chapter. Instead, I focus on the areas of Python that form the foundation of the rest of this book.

Printing

I begin here with a bit of Python that I show you earlier in this chapter — `print()`. It's pretty straightforward — in my "Hello World" example, this function prints onscreen the quoted text in the parentheses.

The `print()` function is an example of one that's built into Python. What's inside the parentheses is called an *argument*.

I can tell Python what to print in a slightly different way. If I type these lines into a code cell:

```
message = "Welcome to Python"
print(message)
```

and then click the Run arrow, this line appears below the cell:

```
Welcome to Python
```

In this example, message is a variable to which I've assigned a value, and print() happily prints the value.

Quoted text is called a *string*.

Another way to use print() is with *f-strings* (which is short for *formatted string literals*). The easiest way to explain it is to just show you how it works:

```
x=17
print(f"The value of x is {x}")
```

Running this snippet produces:

```
The value of x is 17
```

Placing the *x* inside curly braces within the string produces the output with the value of *x*.

Within the curly braces, I can format what I want to print — and this is a great convenience. For example, if *y*=68.67469943 and I want to print *y* rounded to three decimal places, here's how I do it:

```
y = 68.67469943
print(f"The value of y is {y:.3f}")
```

The syntax inside the curly braces (:.3f) instructs Python to round *y* to three decimal places. Running the two lines of code produces:

```
The value of y is 68.675
```

REMEMBER

Moving forward, I don't show code snippets and then say "running the code produces." Instead, you see this:

```
y = 68.67469943
print(f"The value of y is {y:.3f}")

The value of y is 68.675
```

TIP

Get used to seeing `print(f" ... ")`. I use it often throughout this book.

Variable names

As I mention in Chapter 1, a variable can take on different values at different times. The Python version: A *variable* is a container for holding values. Python has some requirements for naming a variable:

» A variable name must start with an uppercase letter, a lowercase letter, or an underscore.

» A variable name can include a number but must not begin with a number.

» A variable name cannot be a Python-reserved keyword (like `if`, `while`, or `for`).

TIP

Use underscores to separate words within variable names. Also, variable names are case-sensitive, so `first_name` is a different variable from `FIRST_NAME`.

As the preceding examples show, you assign a value to a variable by placing its name on the left side of an equal (=) sign and the value on the right side. In Python, you can make multiple assignments on the same line of code:

```
c,d,e = 5,6,7
print(c,d,e)

5 6 7
```

Variable types

Here are four Python variable types:

» A *floating-point* (`float`) number can be positive or negative and contains decimal places.

» An *integer* (`int`) is a whole number with no decimal places.

>> A *string* (`str`) is a sequence of characters surrounded by either single quotes or double quotes.

>> A *Boolean* is either `True` or `False`.

Each of these types holds a single value. They are *immutable*, meaning that after you assign a value to one of these variable types, you can't change it.

Python also provides four types of variables that can hold multiple values: lists, sets, tuples, and dictionaries. They're distinguished superficially by the grouping symbols (brackets, parentheses, or curly braces) that surround them:

>> A *list* is a bracketed, ordered sequence of comma-separated values.

>> A *tuple* looks like a list inside parentheses.

>> A *set* looks like a tuple inside curly braces.

>> A *dictionary* looks like a set (it's inside curly braces). Each of its items is a pair. The first member of each pair is called a *key,* and the second is called a *value.*

These types differ on more than just the superficial distinctions, and I explain each one in greater detail later in this chapter.

Here's one point of difference: Sets and tuples are immutable. Lists and dictionaries are *mutable:* You can change their values (and add new ones) after you've created them.

As you code, you might create variables of different types, and it might be difficult to remember them all.

Colab provides an easy way to track the variables (and each one's type) in your notebook. At the bottom of the notebook on the extreme left is a double curly brace icon ({})next to the word *Variables,* as shown in Figure 2-14.

FIGURE 2-14:
The Variables
icon in the lower
left corner
of Colab.

{} Variables   ▶_ Terminal

Click that icon to open the Variables tab in the right-side panel (see Figure 2-15). You'll see a list of the variables currently in use in the current notebook.

It's often useful to convert from one type to another. Here I convert an int to a float and vice versa:

```
a=float(x)
b=int(y)
print(f"The value of a is {a:.2f} \n and the value of b is {b}")

The value of a is 17.00
 and the value of b is 68
```

TIP

The \n in the f-string is the newline character.

Why did I have to create a new variable for each conversion? I couldn't just go ahead and change the original variables — they're immutable!

Lists

A *list* is an ordered collection of items that can be of any type. The items are separated by commas and enclosed in square brackets; for example:

```
beatles = ["John", "Paul", "George", "Ringo"]
```

I retrieve a list item by its position in the list, which is called its *index*. Indexing in Python begins with 0, so Python is said to have *zero-based indexing*:

```
print(f"{beatles[0]}\n{beatles[3]}")

John
Ringo
```

The `len()` function gives the number of items in a list (its length, in other words):

```
len(beatles)

4
```

I can retrieve a subsequence from within the list. This is called *slicing*. I use a colon (`:`) to perform the slice. Here's what I mean:

```
beatles[1:3]

['Paul', 'George']
```

The number to the left of the colon is the starting index; the number to the right of the colon is the up-to-but-not-including ending index.

Here it is in English: The slice starts from index 1 (the second position in the list) and ends at index 2 (the third position) because the slice goes up to but not including index 3 (the fourth position).

A more succinct way to say it is that the starting index is inclusive and the ending index is exclusive.

REMEMBER

The items in a list don't have to all be the same type.

Strings

Although a string is a single-valued variable, Python treats a string as a list of characters, including spaces. Recall from earlier in this chapter:

```
message = "Welcome to Python"
```

I use `len()` to calculate the number of characters:

```
len(message)

17
```

I can slice the string:

```
message[0:7]

'Welcome'
```

I leave it as an exercise for you to come up with some additional slices.

Tuples

A *tuple* is a collection of comma-separated items inside parentheses:

```
my_tuple = ("apples", "peaches", "pumpkin pie", "peaches")
my_tuple[1]

'peaches'
```

As the example shows, a tuple is indexable and duplicates are permitted. A tuple is immutable — once you create one, you can't change, add, or remove items.

TECHNICAL STUFF

A Python function can return multiple values. When it does, it packs those values into a tuple.

Sets

A *set* is a comma-separated collection inside curly braces — which coincides nicely with the way mathematicians show elements in a set.

Here are two sets:

```
fibs = {1,1,2,3,5}
facts = {1,2,6,24,120}
```

TECHNICAL STUFF

The set `fibs` consists of the first five Fibonacci numbers. The first Fibonacci number is 1, as is the second. From then on, each Fibonacci number is the sum of the preceding two numbers. The set `facts` consists of the first five factorials. The first factorial is 1. The second factorial is 2×1, the third is $3 \times 2 \times 1$, and so on.

From a math course, you might remember set intersection — the set of items that are in both sets. Python uses & for intersection:

```
fibs & facts

{1, 2}
```

Note the curly braces. This tells you that the intersection is a set, too.

You might also remember set union — the combination of unique items that are in both sets. Python uses the pipe (|) character for union:

```
fibs | facts

{1, 2, 3, 5, 6, 24, 120}
```

Sets have no defined order, and they're not indexable. A set is immutable — you can't change its items after you create them.

Dictionaries

A Python dictionary consists of key:value pairs separated by commas and surrounded by curly braces. Unlike a list (which is indexed by zero-based numbering), a dictionary is indexed by its keys. Each key must be unique within its dictionary.

In this example, each Beatle's first name is the key, and his last name is the value:

```
beatles_dictionary = {"John":"Lennon", "Paul":"McCartney",
    "George":"Harrison", "Ringo":"Starr"}
beatles_dictionary["George"]

'Harrison'
```

Working with Python Functions

I've shown you the Python functions `print()`, `len()`, `int()`, and `float()`. They're examples of functions built into Python for handling typical tasks. They're often referred to as *standalone* functions.

Do some Python functions not "stand alone"?

Indeed, some do not. Python *methods* are functions associated with built-in variable types. To call a method, you provide the variable it's associated with, followed by a dot (.), followed by the method and its arguments.

I illustrate with a couple of methods associated with lists:

```
flowers = ["aster", "daisy", "hibiscus", "violet"]
print(flowers)

['aster', 'daisy', 'hibiscus', 'violet']
```

To add a flower to the list, I use the list `append()` method:

```
flowers.append("rose")
print(flowers)

['aster', 'daisy', 'hibiscus', 'violet', 'rose']
```

To insert a flower into a specific position within the list, I use `insert()`. In this example, I insert `"tulip"` in front of `flowers[2]`:

```
flowers.insert(2,"tulip")
print(flowers)

['aster', 'daisy', 'tulip', 'hibiscus', 'violet', 'rose']
```

Checking Out Python Libraries

Thus far, I've told you about functions and methods that are built into Python. They (along with many others) make up the Python Standard Library.

One reason for Python's great popularity is its applicability to a wide variety of fields. The functionality that enables you to work in these fields — like statistical analysis — comes from additional libraries you install into your Python environment and then import into your notebook.

Two libraries I work with often are numpy (which stands for *numerical Python* and is pronounced "num-pie)" and pandas (which loosely stands for "Python data analysis"). These libraries (and others that appear in this book) are used so frequently that Colab has already taken care of the installation part. All you have to do is import them.

TIP

Get used to importing Python libraries. You do it almost every time you code. An important part of Python programming is knowing which libraries to import.

To show you how to work numpy and pandas, I use each one to create a specific type of data structure. I use numpy to create an array, and pandas to create a DataFrame.

Creating an array

An *array* is a variable that can hold one or more values. It can consist of rows and columns, as in the example I'm working with here.

I create an array of names of entertainers. The building blocks of the array are three lists. The first list is one I use earlier in this chapter:

```
beatles = ["John", "Paul", "George", "Ringo"]
```

These are the other two:

```
four_tops = ["Levi", "Larry", "Duke", "Obie"]
marx_bros = ["Groucho", "Harpo", "Chico", "Zeppo"]
```

I begin by importing the appropriate library, which is numpy:

```
import numpy as np
```

In the import statement, as np provides a short alias for numpy that makes coding a bit easier.

Next, I use the `array()` method in `numpy` to construct the array:

```
entertainers = np.array([beatles,four_tops,marx_bros])
print(entertainers)

[['John' 'Paul' 'George' 'Ringo']
 ['Levi' 'Larry' 'Duke' 'Obie']
 ['Groucho' 'Harpo' 'Chico' 'Zeppo']]
```

The array has three rows and four columns. To access an element in this array, I provide the row index and the column index. The element `Levi` is in the second row first column:

```
print(entertainers[1][0])

Levi
```

Importing a library and giving it an alias is appropriate when you use more than one method from the library. If you use only one method, another way to import is this:

```
from numpy import array
```

Then I can turn the `marx_bros` list into an array without using the dot notation:

```
marx_array = array(marx_bros)
print(marx_array)

['Groucho' 'Harpo' 'Chico' 'Zeppo']
```

REMEMBER

Items in an array have to be the same type. Items in a list do not.

It's computationally more efficient to store items in an array than in a list.

TECHNICAL
STUFF

Creating a DataFrame

A *DataFrame* is widely used for data manipulation and analysis. Like a table, it has rows and named columns. The data types can differ from column to column.

In this section, I show you how to use the `pandas` library to create a DataFrame that holds information on the names of six children and their ages, genders, and scores on a math exam. As part of the procedure, I use the dictionary structure I show you earlier.

I begin by importing pandas and providing an alias:

```
import pandas as pd
```

The building blocks of the DataFrame are four lists:

```
name = ["Albert","Bobbi","Charlotte","Dan","Edward","Felicia"]
age = [8,7,8,7,8,7]
gender = ["male","female","female","male","male","female"]
math_score =[85,91,90,92,89,88]
```

I create a dictionary of key:value pairs. Each key will be the name of a column in the DataFrame I'm about to create, and each value is the name of one of the four lists:

```
data = {"Name": name, "Age": age, "Gender": gender, "Math
    Score": math_score}
```

Next, I use the dataframe() method in pandas to create the DataFrame:

```
df = pd.DataFrame(data)
print(df)

        Name        Age     Gender      Math Score
0       Albert      8       male        85
1       Bobbi       7       female      91
2       Charlotte   8       female      90
3       Dan         7       male        92
4       Edward      8       male        89
5       Felicia     7       female      88
```

I use this type of data structure throughout the book.

Installing a library

At the beginning of this main section, I mention that Colab comes with a set of preinstalled, frequently used libraries.

Of course, Colab could not have preinstalled every existing Python library. The time might come when you have to use one that's not already in Colab.

In this book, that time comes in Chapter 13 and again in Chapter 15. In those chapters, I use functions that live in a library called `pingouin`, which does not come preinstalled in Colab.

To install a library, you use the `pip` command. Here's how I use it in Chapters 13 and 15:

```
!pip install pingouin
```

What's that exclamation point all about? Unlike other commands and functions I describe, `pip` doesn't indicate something you're asking Python to do. Instead, it's a message to the compute capability that Google has allotted to you. The exclamation is a signal that this command is intended to work outside of Python. You might say it's a way of "escaping" Colab.

TECHNICAL STUFF

The "compute capability that Google has allotted to you" is called a virtual machine (VM). The VM executes the Python code you type into your notebook. Think of Colab as an extremely friendly user interface to the VM.

TIP

As you dig deeper into Python, you'll probably start reading online articles that cover Python projects. If those articles include code, chances are good that they include `pip`, and without the exclamation point if the writer didn't work in a Jupyter environment. If you copy-and-paste the code into Colab, be sure to add the exclamation point to `pip` if it isn't already there.

Going Round and Round with Looping

As is the case with other computer languages, Python provides looping capabilities that handle repetitive tasks.

One such capability is the `for` loop. Use it when you know the number of iterations in advance. In this example, a `for` loop prints all even numbers and their squares from 0 up to but not including 10.

I begin by setting up the `for` loop:

```
for i in range(10):
```

In this line, `i` is the index; `range(10)` means "starting at 0 and going up to but not including 10." Note the colon (`:`) at the end of the line. It signifies that the following block of code is indented.

Next, I use an `if` statement to specify printing the index and its square only if the index is an even number:

```
if i%2 == 0:
```

This line carries quite a bit of information. First, as per the colon at the end of the preceding line, it's indented. In many programming languages, indentation is just a stylistic way to make code easier to read. In Python, indentation is an essential part of the syntax: It indicates the structure of a code block. Here, it means that the indented line is inside the `for` loop. (How many spaces should you indent? The Python community uses four spaces per indent. The Python language doesn't care, as long as you're consistent.)

The % sign is called the *modulo operator,* which is fancy terminology for "divide the first number (i) by the second number (2) and check the remainder." The double equal sign (==) is a comparison operator. In this line, it means "Is the remainder equal to 0?" If it is, i is an even number, and the flow moves to the next line. This line also ends with a colon.

If i isn't an even number, the flow moves back to the beginning of the loop and i increases by 1.

The next line is indented further, which means it's inside the `if` statement:

```
print(i, i**2)
```

The ** operator means "raise to the power of."

Here's the `for` loop, with comments; each comment begins with a pound sign (#). All the text between the # character and the end of a line is a *comment.*

```
# This for loop prints even numbers between 0 and 8
# along with their squares.
for i in range(10):    #Set up the for loop
    if i%2 == 0:       #Check to see if i is even
        print(i, i**2)     #If it is, print i and i-squared

0 0
2 4
4 16
6 36
8 64
```

Use a `while` loop when you aren't certain how many iterations will occur. Here's a `while` loop that does the same thing as the preceding `for` loop:

```
i = 0
while 0 <= i < 10:
  if i%2 == 0:
    print(i, i**2)
  i += 1
```

The first line shows that I have to explicitly set the initial value of the index.

The second line controls the flow as long as the index is greater than or equal to (`<=`) its lower boundary and less than (`<`) its upper boundary.

The last line shows that I have to explicitly increase the index by 1 at the end of the loop. The `+=` operator means "increase the number on the left side by the number on the right side."

Notice that the last line is indented as far as the `if` statement, meaning that it's inside the `while` loop but not inside the `if` statement.

I leave it as an exercise for you to add comments.

TIP

In the remaining chapters, I rarely use comments. Instead, I provide detailed descriptions of the code. In a book like this one, I feel that's the best way to get the message across.

Considering Conditionals

In the preceding section, I included an `if` statement to give you a hint of how Python treats *conditional* statements — statements that allow code execution if certain conditions are satisfied.

Here's an example of a more elaborate set of conditionals:

```
age = 27
registered = True
if age >= 18 and registered == True:
    print("You can vote.")
```

```
elif age >= 18 and registered == False:
    print("Register to vote")
else:
    print("You're not eligible to vote.")

You can vote.
```

As the code snippet shows, the three branches are if, elif, and else. One require-ment (age) is expressed as a number; the other (registration), as a Boolean. The and operator in the if and in the elif indicates the necessity to meet both voting requirements.

Comprehending List Comprehension

You can combine a for loop with a conditional to form a concise way of creating a list. It's called *list comprehension*.

Here's what I mean. I want to create a list of squares of the even numbers from 0 to 8. This is the old-fashioned way:

```
even_squares = []
for i in range(10):
    if i%2 == 0:
        even_squares.append(i**2)
```

The cool, sleek, *happening* list-comprehension way condenses everything into one line:

```
even_squares = [i**2 for i in range(10) if i%2 == 0]
```

Either way produces:

```
[0, 4, 16, 36, 64]
```

Another possibility is just a list of squares (no conditional necessary):

```
squares = [i**2 for i in range(10)]
print(squares)

[0, 1, 4, 9, 16, 25, 36, 49, 64, 81]
```

I can also use list comprehension to create a list from an existing list that I filter according to a condition. From an earlier example in this chapter, I have a list called `flowers`:

```
['aster', 'daisy', 'tulip', 'hibiscus', 'violet', 'rose']
```

I want to create a new list of flowers with the letter *s* in their names:

```
s_flowers =[ x for x in flowers if "s" in x]
print(s_flowers)

['aster', 'daisy', 'hibiscus', 'rose']
```

In the two numerical examples, the `for` loops operated on a range. In the third example, the `for` loop operated on a list. In each case, the `for` loop processed the items (numbers in the range, flower names in the list) one by one. In Python, any structure that a `for` loop can work on is called an *iterable*.

Bottom line: You can use list comprehension to create a list from any existing iterable.

Defining Your Own Functions

Although Python has a huge number of libraries and functions, you might someday encounter a situation that has no preexisting solution. When that happens, you'll have to create a function. In this section, I walk you through the steps to do just that.

In this example, I write a simple function that gives the sum and the sum of the squares of two numbers. I begin with a `def` statement that gives the name of the function and its arguments:

```
def sum_and_sum_of_squares(x,y):
```

The next part is extremely important — documenting the function. More than a comment but less than code, the *docstring* provides important information for anyone who has to read your work. Although it doesn't do any work, the docstring is retained as part of the running program.

I begin the docstring with three quote marks; write the documentation about what the function does, its arguments, and what it returns; and then finish with three quote marks:

```
'''
Calculates the sum of two numbers and the sum of their squares.

Arguments:
2 numbers

Returns:
sum, sum of squares
'''
```

Next, I code the sum and the sum of squares and then finish with a `return` statement:

```
sum = x + y
sum_of_squares = x**2 + y**2
return sum, sum_of_squares
```

In the earlier section on tuples, I mention that when a function returns multiple values, it packs them into a tuple. That's just what this function does, as you can see when I run this code and then use the function:

```
result = sum_and_sum_of_squares(5,7)
```

The variable `result` is an indexable tuple:

```
print(result[0])
print(result[1])

12
74
```

The built-in statistical functions I work with return results this way, and this is how I retrieve them.

What about that docstring? I use help() to access it:

```
help(sum_and_sum_of_squares)

Help on function sum_and_sum_of_squares in module __main__:

sum_and_sum_of_squares(x, y)
    Calculates the sum of two numbers and the sum of
  their squares.

    Arguments:
    2 numbers

    Returns:
    sum, sum of squares
```

The first line of the output is a bit technical, so I let that one go. The rest of the output is the docstring, which provides the description of the function.

TIP

Keep help() in mind when you want to know how a function works.

Wrapping Up

As I mention earlier, Python encompasses many concepts — way more than I can tell you about in a single chapter. The concepts I describe set you up for the rest of this book and will likely help you learn more about Python.

For an in-depth look at the language, consider *Python For Dummies,* by Stef Maruch and Aahz March, and *Python All-in-One For Dummies,* by John C. Shovic, PhD, and Alan Simpson (both titles published by Wiley).

2

Describing Data

Summarize and describe data.

Work with Python graphics.

Determine central tendency and variability.

Work with standard scores.

Understand and visualize normal distributions.

Chapter **3**

Getting Graphic

D ata visualization is an important part of statistics. A good graph enables you to spot trends and relationships you might otherwise miss if you look only at numbers. Graphics are valuable for another reason: They help you present your ideas to groups.

This is especially important in the field of data science. Organizations rely on data scientists to make sense of huge amounts of data so that decision-makers can formulate strategy. Graphics enable data scientists to explain patterns in the data to managers and to nontechnical personnel.

In this chapter, I show you how to use Python's graphical capabilities to draw frequently used graphs that might help you discern patterns.

Getting the Data

I work with data in the Cars93 data frame, which resides in the MASS package. This data frame holds data on 27 variables for 93 car models that were available in 1993. The MASS package is intended as a resource for R programmers, but we can use it in Python, too.

Here's how to get the data:

```
import statsmodels.api as sm
cars_93 = sm.datasets.get_rdataset("Cars93", "MASS")
cars_93.data
```

Figure 3-1 shows part of the data.

	Manufacturer	Model	Type	Min.Price	Price	Max.Price	MPG.city	MPG.highway	AirBags	DriveTrain	...	Passengers	Length	Wheelba
0	Acura	Integra	Small	12.9	15.9	18.8	25	31	NaN	Front	...	5	177	1
1	Acura	Legend	Midsize	29.2	33.9	38.7	18	25	Driver & Passenger	Front	...	5	195	1
2	Audi	90	Compact	25.9	29.1	32.3	20	26	Driver only	Front	...	5	180	1
3	Audi	100	Midsize	30.8	37.7	44.6	19	26	Driver & Passenger	Front	...	6	193	1
4	BMW	535i	Midsize	23.7	30.0	36.2	22	30	Driver only	Rear	...	4	186	1
...	...	...	...	...	...	...	...	...	...	...	...	...	...	...
88	Volkswagen	Eurovan	Van	16.6	19.7	22.7	17	21	NaN	Front	...	7	187	1
89	Volkswagen	Passat	Compact	17.6	20.0	22.4	21	30	NaN	Front	...	5	180	1
90	Volkswagen	Corrado	Sporty	22.9	23.3	23.7	18	25	NaN	Front	...	4	159	
91	Volvo	240	Compact	21.8	22.7	23.5	21	28	Driver only	Rear	...	5	190	1
92	Volvo	850	Midsize	24.8	26.7	28.5	20	28	Driver & Passenger	Front	...	5	184	1

93 rows × 27 columns

FIGURE 3-1:
Part of the
Cars93
data frame.

Looks like it's just crying out to be graphed, doesn't it?

Before I jump in and graph, I have to Pythonize it all. Although this is already a data frame, I invoke pandas:

```
import pandas as pd
cars_93_df = pd.DataFrame(cars_93.data)
```

Notice that some of the column names in Figure 3-1 include dots (like Min.Price). That's okay in R, but in Python, that's a big no-no. (See Chapter 20 for the reasons.) So I replace the dots with underscores:

```
cars_93_df.columns = cars_93_df.columns.str.replace('.', '_',
   regex=False)
```

That last argument (regex = False) tells Python to consider the dot as just a dot and not as a special character.

Let's graph!

Creating a Histogram

One pattern that might be of interest is the distribution of the prices of all cars listed in the Cars93 DataFrame. If you had to examine the entire data frame to determine this, it would be a tedious task. A graph, however, provides the information immediately. Figure 3-2, a *histogram*, shows what I mean. A histogram represents the distribution of numerical data by dividing the data into *bins* (also known as *intervals*) and showing a bar for each bin. The height of a bar corresponds to the number of data points in its bin.

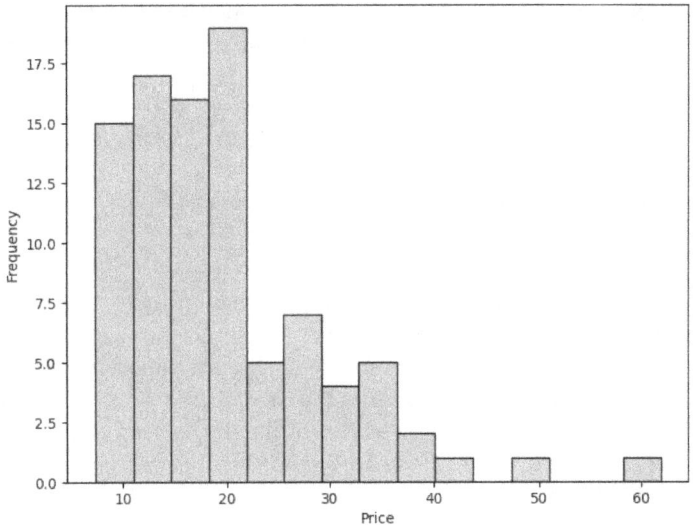

FIGURE 3-2: Histogram of prices of cars in the Cars93 data frame.

The histogram is appropriate when the variable on the *x*-axis is an interval variable or a ratio variable (see Chapter 1). With these types of variables, the numbers have meaning.

In Chapter 1, I distinguish between independent variables and dependent variables. Here, Price is the independent variable, and Frequency is the dependent variable. In most (but not all) graphs, the independent variable is on the *x*-axis, and the dependent variable is on the *y*-axis.

Here's how to draw a histogram. The code for almost all the graphs in this chapter begins with this line

```
import matplotlib.pyplot as plt
```

I import the MatPlotLib library and assign plt as its alias.

TIP

Throughout this chapter — and the book — I begin code snippets with `import` statements. I do this to make each snippet self-contained. While it's not necessary to repeat a specific `import` statement within a notebook, doing so doesn't result in any extra computing: Python just uses the already imported libraries.

Next, I set the dimensions of the plot:

```
plt.figure(figsize=(8, 6))
```

TIP

The "official" unit of the numbers in `figsize` is inches. Supposedly, the code says to produce a figure that measures 8 inches by 6 inches. This, of course, does not happen. Think of those numbers as guidelines: 8 X 6 is a rectangle, 6 X 6 is a square, and an 8 X 6 rectangle is bigger than a 4 X 3 rectangle. If you're ever in doubt, experiment a bit to get the desired appearance.

Next, I set up the histogram. I use the `hist()` method to do it:

```
plt.hist(cars_93_df['Price'], bins=15, color = "lightgray",
    edgecolor='black')
```

The first argument is the relevant variable in the data frame. The second argument (`bins`) specifies the number of intervals into which I divide the data. This is a bit of an art: Too few bins might obscure important details; too many might make the data look noisy. As is the case with `figsize`, you might have to experiment with `bins` when you start creating histograms of your own. The third argument sets the color of the bars, and the fourth argument sets the color of the bars' borders.

Finally, I label each axis and then show the whole thing:

```
plt.xlabel('Price X $1,000')
plt.ylabel('Frequency')
plt.show()
```

The result is shown in Figure 3-2.

Barhopping

For nominal variables (again, see Chapter 1), numbers are just labels. In fact, the levels of a nominal variable (also called a *factor* — see Chapter 2) can be names. Case in point: Another possible point of interest is the amounts of the different types of cars (sporty, midsize, and van, for example) in the DataFrame. So, `Type` is a nominal variable. If you looked at every entry in the DataFrame and created a table of these amounts (or *counts*), it would look like Table 3-1.

TABLE 3-1

Types and Counts of Cars in the Cars93 DataFrame

Type	Count
Midsize	22
Small	21
Compact	16
Sporty	14
Large	11
Van	9

The table shows some trends — more midsize and small car models than large cars and vans. Compact cars and sporty cars are in the middle.

Figure 3-3 shows this information in graphical form. This type of graph is a *bar graph*. The spaces between the bars emphasize that Type, on the *x*-axis, is a nominal variable.

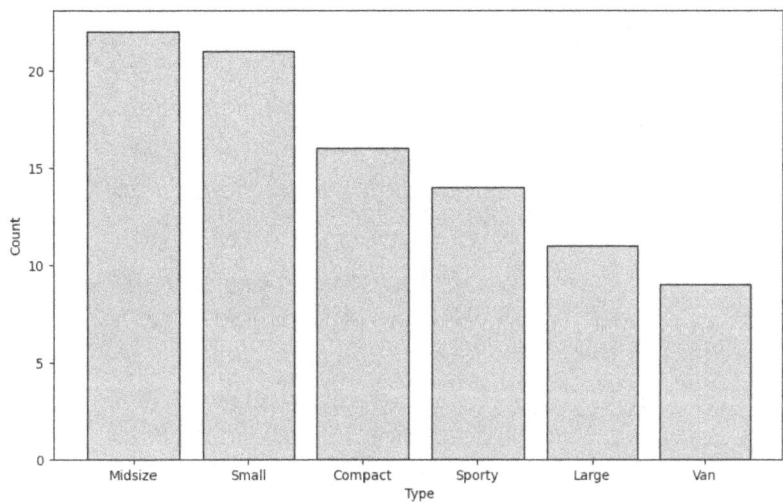

FIGURE 3-3:
Table 3-1 as a
bar graph.

Although the table is pretty straightforward, I think we'd agree that an audience would prefer to see the picture. As I'm fond of saying, eyes that glaze over when looking at numbers often shine brighter when looking at pictures.

To create the bar graph, I begin as before:

```
import matplotlib.pyplot as plt
```

And then I set the figure size:

```
plt.figure(figsize=(10, 6))
```

With cars_93_df as the DataFrame, I start with pandas, using its value_counts() method to produce Table 3-1:

```
car_type_counts = cars_93_df['Type'].value_counts()
```

The car_type_counts object has two properties: index and values. The Type column of Table 3-1 appears in the index property, and the Count in the values property:

```
types = car_type_counts.index
counts = car_type_counts.values
```

Now I create the bar graph

```
plt.bar(types, counts, color = "lightgray", edgecolor='black')
```

and label the axes:

```
plt.xlabel('Type')
plt.ylabel('Count')
```

I use a property called xticks to position the labels on the x-axis, setting rotation = 0 so that they appear horizontal (try values other than 0 and watch what happens):

```
plt.xticks(rotation=0)
```

Then I show the plot to reveal Figure 3-3:

```
plt.show()
```

Slicing the Pie

The *pie graph* shows the same data in a slightly different way: Each count appears as a slice of a pie. Figure 3-4 shows what I mean. In a pie graph, the area of the slice represents the count.

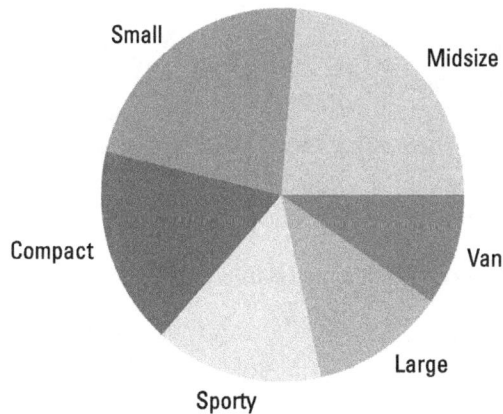

FIGURE 3-4:
Table 3-1 as a
pie graph.

Here's how I plot the pie graph. I start with the import:

```
import matplotlib.pyplot as plt
```

Then I set a size for the figure:

```
plt.figure(figsize=(8, 8))
```

I use the `value_counts()` method as I did in the preceding example:

```
car_type_counts = cars_93_df['Type'].value_counts()
```

Now I have to get the set of gray shades from which I select the colors for the graph:

```
gray_cmap = plt.get_cmap('Grays')
```

Next, I pick the colors:

```
pie_colors = gray_cmap([0.3, 0.5, 0.7, 0.2, 0.4, 0.6])
```

TIP

As an exercise, see what happens when you reorder the colors or choose new ones.

I create the pie graph:

```
plt.pie(car_type_counts, labels=car_type_counts.index,
    colors=pie_colors)
```

I make sure the pie appears as a circle. This is called setting an *equal aspect ratio:*

```
plt.axis('equal')
```

Finally, I show the graph that appears in Figure 3-4:

```
plt.show()
```

PIE GRAPH GUIDELINES

Pardon me if you've heard this one before. It's a cute anecdote that serves as a rule of thumb for pie graphs.

The late, great Yogi Berra often made lovable misstatements that became part of our culture. He once reputedly walked into a pizzeria and ordered a whole pizza.

"Should I cut that into four slices or eight?" asked the waitress.

"Better make it four," said Yogi. "I'm not hungry enough to eat eight."

The takeaway: If a factor has a lot of levels, resulting in a pie graph with a lot of slices, it's probably information overload. The message would come across better in a bar graph.

(Did that Yogi incident really happen? It's not clear. Summarizing a lifetime of sayings attributed to him, Mr. Berra said: "Half the lies they tell about me aren't true.")

The Plot of Scatter

Another potential pattern of interest is the relationship between miles per gallon for city driving and horsepower. This type of graph is a *scatterplot*. Figure 3-5 shows the scatterplot for these two variables.

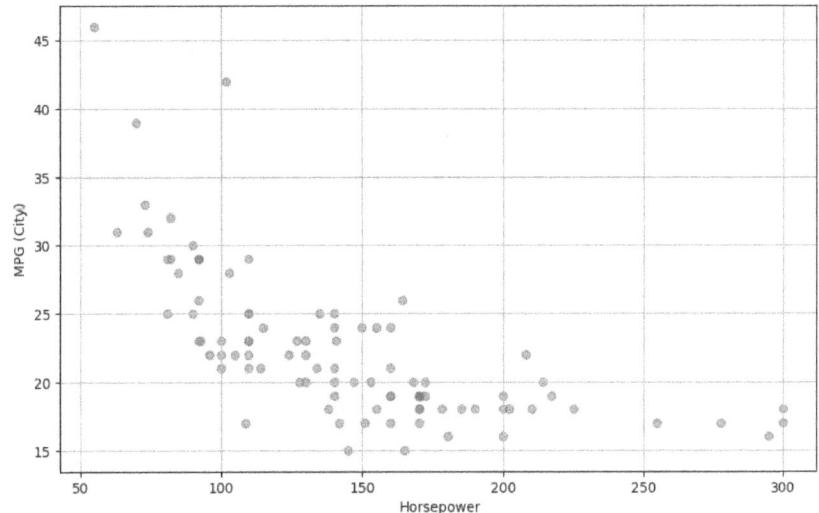

FIGURE 3-5: MPG in city driving and horsepower for the data in Cars93.

Each small circle represents one of the 93 cars. A circle's position along the *x*-axis (its *x-coordinate*) is its horsepower, and its position along the *y*-axis (its *y-coordinate*) is its MPG for city driving.

A quick look at the shape of the scatterplot suggests a relationship: As horsepower increases, MPG-city seems to decrease. (Statisticians would say "MPG-city decreases with horsepower.") Is it possible to use statistics to analyze this relationship and perhaps make predictions? Absolutely! (See Chapter 14.)

Plotting the plot is a snap. First, the import:

```
import matplotlib.pyplot as plt
```

Then the dimensions of the figure:

```
plt.figure(figsize=(10, 6))
```

Next, I specify the type of plot, the variables, and a parameter called `alpha`. Setting `alpha` to `0.5` makes the points in the plot semitransparent, which makes it easier to show overlapping points:

```
plt.scatter(cars_93_df['Horsepower'], cars_93.data['MPG.city'],
    alpha=0.5)
```

Finally, I label the axes, make a grid visible, and show the plot:

```
plt.xlabel('Horsepower')
plt.ylabel('MPG (City)')
plt.grid(True)
plt.show()
```

Of Boxes and Whiskers

What about the relationship between horsepower and the number of cylinders in a car's engine? You would expect horsepower to increase with cylinders, and Figure 3-6 shows that this is indeed the case. Invented by the famed statistician John Tukey, this type of graph is called a *box plot*, and it's a nice, quick way to visualize data.

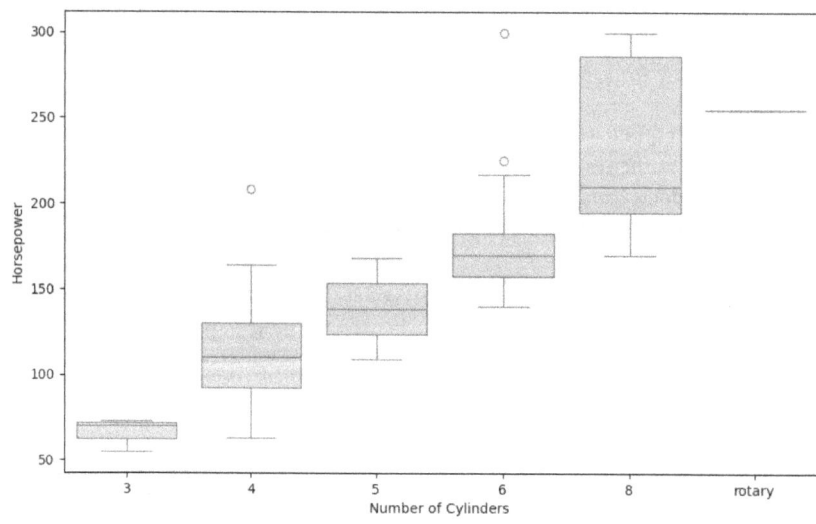

FIGURE 3-6:
Box plot of horsepower versus number of cylinders in the Cars93 data frame.

Each box represents a group of numbers. The leftmost box, for example, represents the horsepower of cars with three cylinders. The black solid line inside the box is the *median:* the horsepower-value that falls between the lower half of the numbers and the upper half. The lower and upper edges of the box are called *hinges.* The lower hinge is the *lower quartile,* the number below which 25 percent of the numbers fall. The upper hinge is the *upper* quartile, the number that exceeds 75 percent of the numbers. (I discuss medians in Chapter 4 and percentiles in Chapter 6.)

The elements sticking out of the hinges are called *whiskers* (so you sometimes see this type of graph referred to as a *box-and-whiskers* plot). The whiskers include data values outside the hinges. The upper whisker boundary is either the maximum value or the upper hinge plus 1.5 times the length of the box, whichever is *smaller.* The lower whisker boundary is either the minimum value or the lower hinge minus 1.5 times the length of the box, whichever is *larger.* Data points outside the whiskers are *outliers.* The box plot shows that the data for four cylinders and for six cylinders have outliers.

Note that the graph shows only a solid line for `rotary`, an engine type that occurs just once in the data.

Here's how to code this informative plot. As always, I begin by importing `matplotlib.pyplot`:

```
import matplotlib.pyplot as plt
```

For this one, I import `seaborn`, an additional graphics library:

```
import seaborn as sns
```

[The alias is `sns` because the library is named after Samuel Norman Seaborn, a character in the classic TV series "The West Wing".] It's a bit easier to create a boxplot in `seaborn` than it is in `matplotlib`.

I'm still working with `cars_93_df`, so

```
data = cars_93_df
```

The next order of business is the business of order — I retrieve the unique cylinder values and sort them:

```
cylinders_order = sorted(data['Cylinders'].unique())
```

Once again, I set the dimensions of the figure:

```
plt.figure(figsize=(10, 6))
```

Now I use the `seaborn.boxplot()` method to set up the boxplot:

```
sns.boxplot(x='Cylinders', y='Horsepower', data=data, color =
    "lightgray", order=cylinders_order)
```

And I finish with axis labels and then the code that renders the plot shown in Figure 3-6:

```
plt.xlabel('Number of Cylinders')
plt.ylabel('Horsepower')
plt.show()
```

Continuous Variables

In the preceding sections, the values on the *x*-axis were discrete (like Type of Car or Number of Cylinders). Sometimes you have to plot a continuous variable, and here's where I show you how to do just that.

I'll keep it simple. In Chapter 14, I show you how a line represents

$$y = 4 + 2x$$

(If you're hazy on how that works, take a look at the discussion in Chapter 14 about graphing lines.) The point here is that the *x*-axis consists of continuous values, and to graph them, I have to use a numpy method called `linspace()`:

Here's what I mean. After the imports

```
import matplotlib.pyplot as plt
import numpy as np
```

I have to define a range for plotting *x*. To stay consistent with Chapter 14, I plot y as x goes from 0 to 6. That range (or any other) holds an infinite number of values. I can't specify an infinite number of values to plot, but 100 values gives us a pretty good picture.

So I use `linspace()` to set up 100 equally spaced points between 0 and 6.01. (To include 6 in the range, I have to go a bit over.):

```
x = np.linspace(0, 6.01, 100)
```

Next, I define the relationship between x and y:

```
y = 4 + 2*x
```

Then I set the dimensions of the figure

```
plt.figure(figsize=(8, 6))
```

I then create the plot of y values that correspond to each of the 100 equally spaced points I specified with `linspace()`:

```
plt.plot(x, y)
```

I label the axes and specify a grid

```
plt.xlabel('x')
plt.ylabel('y')
plt.grid(True)
```

Just to stay consistent with Figure 14-2, I set the lower limit of the x-axis to 0 and the lower limit of the y-axis to 0:

```
plt.xlim(0, plt.xlim()[1])
plt.ylim(0, plt.ylim()[1])
```

And then I show the whole thing:

```
plt.show()
```

The result is shown in Figure 3-7.

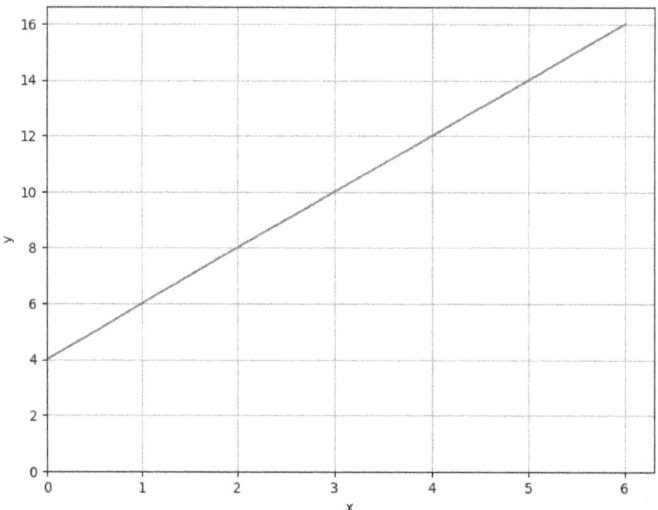

FIGURE 3-7:
Plotting y = 4 + 2x.

Wrapping Up

As far as graphics go, I've just scratched the surface. Python has a rich set of graphics tools and packages — way more than I could show you in this chapter.

What I did show you comes in handy, as you'll see: In the chapters to come, every time I show you an analytic technique, I also show you how to visualize its results.

Chapter **4**

Finding Your Center

I f you've ever worked with a set of numbers and had to figure out how to summarize them with a single number, you've faced a situation that statisticians deal with all the time: Where would this ideal "single number" come from?

A good idea might be to select a number from somewhere in the middle of the set. That number could then represent the entire set of numbers. When you're looking around in the middle of the set, you're looking at *central tendency*. You can address central tendency in a variety of ways.

Means: The Lure of Averages

We've all used averages. Statisticians refer to the average as the *mean*. The mean is an easy way to summarize your spending, your school grades, or your performance in a sport over time.

In the course of their work, scientists calculate means. When a researcher does a study, they apply some kind of treatment or procedure to a small sample of people or things. Then they measure the results and estimate the effects of the procedure on the population that produced the sample. Statisticians have shown that the sample mean is the estimate of the mean of the population.

I think you know how to calculate the mean, but I'll walk you through it anyway. Then I'll show you the statistical formula. My objective is for you to understand statistical formulas in general, and then I'll show you how Python calculates means.

A *mean* is just the sum of a set of numbers divided by how many numbers you added. Suppose you measure the heights (in inches) of six 5-year-old children and find that their heights are

36, 42, 43, 37, 40, 45

The average height of these six children is

$$\frac{36, 42, 43, 37, 40, 45}{6} = 40.5$$

The mean of this sample, then, is 40.5 inches.

A first attempt at a formula for the mean might be

$$\text{Mean} = \frac{\text{Sum of Numbers}}{\text{Amount of Numbers You Added Up}}$$

Formulas, though, usually involve abbreviations. A common abbreviation for "Number" is *X*. Statisticians usually abbreviate "Amount of Numbers You Added Up" as *N*. So the formula becomes

$$\text{Mean} = \frac{\text{Sum of } X}{N}$$

Statisticians also use an abbreviation for *Sum of* — the uppercase Greek letter for S. Pronounced "sigma," it looks like this: Σ. So the formula with the sigma is

$$\text{Mean} = \frac{\sum X}{N}$$

I'm not done yet. Statisticians abbreviate *mean*, too. You might think that *M* would be the abbreviation, and some statisticians agree with you, but most prefer a symbol that's related to *X*. For this reason, the most popular abbreviation for the mean is $\bar{X}$, which is pronounced "X bar." And here's the formula:

$$\bar{X} = \frac{\sum X}{N}$$

I have to tie up one more loose end. In Chapter 1, I discuss samples and populations. Symbols in formulas have to reflect the distinction between the two. The convention is that English letters, like $\bar{X}$, stand for characteristics of samples, and Greek letters stand for characteristics of populations. For the population mean, the symbol is the Greek equivalent of *M*, which is μ. It's pronounced like "you" but with "m" in front of it. The formula for the population mean, then, is

$$\mu = \frac{\sum X}{N}$$

The Average in Python

Python provides a straightforward method for calculating the mean of a set of numbers: mean(). I apply it to the example of the heights of six children.

This method lives in the numpy library, so I begin by importing numpy:

```
import numpy as np
```

Then I create the data in a variable called heights:

```
heights = [36,42,43,37,40,45]
```

Finally, I can calculate np.mean(heights) inside a print(f ...) statement:

```
print(f"Mean of the heights = {np.mean(heights)}")

Mean of the heights = 40.5
```

TIP

All those lines of code can go into one Colab cell.

What's your condition?

When you work with a DataFrame, sometimes you want to calculate the mean of just the cases (rows) that meet certain conditions rather than the mean of all the cases. This is easy to do in Python.

For the discussion that follows, I use the same Cars93 DataFrame that I use in Chapter 3. It's the one that has data for a sample of 93 cars from 1993. It's in the MASS package. This is a dataset associated with R, but as I point out in Chapter 3, it's easy to use R datasets in Python.

The necessary tools reside in the `statsmodel` library, so I begin with

```
import statsmodels.api as sm
```

Next, I retrieve the `Cars93` data:

```
cars_93 = sm.datasets.get_rdataset("Cars93", "MASS")
```

I want to cast the data into a pandas DataFrame, so I import pandas:

```
import pandas as pd
```

and then set up the DataFrame:

```
cars_93df = pd.DataFrame(cars_93.data)
```

To get an idea of what's in the DataFrame, I take a quick look at the columns:

```
print(cars_93df.columns)
```

Here's the result:

```
Index(['Manufacturer', 'Model', 'Type', 'Min.Price', 'Price',
   'Max.Price',
       'MPG.city', 'MPG.highway', 'AirBags', 'DriveTrain',
   'Cylinders',
       'EngineSize', 'Horsepower', 'RPM', 'Rev.per.mile',
   'Man.trans.avail',
       'Fuel.tank.capacity', 'Passengers', 'Length',
   'Wheelbase', 'Width',
       'Turn.circle', 'Rear.seat.room', 'Luggage.room',
   'Weight', 'Origin',
       'Make'],
     dtype='object')
```

The goal here is to calculate the mean horsepower of cars made in the USA and the mean horsepower of cars made elsewhere.

I begin by partitioning the data into USA cars and non-USA cars.

```
USA_cars_93 = cars_93df[cars_93df['Origin'] == 'USA']
nonUSA_cars_93 = cars_93df[cars_93df['Origin'] != 'USA']
```

Next, I calculate the horsepower means (rounded off to two decimal places in the print() statement) and then print them:

```
Average_USA_HP = USA_cars_93.Horsepower.mean()
Average_nonUSA_HP = nonUSA_cars_93.Horsepower.mean()
print(f"Average USA Horsepower = {Average_USA_HP:.2f}, and
    Average nonUSA Horsepower = {Average_nonUSA_HP:.2f}")
```

Running this code results in:

```
Average USA Horsepower = 147.52, and Average nonUSA
    Horsepower = 139.89
```

So the averages differ a bit. (Can we examine that difference more closely? Yes, we can, which is just what I show you how to do in Chapter 11.)

REMEMBER

The :.2f at the end of each expression inside the curly braces means "round off to two decimal places."

Exploring the data

Now that I've shown you how to calculate the horsepower means of USA and non-USA cars, how about the overall horsepower distributions? Are they alike? Do they differ?

That calls for a little data exploration — a couple of histograms do the trick. For an easy comparison, I'll put them side by side. The finished product looks like Figure 4-1.

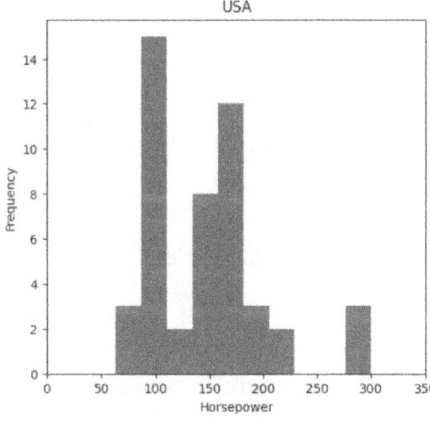
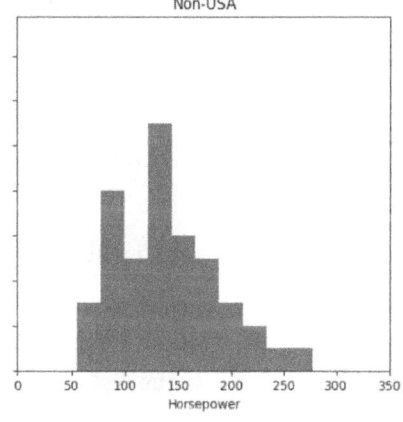

FIGURE 4-1:
The horsepower histograms for USA cars and non-USA cars.

The graphics tools are in `matplotlib`, so I begin by importing that library:

```
from matplotlib import pyplot as plt
```

Then I divide the figure into two subplots that I refer to as `ax1` and `ax2`. Think of them as two pairs of axes:

```
fig, (ax1,ax2) = plt.subplots(1,2, figsize=(12,5), sharey=True)
```

The pair of values 1,2 defines the layout of 1 row and 2 columns (side-by-side). For one above the other, that would be 2,1. The next argument, `figsize`, unsurprisingly sets dimensions for the plots, and the final argument means that the two histograms share the y-axis.

Next, I define the histograms for the USA cars and the non-USA cars:

```
USA_cars_93['Horsepower'].plot(kind='hist',bins=20,
    title='USA',ax=ax1)
nonUSA_cars_93['Horsepower'].plot(kind='hist',bins=20,
    title='Non-USA',ax=ax2)
```

In each `plot()`, the first argument determines the kind of plot it is, the second sets the number of bins (intervals in which I group the data), and the third argument sets the title for the plot. The fourth argument determines which axes get which histogram.

Then I add the code for the axis titles,

```
ax1.set_xlabel('Horsepower')
ax2.set_xlabel('Horsepower')
ax1.set_ylabel('Frequency')
ax2.set_ylabel('Frequency')
```

set lower and upper limits for the x-axes,

```
ax1.set_xlim(0,350)
ax2.set_xlim(0,350)
```

and, finally, add the code that shows the whole thing:

```
plt.show()
```

As the histograms in Figure 4-1 show, the distributions are quite different.

Outliers: The flaw of averages

An *outlier* is an extreme value in a dataset. If the dataset is a sample and you're trying to estimate the population mean, the outlier might bias the estimate.

Statisticians deal with outliers by *trimming* the mean — eliminating extreme values at the low end and the high end before calculating the sample mean. The amount of trim is a percentage, like the upper and lower 5 percent of the scores.

For example, the histogram on the left in Figure 4-1 shows some extreme values, and, consequently, we might want to trim the data a bit. The numpy library has no function for trimming the mean, but the scipy library has one called trim_mean():

```
from scipy import stats
trim_pct = 0.05
trimmed_mean = stats.trim_mean(USA_cars_93.Horsepower, trim_pct)
print(f"Mean of USA horsepower with extreme {100 * trim_pct}%
    trimmed = {trimmed_mean:.2f}")

Mean of USA horsepower with extreme 5.0% trimmed = 144.18
```

I trimmed 5% from each extreme and rounded to two decimal places to make the output prettier.

The result is a bit lower than the untrimmed mean.

TIP

I set up trim_pct to make it easy for you to experiment with a variety of trim percentages.

REMEMBER

What's the appropriate percentage for trim_mean()? That's up to you. It depends on what you're measuring, how extreme your scores can be, and how well you know the area you're studying. When you report a trimmed mean, let your audience know that you've done this and tell them the percentage you've trimmed.

In the upcoming section about the median, I show you another way to deal with extreme scores.

Other means to an end

In this section, I tell you about two additional averages that are different from the mean you're accustomed to working with.

The everyday, garden-variety mean is called the *arithmetic* (pronounced "airith-MET-ic") *mean.*

Geometric mean

Suppose you have a 5-year investment that yields these percentages: 10 percent, 15 percent, 10 percent, 20 percent, and 5 percent. (Yes, yes. I know. This is fiction.) What's the average annual rate of return?

Your first guess might be to average those percentages. That average is 12 percent. And it would be incorrect.

Why? It misses an important point. At the end of the first year, you *multiply* your investment by 1.10 — you don't add 1.10 to your investment. At the end of the second year, you multiply the first-year result by 1.15, and so on.

The arithmetic mean won't give you the average rate of return. Instead, you calculate that average this way:

$$\text{Average Rate of Return} = \sqrt[5]{1.10 \times 1.15 \times 1.10 \times 1.20 \times 1.05} = 1.118847$$

The average rate of return is a little less than 12 percent — 11.118847 percent, to be exact. This kind of average is called the *geometric mean.*

In this example, the geometric mean is the fifth root of the product of five numbers. Is it always the *n*th root of the product of *n* numbers? Yep.

The function I use, gmean() is in scipy, from which I've already imported stats.

I begin with a variable to hold the numbers in the example:

```
rates = [1.10,1.15,1.10,1.20,1.05]
```

The calculation is

```
print(f"Geometric mean of rates = {stats.gmean(rates):.6f}")

Geometric mean of rates = 1.118847
```

Harmonic mean

Here's a situation you sometimes encounter in real life, but more often in algebra textbooks.

Suppose you're in no hurry to get to work in the morning and you drive from your home to your workplace at a rate of 30 miles per hour. At the end of the day, on the other hand, you'd like to get home quickly. So, on the return trip (over exactly the same distance), you drive from your job to your home at 50 miles per hour. What is the average rate for your total time on the road?

It's not 40 miles per hour, because you're on the road a different amount of time for each leg of the trip. Without going into this distinction too deeply, the formula for figuring it out is

$$\frac{1}{\text{Average}} = \frac{1}{2}\left[\frac{1}{30} + \frac{1}{50}\right] = \frac{1}{37.5}$$

The average is 37.5. This type of average is called a *harmonic mean*. This example consists of two numbers, but you can calculate it for any amount of numbers. Just put each number in the denominator of a fraction with 1 as the numerator. Mathematicians call this the *reciprocal* of a number. (So 1/30 is the reciprocal of 30.) Add all the reciprocals together and take their average. The result is the reciprocal of the harmonic mean.

The hmean() function is also in scipy stats:

```
speeds = [30,50]
print(f"Harmonic mean of speeds = {stats.hmean(speeds):.2f}")


Harmonic mean of speeds = 37.50
```

Medians: Caught in the Middle

The mean is a useful way to summarize a group of numbers. One drawback ("the flaw of averages") is that it's sensitive to extreme values. If one number is out of whack, the mean is out of whack, too. When that happens, the mean might not be a good representative of the group.

Here, for example, are the reading speeds (in words per minute) for a group of children:

56, 78, 45, 49, 55, 62

The mean is

```
reading_speeds = [56,78,45,49,55,62]
print(f"Mean reading speed = {np.mean(reading_speeds)}")

Mean reading speed = 57.5
```

Suppose the child who reads 78 words per minute leaves the group and an exceptionally fast reader replaces him. Her reading speed is a phenomenal 180 words per minute, which drastically changes the mean:

```
reading_speeds_new = reading_speeds
reading_speeds_new[1] = 180
print(f"Mean reading speed with new child in the group =
    {np.mean(reading_speeds_new)}")

Mean reading speed with new child in the group = 74.5
```

The new average is misleading. Except for the new child, no one else in the group reads nearly that fast. In a case like this, it's a good idea to use a different measure of central tendency — the median.

Median is a fancy name for a simple concept: It's the middle value in a group of numbers. Arrange the numbers in order (via the numpy sort() method), and the median is the value below which half the scores fall and above which half the scores fall:

```
print(f"Sorted reading speeds in the original group =
    {np.sort(reading_speeds)}")

print(f"Sorted reading speeds in the new group =
    {np.sort(reading_speeds_new)}")
Sorted reading speeds in the original group =
    [45 49 55 56 62 78]
Sorted reading speeds in the new group = [ 45  49  55
    56  62 180]
```

In each case, the median is halfway between 55 and 56, or 55.5.

The Median in Python

So it's no big mystery how to use Python to find a median — np.median() gets it done:

```
print(f"Median reading speed in the original group = {np.
    median(reading_speeds)}")
print(f"Median reading speed in the new group = {np.
    median(reading_speeds_new)}")
```

```
Median reading speed in the original group = 55.5
Median reading speed in the new group = 55.5
```

With larger datasets, you might encounter replication of scores. In any case, the median is still the middle value. For example, here are the horsepower values for all the cars in the cars93 DataFrame:

```
print(f"Sorted Horsepower of cars_93:\n {np.sort(cars_93df.
    Horsepower)}")
Sorted Horsepower of cars_93:
 [ 55  63  70  73  74  81  81  82  82  85  90  90  92  92  92
   92  92  93
   96 100 100 100 102 103 105 109 110 110 110 110 110 110 110
   114 115 124
  127 128 130 130 130 134 135 138 140 140 140 140 140 141 142
   145 147 150
  151 153 155 155 160 160 160 160 160 164 165 168 170 170 170
   170 170 170
  170 172 172 178 180 185 190 200 200 200 202 208 210 214 217
   225 255 278
  295 300 300]
```

And here's the median:

```
print(f"Median horsepower of cars_93= {np.median(cars_93df.
    Horsepower)}")

Median horsepower of cars_93 = 140.0
```

In the preceding print() statement, the \n is a newline character. I used it to make the output look better on the page.

TIP

Statistics à la Mode

One more measure of central tendency, the *mode*, is important. It's the score that occurs most frequently in a group of scores.

Sometimes, the mode is the best measure of central tendency to use. Imagine a small company that consists of 30 consultants and two high-ranking officers. Each consultant has an annual salary of $40,000. Each officer has an annual salary of $250,000. The mean salary in this company is $53,125.

Does the mean give you a clear picture of the company's salary structure? If you were looking for a job with that company, would the mean influence your expectations? You're probably better off if you consider the mode, which in this case is $40,000 (unless you happen to be high-priced executive talent!).

Nothing is complicated about finding the mode. Look at the scores and find the one that occurs most frequently, and you've found the mode. Do two scores tie for that honor? In that case, your set of scores has two modes. (The technical name is *bimodal*.)

Can you have more than two modes? Absolutely.

If every score occurs equally often, you have no mode.

The Mode in Python

The scipy stats.mode() function works on an array of data and returns an array of results. The returned array provides the mode and how many times it occurs in the data.

I begin by casting the list of horsepower values into an array:

```
Horsepower_array = np.array(cars_93df.Horsepower)
```

Then stats.mode() can do its thing:

```
Horsepower_mode = stats.mode(Horsepower_array)
print(f"Modal horsepower of cars_93 = {Horsepower_mode[0]}")
print(f"Frequency of modal horsepower of cars_93 =
   {Horsepower_mode[1]}")

Modal horsepower of cars_93 = 110
Frequency of modal horsepower of cars_93 = 7
```

This function, however, has a quirk: If the data has more than one modal value, it returns only one — the lowest one. Go back to the sorted horsepower values in the preceding section on the median. You'll see that 110 is not the only mode. Can you spot the other one?

Chapter **5**

Deviating from the Average

ere's a well-known statistician joke: Three statisticians go deer hunting with bows and arrows. They spot a deer and take aim. One shoots, and the arrow flies off ten feet to the left. The second shoots, and the arrow flies ten feet to the right. The third statistician happily yells out, "We got him!"

Moral of the story: Calculating the mean is a helpful way to summarize a set of numbers, but the mean might mislead you. How? By not giving you all the information you typically need. If you rely only on the mean, you might miss important information about the set of numbers.

To avoid missing important information, another type of statistic is necessary — a statistic that measures variation. Think of *variation* as a kind of average of how much each number in a group of numbers differs from the group mean. Several statistics are available for measuring variation. They all work the same way: The larger the value of the statistic, the more the numbers differ from their mean. The smaller the value, the less they differ.

Measuring Variation

Suppose you measure the heights of a group of children, and you find that their heights (in inches) are

48, 48, 48, 48, and 48

Then you measure another group and find that their heights are

50, 47, 52, 46, and 45

If you calculate the mean of each group, you'll find they're the same — 48 inches. Just looking at the numbers tells you the two groups of heights are different: The heights in the first group are all the same, whereas the heights in the second vary quite a bit.

Averaging squared deviations: Variance and how to calculate it

One way to show the dissimilarity between the two groups is to examine the deviations in each one. Think of a *deviation* as the difference between a score and the mean of all scores in a group.

Here's what I'm talking about. Table 5-1 shows the first group of heights and their deviations.

TABLE 5-1

The First Group of Heights and Their Deviations

Height	Height-Mean	Deviation
48	48-48	0
48	48-48	0
48	48-48	0
48	48-48	0
48	48-48	0

One way to proceed is to average the deviations. Clearly, the average of the numbers in the Deviation column is 0.

Table 5-2 shows the second group of heights and their deviations.

TABLE 5-2

The Second Group of Heights and Their Deviations

Height	Height-Mean	Deviation
50	50-48	2
47	47-48	−1
52	52-48	4
46	46-48	−2
45	45-48	−3

What about the average of the deviations in Table 5-2? That's . . . 0!

Now what?

Averaging the deviations doesn't help you see a difference between the two groups, because the average of deviations from the mean in any group of numbers is always zero. In fact, veteran statisticians will tell you that's a defining property of the mean.

The joker in the deck here is the negative numbers. How do statisticians deal with them?

The trick is to use something you might recall from algebra class: A minus times a minus is a plus. Sound familiar?

So . . . does this mean that you multiply each deviation times itself and then average the results? Absolutely. Multiplying a deviation times itself is called *squaring a deviation.* The average of the squared deviations is so important that it has a special name: *variance.*

Table 5-3 shows the group of heights from Table 5-2, along with their deviations and squared deviations.

The variance — the average of the squared deviations for this group — is $(4+1+16+4+9)/5 = 34/5 = 6.8$. This, of course, is quite different from the first group, whose variance is 0.

To develop the variance formula for you and show you how it works, I use symbols to show all this: X represents the Height heading in the first column of the table, and $\bar{X}$ represents the mean.

TABLE 5-3

The Second Group of Heights and Their Squared Deviations

Height	Height-Mean	Deviation	Squared Deviation
50	50-48	2	4
47	47-48	–1	1
52	52-48	4	16
46	46-48	–2	4
45	45-48	–3	9

A deviation is the result of subtracting the mean from each number, so

$$\left(X - \bar{X} \right)$$

symbolizes a deviation. How about multiplying a deviation by itself? That's

$$\left(X - \bar{X} \right)^2$$

To calculate variance, you square each deviation, add them up, and find the average of the squared deviations. If N represents the amount of squared deviations you have (in this example, five), the formula for calculating the variance is

$$\frac{\sum \left(X - \bar{X} \right)^2}{N}$$

The Σ character is the uppercase Greek letter *sigma*, and it means "the sum of."

What's the symbol for variance? As I mention in Chapter 1, Greek letters represent population parameters, and English letters represent sample statistics. Imagine that our little group of five numbers is an entire population. Does the Greek alphabet have a letter that corresponds to V in the same way that μ (the symbol for the population mean) corresponds to M?

Nope. Instead, you use the lowercase sigma! It looks like this: σ. And, on top of that, because you're talking about squared quantities, the symbol for population variance is σ^2.

Bottom line: The formula for calculating population variance is

$$\sigma^2 = \frac{\sum \left(X - \bar{X} \right)^2}{N}$$

REMEMBER

A large value for the variance tells you that the numbers in a group vary greatly from their mean. A small value for the variance tells you that the numbers are similar to their mean.

Sample variance

The variance formula I show you in the preceding section is appropriate if the group of five measurements is a population. Does this mean that variance for a sample is different? It does, and here's why.

If your set of numbers is a sample drawn from a large population, your objective is most likely to use the variance of the sample to estimate the variance of the population.

The formula in the preceding section doesn't work as an estimate of the population variance. Although the mean calculated in the usual way is an accurate estimate of the population mean, that's not the case for the variance, for reasons far beyond the scope of this book.

REMEMBER

It's pretty easy to calculate an accurate estimate of the population variance. All you have to do is use $N - 1$ in the denominator rather than N (again, for reasons way beyond this book's scope).

And, because you're working with a characteristic of a sample (rather than of a population), you use the English equivalent of the Greek letter — s rather than σ. This means that the formula for the sample variance (as an estimate of the population variance) is

$$s^2 = \frac{\sum(X - \bar{X})^2}{N - 1}$$

The value of s^2, given the squared deviations in the set of five numbers, is

$$(4 + 1 + 16 + 4 + 9)/4 = 34/4 = 8.5$$

So, if these numbers

50, 47, 52, 46, and 45

are an entire population, their variance is 6.8. If they're a sample drawn from a larger population, the best estimate of that population's variance is 8.5.

Variance in Python

Python provides a couple of different ways to calculate variance. The two I show you are both called var(), but they live in different libraries and they give different results. The one that lives in numpy uses N in the denominator; the one that lives in pandas uses *N*-1 in the denominator.

I begin by importing the two libraries:

```
import numpy as np
import pandas as pd
```

Next, I create a list of the data in the Heights example:

```
heights = [50,47,52,46,45]
```

The pandas function requires the data to be in the form of a *Series* (an array that's kind of like a column in a pandas DataFrame). So:

```
heights_series = pd.Series(heights)
```

The syntaxes of the two functions are different. The numpy function is np.var(heights), the pandas function is heights_series.var().

I embed the var() functions inside print() statements:

```
print(f"Numpy calculates variance as {np.var(heights)}")
print(f"Pandas calculates variance as {heights_series.var()}")

Numpy calculates variance as 6.8
Pandas calculates variance as 8.5
```

REMEMBER

For reasons that will become clear later, I'd like you to think of the denominator of a variance estimate (like $N - 1$) as *degrees of freedom*. Why? Stay tuned. (Chapter 12 reveals all!)

TIP

If you use pandas, this degrees-of-freedom thing I just mentioned comes in handy. You can set a parameter called ddof to make the pandas variance function use N instead of $N - 1$. The parameter name ddof stands for "delta degrees of freedom" — meaning the change in degrees of freedom from N. The default value is 1, so that pandas `var()` uses $N - 1$. Change that value to 0 (no change from N, in other words), and the function uses N:

```
print(f"Pandas calculates population variance as {heights_
    series.var(ddof = 0)}")

Pandas calculates population variance as 6.8
```

Back to the Roots: Standard Deviation

After you calculate the variance of a set of numbers, you have a value whose units are different from your original measurements. For example, if your original measurements are in inches, their variance is in square inches. This is because you square the deviations before you average them. So the variance in the 5-score population in the preceding example is 6.8 square inches.

It might be hard to grasp what that statement means. Often, it's more intuitive if the variation statistic is in the same units as the original measurements. It's easy to turn variance into that kind of statistic. All you have to do is take the square root of the variance.

Like the variance, this square root is so important that it has a special name: standard deviation.

Population standard deviation

The *standard deviation* of a population is the square root of the population variance. The symbol for the population standard deviation is σ (lowercase sigma). Its formula is

$$\sigma = \sqrt{\sigma^2} = \sqrt{\frac{\sum(X - \bar{X})^2}{N}}$$

For this 5-score population of measurements (in inches):

50, 47, 52, 46, and 45

the population variance is 6.8 square inches, and the population standard deviation is 2.61 inches (rounded off).

Sample standard deviation

The standard deviation of a sample — an estimate of the standard deviation of a population — is the square root of the sample variance. Its symbol is s, and its formula is

$$s = \sqrt{s^2} = \sqrt{\frac{\sum(X - \bar{X})^2}{N-1}}$$

For this sample of measurements (in inches):

50, 47, 52, 46, and 45

the estimated population variance is 8.4 square inches, and the estimated population standard deviation is 2.92 inches (rounded off).

Standard Deviation in Python

As is the case with variance, you can find functions for standard deviation in numpy and in pandas. Both are called std(), the syntaxes are different, and numpy uses N whereas pandas uses N − 1.

How about I cut to the chase?

```
print(f"Numpy calculates standard deviation as {np.
    std(heights):.2f}")
print(f"Pandas calculates standard deviation as {heights_series.
    std():.2f}")

Numpy calculates standard deviation as 2.61
Pandas calculates standard deviation as 2.92
```

REMEMBER

The :.2f inside each right curly brace means "round off to two decimal places."

Conditions, Conditions, Conditions . . .

In Chapter 4, I point out that with larger DataFrames, you sometimes want to calculate statistics on rows that meet certain conditions rather than on all the rows.

As in Chapters 3 and 4, I use the Cars93 DataFrame for the discussion that follows. That DataFrame has data for a sample of 93 cars from 1993. You'll find it in the MASS package. This package is associated with R, so again I have to use a little trickery to open it in Python:

```
import statsmodels.api as sm
cars_93 = sm.datasets.get_rdataset("Cars93", "MASS")
```

Next, I cast the data into a pandas DataFrame:

```
cars_93df = pd.DataFrame(cars_93.data)
```

My objective is to find the variance in horsepower of cars made in the USA:

```
USA_cars_93 = cars_93df[cars_93df['Origin'] == 'USA']
Variance_USA_HP = USA_cars_93.Horsepower.var()
print(f"Variance of horsepower of USA cars is
    {Variance_USA_HP:.2f}")

Variance of horsepower of USA cars is 2965.32
```

Notice I didn't have to turn the horsepower data into a pandas Series to use the pandas var() function — the data is already in a column in a pandas DataFrame.

What about the non-USA cars?

```
nonUSA_cars_93 = cars_93df[cars_93df['Origin'] != 'USA']
Variance_nonUSA_HP = nonUSA_cars_93.Horsepower.var()
print(f"Variance of horsepower of non-USA cars is
    {Variance_nonUSA_HP:.2f}")

Variance of horsepower of non-USA cars is 2537.28
```

Can you compare these variances? Sure — but not until Chapter 11.

Chapter **6**

Meeting Standards and Standings

n my left hand, I hold 100 Philippine pesos. In my right, I hold 1,000 Colombian pesos. Which is worth more? Both are called *pesos*, right? So, shouldn't the 1,000 be greater than the 100? Not necessarily. *Peso* is just a coincidence of names. Each one comes out of a different country, and each country has its own economy.

To compare the two amounts of money, you have to convert each currency into a standard unit. The most intuitive standard for US citizens is our own currency. How much is each amount worth in dollars and cents? As I write this chapter, 100 Philippine pesos are worth $1.75. One thousand Colombian pesos are worth 23 cents.

So, when you compare numbers, context is important. To make valid comparisons across contexts, you often have to convert numbers into standard units. In this chapter, I show you how to use statistics to do just that. Standard units show you where a score stands in relation to other scores within a group. I also show you other ways to determine a score's standing within a group.

Catching Some Z's

A number in isolation doesn't provide much information. To fully understand what a number means, you have to take into account the process that produced it. To compare one number to another, they have to be on the same scale.

When you're converting currency, it's easy to figure out a standard. When you convert temperatures from Fahrenheit to Celsius, or lengths from feet to meters, a formula guides you.

When it's not so clear-cut, you can use the mean and standard deviation to standardize scores that come from different processes. The idea is to take a set of scores and use its mean as a zero point and its standard deviation as a unit of measure. Then you make comparisons: You calculate the deviation of each score from the mean, and then you compare that deviation to the standard deviation. You're asking, "How big is a particular deviation relative to (something like) an average of all the deviations?"

To make a comparison, you divide the score's deviation by the standard deviation. This transforms the score into another kind of score. The transformed score is called a *standard score*, or a *z-score*.

The formula for this is

$$z = \frac{X - \bar{X}}{s}$$

if you're dealing with a sample, and it's

$$z = \frac{X - \mu}{\sigma}$$

if you're dealing with a population. In either case, x represents the score you're transforming into a z-score.

Characteristics of z-scores

A z-score can be positive, negative, or 0. A negative z-score represents a score that's less than the mean, and a positive z-score represents a score that's greater than the mean. When the score is equal to the mean, its z-score is 0.

When you calculate the z-score for every score in the set, the mean of the z-scores is 0, and the standard deviation of the z-scores is 1.

After you do this for several sets of scores, you can legitimately compare a score from one set to a score from another. If the two sets have different means and different standard deviations, comparing without standardizing is like comparing apples with kumquats.

In the examples that follow, I show how to use z-scores to make comparisons.

Bonds versus the Bambino

Here's an important question that often comes up in the context of serious metaphysical discussions: Who is the greatest home run hitter of all time: Barry Bonds or Babe Ruth? Although this is a difficult question to answer, one way to get your hands around it is to look at each player's best season and compare the two. Bonds hit 73 home runs in 2001, and Ruth hit 60 in 1927. On the surface, Bonds appears to be the more productive hitter.

The year 1927 was quite different from 2001, however. Baseball (and everything else) went through huge, long-overdue changes in the intervening years, and player statistics reflect those changes. A home run was harder to hit in the 1920s than in the 2000s. Still, 73 versus 60? Hmmm. . . .

Standard scores can help decide whose best season was better. To standardize, I took the top 50 home run hitters of 1927 and the top 50 from 2001. I calculated the mean and standard deviation of each group and then turned Ruth's 60 and Bonds's 73 into z-scores.

The average from 1927 is 12.68 homers with a standard deviation of 10.49. The average from 2001 is 37.02 homers with a standard deviation of 9.64. Although the means differ greatly, the standard deviations are pretty close.

And the z-scores? Ruth's is

$$z = \frac{60 - 12.68}{10.49} = 4.51$$

Bonds's is

$$z = \frac{73 - 37.02}{9.64} = 3.73$$

The clear winner in the z-score best-season home run derby is Babe Ruth. Period.

Just to show you how times have changed, Lou Gehrig hit 47 home runs in 1927 (finishing second to Ruth) for a z-score of 3.27. In 2001, 47 home runs amounted to a z-score of 1.04.

Exam scores

Moving away from sports debates, one practical application of z-scores is the assignment of grades to exam scores. Based on percentage scoring, instructors traditionally evaluate a score of 90 points or higher (out of 100) as an A, 80–89 points as a B, 70–79 points as a C, 60–69 points as a D, and fewer than 60 points as an F. Then they average scores from several exams together to assign a course grade.

Is that fair? Just as a peso from the Philippines is worth more than a peso from Colombia, and a home run was harder to hit in 1927 than in 2001, is a point on one exam worth the same as a point on another? Like "pesos," isn't "points" just a coincidence?

Absolutely. A point on a difficult exam is, by definition, harder to come by than a point on an easy exam. Because points might not mean the same thing from one exam to another, the fairest thing to do is convert scores from each exam into z-scores before averaging them. That way, you're averaging numbers on a level playing field.

I did that in the classroom courses I taught. I often found that a lower numerical score on one exam resulted in a higher z-score than a higher numerical score from another exam. For example, on an exam where the mean is 65 and the standard deviation is 12, a score of 71 results in a z-score of .5. On another exam, with a mean of 69 and a standard deviation of 14, a score of 75 is equivalent to a z-score of .429. (Yes, it's like Ruth's 60 home runs versus Bonds' 73.) Moral of the story: Numbers in isolation tell you very little. You have to understand the process that produces them.

z-Scores in Python

Unsurprisingly, the Python function for calculating z-scores is called `zscore()` It's in `scipy stats`.

I begin by importing the necessary libraries:

```
import numpy as np
import pandas as pd
from scipy import stats
```

I work with a small set of data — the horsepower values of six cars:

```
HP = [200,295,170,300,190,210]
```

Then I apply stats.zscore():

```
HP_z = stats.zscore(HP)
print(HP_z)

[-0.53953558  1.32431459 -1.12811984  1.42241197 -0.73573033
  -0.34334082]
```

The stats.zcore() function considers the data as a population. Thus, it uses σ as the denominator for the z-scores. If your data constitutes a sample and you have to use s as the denominator, reset the ddof parameter (see Chapter 5):

```
HP_z_sample = stats.zscore(HP, ddof = 1)
print(HP_z_sample)

[-0.49252634  1.20892829 -1.02982781  1.29847854 -0.67162683
  -0.31342585]
```

Each of these six numbers is the horsepower of an 8-cylinder USA automobile in the Cars93 dataset in the MASS library. If you'd like to verify:

```
import statsmodels.api as sm
cars_93 = sm.datasets.get_rdataset("Cars93", "MASS")
cars_93df = pd.DataFrame(cars_93.data)
USA_cars_93_8 = cars_93df[(cars_93df['Origin'] == 'USA') &
    (cars_93df['Cylinders'] == '8')]
Horsepower_USA_8 = USA_cars_93_8.Horsepower
print(Horsepower_USA_8)
```

Don't forget the quote marks around the 8 at the end of the fourth statement.

CACHING SOME Z'S

Because negative z-scores might have connotations that are, well, negative, educators sometimes change the z-score when they evaluate students. In effect, they're hiding the z-score, but the concept is the same — standardization with the standard deviation as the unit of measure.

One popular transformation is the T-score: It eliminates negative scores because a set of T-scores has a mean of 50 and a standard deviation of 10. The idea is to give an exam, grade all the tests, and calculate the mean and standard deviation. Next, turn each score into a z-score. Then follow this formula:

$$T = (z)(10) + 50$$

People who use the T-score often like to round to the nearest whole number.

Here's how to transform the z-scores from the example into a set of T-scores:

T_HP_z = np.round((HP_z*10 + 50),0)

Setting the second argument of the round( ) function to 0 rounds off the result to the nearest whole number.

SAT scores are another transformation of the z-score. (Some refer to the SAT as a C-score.) Under the old scoring system, the SAT has a mean of 500 and a standard deviation of 100. After the exams are graded and their mean and standard deviation calculated, each exam score becomes a z-score in the usual way. This formula converts the z-score into a SAT score:

$$SAT = (z)(100) + 500$$

Rounding to the nearest whole number is part of the procedure here, too.

The IQ score is still another transformed z. Its mean is 100, and its standard deviation is 15. What's the procedure for computing an IQ score? You guessed it. In a group of IQ scores, calculate the mean and standard deviation, and then calculate the z-score. Then it's

$$IQ = (z)(15) + 100$$

As with the other two, IQ scores are rounded to the nearest whole number.

Where Do You Stand?

Standard scores show you how a score stands in relation to other scores in the same group. To do this, they use the standard deviation as a unit of measure.

If you don't want to use the standard deviation, you can show a score's relative standing in a simpler way. You can determine the score's rank within the group: In ascending order, the lowest score has a rank of 1, the second lowest has a rank of 2, and so on. In descending order, the highest score is ranked 1, the second highest is ranked 2, and so on.

Ranking in Python

To rank scores in ascending order, I use the rankdata() function from scipy stats:

```
print(HP)

[200, 295, 170, 300, 190, 210]

from scipy.stats import rankdata
ranked_HP = rankdata(HP)
print(ranked_HP)

[3. 5. 1. 6. 2. 4.]
```

Tied scores

By default, the rankdata() function handles tied scores by assigning each one the average of the ranks they would have attained. To show you how this works, I create a new list that replaces the sixth value in HP with 200 and ties it with the first value:

```
HP_ties = HP
HP_ties[5] = 200
print(HP_ties)

[200, 295, 170, 300, 190, 200]

ranked_HP_ties = rankdata(HP_ties)
print(ranked_HP_ties)

[3.5 5.  1.  6.  2.  3.5]
```

Assigning the average is just one way to deal with ranks. The rankdata() function provides an optional argument called method that allows you to specify other ways of working with tied scores. One, for example, assigns the minimum value as the rank for every tied score:

```
ranked_HP_ties = rankdata(HP_ties, method = 'min')
print(ranked_HP_ties)

[3 5 1 6 2 3]
```

Another assigns the maximum:

```
ranked_HP_ties = rankdata(HP_ties, method = 'max')
print(ranked_HP_ties)

[4 5 1 6 2 4]
```

Additional methods are available, but I'm pretty sure the ones I've shown you cover most every possibility you'll encounter.

Percentiles

Closely related to rank is the *percentile*, which represents a score's standing in the group as the percent of scores below it. If you've taken standardized tests, you've encountered percentiles. A score in the 80th percentile is higher than 80 percent of the scores of the other test-takers.

The percentile() method lives in numpy. Give it some data and a percentile, and percentile() tells you the value at that percentile in the data. (It might not necessarily be an existing score.)

I use this method. to calculate percentiles in the horsepower data I work with in this chapter. To calculate the score at the 75th percentile:

```
pctile = np.percentile(HP, 75)
print(pctile)

271.25
```

You can calculate more than one percentile at a time:

```
pctile_values = [25,50,75]
pctiles = np.percentile(HP, pctile_values)
print(pctiles)

[192.5  200.     271.25]
```

The numpy quantile() function gives the same results.

TIP

To calculate the percentile value of a score, you use the percentileofscore() method in scipy stats:

```
from scipy.stats import percentileofscore
score_pctile = percentileofscore(HP, 210)
print(score_pctile)

66.66666666666667
```

IN THIS CHAPTER

» **Working with things great and small**

» **Understanding symmetry, peaks, and plateaus**

» **Experiencing special moments**

» **Finding frequencies**

» **Getting descriptive**

Chapter **7**

Summarizing It All

The measures of central tendency and variability that I discuss in earlier chapters aren't the only ways of summarizing a set of scores. These measures are a subset of descriptive statistics. Some descriptive statistics — like maximum, minimum, and range — are easy to understand. Some — like skewness and kurtosis — are not.

This chapter covers descriptive statistics and shows you how to calculate them in Python.

How Many?

As in earlier chapters, I work with the Cars93 DataFrame, which is in the MASS package in R World. To bring it into Planet Python:

```
import pandas as pd
import statsmodels.api as sm
cars_93 = sm.datasets.get_rdataset("Cars93", "MASS")
cars_93df = pd.DataFrame(cars_93.data)
```

Perhaps the fundamental descriptive statistic is the number of scores in a set of data. Now I already know the number of scores in this DataFrame, but if I had to find that number, len() would get it done:

```
rows_in_cars_93df = len(cars_93df)
print(rows_in_cars_93df)

93
```

To count the number of rows that meet a condition, submit that condition as an argument to len(). Here, for example, is the number of USA cars in the DataFrame:

```
USA_cars = cars_93df[cars_93df['Origin'] == 'USA']
number_of_USA_cars = len(USA_cars)
print(number_of_USA_cars)

48
```

More complex conditions are possible. For the number of 4-cylinder USA cars:

```
USA_4_cylinder_cars = USA_cars[USA_cars['Cylinders'] == '4']
number_of_4_cylinder_USA_cars = len(USA_4_cylinder_cars)
print(number_of_4_cylinder_USA_cars)

22
```

The High and the Low

Two descriptive statistics that need no introduction are the maximum and minimum value in a set of scores:

```
max_Horsepower_USA_4_cylinder_cars = USA_4_cylinder_
    cars['Horsepower'].max()
print(max_Horsepower_USA_4_cylinder_cars)

155

min_Horsepower_USA_4_cylinder_cars = USA_4_cylinder_
    cars['Horsepower'].min()
print(min_Horsepower_USA_4_cylinder_cars)

63
```

Living in the Moments

In statistics, *moments* are quantities that are related to the shape of a set of numbers. By "shape of a set of numbers," I mean "what a histogram based on the numbers looks like" — how spread out it is, how symmetric it is, and more.

A *raw moment* of order *k* is the average of all numbers in the set, with each number raised to the *k*th power before you average it. So the *first* raw moment is the arithmetic mean. The *second* raw moment is the average of the squared scores. The *third* raw moment is the average of the cubed scores, and so on.

A *central moment* is based on the average of *deviations* of numbers from their mean. (Beginning to sound vaguely familiar?) If you square the deviations before you average them, you have the *second* central moment. If you cube the deviations before you average them, that's the *third* central moment. Raise each one to the fourth power before you average them, and you have the *fourth* central moment. I could go on and on, but you get the idea.

Two quick questions:

1. For any set of numbers, what's the first central moment?
2. By what other name do you know the second central moment?

Two quick answers:

1. Zero.
2. Population variance.

Read or reread Chapter 5 if you don't believe me.

A teachable moment

Before I proceed, I think it's a good idea to translate everything I've said so far in this chapter into Python. I work with the horsepower of USA cars and the horsepower of non-USA cars, so I begin by filtering out that data from `cars93_df`:

```python
Horsepower_USA = USA_cars['Horsepower']
non_USA_cars = cars_93df[cars_93df['Origin'] != 'USA']
Horsepower_non_USA = non_USA_cars['Horsepower']
```

The `moment()` function, which calculates central moments, resides in `scipy.stats`. Its first argument is the data; its second argument is which central moment it is. Here, for example, is the third moment of the `Horsepower_USA` data:

```
from scipy.stats import moment

third_moment_HP_USA = moment(Horsepower_USA, moment=3)
print(f"{third_moment_HP_USA:.0f}")
177269
```

Back to descriptives

What does all this talk about moments have to do with descriptive statistics? As I said . . . well . . . a moment ago, think of a histogram based on a set of numbers. The first raw moment (the mean) locates the *center* of the histogram. The second central moment indicates the *spread* of the histogram. The third central moment is involved in the *symmetry* of the histogram, which is called *skewness*. The fourth central moment figures into how fat or thin the tails (extreme ends) of the histogram are. This is called *kurtosis*. Getting into moments of higher order than that is way beyond the scope of this book.

But let's get into symmetry and tailedness.

Skewness

Figure 7-1 shows three histograms. The first is symmetric; the other two are not. The symmetry and the asymmetry are reflected in the skewness statistic.

For the symmetric histogram, the skewness is 0. For the second histogram — the one that tails off to the right — the value of the skewness statistic is *positive*. It's also said to be "skewed to the right." For the third histogram (which tails off to the left), the value of the skewness statistic is *negative*. It's also said to be "skewed to the left."

Now for a formula. I'll let M_k represent the *k*th central moment. To calculate skewness, it's

$$skewness = \frac{\sum(X - \bar{X})^3}{(N-1)s^3} = \frac{M_3}{M_2^{1.5}}$$

In English, the *skewness* of a set of numbers is the third central moment divided by the second central moment raised to the 1.5 power.

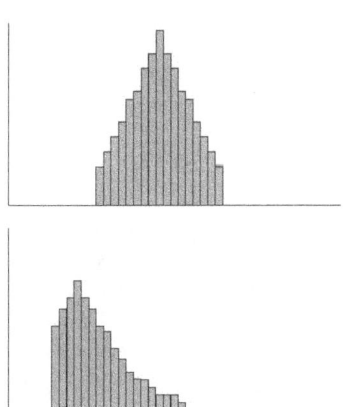

Symmetric: Skewness = 0

Skewed to the right: Skewness is positive

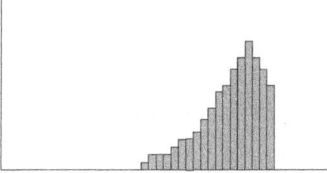

Skewed to the left: Skewness is negative

FIGURE 7-1:
Three histograms,
showing three
kinds
of skewness.

With the moment function, it's easier done than said:

```
skewness_HP_USA = moment(Horsepower_USA, moment=3) /
    moment(Horsepower_USA, moment=2)**1.5
print(f"{skewness_HP_USA:.2f}")
1.13
```

So the skew is positive. How does that compare with the horsepower for non-USA cars?

```
skewness_HP_non_USA = moment(Horsepower_non_USA, moment=3) /
    moment(Horsepower_non_USA, moment=2)**1.5
print(f"{skewness_HP_non_USA:.2f}")
0.64
```

The skew is more positive for USA cars than for non-USA cars. What do the two histograms look like?

I produce them side-by-side in Figure 4-1, over in Chapter 4. For convenience, I show them here as Figure 7-2.

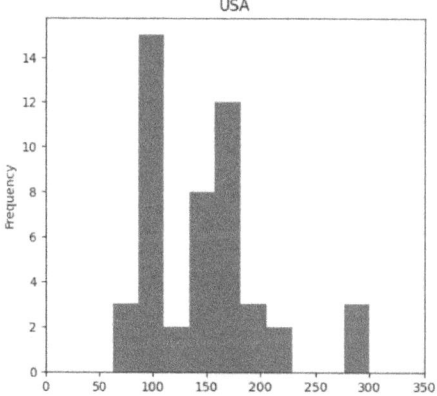
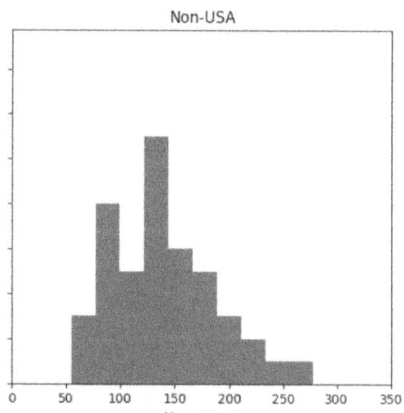

FIGURE 7-2:
Horsepower
histograms for
USA cars and
non-USA cars.

The code for producing them is

```
import matplotlib.pyplot as plt
fig,(ax1,ax2) = plt.subplots(1,2, figsize=(12,5), sharey=True)
Horsepower_USA.plot(kind='hist', title='USA',ax=ax1)
Horsepower_non_USA.plot(kind='hist', title='Non-USA', ax=ax2)
ax1.set_xlabel('Horsepower')
ax2.set_xlabel('Horsepower')
ax1.set_ylabel('Frequency')
ax2.set_ylabel('Frequency')
ax1.set_xlim(0,350)
ax2.set_xlim(0,350)
plt.show()
```

Consistent with the skewness values, the histograms show that in the USA cars, the scores are more bunched up on the left than they are in the non-USA cars.

TIP

It's sometimes easier to see trends in a density plot rather than in a histogram. A *density plot* shows the proportions of scores between a given lower boundary and a given upper boundary (like the proportion of cars with horsepower between 100 and 140). I discuss density in more detail in Chapter 8.

Making a couple of changes to the histogram code produces the density plots:

```
fig,(ax1,ax2) = plt.subplots(1,2, figsize=(12,5), sharey=True)
Horsepower_USA.plot(kind='density', title='USA',
    ylabel='Density',ax=ax1)
Horsepower_non_USA.plot(kind='density',
    title='Non-USA',ylabel='Density',ax=ax2)
ax1.set_xlabel('Horsepower')
```

```
ax2.set_xlabel('Horsepower')
ax1.set_xlim(0,350)
ax2.set_xlim(0,350)
plt.show()
```

Figure 7-3 shows the two density plots.

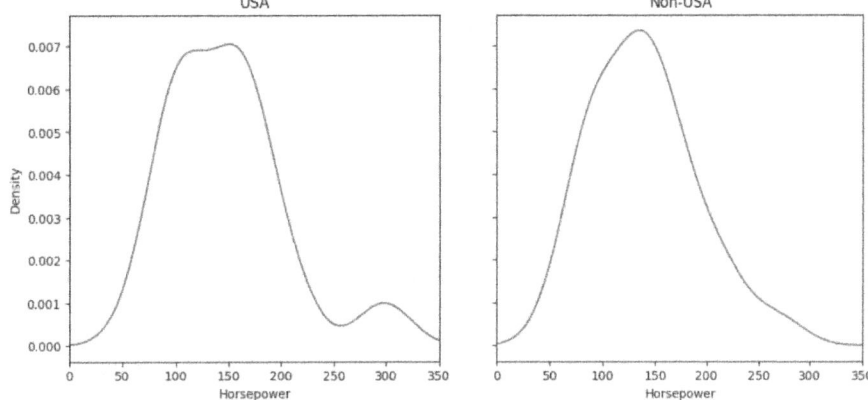

FIGURE 7-3:
Horsepower
density plots for
USA cars and
non-USA cars.

With the density plots, it seems to be easier (for me, anyway) to see the more leftward tilt (and hence, more positive skew) in the plot on the left.

Kurtosis

Figure 7-4 shows two histograms. The first has fatter tails than the second. The first is said to be *leptokurtic.* The second is *platykurtic.* The kurtosis for the first histogram is greater than for the second.

The formula for kurtosis is

$$kurtosis = \frac{\sum (X - \bar{X})^4}{(N-1)s^4} = \frac{M_4}{M_2^2}$$

where M_4 is the fourth central moment and M_2 is the second central moment. So kurtosis is the fourth central moment divided by the square of the second central moment.

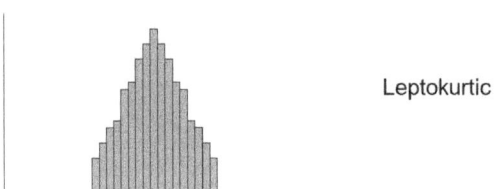

Leptokurtic

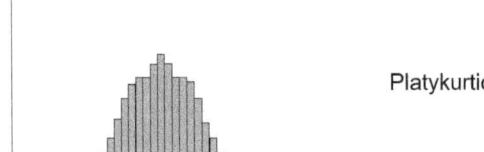

FIGURE 7-4:
Two histograms, showing two kinds of kurtosis.

Platykurtic

I use the moment() function to calculate kurtosis of the horsepower distributions. For the USA cars, it's

```
kurtosis_HP_USA = moment(Horsepower_USA,4)/moment
    (Horsepower_USA,2)**2
print(f"{kurtosis_HP_USA:.2f}")
4.40
```

The fatter tail in the left-side density plot in Figure 7-3 suggests that the USA cars have a higher kurtosis than the non-USA cars. Is this true?

```
kurtosis_HP_non_USA = moment(Horsepower_non_USA,4)/moment
    (Horsepower_non_USA,2)**2
print(f"{kurtosis_HP_non_USA:.2f}")
3.10
```

Yes, it is!

Tuning in the Frequency

A good way to explore data is to find out the frequencies of occurrence for each category of a nominal variable and for each interval of a numerical variable.

Nominal variables

For nominal variables, like Type of automobile in Cars93, the easiest way to find the frequencies is to use the pandas value_counts() method:

```
car_types = cars_93df['Type'].value_counts()
print(car_types)
Type
Midsize     22
Small       21
Compact     16
Sporty      14
Large       11
Van          9
Name: count, dtype: int64
```

Numerical variables

In a similar way, I can set interval values in numerical data and tabulate the frequency in each interval. Here, I use values_counts() to count frequencies for Price in Cars93, in intervals that I set.

Python refers to intervals as *bins.*

REMEMBER Each interval number represents a price in thousands of dollars — and these are 1993 prices!

```
data = cars_93df['Price']
intervals = [5,15,25,35,45,55,65]
frequencies = pd.value_counts(data,bins=intervals,sort=False)
print(frequencies)
(4.999, 15.0]     33
(15.0, 25.0]      39
(25.0, 35.0]      14
(35.0, 45.0]       5
(45.0, 55.0]       1
(55.0, 65.0]       1
```

Additional lines, which you can safely ignore, appear below the output.

In the output, each interval has a left parenthesis and a right square bracket. This means that prices in that interval are greater than the lower bound and less than or equal to the higher bound. To prepare for a possible score of exactly 5, `value_count()` subtracts a tiny bit from the lower bound of the lowest interval.

Mathematicians refer to each of these intervals as either *half-open* or *half-closed* (whichever term you care to use). In this case, they're said to be "open on the left and closed on the right."

The argument `sort = False` tells `value_counts()` not to order the frequencies in descending order. (Try omitting it and watch what happens.)

If you prefer frequencies expressed as proportions, add `normalize = True`:

```
frequencies = pd.value_counts(data,bins=intervals,sort=False,nor
    malize=True)
```

That makes the output look like this:

```
(4.999, 15.0]    0.354839
(15.0, 25.0]     0.419355
(25.0, 35.0]     0.150538
(35.0, 45.0]     0.053763
(45.0, 55.0]     0.010753
(55.0, 65.0]     0.010753
```

Numerical and nominal together

It's sometimes helpful to break out the interval frequencies across the categories in a nominal variable:

Type Price X $1,000	Compact	Large	Midsize	Small	Sporty	Van
(4.99–15]	6	0	2	20	5	0
(15–25]	7	8	8	1	6	9
(25–35]	3	2	7	0	2	0
(35–45]	0	1	3	0	1	0
(45–55]	0	0	1	0	0	0
(55–65]	0	0	1	0	0	0

Here's how to do it. I begin by setting up the data, the intervals, and the labels for the intervals:

```
data = cars_93df['Price']
intervals = [5,15,25,35,45,55,65]
interval_labels = ['(4.99-15]', '(15-25]', '(25-35]', '(35-45]',
   '(45-55]', '(55-65]']
```

Then comes the business end — creating a DataFrame column with the data placed in the intervals. The pandas cut() method gets this done:

```
cars_93df['Price X $1,000'] = pd.cut(data, bins=intervals,
   labels= interval_labels)
```

Next, I use the pandas crosstab() method to create a frequency table that breaks out each frequency across Type of car, and then I print the table:

```
frequency_table = pd.crosstab(cars_93df['Price X $1,000'],
   cars_93df['Type'])
print(frequency_table)
```

Summarizing a DataFrame

If you're looking for descriptive statistics for the numerical variables in a pandas DataFrame, the pandas describe() method will find them for you. I illustrate with a subset of cars93_df. You use double square brackets to create a subset of a pandas DataFrame:

```
MPG_subset = cars_93df[['MPG.city','MPG.highway']]
```

Then apply describe(), and print the results:

```
descriptives = MPG_subset.describe()
print(descriptives)
           MPG.city      MPG.highway
count     93.000000       93.000000
mean      22.365591       29.086022
std        5.619812        5.331726
```

min	15.000000	20.000000
25%	18.000000	26.000000
50%	21.000000	28.000000
75%	25.000000	31.000000
max	46.000000	50.000000

You get the count, the mean, and the standard deviation. The minimum and maximum enclose the 25th, 50th, and 75th percentiles.

To calculate the descriptives for all the numerical variables, it's

```
all_descriptives = cars_93df.describe()
print(all_descriptives)
```

Try it — and you'll see why I didn't put the results on this page!

IN THIS CHAPTER

» Meeting the normal
distribution family

» Working with standard deviations
and the normal distribution

» Understanding Python's normal
distribution functions

Chapter **8**

What's Normal?

O ne of the main jobs of a statistician is to estimate characteristics of a population. The job becomes easier if the statistician can make some assumptions about the populations they study.

Here's an assumption that works over and over again: A specific attribute, ability, or trait is distributed throughout a population so that (1) most people have an average or near-average amount of the attribute and (2) progressively fewer people have increasingly extreme amounts of the attribute. In this chapter, I discuss this assumption and its implications for statistics. I also discuss Python functions related to this assumption.

Hitting the Curve

Attributes in the physical world, like length or weight, are all about objects you can see and touch. It's not that easy in the world of social scientists, statisticians, market researchers, and businesspeople. They have to be creative when they measure traits they can't put their hands around — like intelligence, musical ability, or willingness to buy a new product.

The assumption I mention in this chapter's introduction — that most people are around the average and progressively fewer people are toward the extremes — seems to work out well for those intangible traits. Because this happens often, it has become an assumption about how most traits are distributed.

It's possible to capture this assumption in a graphical way. Figure 8-1 shows the well-known *bell curve* that describes the distribution of a wide variety of attributes. The horizontal axis represents measurements of the ability under consideration. A vertical line drawn down the center of the curve would correspond to the average of the measurements.

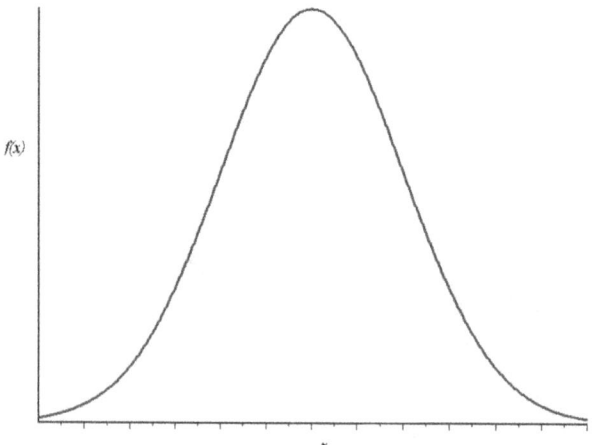

FIGURE 8-1:
The bell curve.

Assume that it's possible to measure a trait like intelligence, and assume that this curve represents the distribution of intelligence in the population: The bell curve shows that most people have about average intelligence, only a few have little intelligence, and only a few are geniuses. That seems to fit nicely with what we know about people, doesn't it?

Digging deeper

On the horizontal axis of Figure 8-1 you see x, and on the vertical axis, $f(x)$. What do these symbols mean? The horizontal axis, as I mention, represents measurements, so think of each measurement as an x.

The explanation of $f(x)$ is a little more involved. A mathematical relationship between x and $f(x)$ creates the bell curve and enables you to visualize it. The relationship is rather complex, and I won't burden you with it right now. (I discuss it in a little while.) Just understand that $f(x)$ represents the height of the curve for a specified value of x. This means that you supply a value for x (and for a couple of other things), and then that complex relationship returns a value of $f(x)$.

Let me get into specifics. The formal name for *bell curve* is *normal distribution*. The term *f(x)* is called *probability density*, so a normal distribution is an example of a *probability density function*. Rather than give you a technical definition of probability density, I ask you to think of probability density as something that allows you to think about the area under the curve as probability. Probability of . . . what? That's coming up in the next section.

Parameters of a normal distribution

You often hear people talk about *the* normal distribution. That's a misnomer. It's really a *family* of distributions. The members of the family differ from one another in terms of two parameters — yes, *parameters* because I'm talking about populations. Those two parameters are the mean (μ) and the standard deviation (σ). The *mean* tells you where the center of the distribution is, and the *standard deviation* tells you how spread out the distribution is around the mean. The mean is in the middle of the distribution. Every member of the normal distribution family is symmetric — the left side of the distribution is a mirror image of the right. (Remember skewness, from Chapter 7? *Symmetric* means that the skewness of a normal distribution is 0.)

The characteristics of the normal distribution family are well known to statisticians. More importantly, you can apply those characteristics to your work.

How? This brings me back to probability. You can find some useful probabilities if you

>> Can lay out a line that represents the *scale* of the attribute you're measuring (the *x*-axis, in other words)

>> Can indicate on the line where the mean of the measurements is

>> Know the standard deviation

>> Can assume that the attribute is normally distributed throughout the population

I work with IQ scores to show you what I mean. Scores on the IQ test follow a normal distribution. The mean of the distribution of these scores is 100, and the standard deviation is 15. Figure 8-2 shows the probability density for this distribution.

TECHNICAL
STUFF

You might have read elsewhere that the standard deviation for IQ is 16 rather than 15. That's the case for the Stanford–Binet version of the IQ test. For other versions, the standard deviation is 15.

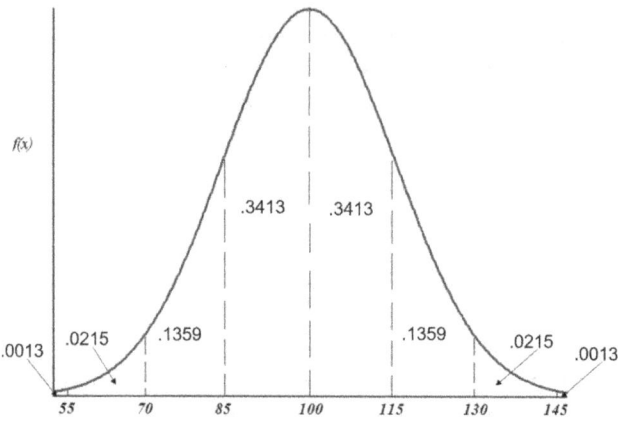

FIGURE 8-2:
The normal
distribution of IQ,
divided into
standard
deviations.

As Figure 8-2 shows, I've laid out a line for the IQ scale (the *x*-axis). Each point on the line represents an IQ score. With the mean (100) as the reference point, I've marked off every 15 points (the standard deviation). I've drawn a dashed line from the mean up to *f*(100) (the height of the distribution where *x* = 100) and drawn a dashed line from each standard deviation point.

The figure also shows the proportion of area bounded by the curve and the horizontal axis, and by successive pairs of standard deviations. It also shows the proportion beyond three standard deviations on either side (55 and 145). Note that the curve never touches the horizontal. It gets closer and closer, but it never touches. (Mathematicians say that the curve is *asymptotic* to the horizontal.)

So, between the mean and one standard deviation — between 100 and 115 — are .3413 (or 34.13 percent) of the scores in the population. Here's another way to say this: The probability that an IQ score is between 100 and 115 is .3413. At the extremes, in the tails of the distribution, .0013 (.13 percent) of the scores are on each side (less than 55 or greater than 145).

REMEMBER

The proportions in Figure 8-2 hold for every member of the normal distribution family, not just for IQ scores. For example, in the "Caching some z's" sidebar in Chapter 6, I mention SAT scores, which have a mean of 500 and a standard deviation of 100. They're normally distributed, too. That means 34.13 percent of SAT scores are between 500 and 600, 34.13 percent are between 400 and 500, and, well, you can use Figure 8-2 as a guide for other proportions.

Working with Normal Distributions

The complex relationship I told you about between *x* and *f(x)* is

$$f(x) = \frac{1}{\sigma\sqrt{2\pi}} e^{-\left[\frac{(x-\mu)^2}{2\sigma^2}\right]}$$

If you supply values for μ (the mean), σ (the standard deviation), and *x* (a score), the equation gives you back a value for *f(x)*, the height of the normal distribution at *x*. The constants π and *e* are important in mathematics: π is approximately 3.1416 (the ratio of a circle's circumference to its diameter); *e* is approximately 2.71828. It's related to something called natural logarithms (described in Chapter 16) and to numerous other mathematical concepts.

Distributions in Python

The normal distribution family is one of many distribution families that reside in `scipy.stats`. It's an example of what mathematicians call a *continuous random variable* — a variable that can take on an infinite number of values.

The `scipy.stats` library holds a class that represents continuous random variables. It's called `rv_continuous`. (Think of a class as a category of things, like human or automobile.) The normal distribution family is a subclass of `rv_continuous`. Its `scipy.stats` name is `norm`. In software lingo, a specific member of a family is called an object. Here's more software lingo: An object is an *instance* of a class.

Some of the other many subclasses in `rv_continuous` are `f`, `t`, and `chi`. These are distribution families I use in this book. All these subclasses inherit methods from `rv_continuous`. A *method* is a function you use with a member of a distribution family. So a method is a way to perform actions on an object. In Python, it looks like this:

```
object.method()
```

In the next section, I use methods with an object that is a member of the normal distribution family.

One more thing before I proceed. Another class in `scipy.stats` is called `rv_discrete`. This class represents *discrete random variables* — variables that can take on a finite number of values, like tosses of a coin, rolls of dice, or cylinders in a car's engine. I work with subclasses of `rv_discrete`, too, but that comes later on.

Normal density function in Python

To work with the normal distribution family, I begin with

```
from scipy.stats import norm
```

Next, I identify the member of the family I want to work with. For this example, I use the IQ distribution, so

```
mu,sigma = 100,15
IQ_dist = norm(mu,sigma)
```

REMEMBER

In the terminology of the preceding section, IQ_dist is an object — an instance of the norm class.

To find the value of the probability density function when IQ = 100, I use the pdf() method:

```
pdf_IQ_100 = IQ_dist.pdf(100)
print(pdf_IQ_100)
0.02659615202676218
```

REMEMBER

This does *not* mean that the probability of finding an IQ score of 100 is .027. Probability density is *not* the same as probability. With a probability density function, it only makes sense to talk about the probability of a score between two values — like the probability of a score between 100 and 115.

Plotting a normal curve

I can use pdf() as a tool for plotting a normal distribution. For that, I also need the numpy library and the matplotlib library:

```
import numpy as np
import matplotlib.pyplot as plt
```

Next, I generate a sequence of values for the *x*-axis. To do this, I use the numpy library's linspace():

```
x = np.linspace(mu - 3*sigma, mu + 3*sigma, 100)
```

The arguments are in a format you see a lot in Python — start, stop, and step: The first argument is the starting value, the second argument is the ending value, and the third argument is the size of each step in between. So linspace() starts creating points at mu-3*sigma (55), finishes at mu+3*sigma (145), and creates 100 evenly spaced points between the two.

Next, I use pdf() to set the y value for each of those 100 x values:

```
y = IQ_dist.pdf(x)
```

With my *xy* pairs in place, plotting the curve is straightforward:

```
plt.plot(x, y)
```

One idiosyncrasy of plt.plot() is that it leaves a gap between the bottom of the plot and the x-axis. To eliminate the gap, I set the limits for *y*:

```
plt.ylim(bottom = 0, top = None)
```

The second argument top = None means that matplotlib determines the upper limit.

On the x-axis, I'd like to mark where the standard deviation values are and label them accordingly. The marks are called tick marks, and I use np.arange() to set the range and step size for the tick marks:

```
xtick_marks= np.arange(mu - 3*sigma, mu + 3*sigma +1, sigma)
```

Wait a minute. It's start-stop-step, so why is the end-value mu +3*sigma + 1 and not just mu + 3*sigma? The arange() function goes up to the stop value but doesn't include it, so I add a little bit to make sure that mu + 3*sigma is invited to the party. (Leave out the +1 and watch what happens.)

Then I use plt.xticks to plot the tick marks:

```
plt.xticks(xtick_marks)
```

All that's left is to label the axes and set a title for the graph:

```
plt.xlabel('IQ')
plt.ylabel('f(IQ)')
plt.title('IQ Probabiity Density')
```

and then show the finished product:

```
plt.show()
```

The result is shown in Figure 8-3.

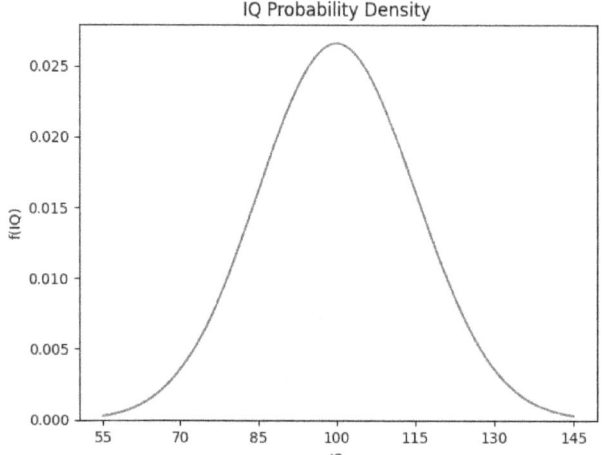

FIGURE 8-3:
The plot of the
normal density
function for IQ.

One more graphic touch. I just mentioned that in a density function, it makes sense to talk about the probability of a score in an interval, like the probability of an IQ between 100 and 115. To visualize that interval on the distribution, I define an area that I want to shade and use plt.fill_between():

```
shade_area = (100 <= x) & (x <= 115)
plt.fill_between(x,y, where= shade_area)
```

Add those two lines to the code for Figure 8-3, anywhere between

```
plt.plot(x,y)
```

and

```
plt.show()
```

and you produce Figure 8-4.

I show you how to compute this probability in the next section.

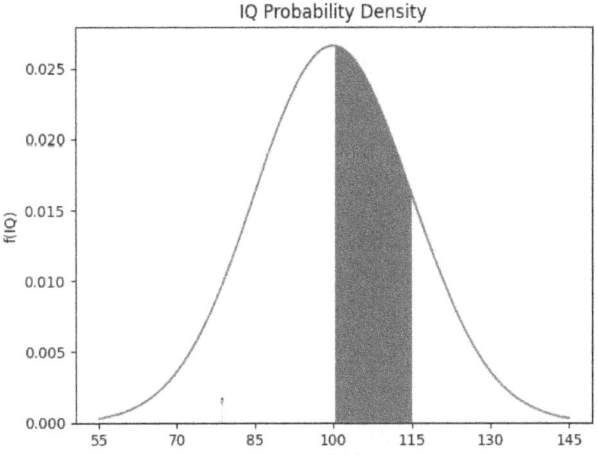

FIGURE 8-4:
Visualizing the probability of an IQ between 100 and 115.

Calculating cumulative density

The cumulative density method `cdf()` returns the probability of a score less than a specified score in a distribution.

This is the IQ distribution I've been working with:

```
cdf_IQ_100 =IQ_dist.cdf(100)
print(cdf_IQ_100)
0.5
```

In the section about normal density functions in Python, I mention a couple of times that it makes sense to talk about the probability of a score in an interval — say, between 100 and 115. You use `cdf()` to find that probability:

```
IQ_between_100_115 = IQ_dist.cdf(115) - IQ_dist.cdf(100)
print(IQ_between_100_115)
0.3413447460685429
```

The plot of the cumulative density function for the IQ distribution is shown in Figure 8-5.

I leave it as an exercise for you to examine the code that produced Figure 8-3 and make the changes to produce Figure 8-5.

TIP

Note the uppercase *F* on the *y*-axis in Figure 8-5. It's what you would see on the left side of the (extremely complicated) equation of the cumulative density function for the normal distribution.

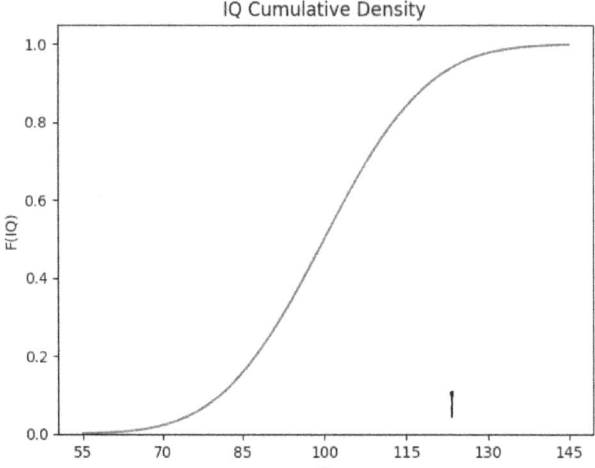

FIGURE 8-5:
The plot of the cumulative density function for IQ.

Percentiles and cumulative density

Closely related to cumulative density is the percentile, which I cover in Chapter 6. That's the percentage of scores in a distribution that are below a given value. In the IQ distribution, for example, 100 is at the 50th percentile.

Looking at it from the opposite direction, what's the score at a given percentile? You use ppf() (percent point function) to find out. Think of it as the inverse of cdf().

Here is the 95th percentile score in the IQ distribution:

```
IQ_95th_percentile = IQ_dist.ppf(0.95)
print(f'{IQ_95th_percentile:.0f}')
125
```

You can use ppf() and a for loop to find the quartiles (25th, 50th, and 75th percentiles) of the IQ distribution:

```
for i in range(25, 75 + 1, 25):
    print(f'{i}th percentile = {IQ_dist.ppf(i/100):.0f}')
25th percentile = 90
50th percentile = 100
75th percentile = 110
```

Once again, you see the start-stop-step of the range. And notice that the stop is the desired upper limit + 1.

REMEMBER

You can use `print(f'{ ... } ')`, as I did here, to round off the results and make them a little prettier.

Random sampling

You use the `rvs()` ("random variates") method to generate random numbers from a probability distribution.

Here are five random numbers from the IQ distribution:

```
sample = IQ_dist.rvs(5)
print(sample)

[ 81.52704522  84.99354277  99.01974293  86.46783787
  120.31083628]
```

When I run that code again, this is the result:

```
[115.17001655  96.28456639 102.11515795  93.63154458
  101.84011852]
```

Yes, the numbers are all different. (In fact, when you run this code, I can almost guarantee that your numbers will be different from mine.) Each time you run the `rvs()` method, it generates a new set of random numbers. The randomization process starts with a number called a *seed*. If you want to reproduce randomization results, use `np.random.seed()` to set the seed to a particular number before randomizing:

```
np.random.seed(2352632)
sample = IQ_dist.rvs(5)
print(sample)
[ 99.54103266  77.25078354 117.99441074 106.60293584
  119.51685651]
```

REMEMBER

If you set the seed to that same number the next time you randomize, you produce the same results. If you don't, you won't.

Randomization is the foundation of simulation, which comes up in Chapters 9 and 18. Bear in mind that Python (or most any other software) doesn't generate true random numbers. Python generates pseudorandom numbers, which are sufficiently unpredictable for most tasks that require randomization — like the simulations I discuss later in this book.

A Distinguished Member of the Family

To standardize a set of scores so that you can compare them to other sets of scores, you convert each one to a z-score. (I discuss z-scores in Chapter 6.) The formula for converting a score to a z-score (also known as a standard score) is

$$z = \frac{x - \mu}{\sigma}$$

The idea is to use the standard deviation as a unit of measure. For example, the Wechsler version of the IQ test (among others) has a mean of 100 and a standard deviation of 15. The Stanford-Binet version has a mean of 100 and a standard deviation of 16. How does a Wechsler score of, say, 110, stack up against a Stanford-Binet score of 110?

One way to answer this question is to put the two versions on a level playing field by standardizing both scores. For the Wechsler:

$$z = \frac{110 - 100}{15} = .667$$

For the Stanford-Binet:

$$z = \frac{110 - 100}{16} = .625$$

So 110 on the Wechsler is a slightly higher score than 110 on the Stanford-Binet.

Now, if you standardize all the scores in a normal distribution (such as either version of the IQ), you have a normal distribution of z-scores. Any set of z-scores (normally distributed or not) has a mean of 0 and a standard deviation of 1. If a normal distribution has those parameters, it's a *standard normal distribution* — a normal distribution of standard scores. Its equation is

$$f(z) = \frac{1}{\sqrt{2\pi}} e^{\left[\frac{-z^2}{2}\right]}$$

Figure 8-6 shows the standard normal distribution. It looks like Figure 8-2, except that I've substituted 0 for the mean and entered standard deviation units in the appropriate places.

WARNING

The standard normal distribution is the member of the normal distribution family that most people are familiar with. It's the one they remember most from statistics courses, and it's the one that most people have in mind when they (mistakenly) say *the* normal distribution. It's also what people think of when they hear about the term z-*scores*. This distribution leads many to the mistaken idea that converting to z-scores somehow transforms a set of scores into a normal distribution.

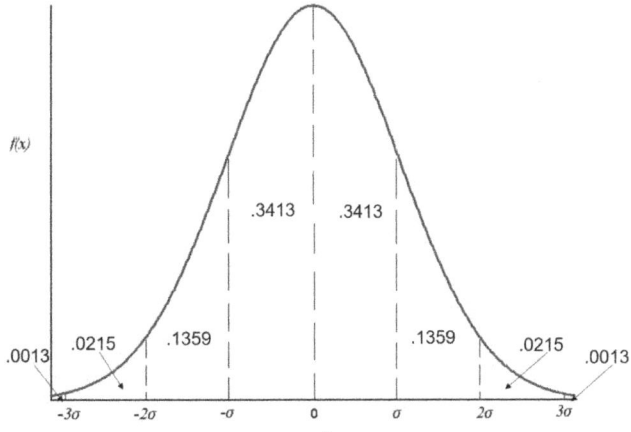

FIGURE 8-6:
The standard normal distribution, divvied up by standard deviations.

Setting up the standard normal distribution in Python

The standard normal distribution in Python couldn't be easier to set up. The only change you make to norm is to *not* specify a mean and a standard deviation — the defaults are 0 and 1:

```
standard_normal_dist = norm()
standard_normal_dist = norm()
```

To demonstrate that I have indeed set up the standard normal distribution, here's its mean and standard deviation:

```
standard_mu = standard_normal_dist.mean()
standard_sigma = standard_normal_dist.std()
print(f'mean of the standard normal = {standard_mu:.2f}')
print(f'standard deviation of the standard normal =
    {standard_sigma:.2f}')
mean of the standard normal = 0.00
standard deviation of the standard normal = 1.00
```

Plotting the standard normal distribution

Rather than just go through the motions of changing the code for Figure 8-3 to accommodate mean = 0 and standard deviation = 1, I show you a couple of tricks to produce a graphic that resembles Figure 8-6.

To show you what I mean, take a look at Figure 8-7.

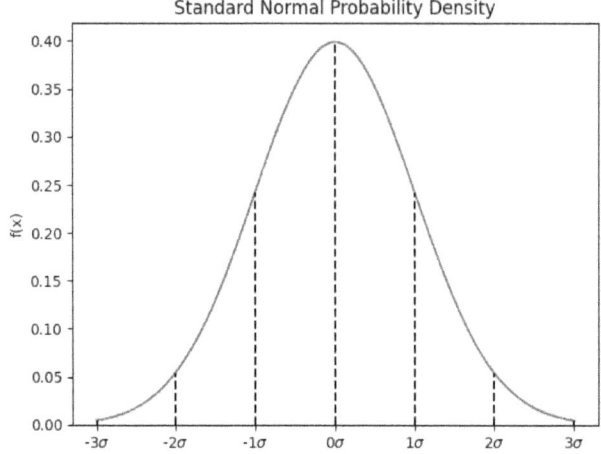

Here's how to do it. I begin, once again, by generating 100 equally spaced points for the x-axis:

```
x = np.linspace(standard_mu - 3*standard_sigma, standard_mu +
    3*standard_sigma, 100)
```

Then I use those 100 x-values to generate the corresponding y-values:

```
y = standard_normal_dist.pdf(x)
```

Next, I plot the distribution

```
plt.plot(x, y)
```

and eliminate the gap between the bottom of the plot and the x-axis:

```
plt.ylim(bottom = 0, top = None)
```

Now I address the tick marks:

```
xtick_marks = np.arange(standard_mu - 3*standard_sigma,
    standard_mu + 3*standard_sigma + .1, standard_sigma)
```

And now it's time for a little Python magic to produce those sigmas on the x-axis:

```
xtick_labels = [f'{i:.0f}$\\sigma$' for i in range(-3, 4)]
```

The bracketed expression on the right is an example of a neat feature called *list comprehension* — using a `for` loop to create a list. The *f*-string instructs the `for` loop to add each sigma (preceded by the *i*-th range value) to the list.

This is the created list:

```
['-3$\\sigma$', '-2$\\sigma$', '-1$\\sigma$', '0$\\sigma$',
  '1$\\sigma$', '2$\\sigma$', '3$\\sigma$']
```

Then I plot the tick marks and the sigmas:

```
plt.xticks(xtick_marks, xtick_labels)
```

I use a `for` loop along with `plt.vlines()` to plot the dashed vertical line at each tick mark:

```
for tick in xtick_marks:
        plt.vlines(tick, 0, standard_normal_dist.pdf(tick),
    linestyles='--', colors='black')
```

The first argument gives the *x*-axis location to plot the line, the second is the *y*-location where the line starts, and the third is where the line stops.

Then I label the axes, supply a title, and show the plot:

```
plt.xlabel('x')
plt.ylabel('f(x)')
plt.title('Standard Normal Probability Density')

plt.show()
```

Voilà! It's Figure 8-7.

For your convenience, here it is, all together:

```
# Generate 100 x values
x = np.linspace(standard_mu - 3*standard_sigma, standard_mu +
    3*standard_sigma, 100)

# Generate the corresponding y values
y = standard_normal_dist.pdf(x)

# Plot the points
plt.plot(x, y)
```

```
# Eliminate the gap between the bottom of the plot and
   the x-axis
plt.ylim(bottom = 0, top = None)

# Create the tick marks and the sigma labels, and plot them
xtick_marks = np.arange(standard_mu - 3*standard_sigma,
   standard_mu + 3*standard_sigma + .1, standard_sigma)
xtick_labels = [f'{i:.0f}$\\sigma$' for i in range(-3, 4)]
plt.xticks(xtick_marks,xtick_labels)

# Plot the vertical dashed lines
for tick in xtick_marks:
        plt.vlines(tick, 0, standard_normal_dist.pdf(tick),
   linestyles='--', colors='black')

# Label the axes, title the graph, and show the plot
plt.xlabel('x')
plt.ylabel('f(x)')
plt.title('Standard Normal Probability Density')
plt.show()
```

3
Drawing Conclusions from Data

Create sampling distributions.

Figure out confidence limits.

Work with t-tests.

Work with analysis of variance.

Visualize t, chi-square, and F distributions.

Understand correlation and regression.

Chapter **9**

The Confidence Game: Estimation

opulation and *sample* are pretty easy concepts to understand. A *population* is a huge collection of individuals, and a *sample* is a group of individuals you draw from a population. Measure the sample-members on some trait or attribute, calculate statistics that summarize the sample, and you're off and running.

In addition to those summary statistics, you can use the statistics to estimate the population parameters. This is a big deal: Just on the basis of a small percentage of individuals from the population, you can draw a picture of the entire population.

How definitive is that picture? In other words, how much confidence can you have in your estimates? To answer this question, you have to have a context for your estimates. How probable are they? How likely is the true value of a parameter to be within a particular lower bound and upper bound?

In this chapter, I introduce the context for estimates, show how that context plays into confidence in those estimates, and show how to use Python to calculate confidence levels.

Understanding Sampling Distributions

So you have a population, and you pull a sample out of this population. You measure the sample-members on some attribute and calculate the sample mean. You then return the sample-members to the population, draw another sample, assess the new sample-members, and then calculate *their* mean. Repeat this process again and again, always with the same number of individuals as in the original sample. If you could do this an infinite number of times (with the same sample size every time), you'd have an infinite number of means. Those sample means form a distribution of their own. This distribution is called *the sampling distribution of the mean.*

For a sample mean, this is the *context* I mention at the beginning of this chapter. Like any other number, a statistic makes no sense by itself. You have to know where it comes from in order to understand it. Of course, a statistic *comes from* a calculation performed on sample data. In another sense, a statistic is part of a sampling distribution.

REMEMBER

In general, *a sampling distribution is the distribution of all possible values of a statistic for a given sample size.*

I've italicized the definition for a reason: It's extremely important. After many years of teaching statistics, I can tell you that this concept usually sets the boundary line between people who understand statistics and people who don't.

So . . . if you understand what a sampling distribution is, you'll understand what the field of statistics is all about. If you don't, you won't. It's almost that simple.

If you don't know what a sampling distribution is, statistics will be a cookbook-type of subject for you: Whenever you have to apply statistics, you'll find yourself plugging numbers into formulas and hoping for the best. On the other hand, if you're comfortable with the idea of a sampling distribution, you'll grasp the big picture of inferential statistics.

To help clarify the idea of a sampling distribution, take a look at Figure 9-1. It summarizes the steps in creating a sampling distribution of the mean.

A sampling distribution — like any other group of scores — has a mean and a standard deviation. The symbol for the mean of the sampling distribution of the mean (yes, I know that's a mouthful) is $\mu_{\bar{x}} = \mu$.

REMEMBER

The standard deviation of a sampling distribution is a pretty hot item. It has a special name: *standard error.* For the sampling distribution of the mean, the standard deviation is called *the standard error of the mean.* Its symbol is $\sigma_{\bar{x}} = \sigma/\sqrt{N}$.

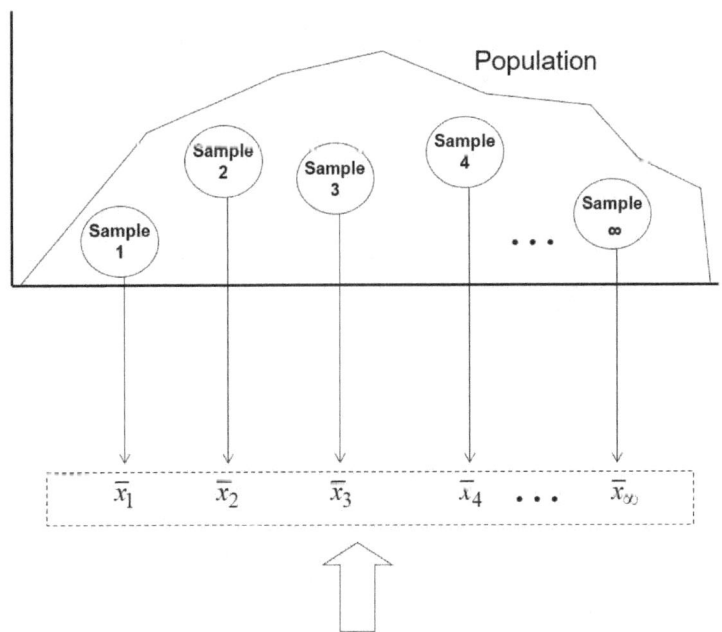

FIGURE 9-1:
Creating the
sampling
distribution
of the mean.

Sampling Distribution of the Mean

An EXTREMELY Important Idea:
The Central Limit Theorem

The situation I asked you to imagine never happens in the real world. You never take an infinite number of samples and calculate their means, and you never actually create a sampling distribution of the mean. Typically, you draw one sample and calculate its statistics.

So if you have only one sample, how can you ever know anything about a sampling distribution — a theoretical distribution that encompasses an infinite number of samples? Is this all just a wild goose chase?

No, it's not. You can figure out a lot about a sampling distribution because of a wonderful gift from mathematicians to the field of statistics: the central limit theorem.

REMEMBER

According to the *central limit theorem:*

>> The sampling distribution of the mean is approximately a normal distribution if the sample size is large enough.

Large enough means about 30 or more.

» The mean of the sampling distribution of the mean is the same as the population mean.

In equation form, that's

$$\mu_{\bar{x}} = \mu$$

» The standard deviation of the sampling distribution of the mean (also known as the standard error of the mean) is equal to the population standard deviation divided by the square root of the sample size.

The equation for the standard error of the mean is

$$\sigma_{\bar{x}} = \sigma / \sqrt{N}$$

Notice that the central limit theorem says nothing about the population. All it says is that if the sample size is large enough, the sampling distribution of the mean is a normal distribution, with the indicated parameters. The population that supplies the samples doesn't have to be a normal distribution for the central limit theorem to hold.

What if the population is a normal distribution? In that case, the sampling distribution of the mean is a normal distribution, regardless of the sample size.

Figure 9-2 shows a general picture of the sampling distribution of the mean, partitioned into standard error units.

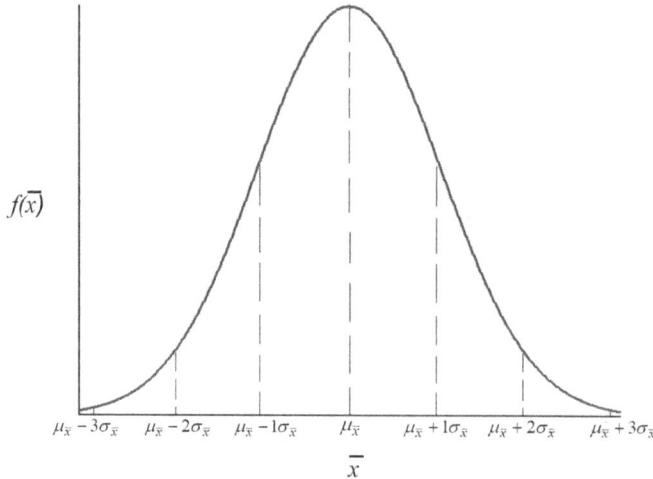

$f(\bar{x})$

$\mu_{\bar{x}} - 3\sigma_{\bar{x}}$ $\mu_{\bar{x}} - 2\sigma_{\bar{x}}$ $\mu_{\bar{x}} - 1\sigma_{\bar{x}}$ $\mu_{\bar{x}}$ $\mu_{\bar{x}} + 1\sigma_{\bar{x}}$ $\mu_{\bar{x}} + 2\sigma_{\bar{x}}$ $\mu_{\bar{x}} + 3\sigma_{\bar{x}}$

$\bar{x}$

FIGURE 9-2:
The sampling distribution of the mean, partitioned.

(Approximately) Simulating the central limit theorem

It almost doesn't sound right: How can a population that's not normally distributed produce a normally distributed sampling distribution?

To give you an idea of how the central limit theorem works, I walk you through a simulation. This simulation creates something like a sampling distribution of the mean for a very small sample, based on a population that's not normally distributed. As you'll see, even though the population is not a normal distribution, and even though the sample is small, the sampling distribution of the mean looks quite a bit like a normal distribution.

Imagine a huge population that consists of just three scores — 1, 2, and 3, and each one is equally likely to appear in a sample. That kind of population is definitely *not* a normal distribution.

Imagine also that you can randomly select a sample of three scores from this population. Table 9-1 shows all possible samples and their means.

TABLE 9-1 **ALL Possible Samples of Three Scores (and Their Means) from a Population Consisting of the Scores 1, 2, and 3**

Sample	Mean	Sample	Mean	Sample	Mean
1,1,1	1.00	2,1,1	1.33	3,1,1	1.67
1,1,2	1.33	2,1,2	1.67	3,1,2	2.00
1,1,3	1.67	2,1,3	2.00	3,1,3	2.33
1,2,1	1.33	2,2,1	1.67	3,2,1	2.00
1,2,2	1.67	2,2,2	2.00	3,2,2	2.33
1,2,3	2.00	2,2,3	2.33	3,2,3	2.67
1,3,1	1.67	2,3,1	2.00	3,3,1	2.33
1,3,2	2.00	2,3,2	2.33	3,3,2	2.67
1,3,3	2.33	2,3,3	2.67	3,3,3	3.00

If you look closely at the table, you can almost see what's about to happen in the simulation. The sample mean that appears most frequently is 2.00. The sample means that appear least frequently are 1.00 and 3.00. Hmmm. . . .

In the simulation, you randomly select a score from the population, put it back into the population, and then randomly select two more, putting each one back after you select it. That group of three scores is a sample. Then you calculate the mean of that sample. You repeat this process for a total of 1,000 samples, resulting in 1,000 sample means. Finally, you graph the distribution of the sample means.

REMEMBER

Putting a score back into the population after you select it is called *sampling with replacement*.

What does the simulated sampling distribution of the mean look like? I walk you through it in Python.

I begin by importing the required libraries:

```
import numpy as np
import random
import matplotlib.pyplot as plt
```

Next, I define the population:

```
population = [1, 2, 3]
```

Because I sample with replacement from these three numbers, you can think of this as an infinite population where each number has a ⅓ chance of being sampled.

Next, I set the sample size

```
sample_size = 3
```

and the number of samples:

```
num_samples = 1000
```

I need an empty list for the sample means:

```
sample_means = []
```

Now for the business end — a for loop that generates the sampling distribution:

```
for i in range(num_samples):
    sample = random.choices(population, k=sample_size)
    mean_of_the_sample = np.mean(sample)
    sample_means.append(mean_of_the_sample)
```

The `random.choices()` function does the sampling with replacement. After it takes each sample, I calculate that sample's mean and append the mean to the `sample_means` list.

After 1,000 samples (and their means), I prepare to plot the sampling distribution. I begin by creating a list of the possible sample means:

```
means_list = np.unique(sample_means)
```

I do this because I want those values to appear as tick marks on the *x*-axis:

```
plt.xticks(means_list)
```

I lay out the plot — a histogram that shows the frequency of each sample mean. For the histogram, I have to divide the 1,000 (sorted) sample means into equally sized intervals called *bins*. Each bin covers a range of sample means. I could specify the number of bins, but I prefer to let `matplotlib` do it for me:

```
plt.hist(sample_means, bins='auto')
```

Finally, I label the axes and show the plot:

```
plt.xlabel("Sample Mean")
plt.ylabel("Frequency")
plt.show()
```

The result is shown in Figure 9-3.

Looks a lot like the beginnings of a normal distribution, right?

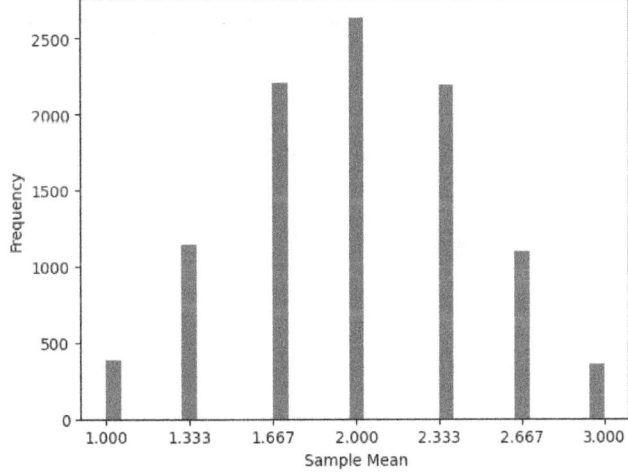

FIGURE 9-3: Sampling distribution of the mean based on 1,000 samples of size 3 from a population consisting of the equally probable scores 1, 2, and 3.

Predictions of the central limit theorem

How do the characteristics of the sampling distribution match up with what the central limit theorem predicts?

To derive the predictions, you have to start with the population. Think of each population value (1, 2, or 3) as an X, and think of each probability as $pr(X)$. Mathematicians would refer to X as a *discrete random variable*.

The mean of a discrete random variable is called its *expected value*. The notation for the expected value of X is $E(X)$.

To find $E(X)$, you multiply each X by its probability and then add all those products together. Remember, the probability of selecting any of the three numbers from the population is $\frac{1}{3}$.

For this example, then, the expected value is

$$E(X) = \sum X(pr(X)) = 1\left(\frac{1}{3}\right) + 2\left(\frac{1}{3}\right) + 3\left(\frac{1}{3}\right) = 2$$

In Python, that's

```
probabilities = [1/3, 1/3, 1/3]
expected_value = np.sum(np.multiply(population, probabilities))
print(expected_value)
2.0
```

To find the variance of X, subtract $E(X)$ from each X, square each deviation, multiply each squared deviation by the probability of X, and add the products. For this example:

$$\text{var}(X) = \sum (X - E(X))^2 (pr(x)) = (1-2)^2\left(\frac{1}{3}\right) + (2-2)^2\left(\frac{1}{3}\right) + (3-2)^2\left(\frac{1}{3}\right) = .67$$

In Python:

```
variance = np.sum(np.multiply((np.subtract(population, expected_
    value)**2), probabilities))
print(variance)
0.6666666666666666
```

As always, the standard deviation is the square root of the variance:

$$\sigma = \sqrt{\text{var}(X)} = \sqrt{.67} = .82$$

Again, in Python:

```
stdev = np.sqrt(variance)
print(stdev)
0.816496580927726
```

According to the central limit theorem, the mean of the sampling distribution should be

$$\mu_{\bar{x}} = \mu = 2$$

and the standard deviation should be

$$\sigma_{\bar{x}} = \sigma\big/\sqrt{N} = .82\big/\sqrt{3} = .4714$$

How do these predicted values match up with the characteristics of the sampling distribution I created?

```
mean_of_sampling_dist = np.mean(sample_means)
print(mean_of_sampling_dist)
1.9936666666666665

standard_deviation_of_sampling_dist = np.std(sample_means)
print(standard_deviation_of_sampling_dist)
0.4713148275480697
```

Spot on! Even with a non-normally distributed population and a small sample size, the central limit theorem paints an accurate picture of the sampling distribution of the mean.

If you go through this exercise, your results will most likely be a little different from mine. Why? Random sampling!

REMEMBER

Confidence: It Has Its Limits!

I tell you about sampling distributions because they help answer the question I pose at the beginning of this chapter: How much confidence can you have in the estimates you create?

The procedure is to calculate a statistic and then use that statistic to establish upper and lower bounds for the population parameter with, say, 95 percent confidence. (The interpretation of confidence limits is a bit more involved than that, as you'll see.) You can do this only if you know the sampling distribution of the statistic and the standard error of the statistic. In the next section, I show how to do this for the mean.

Finding Confidence Limits for a Mean

The FarBlonJet Corporation manufactures navigation systems. (Corporate motto: "Taking a trip? Get FarBlonJet.") The company has developed a new battery to power its portable model. To help market this system, FarBlonJet wants to know how long, on average, each battery lasts before it burns out.

The FarBlonJet employees like to estimate that average with 95 percent confidence. They test a sample of 100 batteries and find that the sample mean is 60 hours, with a standard deviation of 20 hours. The central limit theorem, remember, says that with a large enough sample (30 or more), the sampling distribution of the mean approximates a normal distribution. The standard error of the mean (the standard deviation of the sampling distribution of the mean) is

$$\sigma_{\bar{x}} = \sigma / \sqrt{N}$$

The sample size, N, is 100. What about σ? That's unknown, so you have to estimate it. If you know σ, that would mean you know μ, and establishing confidence limits would be unnecessary.

The best estimate of σ is the standard deviation of the sample. In this case, that's 20. This leads to an estimate of the standard error of the mean:

$$s_{\bar{x}} = s / \sqrt{N} = 20 / \sqrt{100} = 20 / 10 = 2$$

The best estimate of the population mean is the sample mean: 60. Armed with this information — estimated mean, estimated standard error of the mean, normal distribution — you can envision the sampling distribution of the mean, which is shown in Figure 9-4. Consistent with Figure 9-2, each standard deviation is a standard error of the mean.

Now that you have the sampling distribution, you can establish the 95 percent confidence limits for the mean. Starting at the center of the distribution, how far out to the sides do you have to extend until you have 95 percent of the area under the curve? (For more on the area under a normal distribution and what it means, see Chapter 8.)

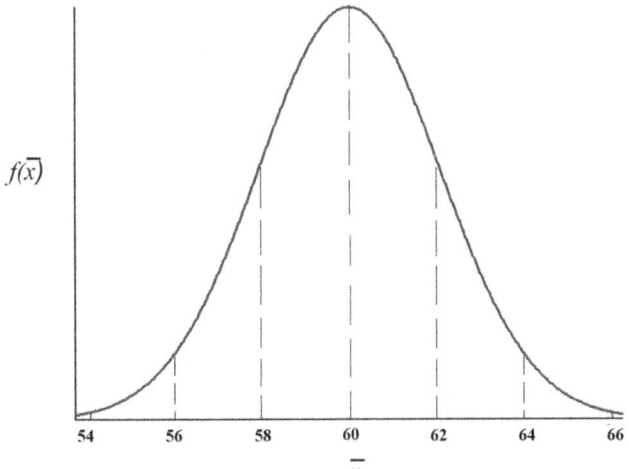

FIGURE 9-4:
The sampling
distribution of the
mean for the
FarBlonJet
battery.

One way to answer this question is to work with the standard normal distribution and find the z-score that cuts off 2.5 percent of the area in the upper tail. Then multiply that z-score by the standard error. Add the result to the sample mean to calculate the upper confidence limit and then subtract the result from the mean to calculate the lower confidence limit.

The `norm.interval()` method from `scipy.stats` handles all that computation. First, the setup:

```
from scipy.stats import norm
battery_mean = 60
battery_std_error = 2
```

Now for the heavy lifting:

```
confidence_interval_95 = norm.interval(0.95, battery_mean,
    battery_std_error)
```

The result, `confidence_interval_95`, is a tuple consisting of two numbers, the lower bound and the upper bound of the confidence interval

For pretty-looking results:

```
lower_bound_95 = confidence_interval_95[0]
upper_bound_95 = confidence_interval_95[1]
print(f'The 95% confidence limits are {lower_bound_95:.2f} and
    {upper_bound_95:.2f}')
The 95% confidence limits are 56.08 and 63.92
```

Figure 9-5 shows these bounds on the sampling distribution.

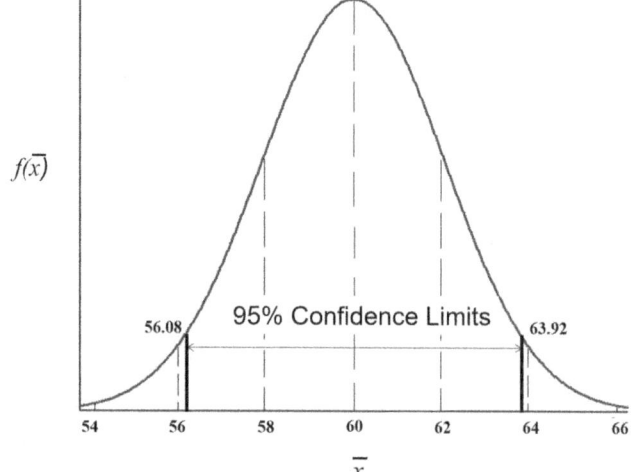

FIGURE 9-5:
The 95 percent
confidence limits
on the FarBlonJet
sampling
distribution.

What does this tell you, exactly? One interpretation is that if you repeat this sampling and estimation procedure many times, the confidence intervals you calculate (which would be different every time you do it) would include the population mean 95 percent of the time.

Fit to a t

The central limit theorem specifies (approximately) a normal distribution for large samples. In the real world, however, you typically deal with smaller samples, and the normal distribution isn't appropriate. What do you do?

First of all, you pay a price for using a smaller sample — you have a larger standard error. Suppose the FarBlonJet Corporation found a mean of 60 and a standard deviation of 20 in a sample of 25 batteries. The estimated standard error is

$$s_{\bar{x}} = s / \sqrt{N} = 20 / \sqrt{25} = 20 / 5 = 4$$

which is twice as large as the standard error for N=100.

Second, you don't get to use the standard normal distribution to characterize the sampling distribution of the mean. For small samples, the sampling distribution of the mean is a member of a family of distributions called the t-*distribution*. The parameter that distinguishes members of this family from one another is called *degrees of freedom*.

REMEMBER

As I say in Chapter 5, think of *degrees of freedom* as the denominator of your variance estimate. For example, if your sample consists of 25 individuals, the sample variance that estimates population variance is

$$s^2 = \frac{\sum(x-\bar{x})^2}{N-1} = \frac{\sum(x-\bar{x})^2}{25-1} = \frac{\sum(x-\bar{x})^2}{24}$$

The number in the denominator is 24, and that's the value of the degrees of freedom parameter. In general, degrees of freedom (*df*) = *N* − 1 (*N* is the sample size) when you use the *t*-distribution the way I show you in this section.

Figure 9-6 shows two members of the *t*-distribution family (*df* = 3 and *df* = 10), along with the normal distribution for comparison. As the figure shows, the greater the *df*, the more closely *t* approximates a normal distribution.

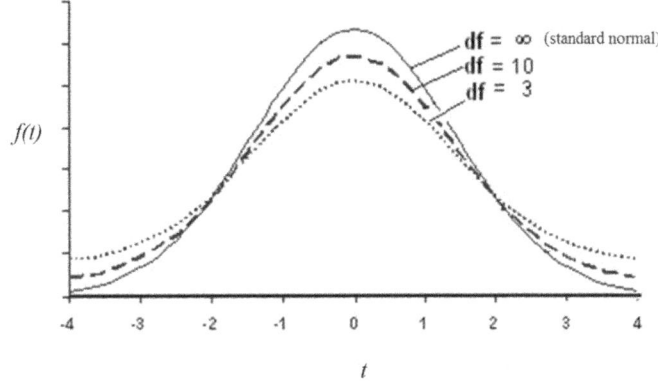

FIGURE 9-6:
Some members
of the
t-distribution
family.

To determine the lower and upper bounds for the 95 percent confidence level for a small sample, work with the member of the *t*-distribution family that has the appropriate *df*. Find the value that cuts off the upper 2.5 percent of the area in the upper tail of the distribution. Then multiply that value by the standard error.

Add the result to the mean to get the upper confidence limit; subtract the result from the mean to get the lower confidence limit.

This time, t.interval() does the work. To begin, I import the *t*-distribution family from scipy.stats:

```
from scipy.stats import t
```

Then I set it all up:

```
degrees_of_freedom = 24
battery_mean = 60
battery_std_error_t = 4
```

And finally, I hand it off to my friend `t.interval()`:

```
confidence_interval_95_with_t = t.interval(0.95, degrees_of_
    freedom, battery_mean, battery_std_error_t)
lower_bound_95_t = confidence_interval_95_with_t[0]
upper_bound_95_t = confidence_interval_95_with_t[1]
print(f'The 95% confidence limits are {lower_bound_95_t:.2f} and
    {upper_bound_95_t:.2f}')
The 95% confidence limits are 51.74 and 68.2
```

Chapter **10**

One-Sample Hypothesis Testing

Whatever your occupation, you often have to assess whether something new and different has happened. Sometimes you start with a population that you know a lot about (like its mean and standard deviation) and you draw a sample. Is that sample like the rest of the population, or does it represent something out of the ordinary?

To answer that question, you measure each individual in the sample and calculate the sample's statistics. Then you compare those statistics with the population's parameters. Are they the same? Are they different? Is the sample extraordinary in some way? Proper use of statistics helps you make the decision.

Sometimes, though, you don't know the parameters of the population that the sample came from. What happens then? In this chapter, I discuss statistical techniques and Python functions for dealing with both cases.

Hypotheses, Tests, and Errors

A *hypothesis* is a guess about the way the world works. It's a tentative explanation of some process, whether that process occurs in nature or in a laboratory.

REMEMBER

Before studying and measuring the individuals in a sample, a researcher formulates hypotheses that predict what the data should look like.

Generally, one hypothesis predicts that the data won't show anything new or out of the ordinary. This is called the *null hypothesis* (abbreviated H_0). According to the null hypothesis, if the data deviates from the norm in any way, that deviation is due strictly to chance. Another hypothesis, the *alternative hypothesis* (abbreviated H_1), explains things differently. According to the alternative hypothesis, the data shows something important.

After gathering the data, it's up to the researcher to make a decision. The way the logic works, the decision centers around the null hypothesis. The researcher must decide whether to either reject the null hypothesis or not reject the null hypothesis.

In *hypothesis testing*, you

» Formulate null and alternative hypotheses.

» Gather data.

» Decide whether to reject or not reject the null hypothesis.

REMEMBER

Nothing in the logic involves *accepting* either hypothesis. Nor does the logic involve making any decisions about the alternative hypothesis. It's all about rejecting or not rejecting H_0.

Regardless of the reject-don't-reject decision, an error is possible. One type of error occurs when you believe that the data shows something important and you reject H_0, but in reality, the data are due just to chance. This is called a *Type I error*. At the outset of a study, you set the criteria for rejecting H_0. In so doing, you set the probability of a Type I error. This probability is called *alpha* (α).

The other type of error occurs when you don't reject H_0, and the data is due to something out of the ordinary. For one reason or another, you happened to miss it. This is called a *Type II error*. Its probability is called *beta* (β). Table 10-1 summarizes the possible decisions and errors.

Note that you never know the true state of the world. (If you do, it's not necessary to do the study!) All you can ever do is measure the individuals in a sample, calculate the statistics, and make a decision about H_0. (I discuss hypotheses and hypothesis testing in Chapter 1.)

TABLE 10-1   **Decisions and Errors in Hypothesis Testing**

		"True State" of the World	
		H_0 is True	H_1 is True
	Reject H_0	Type I Error	Correct Decision
Decision			
	Do Not Reject H_0	Correct Decision	Type II Error

Hypothesis Tests and Sampling Distributions

In Chapter 9, I discuss sampling distributions. A sampling distribution, remember, is the set of all possible values of a statistic for a given sample size.

Also in Chapter 9, I discuss the central limit theorem. This theorem tells you that the sampling distribution of the mean approximates a normal distribution if the sample size is large enough (for practical purposes, at least 30). This works whether or not the population is normally distributed. If the population is a normal distribution, the sampling distribution is normal for any sample size. Here are two other points from the central limit theorem:

>> The mean of the sampling distribution of the mean is equal to the population mean.

   The equation for this is

   $\mu_{\bar{x}} = \mu$

>> The standard error of the mean (the standard deviation of the sampling distribution) is equal to the population standard deviation divided by the square root of the sample size.

   This equation is

   $\sigma_{\bar{x}} = \sigma / \sqrt{N}$

The sampling distribution of the mean figures prominently into the type of hypothesis testing I discuss in this chapter. Theoretically, when you test a null hypothesis versus an alternative hypothesis, each hypothesis corresponds to a separate sampling distribution.

Figure 10-1 shows what I mean. The figure shows two normal distributions. I placed them arbitrarily. Each normal distribution represents a sampling distribution of the mean. The one on the left represents the distribution of possible sample means if the null hypothesis is truly how the world works. The one on the right represents the distribution of possible sample means if the alternative hypothesis is truly how the world works.

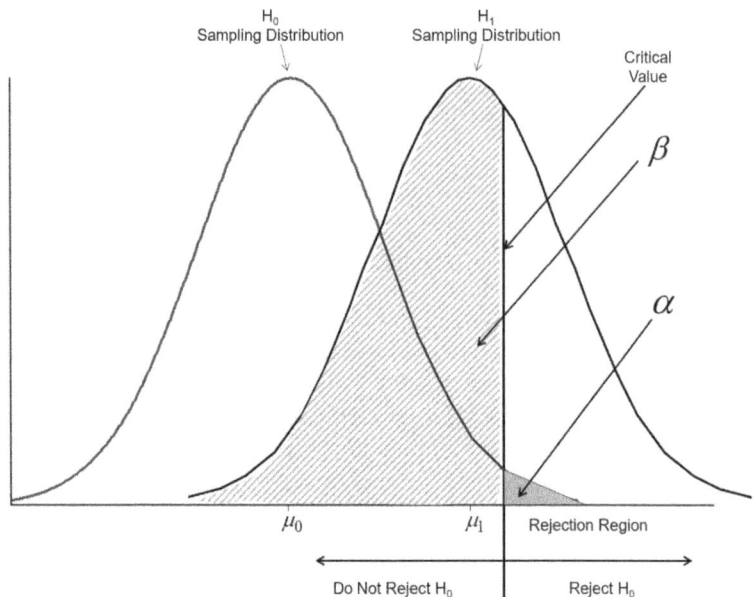

Of course, when you do a hypothesis test, you never know which distribution produces the results. You work with a sample mean — a point on the horizontal axis. The reject-or-don't reject decision boils down to deciding which distribution the sample mean is part of. You set up a *critical value* — a decision criterion. If the sample mean is on one side of the critical value, you reject H_0. If not, you don't.

In this vein, the figure also shows α and β. These, as I mention earlier in this chapter, are the probabilities of decision errors. The area that corresponds to α is in the H_0 distribution. I've shaded it in dark gray. It represents the probability that a sample mean comes from the H_0 distribution, but it's so extreme that you reject H_0.

REMEMBER

Where you set the critical value determines α. In most hypotheses testing, you set α at .05. This means you're willing to tolerate a Type I error (rejecting H_0 when you shouldn't) 5 percent of the time. Graphically, the critical value cuts off 5 percent of the area of the sampling distribution. By the way, if you're talking about the 5 percent of the area that's in the right tail of the distribution (refer to Figure 10-1), you're talking about the *upper* 5 percent. If it's the 5 percent in the left tail you're interested in, that's the *lower* 5 percent.

The area that corresponds to β is in the H_1 distribution. I've shaded it in light gray. This area represents the probability that a sample mean comes from the H_1 distribution, but it's close enough to the center of the H_0 distribution that you don't reject H_0 (but you should have). You don't get to set β. The size of this area depends on the separation between the means of the two distributions, and that's up to the world we live in — not up to you.

These sampling distributions are appropriate when your work corresponds to the conditions of the central limit theorem: if you know that the population you're working with is a normal distribution or if you have a large sample, in other words.

Catching Some Z's Again

Here's an example of a hypothesis test that involves a sample from a normally distributed population. Because the population is normally distributed, any sample size results in a normally distributed sampling distribution. Because it's a normal distribution, you use z-scores in the hypothesis test:

$$z = \frac{\bar{x} - \mu}{\sigma / \sqrt{N}}$$

One more *because:* Because you use the z-score in the hypothesis test, the z-score here is called the *test statistic.*

Suppose you think that people living in a particular zip code have higher-than-average IQs. You take a sample of nine people from that zip code, give them IQ tests, tabulate the results, and calculate the statistics. For the population of IQ scores, $\mu = 100$ and $\sigma = 15$.

The hypotheses are

$H_0: \mu_{ZIP\ code} \le 100$

$H_1: \mu_{ZIP\ code} > 100$

Assume that $\alpha = .05$. That's the shaded area in the tail of the H_0 distribution earlier, in Figure 10-1.

Why the ≤ in H_0? You use that symbol because you'll reject H_0 only if the sample mean is larger than the hypothesized value. Anything else is evidence in favor of not rejecting H_0.

Suppose the sample mean is 108.67. Can you reject H_0?

The test involves turning 108.67 into a standard score in the sampling distribution of the mean:

$$z = \frac{\bar{x} - \mu}{\sigma / \sqrt{N}} = \frac{108.67 - 100}{\left(15 / \sqrt{9}\right)} = \frac{8.67}{\left(15 / 3\right)} = \frac{8.67}{5} = 1.73$$

Is the value of the test statistic large enough to enable you to reject H_0 with σ = .05? It is. The critical value — the value of z that cuts off 5 percent of the area in a standard normal distribution — is 1.645. (After years of working with the standard normal distribution, I happen to know this. Read Chapter 8 and find out about Python's norm.ppf() method, and then you can have information like that at your fingertips, too.) The calculated value, 1.73, exceeds 1.645, so it's in the rejection region. The decision is to reject H_0.

This means that if H_0 is true, the probability of getting a test statistic value that's at least this large is less than .05. That's strong evidence in favor of rejecting H_0.

REMEMBER

In statistical parlance, anytime you reject H_0, the result is said to be *statistically significant*.

This type of hypothesis testing is called *one-tailed* because the rejection region is in one tail of the sampling distribution.

A hypothesis test can be one-tailed in the other direction. Suppose you have reason to believe that people in that zip code have lower-than-average IQs. In that case, the hypotheses are

$H_0: \mu_{ZIP\ code} \geq 100$

$H_1: \mu_{ZIP\ code} < 100$

For this hypothesis test, the critical value of the test statistic is −1.645 if α = .05.

A hypothesis test can be *two-tailed,* meaning that the rejection region is in both tails of the H_0 sampling distribution. That happens when the hypotheses look like this:

$H_0: \mu_{ZIP\ code} = 100$

$H_1: \mu_{ZIP\ code} \neq 100$

In this case, the alternative hypothesis just specifies that the mean is different from the null-hypothesis value, without saying whether it's greater or whether it's less. Figure 10-2 shows what the two-tailed rejection region looks like for α = .05. The 5 percent is divided evenly between the left tail (also called the *lower tail*) and the right tail (the *upper tail*).

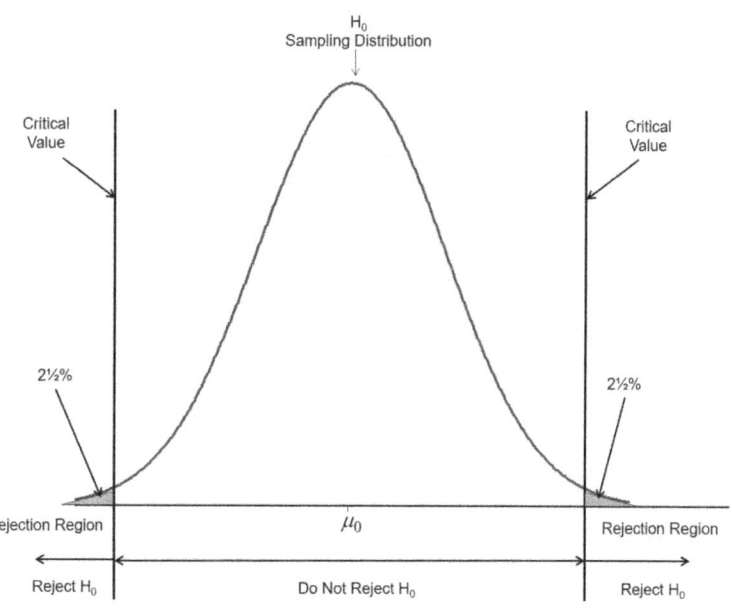

FIGURE 10-2:
The two-tailed rejection region for α = .05.

For a standard normal distribution, incidentally, the z-score that cuts off 2.5 percent in the right tail is 1.96. The z-score that cuts off 2.5 percent in the left tail is −1.96. (Again, I happen to know these values after years of working with the standard normal distribution.) The z-score in the preceding example, 1.73, doesn't exceed 1.96. The decision, in the two-tailed case, is *not* to reject H_0.

TIP

This brings up an important point: A one-tailed hypothesis test can reject H_0, whereas a two-tailed test on the same data might not. A two-tailed test indicates that you're looking for a difference between the sample mean and the null-hypothesis mean, but you don't know in which direction. A one-tailed test shows that you have a pretty good idea of how the difference should come out. For practical purposes, this means you should try to have enough knowledge to be able to specify a one-tailed test: That gives you a better chance of rejecting H_0 when you should.

z-Testing in Python

A Python function called `z_test()` would be useful for doing the kind of testing I discuss in the previous section. One problem: That function doesn't exist in Python. It's easy enough to define one on your own and learn a bit about Python programming in the process.

The function will work like this:

```
IQ_data = [100,101,104,109,125,116,105,108,110]
my_z_test = z_test(IQ_data,100,15)
z = 1.73
one-tailed probability = 0.042
two-tailed probability = 0.084
```

Begin by importing `norm` and creating the function name and its arguments:

```
from scipy.stats import norm
def z_test(data,mu,sigma):
```

Next, we implement a best practice — documentation inside the function. This type of embedded document is called a *docstring*, and it's a good idea to get acquainted with it right off the bat. Three quote marks precede the docstring, and three follow it. (It's something like # on steroids.) The docstring tells the reader what the function does, its arguments, and what it returns:

```
"""
Given a list of sample data, this function performs a z-test
 and returns the z-score,
one-tailed p-value, and two-tailed p-value
The function assumes that the population is normally
 distributed.

Args:
  data: list of sample data
  mu: mean of the normally distributed population
  sigma: standard deviation of the normally distributed
population

Returns:
  z_score: z-score of the sample data
  one_tailed_p_value: p-value of the sample data
  two_tailed_p_value: two-tailed p-value of the sample data
"""
```

Next, I start calculating. First, the sample size and the sample mean:

```
sample_size = len(data)
sample_mean = sum(data) / sample_size
```

and then the z-score, based on the standard error of the mean:

```
z_score = (sample_mean - mu) / (sigma / (sample_size**0.5))
```

I use the `norm.sf()` method to compute the proportion of area under the normal curve that lies beyond the absolute value of the z-score. The name `sf` stands for *survival function* and it's `1-cdf`:

```
one_tailed_p_value = norm.sf(abs(z_score))
```

Why the absolute value? If the z-score is negative, I want to know the proportion that's more extreme in the negative direction (in the left tail, in other words).

I multiply the one-tailed p-value by 2 to calculate the two-tailed p-value:

```
two_tailed_p_value = one_tailed_p_value * 2
```

Finally, I print the results and return them.

```
print(f"z = {z_score:.2f}")
print(f"one-tailed_p = {one_tailed_p_value:.3f}")
print(f"two-tailed_p = {two_tailed_p_value:.3f}")
return z_score, one_tailed_p_value, two_tailed_p_value
```

Running all that code produces what you see at the beginning of this section.

Returning the values enables a user to retrieve them. For example, if the user wants to work further with the z-score, that's

```
my_z_score = my_z_test[0]
print(my_z_score)
1.7333333333333343
```

One more thing:

```
help(z_test)
z_test(data, mu, sigma)
    Given a list of sample data, this function performs a z-test
    and returns the z-score,
```

```
   one-tailed p-value, and two-tailed p-value
   The function assumes that the population is normally
distributed.
   Args:
      data: list of sample data
      mu: mean of the normally distributed population
      sigma: standard deviation of the normally distributed
population
   Returns:
      z_score: z-score of the sample data
      one_tailed_p_value: p-value of the sample data
      two_tailed_p_value: two-tailed p-value of the sample data
```

And that's why you write a docstring when you create a function.

t for One

In the preceding example, you work with IQ scores. The population of IQ scores is a normal distribution with a well-known mean and standard deviation. Thus, you can work with the central limit theorem and describe the sampling distribution of the mean as a normal distribution. You can then use z as the test statistic.

In the real world, however, you usually don't have the luxury of working with well-defined populations. You usually have small samples, and you're typically measuring something that isn't as well-known as IQ. The bottom line is that you often don't know the population parameters, nor do you know whether the population is normally distributed.

When that's the case, you use the sample data to estimate the population standard deviation, and you treat the sampling distribution of the mean as a member of a family of distributions called the t-distribution. You use t as a test statistic. In Chapter 9, I introduce this distribution and mention that you distinguish members of this family by a parameter called *degrees of freedom* (df).

The formula for the test statistic is

$$t = \frac{\bar{x} - \mu}{s / \sqrt{N}}$$

Think of *df* as the denominator of the estimate of the population variance. For the hypothesis tests in this section, that's $N - 1$, where N is the number of scores in the sample. The higher the df, the more closely the t-distribution resembles the normal distribution.

Here's an example. FarKlempt Robotics, Inc., markets microrobots. The company claims that its product averages four defects per unit. A consumer group believes this average is higher. The consumer group takes a sample of nine FarKlempt microrobots and finds an average of seven defects, with a standard deviation of 3.12. The hypothesis test is

$H_0: \mu \leq 4$

$H_1: \mu > 4$

$\alpha = .05$

The formula is

$$t = \frac{\bar{x} - \mu}{s/\sqrt{N}} = \frac{7 - 4}{3.12/\sqrt{9}} = \frac{3}{3.12/3} = 2.88$$

Can you reject H_0? The function in the next section tells you.

t Testing in Python

The `scipy.stats` function `ttest_1samp()` does the honors.

I begin with the necessary imports:

```
import numpy as np
from scipy.stats import ttest_1samp
```

Here's the data:

```
FarKlempt_data = [3,6,9,9,4,10,6,4,12]
```

and the hypothesized population mean:

```
pop_mean = 4
```

Now I carry out the t-test and print the results:

```
t_statistic, p_value = ttest_1samp(FarKlempt_data, pop_mean)

print(f"t-statistic: {t_statistic:.2f}")
print(f"p-value: {p_value:.3f}")
t-statistic: 2.88
p-value: 0.020
```

Because *p*-value is less than .05, the decision is to reject the null hypothesis with α = .05.

Working with *t*-Distributions

Just as you can use the `pdf()`, `cdf()`, `sf()`, `ppf()`, and `rng()` methods for the normal distribution family, you can use them for the *t*-distribution family and any other distribution family that resides in `scipy.stats`.

Here are `t.pdf()` and `t.cdf()` at work in a *t*-distribution with 12 df:

```
from scipy.stats import t
import numpy as np

t_values = list(range(-4, 5,1))
t_list = t.pdf(t_values, 12)
print(t_list)
[0.00158498 0.01028313 0.06022418 0.23223034 0.39072631
  0.23223034
 0.06022418 0.01028313 0.00158498]

cum_t_list = t.cdf(t_values, 12)
print(cum_t_list)
[8.80848122e-04 5.53334784e-03 3.43275070e-02 1.68524529e-01
 5.00000000e-01 8.31475471e-01 9.65672493e-01 9.94466652e-01
 9.99119152e-01]
```

I use `t.ppf()` to calculate quartiles:

```
for i in range(25, 75 + 1, 25):
    print(f'{i}th percentile = {t(12).ppf(i/100):.3f}')
25th percentile = -0.695
50th percentile = 0.000
75th percentile = 0.695
```

and `t.rvs()` to generate eight random numbers:

```
random_t_numbers = t.rvs(12, size=8)
print(random_t_numbers)
[ 0.94275631 -1.74438257  1.26800223  1.32953943 -1.90615579
  0.52935364
  0.60583235 -0.81033282]
```

Visualizing *t*-Distributions

Visualizing a distribution often helps you understand it. The process is pretty straightforward in Python. Over in Chapter 9, Figure 9-6 shows three members of the *t*-distribution family on the same graph. The first has df = 3, the second has df = 10, and the third is the standard normal distribution (df = infinity).

In this section, I show you how to create that graph in `matplotlib`. Figure 10-3 shows the finished product.

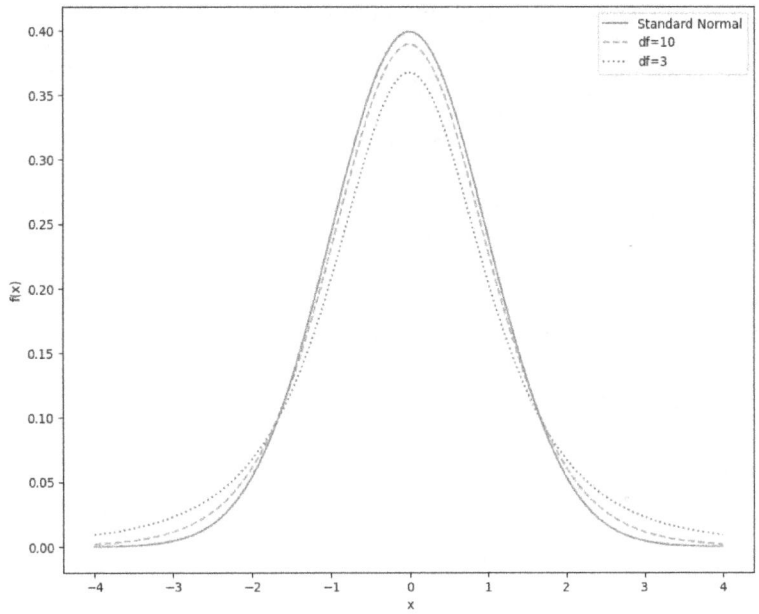

FIGURE 10-3: Two *t*-distributions and the standard normal distribution.

First, I import what I need:

```
import numpy as np
import matplotlib.pyplot as plt
from scipy.stats import t, norm
```

Next, I create the values for the *x*-axis:

```
x = np.linspace(-4, 4, 100)
```

Then I set the degrees of freedom for the t-distributions:

```
df1 = 3
df2 = 10
```

Now I compute the three density functions:

```
t_pdf1 = t.pdf(x, df1)
t_pdf2 = t.pdf(x, df2)
normal_pdf = norm.pdf(x)  # Standard normal (df = infinity)
```

Then I set the dimensions of the figure

```
plt.figure(figsize=(10, 8))
```

and plot the three distributions:

```
plt.plot(x, t_pdf1, linestyle = ':', label=f'df={df1}')
plt.plot(x, t_pdf2, linestyle = '--',label=f'df={df2}')
plt.plot(x, normal_pdf, label='Standard Normal')
```

Note the different `linestyle` for each curve.

I label the axes

```
plt.xlabel('x')
plt.ylabel('f(x)')
```

and set up the legend:

```
plt.legend(reverse = True)
```

The `reverse = True` argument orders the items on the legend the same as the arrangement of the curves on the graph.

Finally, I show the plot, which is what you see in Figure 10-3:

```
plt.show()
```

Testing a Variance

So far, I discuss one-sample hypothesis testing for means. You can also test hypotheses about variances.

This topic sometimes comes up in the context of manufacturing. Suppose that FarKlempt Robotics, Inc., produces a part that has to be a certain length with a very small variability. You can take a sample of parts, measure them, find the sample variability, and perform a hypothesis test against the desired variability.

The family of distributions for the test is called *chi-square*. Its symbol is χ^2. I won't go into all the mathematics. I'll just tell you that, once again, df is the parameter that distinguishes one member of the family from another. Figure 10-4 shows two members of the chi-square family.

As the figure shows, chi-square isn't like the previous distribution families I showed you. Members of this family can be skewed, and none of them can take a value less than 0.

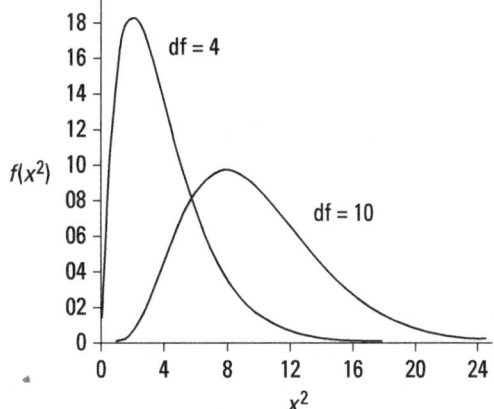

FIGURE 10-4:
Two members
of the chi-square
family.

The formula for the test statistic is

$$\chi^2 = \frac{(N-1)s^2}{\sigma^2}$$

N is the number of scores in the sample, s^2 is the sample variance, and σ^2 is the population variance specified in H_0.

With this test, you have to assume that what you're measuring has a normal distribution.

Suppose the process for the FarKlempt part has to have, at most, a standard deviation of 1.5 inches for its length. (Notice that I use *standard deviation*. This allows me to speak in terms of inches. If I use *variance,* the units would be square inches.) After measuring a sample of ten parts, you find a standard deviation of 1.80 inches.

The hypotheses are

H_0: $\sigma^2 \leq 2.25$ (remember to square the "at-most" standard deviation of 1.5 inches)

H_1: $\sigma^2 > 2.25$

$\alpha = .05$

Working with this formula:

$$\chi^2 = \frac{(N-1)s^2}{\sigma^2} = \frac{(10-1)(1.80)^2}{(1.5)^2} = \frac{(9)(3.25)}{2.25} = 12.96$$

can you reject H_0? Read on.

Testing a Variance in Python

Just as `scipy.stats` supplies `norm` and `t`, it also supplies `chi2`. Unlike `ttest_1samp()`, however, `chi2_1samp()` doesn't exist.

So let's make one of our own. The objective is a function that takes as its arguments sample data, the alternative hypothesis ('greater', 'less', or 'not equal'), and the hypothesized population variance. I want it to return the calculated chi-square, the *p*-value, and whether the *p*-value is one-tailed (if the alternative hypothesis is 'greater' or it's 'less') or two-tailed (if the alternative hypothesis is 'not equal').

I begin with the imports:

```
from scipy.stats import chi2
import numpy as np
```

Then I define the function and add a docstring:

```
def chi2_1sample(data, alternative, pop_variance):
    """
    Performs a chi-squared test for one sample variance.
    It's analogous to the one-sample t-test, but for variance.
```

```
Args:
    data: A list or NumPy array of sample data.
    alternative: The alternative hypothesis ('greater',
'less', or 'not equal').
    pop_variance: The hypothesized population variance.

Returns:
    chi2_statistic: The chi-squared test statistic.
    p_value: The p-value of the test.
"""
```

I list all possible alternative hypotheses as well as the action to take if the input isn't one of them:

```
alternatives = ['greater', 'less', 'not equal']
if alternative not in alternatives:
    raise ValueError(f"Invalid alternative hypothesis. Must
be one of {alternatives}.")
    return
```

Next, it's the computations for *N* and for the sample variance:

```
n = len(data)
sample_variance = np.var(data, ddof=1)
```

That second argument for np.var() gives the variance estimate with $N - 1$ in the denominator (see Chapter 5).

I calculate the value of chi-square

```
chi2_statistic = (n - 1) * sample_variance / pop_variance
```

and set a default value for the number of distribution tails that figure into the *p*-value:

```
tails = 1
```

Unlike the *t*-distribution, the chi-square distribution is skewed. For this reason, the alternative hypothesis determines how I calculate the *p*-value:

>> If the alternative hypothesis is 'greater' (alternatives[0]), I use the sf() method to compute the *p*-value because that gives the area under the chi-square distribution that's to the right of chi2_statistic.

>> If the alternative hypothesis is 'less' (alternatives[1]), I use the cdf() method to compute the *p*-value because that gives the area under the chi-square distribution that's to the left of ch2_statistic.

>> If the alternative hypothesis is 'not equal' (alternatives[2]), I don't know in advance whether to use cdf() or sf(). So I calculate both, find the minimum of the two, and multiply the minimum by 2 to find the *p*-value. In this case, I also reset tails to 2:

```
if alternative == alternatives[0]:
    p_value = chi2.sf(chi2_statistic, df=n - 1)
elif alternative == alternatives[1]:
    p_value = chi2.cdf(chi2_statistic, df=n - 1)
elif alternative == alternatives[2]:
    tails = 2
    p_value = 2* min(chi2.cdf(chi2_statistic, df=n - 1),
chi2.sf(chi2_statistic, df=n - 1))
```

Then I print the results and I return them:

```
print(f"chi-square = {chi2_statistic:.2f}")
print(f"{tails}-tailed p-value = {p_value:.3f}")
return chi2_statistic, p_value
```

Here's a look at this function in action. First, a list of the sample data:

```
FarKlempt2_data = [12.43,11.71,14.41,11.05,9.53,11.66,9.33,
    11.71,14.35,13.81]
```

And now the function call:

```
chi2_statistic, p_value = chi2_1sample(FarKlempt2_data,
    'greater',2.25)
chi-square = 12.98
1-tailed p-value = 0.163
```

The chi-square value in the previous section is a bit lower because of rounding. The *p*-value is greater than .05. Therefore, I cannot reject the null hypothesis with α = .05.

TIP

Try calling the function with 'less' and with 'not equal' as the second argument to check the output. Also, try calling it with a nonsense string as the second argument and watch what happens.

How high would chi-square (with df = 9) have to be in order to reject H_0? Hmmm . . . .

Working with Chi-Square Distributions

As is the case for the distribution families I discuss in this chapter, `scipy.stats` methods work with the chi-square family: `pdf()` (for the density function), `cdf()` (for the cumulative density function), `ppf()` (for percentiles in general and quartiles in particular), and `rvs()` (for random-number generation).

To answer the question I pose at the end of the previous section, I use `ppf()`:

```
alpha = 0.05
df = len(FarKlempt2_data) - 1
rejection_criteria_for_05 = chi2.ppf(1-alpha,9)
print(f'the chi-square value needed to reject H0 with df = {df}
    and alpha = {alpha} is {rejection_criteria_for_05:.2f}')
the chi-square value needed to reject H0 with df = 9 and alpha =
    0.05 is 16.92
```

The observed value missed that critical value by quite a bit.

Here are examples of other `scipy.stats` functions for chi-square with df = 9. I begin by creating a set of values to work with:

```
chi_square_values = np.arange(0,9,2)
print(chi_square_values)
[0 2 4 6 8]
```

To get the probability density for each value, I apply `pdf()`:

```
densities=chi2.pdf(chi_square_values,9)
print(densities)
[0.         0.01581362 0.06581756 0.10008447 0.10077616]
```

A little Python magic can snazz up the output. I use Python's `zip()` function to pair up the `chi_square_values` with their corresponding `densities`. A `for` loop prints the pairs:

```
for value, density in zip(chi_square_values, densities):
    print(f"When chi-square with 9 df = {value}, density =
    {density:.3f}")
When chi-square with 9 df = 0, density = 0.000
When chi-square with 9 df = 2, density = 0.016
When chi-square with 9 df = 4, density = 0.066
When chi-square with 9 df = 6, density = 0.100
When chi-square with 9 df = 8, density = 0.101
```

I leave it as an exercise for you to produce this output:

```
When chi-square with 9 df = 0, cumulative density = 0.000
When chi-square with 9 df = 2, cumulative density = 0.009
When chi-square with 9 df = 4, cumulative density = 0.089
When chi-square with 9 df = 6, cumulative density = 0.260
When chi-square with 9 df = 8, cumulative density = 0.466
```

Here are six random numbers selected from this chi-square distribution:

```
six_random_numbers = chi2.rvs(df=9, size=6)
print(six_random_numbers)
[10.12333199  4.31869443  6.06748709  5.90810708  8.05184715
  11.71543698]
```

Visualizing Chi-Square Distributions

Figure 10-4, earlier in this chapter, nicely shows a couple of members of the chi-square family, with each member annotated with its degrees of freedom. In this section, I show you how to use matplotlib to re-create that picture.

First, the necessary imports:

```
import matplotlib.pyplot as plt
from scipy.stats import chi2
import  numpy as np
```

Then I set the figure size

```
plt.figure(figsize=(10, 6))
```

and create 100 evenly spaced points on the *x*-axis from x = 0 to x = 25:

```
x = np.linspace(0,25,100)
```

Then I calculate the chi-square densities for both distributions — one with 4 df and the other with 9:

```
y1=chi2.pdf(x,4)
y2=chi2.pdf(x,9)
```

I plot them both

```
plt.plot(x, y1, label='df=4')
plt.plot(x, y2, label='df=9')
```

and then comes the new wrinkle — annotation instead of a legend:

```
plt.annotate('df=4', xy=(4, 0.14), xytext=(5, 0.15))
plt.annotate('df=9', xy=(14, 0.04), xytext=(15, 0.05))
```

In each `annotate()` method, the first argument is what the annotation says, the second argument is the *xy* coordinates of where an arrow would point if I wanted an arrow, and the third argument is the *xy* coordinates where the annotation goes. Seems a bit quirky to need that second argument even if I'm not including an arrow, but there you have it.

Now I label the axes and show the figure:

```
plt.xlabel('x')
plt.ylabel('f(x)')
plt.show()
```

The result is shown in Figure 10-5.

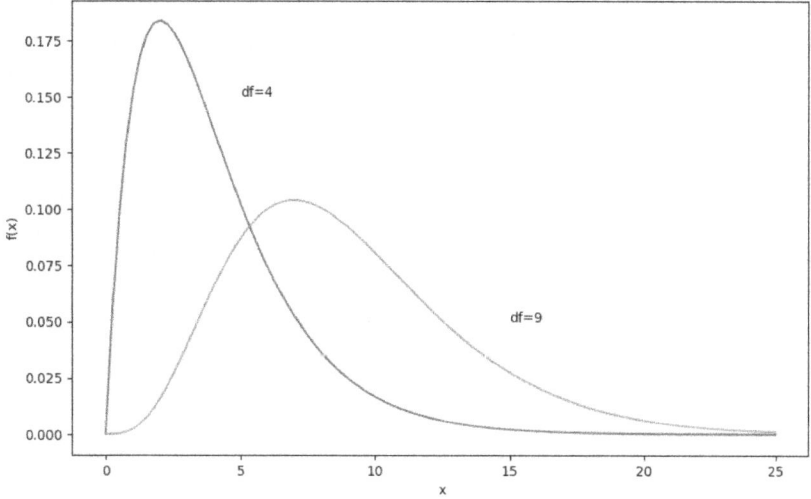

FIGURE 10-5:
Two members of the chi-square family, plotted in matplotlib.

Chapter **11**

Two-Sample Hypothesis Testing

I n a variety of fields, the need often arises to compare one sample with another. Sometimes the samples are independent, and sometimes they're matched in some way. Each sample comes from a separate population. The objective is to decide whether these populations are different from one another.

Usually, this involves tests of hypotheses about population means. You can also test hypotheses about population variances. In this chapter, I show you how to carry out these tests as well as how to use Python to get the job done.

Hypotheses Built for Two

As in the one-sample case (see Chapter 10), hypothesis testing with two samples starts with a null hypothesis (H_0) and an alternative hypothesis (H_1). The null hypothesis specifies that any differences you see between the two samples are due strictly to chance. The alternative hypothesis says, in effect, that any differences you see are real and not due to chance.

It's possible to have a *one-tailed test,* in which the alternative hypothesis specifies the direction of the difference between the two means, or a *two-tailed test* in which the alternative hypothesis does not specify the direction of the difference.

For a one-tailed test, the hypotheses look like this:

$$H_0 : \mu_1 - \mu_2 = 0$$
$$H_1 : \mu_1 - \mu_2 > 0$$

or like this:

$$H_0 : \mu_1 - \mu_2 = 0$$
$$H_1 : \mu_1 - \mu_2 < 0$$

For a two-tailed test, the hypotheses are

$$H_0 : \mu_1 - \mu_2 = 0$$
$$H_1 : \mu_1 - \mu_2 \neq 0$$

The 0 in these hypotheses is the typical case. It's possible, however, to test for any value — just substitute that value for 0.

To carry out the test, you first set α — the probability of a Type I error that you're willing to live with (see Chapter 10). Then you calculate the mean and standard deviation of each sample, subtract one mean from the other, and use a formula to convert the result into a test statistic. With that out of the way, you compare the test statistic to a sampling distribution of test statistics. If it's in the rejection region that α specifies (again, see Chapter 10), reject H_0. If it's not, don't reject H_0.

Sampling Distributions Revisited

In Chapter 9, I introduce the idea of a sampling distribution — a distribution of all possible values of a statistic for a particular sample size. In that chapter, I describe the sampling distribution of the mean. In Chapter 10, I show its connection with one-sample hypothesis testing.

For two-sample hypothesis testing, another sampling distribution is necessary. This one is the sampling distribution of the difference between means.

The *sampling distribution of the difference between means* is the distribution of all possible values of differences between pairs of sample means with the sample sizes held constant from pair to pair. (Yes, that's a mouthful.) *Held constant from pair to pair* means that the first sample in the pair always has the same size, and the second sample in the pair always has the same size. The two sample sizes aren't necessarily equal.

REMEMBER

Within each pair, each sample comes from a different population. All samples are independent of one another so that picking individuals for one sample has no effect on picking individuals for another.

Figure 11-1 shows the steps in creating this sampling distribution. This is something you never do in practice. It's all theoretical. As the figure shows, the idea is to take a sample out of one population and a sample out of another, calculate their means, and subtract one mean from the other. You then return the samples to the populations and repeat the same process over and over and over. The result of the process is a set of differences between means. This set of differences is the sampling distribution.

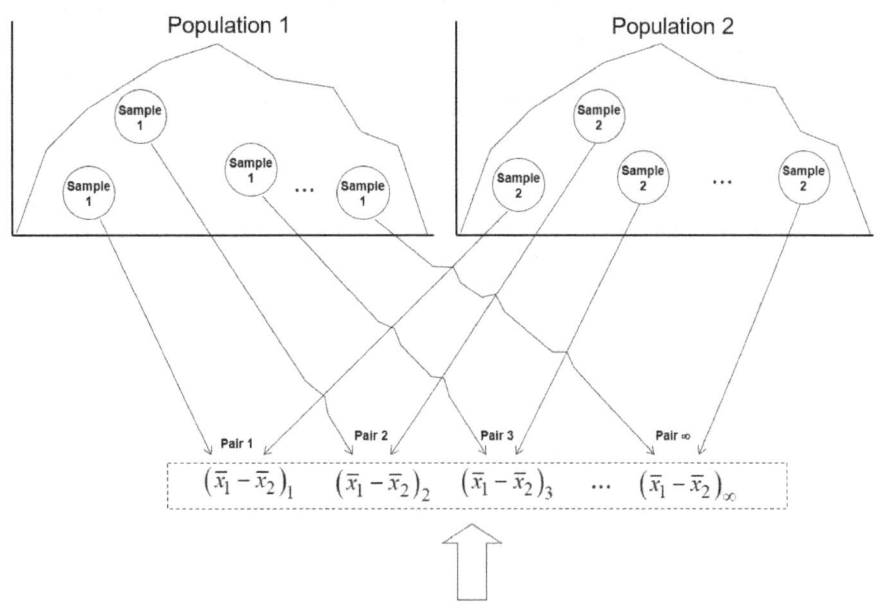

FIGURE 11-1:
Creating the sampling distribution of the difference between means.

Applying the central limit theorem

Like any other set of numbers, this sampling distribution has a mean and a standard deviation. As is the case with the sampling distribution of the mean (see Chapters 9 and 10), the central limit theorem applies here.

According to the central limit theorem, if the samples are large enough, the sampling distribution of the difference between means is approximately a normal distribution. If the populations are normally distributed, the sampling distribution is a normal distribution even if the samples are small.

The central limit theorem also has something to say about the mean and standard deviation of this sampling distribution. Suppose that the parameters for the first population are μ_1 and α_1 and that the parameters for the second population are μ_2 and α_2. The mean of the sampling distribution is

$$\mu_{\bar{x}_1 - \bar{x}_2} = \mu_1 - \mu_2$$

The standard deviation of the sampling distribution is

$$\sigma_{\bar{x}_1 - \bar{x}_2} = \sqrt{\frac{\sigma_1^2}{N_1} + \frac{\sigma_2^2}{N_2}}$$

N_1 is the number of individuals in the sample from the first population, and N_2 is the number of individuals in the sample from the second.

REMEMBER

This standard deviation is called *the standard error of the difference between means*.

Figure 11-2 shows the sampling distribution along with its parameters, as specified by the central limit theorem.

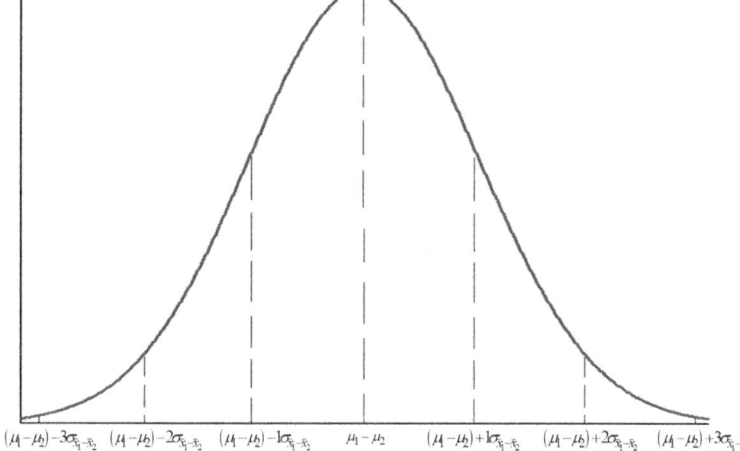

FIGURE 11-2:
The sampling distribution of the difference between means, according to the central limit theorem.

Z's once more

Because the central limit theorem says that the sampling distribution is approximately normal for large samples (or for small samples from normally distributed populations), you use the z-score as your test statistic. Another way to say "use the z-score as your test statistic" is "perform a z-test." Here's the formula:

$$z = \frac{(\bar{x}_1 - \bar{x}_2) - (\mu_1 - \mu_2)}{\sigma_{\bar{x}_1 - \bar{x}_2}}$$

The term $(\mu_1 - \mu_2)$ represents the difference between the means in H_0.

This formula converts the difference between sample means into a standard score. Compare the standard score against a standard normal distribution — a normal distribution with $\mu = 0$ and $\alpha = 1$. If the score is in the rejection region defined by α, reject H_0. If it's not, don't reject H_0.

You use this formula when you know the value of α_1^2 and α_2^2.

Here's an example. Imagine a new training technique designed to increase IQ. Take a sample of nine people and train them under the new technique. Take another sample of nine people and give them no special training. Suppose that the sample mean for the new technique sample is 110.222, and for the no-training sample it's 101. The hypothesis test is

$$H_0 : \mu_1 - \mu_2 \leq 0$$
$$H_1 : \mu_1 - \mu_2 > 0$$

I'll set α at .05.

The IQ is known to have a standard deviation of 15 and I assume that standard deviation would be the same in the population of people trained on the new technique. Of course, that population doesn't exist. The assumption is that if it did, it should have the same value for the standard deviation as the regular population of IQ scores. Does the mean of that (theoretical) population have the same value as the regular population? H_0 says it does. H_1 says it's larger.

The test statistic is

$$z = \frac{(\bar{x}_1 - \bar{x}_2) - (\mu_1 - \mu_2)}{\sigma_{\bar{x}_1 - \bar{x}_2}} = \frac{(\bar{x}_1 - \bar{x}_2) - (\mu_1 - \mu_2)}{\sqrt{\dfrac{\sigma_1^2}{N_1} + \dfrac{\sigma_2^2}{N_2}}} = \frac{(110.222 - 101)}{\sqrt{\dfrac{15^2}{9} + \dfrac{15^2}{9}}} = \frac{9.222}{7.071} = 1.304$$

With $\alpha = .05$, the critical value of z — the value that cuts off the upper 5 percent of the area under the standard normal distribution — is 1.645. (You can use the `norm.ppf()` function from Chapter 8 to verify this.) The calculated value of the test statistic is less than the critical value, so the decision is to not reject H_0. Figure 11-3 summarizes for you.

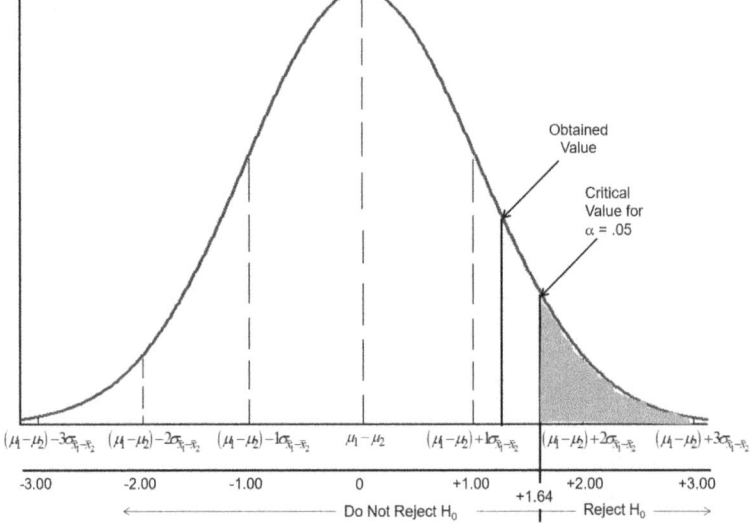

FIGURE 11-3: The sampling distribution of the difference between means, along with the critical value for $\alpha = .05$ and the obtained value of the test statistic in the IQ example.

Obtained Value

Critical Value for $\alpha = .05$

$(\mu_1-\mu_2)-3\sigma_{\bar{x}_1-\bar{x}_2}$ $(\mu_1-\mu_2)-2\sigma_{\bar{x}_1-\bar{x}_2}$ $(\mu_1-\mu_2)-1\sigma_{\bar{x}_1-\bar{x}_2}$ $\mu_1-\mu_2$ $(\mu_1-\mu_2)+1\sigma_{\bar{x}_1-\bar{x}_2}$ $(\mu_1-\mu_2)+2\sigma_{\bar{x}_1-\bar{x}_2}$ $(\mu_1-\mu_2)+3\sigma_{\bar{x}_1-\bar{x}_2}$

-3.00 -2.00 -1.00 0 +1.00 +2.00 +3.00

+1.64

Do Not Reject H_0 Reject H_0

z-testing for two samples in Python

As is the case for one-sample testing (explained in Chapter 10), Python provides no function for a two-sample *z*-test. If this function existed, you'd probably want it to work like this for my IQ example:

```
sample1 = [100,118,97,92,118,125,136,95,111]
sample2 = [91,109,83,88,115,108,127,102,86]

sigma1 = 15
sigma2 = 15

my_2_sample_z = two_sample_z_test(sample1, sample2,
    sigma1, sigma2)

mean1 = 110.222  mean2 = 101.000
standard error = 7.071
z_statistic = 1.304
one-tailed p_value = 0.096
two-tailed p_value = 0.192
```

Because this function isn't available, I show you how to create it. First, I import norm from `scipy.stats`:

```
from scipy.stats import norm
```

Next, I define the function and write a docstring (see Chapter 2):

```
def two_sample_z_test(sample1, sample2, sigma1, sigma2):

"""
    Performs a z-test for the difference between the means of
    two samples.

    Args:
      sample1: A list or numpy array of the data in the
    first sample.
      sample2: A list or numpy array of the data in the
    second sample.
      sigma1: The standard deviation of the population that
    produced the first sample.
      sigma2: The standard deviation of the population that
    produced the second sample.

    Returns:
      the z-statistic, the 1-tailed p-value, mean of sample1, and
    mean of sample2.
    """
```

Then I calculate the sample sizes and the sample means:

```
n1 = len(sample1)
n2 = len(sample2)
mean1 = sum(sample1) / n1
mean2 = sum(sample2) / n2
```

This gives me the information I need to calculate the standard error of the difference between means:

```
std_err = ((sigma1**2 / n1) + (sigma2**2 / n2))**0.5
```

And now I can compute the z-statistic.

```
z_statistic = (mean1 - mean2) / std_err
```

In case `z_statistic` is negative, I use its absolute value (`abs()`) to calculate its *p*-value:

```
p_value = norm.sf(abs(z_statistic))
```

That's pretty much it, except for printing the results and returning them.

```
print(f'mean1 = {mean1:.3f}  mean2 = {mean2:.3f}')
print(f'standard error = {std_err:.3f}')
print(f'z_statistic = {z_statistic:.3f} ')
print(f'one-tailed p_value = {p_value:.3f} ')
print(f'two-tailed p_value = {p_value*2:.3f} ')
return z_statistic, p_value, mean1, mean2
```

Give it a try! Create those lists I showed you for `sample1` and `sample2`, set the values for `sigma1` and `sigma2`, and watch `two_sample_z_test()` do its thing.

t for Two

The example in the preceding section involves a situation you rarely encounter — known population variances. If you know a population's variance, you're likely to know the population mean. If you know the mean, you probably don't have to perform hypothesis tests about it.

Not knowing the variances takes the central limit theorem out of play. This means you can't use the normal distribution as an approximation of the sampling distribution of the difference between means. Instead, you use the *t*-distribution, a family of distributions I introduce in Chapter 9 and apply to one-sample hypothesis testing in Chapter 10. The members of this family of distributions differ from one another in terms of a parameter called *degrees of freedom* (df). Think of *df* as the denominator of the variance estimate you use when you calculate a value of *t* as a test statistic. Another way to say "calculate a value of *t* as a test statistic" is "Perform a *t*-test."

Estimating population variance

When you don't know the population variance, you use the sample variance to estimate it. If you have two samples, you average (sort of) the two sample variances to arrive at the estimate.

Putting sample variances together to estimate a population variance is called *pooling*. With two sample variances, here's how you do it:

$$s_p^2 = \frac{(N_1 - 1)s_1^2 + (N_2 - 1)s_2^2}{(N_1 - 1) + (N_2 - 1)}$$

In this formula, $s_p{}^2$ stands for the pooled estimate. Notice that the denominator of this estimate is $(N_1 - 1) + (N_2 - 1)$. Is this the *df*? Absolutely!

The formula for calculating t is

$$t = \frac{(\bar{x}_1 - \bar{x}_2) - (\mu_1 - \mu_2)}{s_p\sqrt{\dfrac{1}{N_1} + \dfrac{1}{N_2}}}$$

On to an example. FarKlempt Robotics is trying to choose between two machines to produce a component for its new microrobot. Speed is of the essence, so the company has each machine produce ten copies of the component and time each production run. The hypotheses are

$$H_0 : \mu_1 - \mu_2 = 0$$
$$H_1 : \mu_1 - \mu_2 \neq 0$$

They set α at .05. This is a two-tailed test because they don't know in advance which machine might be faster.

Table 11-1 presents the data for the production times in minutes.

TABLE 11-1

Sample Statistics from the FarKlempt Machine Study

	Machine 1	Machine 2
Mean Production Time	23.00	20.00
Standard Deviation	2.71	2.79
Sample Size	10	10

The pooled estimate of α^2 is

$$s_p^2 = \frac{(N_1 - 1)s_1^2 + (N_2 - 1)s_2^2}{(N_1 - 1) + (N_2 - 1)} = \frac{(10 - 1)(2.71)^2 + (10 - 1)(2.79)^2}{(10 - 1) + (10 - 1)}$$

$$= \frac{(9)(2.71)^2 + (9)(2.79)^2}{(9) + (9)} = \frac{66 + 70}{18} = 7.56$$

The estimate of α is 2.75, the square root of 7.56.

The test statistic is

$$t = \frac{(\bar{x}_1 - \bar{x}_2) - (\mu_1 - \mu_2)}{s_p \sqrt{\frac{1}{N_1} + \frac{1}{N_2}}} = \frac{(23 - 20)}{2.75 \sqrt{\frac{1}{10} + \frac{1}{10}}} = \frac{3}{1.23} = 2.44$$

For this test statistic, $df = 18$, the denominator of the variance estimate. In a t-distribution with 18 df, the critical value is 2.10 for the right-side (upper) tail and −2.10 for the left-side (lower) tail. If you don't believe me, apply $t.ppf(0.975, 18)$. (See Chapter 10.) The calculated value of the test statistic is greater than 2.10, so the decision is to reject H_0. The data provides evidence that Machine 2 is significantly different from Machine 1. (You can use the word *significant* whenever you reject H_0.)

t-Testing in Python

Here are a couple of lists for the sample data in the example in the preceding section:

```
machine1 = [24.58, 22.09, 23.70, 18.89, 22.02, 28.71, 24.44,
    20.91, 23.83, 20.83]
machine2 = [21.61, 19.06, 20.72, 15.77, 19, 25.88, 21.48, 17.85,
    20.86, 17.77]
```

These are independent samples, so to carry out the t-test, I use `ttest_ind()`, which lives in `scipy.stats`:

```
from scipy.stats import ttest_ind
my_t, my_t_p_value = ttest_ind(machine1, machine2,
    equal_var=True)
```

The third argument indicates the equal variances assumption. If you can't assume that the two samples come from the same population or from populations with equal variances, set `equal_var = False`. (**Spoiler alert:** For this example, it doesn't make a difference.)

```
print(f'my_t = {my_t:.3f}  my_t_p_value = {my_t_p_value:.3f}')
my_t = 2.440  my_t_p_value = 0.025
```

Bear in mind that this function returns a two-tailed p-value. Though that's appropriate for this example, you have to divide it by 2 for an alternative hypothesis of "greater than" or an alternative hypothesis of "less than."

Visualizing the results

In studies like the one in the preceding section, two ways of presenting the results are bar graphs and boxplots.

Bar graphs

Bar graphs enable you to plot sample means and standard errors. It's easy to do that with `matplotlib`. Figure 11-4 shows what I mean.

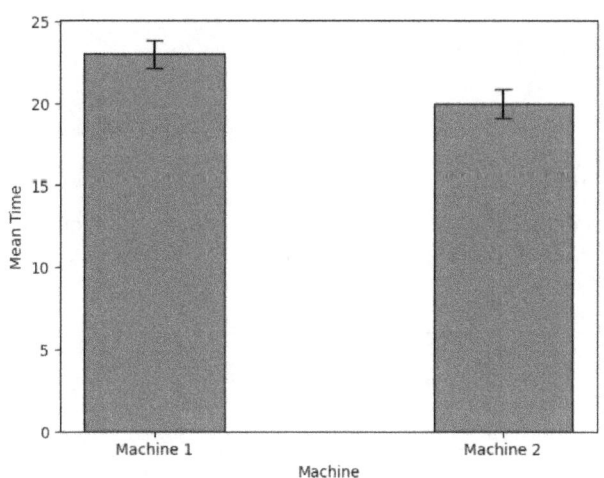

FIGURE 11-4:
FarKlempt
Machines
means and
standard errors.

The lines extending upward and downward from the top of each bar represent the standard error of the mean for that machine.

Here's how to plot it. First, the imports:

```
import matplotlib.pyplot as plt
import numpy as np
```

Next, the data. I reuse the lists from the example:

```
groups = ['Machine 1', 'Machine 2']
means = [np.mean(machine1), np.mean(machine2)]
```

I calculate the standard error of the mean for each sample:

```
st_errors = [np.std(machine1, ddof=1) / np.sqrt(len(machine1)),
    np.std(machine2, ddof=1) / np.sqrt(len(machine2))]
```

Then I set up the plot with the error bars:

```
plt.bar(groups, means, yerr=st_errors, capsize=6, width = 0.4,
    color = 'gray', edgecolor = 'black' )
```

In the preceding statement, the `capsize`, `width`, `color`, and `edgecolor` arguments make the bar graph prettier. Try other values, if you like.

I label the axes and show the plot:

```
plt.ylabel('Mean Time')
plt.xlabel('Machine')
plt.show()
```

Boxplots

Boxplots depict each group's quartiles, as well as the group's range. Figure 11-5 is a boxplot for the data in this example.

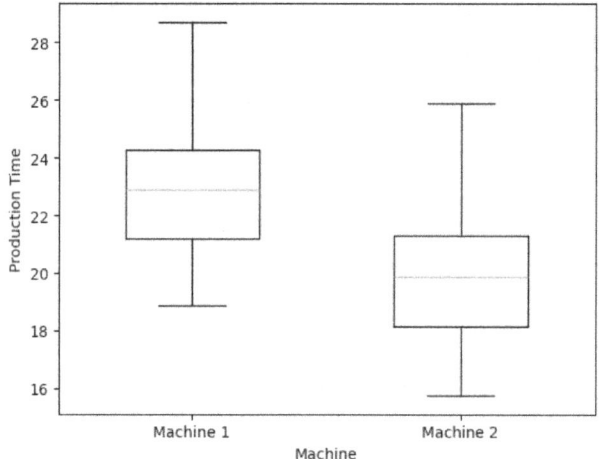

FIGURE 11-5:
Boxplot of
FarKlempt
Machines data.

The bottom of a box is the group's 25th percentile, the top is the 75th percentile, and the line in the middle of the box is the 50th percentile (also known as the median). The downward and upward lines represent the group's range. One line longer than the other indicates skewness — positive if the upper line is longer or negative if the lower line is longer (see Chapter 7).

Here's the `matplotlib` implementation, using the data from this example. I begin with the import and the data:

```
import matplotlib.pyplot as plt
data = [machine1, machine2]
```

Then I set up the plot:

```
plt.boxplot(data, tick_labels=['Machine 1', 'Machine 2'],
    widths = 0.5)
```

I label the axes and show the plot:

```
plt.xlabel('Machine')
plt.ylabel('Production Time')
plt.show()
```

A Matched Set: Hypothesis Testing for Paired Samples

In the hypothesis tests I describe so far, the samples are independent of one another. Choosing an individual for one sample has no bearing on the choice of an individual for the other.

Sometimes, the samples are matched. The most obvious case is when the same individual provides a score under each of two conditions — as in a before-after study. Suppose ten people participate in a weight loss program. They weigh in before they start the program and again after one month on the program. The important data is the set of before-after differences. Table 11-2 shows the data.

TABLE 11-2

Data for the Weight Loss Example

Person	Weight Before Program	Weight After One Month	Difference
1	198	194	4
2	201	203	-2
3	210	200	10
4	185	183	2
5	204	200	4
6	156	153	3

(continued)

TABLE 11-2 *(continued)*

Person	Weight Before Program	Weight After One Month	Difference
7	167	166	1
8	197	197	0
9	220	215	5
10	186	184	2
Mean			2.9
Standard Deviation			3.25

The idea is to think of these differences as a sample of scores and treat them as you would in a one-sample t-test (see Chapter 10).

You carry out a test on these hypotheses:

$$H_0 : \mu_d \leq 0$$
$$H_1 : \mu_d > 0$$

The d in the subscripts stands for *difference*. Set α = .05.

From Table 11-2

$$t = \frac{\bar{d} - \mu_d}{s_d} = \frac{2.9}{(3.25 / \sqrt{10})} = 2.82$$

and with df = 9 (Number of pairs − 1), the critical value for α = .05 is 1.83. (Use t.ppf() to verify.) The calculated value exceeds this value, so the decision is to reject H_0.

Paired Sample *t*-Testing in Python

The scipy.stats function for paired sample t-testing is called ttest_rel(), so

```
from scipy.stats import ttest_rel
```

Next, here are two lists that contain the data from Table 11-2:

```
before = [198,201,210,185,204,156,167,197,220,186]
after = [194,203,200,183,200,153,166,197,215,184]
```

Now I compute the results and print them:

```
t_statistic, p_value = ttest_rel(before, after)
print(f't_statistic = {t_statistic:.3f}  p_value = {p_value:.3f}')
t_statistic = 2.824   p_value = 0.020
```

The function returns a two-tailed *p*-value, so I divide by 2 for the one-tailed *p*-value.

With these results, the decision is to reject H_o.

Testing Two Variances

The two-sample hypothesis testing I describe in this chapter pertains to means. It's also possible to test hypotheses about variances.

In this section, I extend the one-variance manufacturing example I use in Chapter 10. FarKlempt Robotics, Inc., produces a part that has to be a certain length with a very small variability. The company is considering two machines to produce this part, and it wants to choose the one that results in the least variability. FarKlempt Robotics takes a sample of parts from each machine, measures them, finds the variance for each sample, and performs a hypothesis test to see whether one machine's variance is significantly greater than the other's.

The hypotheses are

$$H_0 : \sigma_1^2 = \sigma_2^2$$
$$H_1 : \sigma_1^2 \neq \sigma_2^2$$

As always, an α is a must-have item. As usual, I set it to .05.

When you test two variances, you don't subtract one from the other. Instead, you divide one by the other to calculate the test statistic. Sir Ronald Fisher is a famous statistician who worked out the mathematics (and the family of distributions) for working with variances in this way. The test statistic is named in his honor. It's called an F-*ratio*, and the test is the F-*test*. The family of distributions for the test is called the F-*distribution*.

Without going into all the mathematics, I'll just tell you that, once again, *df* is the parameter that distinguishes one member of the family from another. What's different about this family is that two variance estimates are involved, so each member of the family is associated with two values of *df* rather than one, as in the *t*-test. Another difference between the *F*-distribution and the others you've seen is that the *F* cannot have a negative value. Figure 11-6 shows two members of the *F*-distribution family.

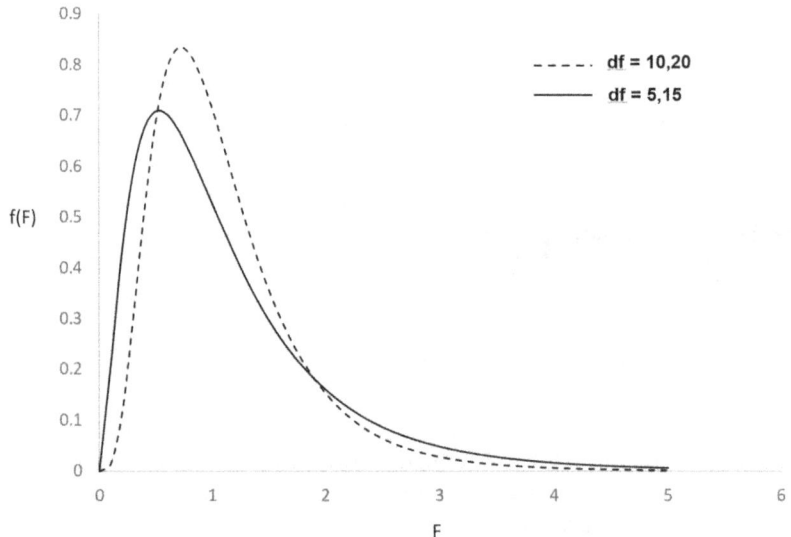

FIGURE 11-6:
Two members of
the *F*-distribution
family.

The test statistic is

$$F = \frac{\text{larger } s^2}{\text{smaller } s^2}$$

Suppose FarKlempt Robotics produces 10 parts with Machine 1 and finds a sample variance of .813 square inches. It produces 15 parts with Machine 2 and finds a sample variance of .635 square inches. Can the company reject H_0?

Calculating the test statistic,

$$F = \frac{.813}{.635} = 1.281$$

the *df*'s are 9 and 14: The variance estimate in the numerator of the *F*-ratio is based on 10 cases, and the variance estimate in the denominator is based on 15 cases.

When the *df*'s are 9 and 14 and it's a two-tailed test at $\alpha = .05$, the critical value of *F* is 3.209. (In a moment, I show you a Python function that computes this.) The calculated value is less than the critical value, so the decision is not reject H_0.

REMEMBER

It makes a difference which *df* is in the numerator and which *df* is in the denominator. The F-distribution for df = 9 and df = 14 is different from the F-distribution for *df* = 14 and *df* = 9. For example, the critical value in the latter case is 3.798, not 3.209.

F-testing in Python

Python has no function for testing the ratio of two variances, but the procedure is straightforward: Find the variances, divide one by the other, and compare against the F-distribution with the appropriate degrees of freedom.

I begin by importing the F family from `scipy.stats` and `numpy` for some calculations:

```
from scipy.stats import f
import numpy as np
```

Then I set up two lists with the data:

```
machine1_parts = [3.8,2.5,2.3,2.1,3.5,3.9,2.0,3.8,4.0,4.4]
machine2_parts = [2.9,3.5,2.2,4.5,3.1,3.8,4.3,2.4,2.7,2.6,3.6,
   4.1,4.8,3.0,3.0]
```

Next, I calculate the variances and the degrees of freedom:

```
m1_variance = np.var(machine1_parts, ddof=1)
m2_variance = np.var(machine2_parts, ddof=1)
df1 = len(machine1_parts) - 1
df2 = len(machine2_parts) - 1
```

Finally, I compute the F statistic and the *p*-values (one-tailed and two-tailed):

```
F_statistic = m1_variance / m2_variance
one_tailed_p_value = f.sf(F_statistic, df1, df2)
two_tailed_p_value = one_tailed_p_value * 2
```

and then print the results:

```
print(f'F_statistic = {F_statistic:.3f}')
print(f'1-tailed p_value = {one_tailed_p_value:.3f}')
print(f'2-tailed p_value = {two_tailed_p_value:.3f}')
```

The low value of the F statistic and the high value of p indicate that you cannot reject H_0.

F in conjunction with t

One use of the F-distribution is in conjunction with the t-test for independent samples. Before you do the t-test, you use F to help decide whether to assume equal variances or unequal variances in the samples.

In the equal variances t-test example I show you earlier in this chapter, the standard deviations are 2.71 and 2.79. The variances are 7.34 and 7.78. The F-ratio of these variances is

$$F = \frac{7.78}{7.34} = 1.06$$

Each sample is based on ten observations, so df = 9 for each sample variance. An F-ratio of 1.06 cuts off the upper 47 percent of the F-distribution whose df are 9 and 9, so it's safe to use the equal variances version of the t-test for these data.

How does all this play out in the context of hypothesis testing? On rare occasions, H_0 is a desirable outcome and you'd rather not reject it. In that case, you stack the deck against *not* rejecting by setting α at a high level so that small differences cause you to reject H_0.

This is one of those rare occasions. It's more desirable to use the equal variances t-test, which typically provides more degrees of freedom than the unequal variances t-test. Setting a high value of α (.20 is a good one) for the F-test enables you to be confident when you assume equal variances.

Working with F-Distributions

Just like the other distribution-families I cover earlier (normal, t, chi-square), Python provides functions for dealing with F-distributions: f.pdf() provides the density, f.cdf() provides the cumulative density, f.ppf() gives percentile information, and f.rvs() generates random numbers.

TIP

Note that throughout this section, I spell out *degrees of freedom* rather than use the abbreviation *df* as I do elsewhere. That's to avoid confusion with the density function f.pdf() and the cumulative density function f.cdf().

That critical value I refer to earlier for a two-tailed F-test with 9 and 14 degrees of freedom is

```
from scipy.stats import f
Critical_F_value = f.ppf(0.975, 9,14)
print(f'Critical F value for df = 9,14 =
   {Critical_F_value:.3f}')
Critical F value for df = 9,14 = 3.209
```

It's a two-tailed test at α = .05, so .025 is in each tail.

Here's f.pdf() calculating densities for F-values from 0 to 4, with 9 and 14 degrees of freedom. I begin by creating a list of F-values for f.pdf() to operate on. Is this a good time for list comprehension? It's *always* a good time for list comprehension!

```
F_values = [x for x in range(0,5,1)]
```

How about some more comprehension?

```
densities = [f.pdf(x, 9, 14) for x in F_values]
```

And now I use a for loop to print the results:

```
for i in range(len(densities)):
   print(f'when F = {F_values[i]}, density = {densities[i]:.3f}')
when F = 0, density = 0.000
when F = 1, density = 0.645
when F = 2, density = 0.164
when F = 3, density = 0.039
when F = 4, density = 0.011
```

I leave it as an exercise for you to produce the results for cumulative density:

```
when F = 0, cumulative density = 0.000
when F = 1, cumulative density = 0.518
when F = 2, cumulative density = 0.882
when F = 3, cumulative density = 0.968
when F = 4, cumulative density = 0.990
```

To generate five random numbers from this member of the F-distribution family, use the following:

```
five_random_F_values = f.rvs(9, 14, size=5)
print(five_random_F_values)
[0.50878715 0.98062611 1.76622406 2.4906664  0.61434359]
```

Visualizing F-Distributions

As I've said, visualizing distributions helps you learn them. F-distributions are no exception, and with the help of density functions and matplotlib, it's easy to plot them. I show you how to use matplotlib to depict an F-distribution with 5 and 15 degrees of freedom and another with 10 and 20 degrees of freedom. The finished product looks just like Figure 11-6, from earlier in this chapter.

I begin by importing numpy and matplotlib, along with f from scipy.stats:

```
import numpy as np
import matplotlib.pyplot as plt
from scipy.stats import f
```

Then I set the degrees of freedom for the first F-distribution

```
df1_1, df1_2 = 5, 10
```

and for the second:

```
df2_1, df2_2 = 10, 20
```

Next, I generate 100 evenly spaced values on the x-axis from 0 to 5:

```
x = np.linspace(0, 5, 100)  # Values from 0 to 5
```

In both F-distributions, I compute the density for each of these 100 values:

```
pdf1 = f.pdf(x, df1_1, df1_2)
pdf2 = f.pdf(x, df2_1, df2_2)
```

Then I plot both distributions, keeping track of the labels for the legend that follows. I also use color and linestyle to add some styling:

```
plt.plot(x, pdf1, label=f'df = {df1_1}, {df1_2}', color
    = 'black')
plt.plot(x, pdf2, label=f'df = {df2_1}, {df2_2}', color =
    'black', linestyle = '--')
```

TIP

The f string in each of the two preceding statements avoids explicit labels like "df = 5, 10" and "df = 10, 20".

I style it up a little more by eliminating the gap between the plotted curves and the *x*-axis:

```
plt.ylim(bottom=0)
```

I label the axes

```
plt.xlabel('F')
plt.ylabel('f(F)')
```

and add the legend:

```
plt.legend(reverse = True)
```

I added `reverse = True` so that the order of the items on the legend reflects the order of the curves on the plot.

All that's left is

```
plt.show()
```

Run the code to produce Figure 11-7.

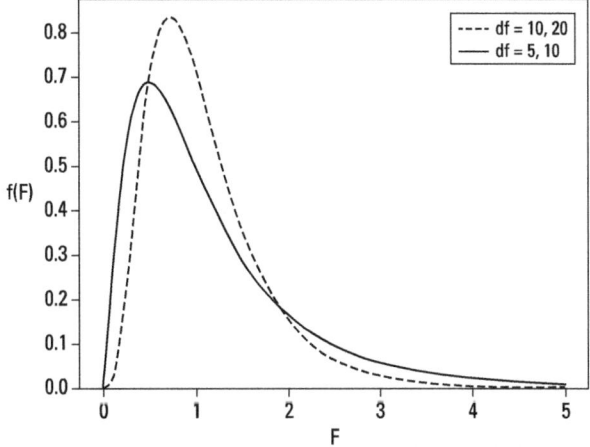

FIGURE 11-7:
Two members of
the *F*-distribution
family, plotted in
matplotlib.

Experiment with other values for degrees of freedom and see what the curves look like.

IN THIS CHAPTER

» Understanding why multiple *t*-tests won't work

» Analyzing variance

» Taking the next step after an ANOVA

» Working with repeated measures

» Performing a trend analysis

Chapter **12**

Testing More than Two Samples

S tatistics would be limited if you could only make inferences about one or two samples. In this chapter, I discuss the procedures for testing hypotheses about three or more samples. I show what to do when samples are independent of one another, and what to do when they're not. In both cases, I discuss what to do after you test the hypotheses. I also discuss Python functions that do the work for you.

Testing More than Two

Imagine this situation. Your company asks you to evaluate three different methods for training its employees to do a particular job. You randomly assign 30 employees to one of the three methods. Your plan is to train them, test them, tabulate the results, and draw some conclusions. Before you can finish the study, three people leave the company — one from the Method 1 group and two from the Method 3 group.

Table 12-1 shows the data.

TABLE 12-1

Data from Three Training Methods

	Method 1	Method 2	Method 3
	95	83	68
	91	89	75
	89	85	79
	90	89	74
	99	81	75
	88	89	81
	96	90	73
	98	82	77
	95	84	
		80	
Mean	93.44	85.20	75.25
Variance	16.28	14.18	15.64
Standard Deviation	4.03	3.77	3.96

Do the three methods provide different results, or are they so similar that you can't distinguish among them? To decide, you have to carry out a hypothesis test

$$H_0 : \mu_1 = \mu_2 = \mu_3$$
$$H_1 : \text{Not } H_0$$

with $\alpha = .05$.

A thorny problem

Finding differences among three groups sounds pretty easy, particularly if you've read Chapter 11. Take the mean of the scores from Method 1 and the mean of the scores from Method 2, and do a t-test to see whether they're different. Follow the same procedure for Method 1 versus Method 3, and for Method 2 versus Method 3. If at least one of those t-tests shows a significant difference, reject H_0.

Nothing to it, right? Wrong. If your α is .05 for each t-test, you're setting yourself up for a Type I error with a probability higher than you planned on. The probability that at least one of the three t-tests results in a significant difference is way above .05. In fact, it's .14, which is way beyond acceptable. (The mathematics behind calculating that number is a little involved, so I won't elaborate.)

With more than three samples, the situation gets even worse. Four groups require six *t*-tests, and the probability that at least one of them is significant is .26. Table 12-2 shows what happens with increasing numbers of samples.

TABLE 12-2

The Incredible Increasing Alpha

Number of Samples t	Number of Tests	Pr (At Least One Significant t)
3	3	.14
4	6	.26
5	10	.40
6	15	.54
7	21	.66
8	28	.76
9	36	.84
10	45	.90

Carrying out multiple *t*-tests is clearly not the answer. What do you do?

A solution

It's necessary to take a different approach. The idea is to think in terms of variances rather than means.

I'd like you to think of variance in a slightly different way. The formula for estimating population variance, remember, is

$$s^2 = \frac{\sum(x - \bar{x})^2}{N - 1}$$

Because the variance is almost a mean of squared deviations from the mean, statisticians also refer to it as *mean square*. In a way, that's an unfortunate nickname: It leaves out "deviation from the mean," but there you have it.

The numerator of the variance — excuse me, mean-square — is the sum of squared deviations from the mean. This leads to another nickname: *sum of squares.* The denominator, as I say in Chapter 10, is *degrees of freedom (df)*. So the slightly different way to think of variance is

$$\text{Mean Square} = \frac{\text{Sum of Squares}}{\text{df}}$$

You can abbreviate this as

$$MS = \frac{SS}{df}$$

Now, on to solving the thorny problem. One important step is to find the mean-squares hiding in the data. Another is to understand that you use these mean-squares to estimate the variances of the populations that produced these samples. In this case, assume that those variances are equal, so you're really estimating one variance. The final step is to understand that you use these estimates to test the hypotheses I show you at the beginning of this chapter.

Three different mean-squares are inside the data in Table 12-1. Start with the whole set of 27 scores, forgetting for the moment that they're divided into three groups. Suppose that you want to use those 27 scores to calculate an estimate of the population variance. (A dicey idea, but humor me.) The mean of those 27 scores is 85. I'll call that mean the *grand mean* because it's the average of everything.

So the mean-square would be

$$\frac{(95-85)^2 + (91-85)^2 + \ldots + (73-85)^2 + (77-85)^2}{(27-1)} = 68.08$$

The denominator has 26 (27−1) degrees of freedom. I refer to that variance as the total variance, or in the new way of thinking about this, the MS_{Total}. It's often abbreviated as MS_T.

Here's another variance to consider. In Chapter 11, I describe the t-test for two samples with equal variances. For that test, you put together the two sample variances to create a *pooled* estimate of the population variance. The data in Table 12-1 provides three sample variances for a pooled estimate: 16.28, 14.18, and 15.64. Assuming that these numbers represent equal population variances, the pooled estimate is

$$s_p^2 = \frac{(N_1-1)s_1^2 + (N_2-1)s_2^2 + (N_3-1)s_3^2}{(N_1-1) + (N_2-1) + (N_3-1)}$$

$$= \frac{(9-1)(16.28) + (10-1)(14.18) + (8-1)(15.64)}{(9-1) + (10-1) + (8-1)} = 15.31$$

Because this pooled estimate comes from the variance within the groups, it's called MS_{Within}, or MS_W.

One more mean-square to go — the variance of the sample means around the grand mean. In this example, that means the variance in these numbers 93.44, 85.20, and 75.25 — sort of. I say "sort of" because these are means, not scores. When you deal with means, you have to take into account the number of scores that produced each mean. To do that, you multiply each squared deviation by the number of scores in that sample.

So this variance is

$$\frac{(9)(93.11-85)^2+(10)(85.20-85)^2+(8)(75.25-85)^2}{3-1} = 701.34$$

The *df* for this variance is 2 (the number of samples − 1).

Statisticians, not known for their crispness of usage, refer to this as the variance *between* sample means. (*Among* is the correct word when you're talking about more than two items.) This variance is known as $MS_{Between}$, or MS_B.

So you now have three estimates of population variance: MS_T, MS_W, and MS_B. What do you do with them?

Remember that the original objective is to test a hypothesis about three means. According to H_0, any differences you see among the three sample means are due strictly to chance. The implication is that the variance among those means is the same as the variance of any three numbers selected at random from the population.

If you could somehow compare the variance among the means (that's MS_B, remember) with the population variance, you could see whether that holds up. If only you had an estimate of the population variance that's independent of the differences among the groups, you'd be in business.

Ah . . . but you do have that estimate. You have MS_W, an estimate based on pooling the variances within the samples. Assuming that those variances represent equal population variances, this is a solid estimate. In this example, it's based on 24 degrees of freedom.

The reasoning now becomes this: If MS_B is about the same as MS_W, you have evidence consistent with H_0. If MS_B is significantly larger than MS_W, you have evidence that's inconsistent with H_0. In effect, you transform these hypotheses

$H_0 : \mu_1 = \mu_2 = \mu_3$
$H_1 : \text{Not } H_0$

into these:

$H_0 : \sigma_B^2 \le \sigma_W^2$
$H_1 : \sigma_B^2 > \sigma_W^2$

Rather than perform multiple *t*-tests among sample means, you perform a test of the difference between two variances.

What is that test? In Chapter 11, I show you the test for hypotheses about two variances. It's called the F-test. To perform this test, you first divide one variance by the other, and you then evaluate the result against a family of distributions called the F-distribution. Because two variances are involved, two values for degrees of freedom define each member of the family.

For this example, F has df = 2 (for the MS_B) and df = 24 (for the MS_W). Figure 12-1 shows what this member of the F family looks like. For our purposes, it's the distribution of possible F-values if H_0 is true. (See the section in Chapter 11 about visualizing F-distributions.)

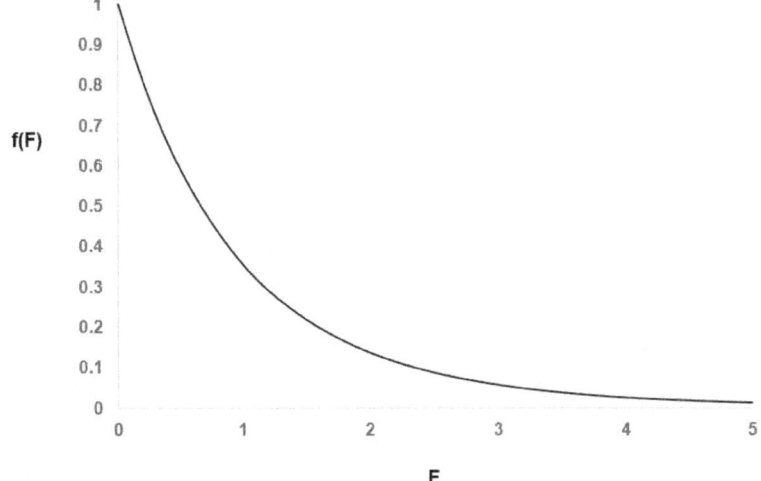

FIGURE 12-1:
The F-distribution with 2 and 24 degrees of freedom.

The test statistic for the example is

$$F = \frac{701.34}{15.31} = 45.82$$

What proportion of area does this value cut off in the upper tail of the F-distribution? From Figure 12-1, you can see that this proportion is microscopic because the values on the horizontal axis only go up to 5. (And the proportion of area beyond 5 is tiny.) It's way less than .05.

This means that it's highly unlikely that differences among the means are due to chance. It means that you reject H_0.

REMEMBER

This whole procedure for testing more than two samples is called the *analysis of variance*, often abbreviated as ANOVA. In the context of an ANOVA, the denominator of an F-ratio has the generic name *error term*. The independent variable is sometimes called a *factor*. So this is a single-factor (or 1-factor) ANOVA.

In this example, the factor is Training Method. Each instance of the independent variable is called a *level*. The independent variable in this example has three levels.

More complex studies have more than one factor, and each factor can have many levels.

Meaningful relationships

Take another look at the mean-squares in this example, each with its sum of squares and degrees of freedom. Before, when I calculated each mean-square for you, I didn't explicitly show you each sum of squares, but here I include them:

$$MS_B = \frac{SS_B}{df_B} = \frac{1402.68}{2} = 701.34$$

$$MS_W = \frac{SS_W}{df_W} = \frac{367.32}{24} = 15.31$$

$$MS_T = \frac{SS_T}{df_T} = \frac{1770}{26} = 68.08$$

Start with the degrees of freedom: $df_B = 2$, $df_W = 24$, and $df_T = 26$. Is it a coincidence that they add up? Hardly. It's always the case that

$$df_B + df_W = df_T$$

How about those sums of squares?

$$1402.68 + 367.32 = 1770$$

Again, this is no coincidence. In the analysis of variance, this always happens:

$$SS_B + SS_W = SS_T$$

In fact, statisticians who work with the analysis of variance speak of partitioning (read "breaking down into non-overlapping pieces") the SS_T into one portion for the SS_B and another for the SS_W and partitioning the df_T into one amount for the df_B and another for the df_W.

ANOVA in Python

In this section, I walk you through the previous section's example and show you how to do an analysis of variance in Python. In fact, I show you two ways to get it done.

Quick and dirty

I begin by creating a list for each method's scores in Table 12-1:

```
method1_scores = [95,91,89,90,99,88,96,98,95]
method2_scores = [83,89,85,89,81,89,90,82,84,80]
method3_scores = [68,75,79,74,75,81,73,77]
```

Then I turn to the `scipy.stats` library and import the function I need to do the analysis.

```
from scipy.stats import f_oneway
```

The function's name indicates an ANOVA that involves just one independent variable ("one-way"). Is it possible to have more than one? Absolutely — and you find out about that in Chapter 13.

For now,

```
F_statistic, p_value = f_oneway(method1_scores, method2_scores,
    method3_scores)
print(f'F-statistic = {F_statistic:.2f}')
print(f'p-value = {p_value}')–
F-statistic = 45.82
p-value = 6.38097789552937e-09
```

So that's all there is to it?

Not so fast. . . .

Slower and more involved

The preceding analysis didn't show any df, SS, or MS. For that kind of information, we have to start with a different data format and download a library called `statsmodels`.

First, the data format. At present, the data is in a format that reflects the three columns of Table 12-1. It's called *wide format.* Our objective is to get the data into *long format.* In this case, long format has two columns: one for Method and one for Score.

To create the Score column, I add the three score lists together:

```
Score = method1_scores + method2_scores + method3_scores
```

Each entry in the Method column must match up with the corresponding score in the Score column. In other words, I need a list with Method 1 repeated nine times, followed by Method 2 repeated ten times, followed by Method 3 repeated eight times:

```
Method = ['Method 1'] * len(method1_scores) + ['Method 2'] *
    len(method2_scores) + ['Method 3'] * len(method3_scores)
```

Now I have to put the two lists together into a DataFrame. For that, I need the pandas library:

```
import pandas as pd
```

I create the DataFrame by using the zip() function to put the two lists together so that pd.DataFrame() can work its magic:

```
method_data_frame = pd.DataFrame(zip(Method, Score),
    columns=['Method', 'Score'])
```

Just to verify that I have a DataFrame:

```
print(method_data_frame.head())
      Method  Score
0   Method 1     95
1   Method 1     91
2   Method 1     89
3   Method 1     90
4   Method 1     99
```

Now, the library. The statsmodels library is where you find lots of tools for statistical analysis, including anova. I import a couple of its capabilities:

```
import statsmodels.formula.api as sm
import statsmodels.stats.anova as stats
```

The first enables me to express the analysis in the kind of format you find in R, which is concise and intuitive. (Shameless plug: If you ever want to learn about R, have I got a book for you!)

The second allows me to cast the analysis into an ANOVA table that shows all the df SS, MS, and F. Here are the two in action:

```
model = sm.ols('Score ~ Method', data=method_data_frame).fit()
anova_table = stats.anova_lm(model)
```

'Score ~ Method' is in the R format I just mentioned. The tilde (~) separates the dependent variable from the independent variable. Read that string as "Score depends on Method."

I defer explaining os, fit(), and lm until Chapter 14.

For now,

```
print(anova_table)
              df        sum_sq      mean_sq           F        PR(>F)
Method       2.0   1402.677778   701.338889   45.823891   6.380978e-09
Residual    24.0    367.322222    15.305093         NaN            NaN
```

The ANOVA table shows the same F and p you saw in the preceding section.

If it's the same, why do we need the additional info? I tell you in a moment, but first. . . .

Visualizing the results

As I point out in Chapter 11, two ways of plotting the findings are to show them as a bar plot (with standard error bars) and as a boxplot.

First, I address the bar plot. It looks like Figure 12-2.

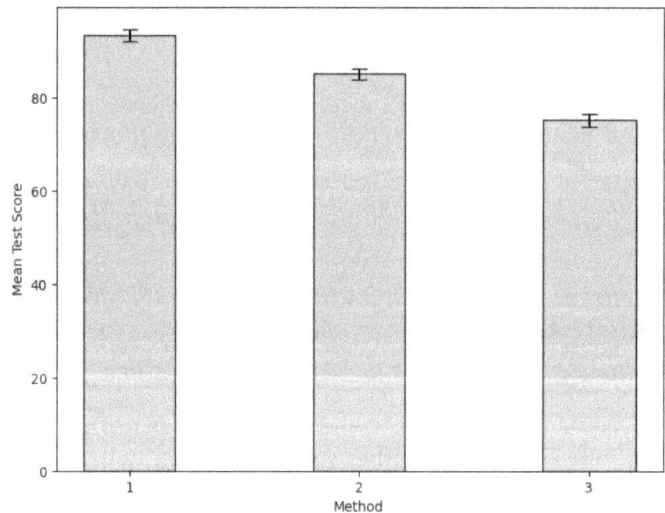

FIGURE 12-2: Bar plot with standard error bars for the methods data.

Here's how to plot it. First, you take care of the imports:

```
import matplotlib.pyplot as plt
import numpy as np
```

Here are the labels to appear on the *x*-axis:

```
groups = ['1', '2', '3']
```

Then I gather the data. I do this a little differently from the two-sample case in Chapter 11. Here, with the DataFrame in long format, I use groupby() to get the means and the standard errors of the mean:

```
means = method_data_frame.groupby('Method')['Score'].mean()
st_errors = method_data_frame.groupby('Method')['Score'].sem()
```

Now I create the plot:

```
plt.figure(figsize=(8, 6))
plt.bar(groups, means, yerr=st_errors, capsize=6, width = 0.4,
    color =  'lightgray',edgecolor = 'black' )
```

I label the axes and show the plot:

```
plt.xlabel('Machine')
plt.ylabel('Mean Time')
plt.show()
```

Refer to Figure 12-2 for the final result.

Now for the boxplot, shown in Figure 12-3.

Here's how to plot that one:

```
import matplotlib.pyplot as plt
```

To gather the data for the boxplot, I revert to the way I do it in Chapter 11 — this is in keeping with what plt.boxplot() expects:

```
data = [method1_scores, method2_scores, method3_scores]
```

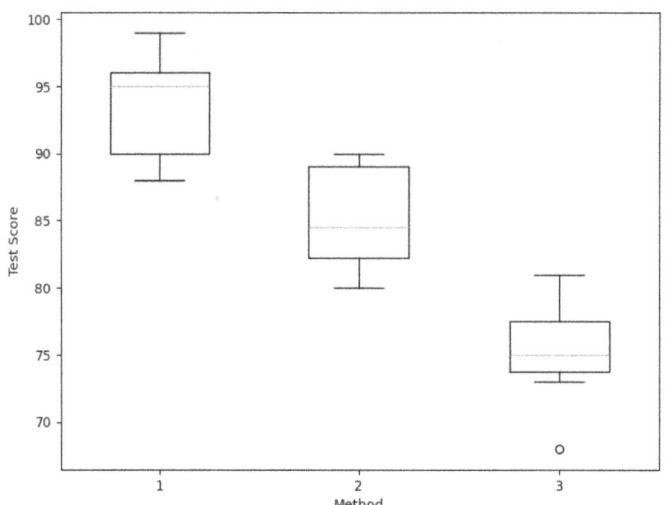

FIGURE 12-3:
Boxplot of the
methods data.

Then I create the plot:

```
plt.figure(figsize=(8, 6))
plt.boxplot(data, tick_labels=['1', '2', '3'], widths = 0.5)
```

Finally, I label the axes and display the plot:

```
plt.xlabel('Method')
plt.ylabel('Test Score')

# Display the plot
plt.show()
```

After the ANOVA

The ANOVA enables you to decide whether to reject H_0. After you decide to reject, then what? All you can say is that somewhere within the set of means, something is different from something else. The analysis doesn't specify what those "somethings" are.

Planned comparisons

To get more specific, you have to do some further tests. Not only that, you have to plan those tests in advance of carrying out the ANOVA.

What are those tests? Given what I mention earlier, this might surprise you: *t*-tests. Though this might sound inconsistent with the increased alpha of multiple *t*-tests, it's not. If an analysis of variance enables you to reject H_0, it's okay to use *t*-tests to turn the magnifying glass on the data and find out where the differences are. And, as I'm about to show you, the *t*-test you use is slightly different from the one I discuss in Chapter 11.

These post-ANOVA *t*-tests are called *planned comparisons*. Some statisticians refer to them as *a priori tests* or *contrasts*. I illustrate by following through with the example. Suppose before you gathered the data, you had reason to believe that Method 1 would result in higher scores than Method 2, and that Method 2 would result in higher scores than Method 3. In that case, you plan in advance to compare the means of those samples in the event your ANOVA-based decision is to reject H_0.

The formula for this kind of *t*-test is

$$t = \frac{\bar{x}_1 - \bar{x}_2}{\sqrt{MS_W \left[\dfrac{1}{n_1} + \dfrac{1}{n_2} \right]}}$$

It's a test of

$H_0: \mu_1 \leq \mu_2$

$H_1: \mu_1 > \mu_2$

MS_W takes the place of the pooled estimate s_p^2 I show you in Chapter 11. In fact, when I introduced MS_W, I showed how it's just a pooled estimate that can incorporate variances from more than two samples. The df for this *t*-test is df_W, rather than $(n_1 - 1) + (n_2 - 1)$.

For this example, the Method 1 versus Method 2 comparison is

$$t = \frac{\bar{x}_1 - \bar{x}_2}{\sqrt{MS_W \left[\dfrac{1}{n_1} + \dfrac{1}{n_2} \right]}} = \frac{93.44 - 85.2}{\sqrt{15.31 \left[\dfrac{1}{9} + \dfrac{1}{10} \right]}} = 4.59$$

With df = 24, this value of *t* cuts off a minuscule portion of area in the upper tail of the *t*-distribution. The decision is to reject H_0.

The planned comparison *t*-test formula I show you matches up with the *t*-test for two samples. You can write the planned comparison *t*-test formula in a way that sets up additional possibilities. Start by writing the numerator

$$\bar{x}_1 - \bar{x}_2$$

a bit differently:

$$(+1)\bar{x}_1 + (-1)\bar{x}_2$$

The +1 and −1 are *comparison coefficients.* I refer to them, in a general way, as c_1 and c_2. In fact, c_3 and $\bar{x}_3$ can enter the comparison, even if you're just comparing $\bar{x}_1$ with $\bar{x}_2$:

$$(+1)\bar{x}_1 + (-1)\bar{x}_2 + (0)\bar{x}_3$$

The important thing is that the coefficients add up to zero.

Here's how the comparison coefficients figure into the planned comparison *t*-test formula for a study that involves three samples:

$$t = \frac{c_1\bar{x}_1 + c_2\bar{x}_2 + c_3\bar{x}_3}{\sqrt{MS_W\left[\dfrac{c_1^2}{n_1} + \dfrac{c_2^2}{n_2} + \dfrac{c_3^2}{n_3}\right]}}$$

Applying this formula to Method 2 versus Method 3 gives us the following:

$$t = \frac{c_1\bar{x}_1 + c_2\bar{x}_2 + c_3\bar{x}_3}{\sqrt{MS_W\left[\dfrac{c_1^2}{n_1} + \dfrac{c_2^2}{n_2} + \dfrac{c_3^2}{n_3}\right]}} = \frac{(0)(93.44) + (+1)(85.2) + (-1)(75.25)}{\sqrt{15.31\left[\dfrac{0^2}{9} + \dfrac{1^2}{10} + \dfrac{(-1)^2}{8}\right]}} = 5.36$$

The value for *t* indicates the results from Method 2 are significantly higher than the results from Method 3.

You can also plan a more complex comparison — say, Method 1 versus the average of Method 2 and Method 3. Begin with the numerator. That would be

$$\bar{x}_1 - \frac{(\bar{x}_2 + \bar{x}_3)}{2}$$

With comparison coefficients, you can write this as

$$(+1)\bar{x}_1 + \left(-\frac{1}{2}\right)\bar{x}_2 + \left(-\frac{1}{2}\right)\bar{x}_3$$

If you're more comfortable with whole numbers, you can write it as

$$(+2)\bar{x}_1 + (-1)\bar{x}_2 + (-1)\bar{x}_3$$

Plugging these whole numbers into the formula gives you

$$t = \frac{c_1\bar{x}_1 + c_2\bar{x}_2 + c_3\bar{x}_3}{\sqrt{MS_W\left[\dfrac{c_1^2}{n_1} + \dfrac{c_2^2}{n_2} + \dfrac{c_3^2}{n_3}\right]}} = \frac{(2)(93.44) + (-1)(85.2) + (-1)(75.25)}{\sqrt{15.31\left[\dfrac{2^2}{9} + \dfrac{(-1)^2}{10} + \dfrac{(-1)^2}{8}\right]}} = 8.26$$

Again, strong evidence for rejecting H_0.

In general, the formula for the test with i groups is

$$t = \frac{\sum c_i \bar{x}_i}{\sqrt{MS_W \left[\sum \frac{c_i^2}{n_i} \right]}}$$

Contrasts in Python

My objective in this section is to create a function that computes a t-test for a contrast. It follows that general formula I show you earlier:

$$t = \frac{\sum c_i \bar{x}_i}{\sqrt{MS_W \left[\sum \frac{c_i^2}{n_i} \right]}}$$

First, the imports:

```
import pandas as pd
from scipy.stats import t
```

I begin with the definition and a docstring:

```
def t_contrast(contrast,independent_variable,dependent_
    variable,data, anova_table):
    '''
 This function calculates the t-statistic and its associated
    p-value for a
 contrast effect. Use it after running anova and printing the
    anova table.

 Args:
 contrast: A list of contrast coefficients.
 independent_variable: The name of the independent variable.
 dependent_variable: The name of the dependent variable.
 data: A pandas DataFrame that holds the data in long format.
 anova_table: A pandas DataFrame of the anova table.

 Returns:
 t_statistic: The t-statistic.
 p_value: The p-value associated with the t-statistic.

    '''
```

I'm using the ANOVA table I computed earlier.

The first step is to calculate the group means and put them in a list:

```
means = list(data.groupby(independent_variable)[dependent_
    variable].mean())
```

Then I calculate the contrast effect, meaning the numerator of the formula:

$$\sum c_i \bar{x}_i$$

That's

```
contrast_effect = sum(contrast[i]*means[i] for i in
    range(len(contrast)))
```

Next, I start working on the denominator. I retrieve the MS_{Within} from the ANOVA table:

```
MS_Within = anova_table.loc['Residual','mean_sq']
```

The ANOVA table refers to "Within" as "Residual."

Next, I get the sample sizes and their reciprocals and put the reciprocals in a list:

```
sample_sizes = data.groupby(independent_variable).size()
recip_sample_sizes = list(1/sample_sizes)
```

Then I square each contrast coefficient

```
squared_contrast = [i**2 for i in contrast]
```

The next step is to use the preceding three lines of code to calculate this segment of the denominator:

$$\sum \frac{c_i^2}{n_i}$$

```
denominator_segment = sum(squared_contrast[i]*recip_sample_
    sizes[i] for i in range(len(squared_contrast)))
```

Now I can calculate the denominator, which looks like this in the formula:

$$\sqrt{MS_W \left[\sum \frac{c_i^2}{n_i} \right]}$$

and like this in Python:

```
denominator = (MS_Within*denominator_segment)**0.5
```

Finally, I calculate the t-statistic:

```
t_statistic = contrast_effect/denominator
```

To evaluate the t-statistic, I retrieve the df_{Within} from the ANOVA table:

```
deg_of_freedom = anova_table.loc['Residual','df']
```

Then I get the p-value:

```
p_value = t.sf(abs(t_statistic), deg_of_freedom)
```

I wrap up by printing t and p and returning their values:

```
print(f't-statistic = {t_statistic:.2f}')
print(f'p-value = {p_value}')
return t_statistic, p_value
```

Here it is in action, testing Method 1 versus the average of Method 2 and Method 3:

```
my_contrast = [2,-1,-1]
my_independent_variable = 'Method'
my_dependent_variable = 'Score'
my_data = method_data_frame
my_anova_table = anova_table
```

```
contrast_result = t_contrast(my_contrast, 'Method', 'Score',
    method_data_frame, my_anova_table)
t-statistic = 8.26
p-value = 8.921754785727027e-09
```

Try it on Method 2 versus Method 3.

Unplanned comparisons

Things would get boring if your post-ANOVA testing were limited to comparisons you had to plan in advance. Sometimes you want to snoop around your data and see whether anything interesting reveals itself. Sometimes something jumps out at you that you didn't anticipate.

When this happens, you can make comparisons you didn't plan on. These comparisons are called *a posteriori tests, post hoc tests,* or *simply unplanned comparisons.* Statisticians have come up with a wide variety of these tests, many of them with exotic names and many of them dependent on special sampling distributions.

The idea behind these tests is that you pay a price for not having planned them in advance. That price has to do with stacking the deck against rejecting H_0 for the particular comparison.

Of all the unplanned tests available, the one I like best is a creation of famed statistician Henry Scheffé. As opposed to esoteric formulas and distributions, you start with the test I already showed you and then add a couple of easy-to-do extras.

The first extra is to understand the relationship between t and F. I've shown you the F-test for three samples. You can also carry out an F-test for two samples. That F-test has $df_B = 1$ and $df_W = (n_1 - 1) + (n_2 - 1)$. The df for the t-test, of course, is $(n_1 - 1) + (n_2 - 1)$. Hmmm. . . . Seems like they should be related somehow.

They are. The relationship between the two-sample t and the two-sample F is

$$F_{1,df} = t_{df}^2$$

Now I can tell you the steps for performing Scheffé's test:

1. **Calculate the planned comparison t-test.**

2. **Square the value to create F.**

3. **Find the critical value of F for df_B and df_W at $\alpha = .05$ (or whatever α you choose).**

4. **Multiply this critical F by the df_B.**

   The result is your critical F for the unplanned comparison. I'll call this F'.

5. **Compare the calculated F to F'.**

   If the calculated F is greater, reject H_0 for this test. If it's not, don't reject H_0 for this test.

Imagine that in the example, you didn't plan in advance to compare the mean of Method 1 with the mean of Method 3. (In a study involving only three samples, that's hard to imagine, I grant you.) The t-test is

$$t = \frac{c_1\bar{x}_1 + c_2\bar{x}_2 + c_3\bar{x}_3}{\sqrt{MS_W\left[\dfrac{c_1^2}{n_1} + \dfrac{c_2^2}{n_2} + \dfrac{c_3^2}{n_3}\right]}} = \frac{(+1)(93.44)+(0)(85.2)+(-1)(75.25)}{\sqrt{15.31\left[\dfrac{1^2}{9} + \dfrac{0^2}{10} + \dfrac{(-1)^2}{8}\right]}} = 9.57$$

Squaring this result gives

$$F = t^2 = (9.57)^2 = 91.61$$

For F with 2 and 24 df and $\alpha = .05$, the critical value is 3.403. So:

$$F' = (df_B)F = (2)(3.403) = 6.806$$

Because the calculated F, 91.61, is greater than F', the decision is to reject H_0. You have evidence that Method 1's results are different from Method 3's results.

Our newly defined function verifies these numbers:

```
my_unplanned_contrast = [1,-0,-1]
my_independent_variable = 'Method'
my_dependent_variable = 'Score'
my_data = method_data_frame
my_anova_table = anova_table
contrast_result = t_contrast(my_unplanned_contrast, 'Method',
    'Score', method_data_frame, my_anova_table)
t_unplanned,_ = t_contrast(my_unplanned_contrast, 'Method',
    'Score', method_data_frame, my_anova_table)
t-statistic = 9.57
p-value = 5.744981203502695e-10


F_unplanned = t_unplanned**2
print(F_unplanned)
91.60627256438131


from scipy.stats import f
F_prime = 2*f.ppf(0.95,2,24)
print(F_prime)
6.805652210700389
```

Another Kind of Hypothesis, Another Kind of Test

The preceding ANOVA works with independent samples. As Chapter 11 explains, sometimes you work with matched samples. For example, sometimes a single individual provides data in a number of different conditions. In this section, I introduce the ANOVA you use when you have more than two matched samples.

This type of ANOVA is called *repeated measures.* You'll see it called other names, too, like *randomized blocks* or *within subjects.*

Working with repeated measures ANOVA

To show how this works, I extend the example from Chapter 11. In that example, ten men participate in a weight loss program. Table 12-3 shows their data over a 3-month period.

TABLE 12-3   Data for the Weight Loss Example

Person	Before	Month 1	Month 2	Month 3	Mean
Al	198	194	191	188	192.75
Bill	201	203	200	196	200.00
Charlie	210	200	192	188	197.50
Dan	185	183	180	178	181.50
Ed	204	200	195	191	197.50
Fred	156	153	150	145	151.00
Gary	167	166	167	166	166.50
Harry	197	197	195	192	195.25
Irv	220	215	209	205	212.25
Jon	186	184	179	175	181.00
Mean	192.4	189.5	185.8	182.4	187.525

Is the program effective? This question calls for a hypothesis test:

$H_0 : \mu_{\text{Before}} = \mu_1 = \mu_2 = \mu_3$

$H_1 : \text{Not } H_0$

Once again, you set $\alpha = .05$.

As in the previous ANOVA, start with the variances in the data. The MS_T is the variance in all 40 scores from the grand mean, which is 187.525:

$$MS_T = \frac{(198 - 187.525)^2 + (201 - 187.525)^2 + \ldots + (175 - 187.525)^2}{(40 - 1)} = 318.20$$

The people participating in the weight loss program also supply variance. Each one's overall mean (their average over the four measurements) varies from the grand mean. Because these data are in the rows, I call this MS_{Rows}:

$$MS_{Rows} = \frac{(192.75-187.525)^2 + (200-187.525)^2 + \ldots + (181-187.525)^2}{(10-1)}$$
$$= 1292.41$$

The means of the columns also vary from the grand mean:

$$MS_{Columns} = \frac{(192.4-187.525)^2 + (189.5-187.525)^2 + (185.8-187.525)^2 + (182.4-187.525)^2}{(4-1)}$$
$$= 189.69$$

One more source of variance is in the data. Think of it as the variance left over after you pull out the variance in the rows and the variance in the columns from the total variance. (Actually, it's more correct to say that it's the sum of squares that's left over when you subtract the SS_{Rows} and the $SS_{Columns}$ from the SS_T.)

This variance is called MS_{Error}. As I say earlier, in the ANOVA the denominator of an F is called an *error term*. So the word *error* here gives you a hint that this MS is a denominator for an F.

To calculate MS_{Error}, you use the relationships among the sums of squares and among the df:

$$MS_{Error} = \frac{SS_{Error}}{df_{Error}} = \frac{SS_T - SS_{Rows} - SS_{Columns}}{df_T - df_{Rows} - df_{Columns}} = \frac{209.175}{27} = 7.75$$

Here's another way to calculate the df_{Error}:

$$df_{Error} = (\text{number of rows} - 1)(\text{number of columns} - 1)$$

To perform the hypothesis test, you calculate the F:

$$F = \frac{MS_{Columns}}{MS_{Error}} = \frac{189.69}{7.75} = 24.49$$

With 3 and 27 degrees of freedom, the critical F for $\alpha = .05$ is 2.96. The calculated F is larger than the critical F, so the decision is to reject H_0.

What about an F involving MS_{Rows}? That one doesn't figure into H_0 for this example. If you find a significant F, all it shows is that people are different from one another with respect to weight loss and that doesn't tell you much.

As is the case with the ANOVA I showed you earlier, you plan comparisons to zero in on the differences. You can use the same formula, except that you substitute MS_{Error} for MS_W:

$$t = \frac{c_1\bar{x}_1 + c_2\bar{x}_2 + c_3\bar{x}_3 + c_4\bar{x}_4}{\sqrt{MS_{Error}\left[\dfrac{c_1^2}{n_1} + \dfrac{c_2^2}{n_2} + \dfrac{c_3^2}{n_3} + \dfrac{c_4^2}{n_4}\right]}} = \frac{c_1\bar{x}_1 + c_2\bar{x}_2 + c_3\bar{x}_3 + c_4\bar{x}_4}{\sqrt{MS_{Error}\left[\dfrac{c_1^2 + c_2^2 + c_3^2 + c_4^2}{n}\right]}}$$

The formula works out to the expression on the right because, in a repeated measures design, all the n's are the same.

The df for this test is df_{Error}.

For Scheffé's post hoc test, you also follow the same procedure as earlier and substitute MS_{Error} for MS_W. The only other change is to substitute df_{Time} for df_B and substitute df_{Error} for df_W when you find F'.

Repeated measures ANOVA in Python

To set the stage for the repeated measures analysis, I put the columns of Table 12-3 into lists:

```
Person = ["Al", "Bill", "Charlie", "Dan", "Ed", "Fred",
    "Gary","Harry","Irv","Jon"]
Before = [198,201,210,185,204,156,167,197,220,186]
Month_1 = [194,203,200,183,200,153,166,197,215,184]
Month_2 = [191,200,192,180,195,150,167,195,209,179]
Month_3 = [188,196,188,178,191,145,166,192,205,175]
```

TIP

When you create labels for the levels of your dependent variable (like Before, Month_1, Month_2, and Month_3), make sure their alphabetical order reflects their logical order. This is important if you use groupby(), which returns its results in alphabetical order. If your labels aren't in alphabetical order, you have to complete the extra steps to reorder those results to fit your analysis.

Next, I make sure I've imported the pandas library

```
import pandas as pd
```

and then I create a pandas DataFrame. When I constructed a DataFrame earlier in this chapter, I created two lists and then used zip() to put the lists together into a long format DataFrame. This time, with all the columns, it's easier to use a dictionary (see Chapter 2) to create a wide-format DataFrame first and then transform it into long format.

202   PART 3 Drawing Conclusions from Data

REMEMBER

Transformation from wide format to long format is called "melting."

Here's the wide format:

```
weight_loss_data = pd.DataFrame({'Person': Person, 'Before':
   Before, 'Month_1': Month_1, 'Month_2': Month_2,
   'Month_3': Month_3})
print(weight_loss_data)
   Person  Before  Month_1  Month_2  Month_3
0  Al         198      194      191      188
1  Bill       201      203      200      196
2  Charlie    210      200      192      188
3  Dan        185      183      180      178
4  Ed         204      200      195      191
5  Fred       156      153      150      145
6  Gary       167      166      167      166
7  Harry      197      197      195      192
8  Irv        220      215      209      205
9  Jon        186      184      179      175
```

The next order of business is to melt this wide-format data format into long format. To do this, I use pd.melt():

```
weight_loss_data_long = pd.melt(weight_loss_data,
   id_vars=['Person'],
            value_vars=['Before', 'Month_1', 'Month_2',
   'Month_3'],
            var_name='Time', value_name='Weight')
```

What does the new DataFrame look like? Here are the first five rows:

```
print(weight_loss_data_long.head())
   Person   Time     Weight
0  Al       Before      198
1  Bill     Before      201
2  Charlie  Before      210
3  Dan      Before      185
4  Ed       Before      204
```

To proceed with the analysis, I first do the following:

```
import statsmodels.formula.api as smf
import statsmodels.stats.anova as stats
```

As I mention earlier, the statsmodels library enables me to use the convenient R-like syntax to set up the ANOVA.

Before I show you the repeated measures ANOVA, let's see what the analysis looks like if I treat it as the type of ANOVA I show you earlier in this chapter. That is, suppose I ignore the variability among Persons and just consider Weight to depend on Time:

```
data =weight_loss_data_long
model = smf.ols('Weight ~ Time', data).fit()
anova_table = stats.anova_lm(model)
print(anova_table)
              df      sum_sq      mean_sq       F          PR(>F)
Time         3.0     569.075     189.691667   0.576721   0.634051
Residual    36.0    11840.900    328.913889   NaN         NaN
```

This analysis shows no significant differences among the levels of Time. The key is to tease out the variability among people — the Person variance, in other words. That breaks down the SS for Residual into two components: one SS for Person (which has nine degrees of freedom) and another SS that has the remaining 27 degrees of freedom. Divide that second SS by its degrees of freedom, and you have the MS_{Error} I mention earlier (although Python calls it Residual).

The repeated measures ANOVA does the division for you:

```
data = weight_loss_data_long
model = smf.ols('Weight ~ Time + Person', data).fit()
rm_anova_table = stats.anova_lm(model)
print(rm_anova_table)
```

	df	sum_sq	mean_sq	F	PR(>F)
Time	3.0	569.075	189.691667	24.485120	7.304701e-08
Person	9.0	11631.725	1292.413889	166.822876	2.709815e-21
Residual	27.0	209.175	7.747222	NaN	NaN

Now, the high F value and low p value for Time lead us to reject H_0.

By accounting for the variability among Persons (pulling it out of the Residual, in other words), the repeated measures ANOVA is more powerful, giving you greater ability to reject H_0.

The high F value for Person just tells us that people are significantly different with respect to weight loss. (Spoiler alert: No one's winning any Nobel prizes for that kind of "discovery.") Because our null and alternative hypotheses were about Time (and not Person), we ignore this result.

REMEMBER

In some fields, the word *subject* means "person": That's why a repeated measures analysis is also called a *within-subjects* analysis, as I point out earlier.

TIP

Python offers other ways to perform a repeated measures analysis. In my view, none of them is as straightforward as this one. Best of all, this one allows us to apply our earlier post-analysis work from this chapter. Post analysis with the other methods can be hard to understand if you don't know some extra mathematics.

Visualizing the results

One way to visualize the results is to plot the mean weight loss on the *y*-axis and the month (0, 1, 2, 3) on the *x*-axis. Figure 12-4 shows the plot, along with the standard error of the mean (reflected in the error bars).

REMEMBER

Notice that I use 0–3 to represent the levels of Time (Before, Month 1, Month 2, Month 3).

Here's how to plot this figure:

```
import matplotlib.pyplot as plt
import numpy as np
```

As per my earlier tip, the next two lines are where it's important to have the alphabetical order of the labels reflect the logical order of the levels:

```
means = weight_loss_data_long.groupby('Time')['Weight'].mean()
st_errors = weight_loss_data_long.groupby('Time')
    ['Weight'].sem()
```

This is how the levels of the independent variable will look on the *x*-axis:

```
times = ['0','1', '2', '3']
```

I set up the plot and label the axes:

```
plt.figure(figsize=(8, 6))
plt.ylabel('Weight (lbs)')
plt.xlabel('Month')
```

The errorbar() method plots the means and the standard errors:

```
plt.errorbar(times, means, yerr=st_errors, capsize=6, fmt='ko',
    markersize=8)
```

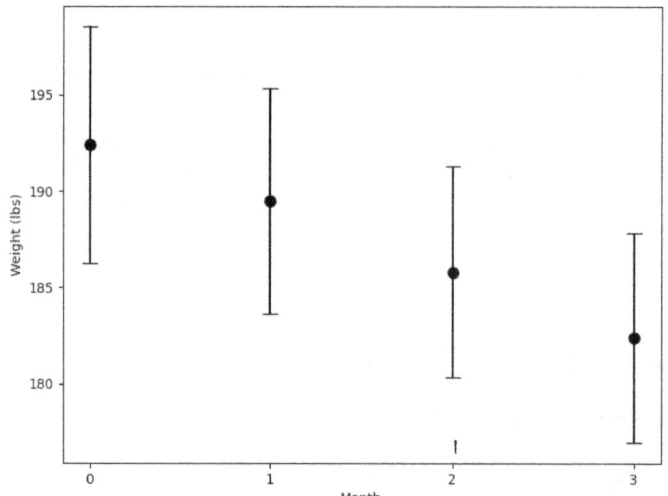

FIGURE 12-4:
The means and
standard errors
for the weight
loss example.

The fmt (format) parameter is a string that sets the color and shape for the means marker: "k" for "black" and "o" for a circle.

Finally,

```
plt.show()
```

Getting Trendy

In situations like the one in the weight loss example, you have an independent variable that's quantitative — its levels are numbers (0 months, 1 month, 2 months, 3 months). Not only that, but in this case, the intervals are equal.

With that kind of an independent variable, it's often a good idea to plan to look for trends in the data rather than just plan comparisons among means. As Figure 12-4 shows, the means in the weight loss example seem to fall along a line.

Trend analysis is the statistical procedure that examines that pattern. The objective is to see whether the pattern contributes to the significant differences among the means.

A trend can be linear, as it apparently is in this example, or nonlinear (in which the means fall on a curve). The two nonlinear types of curves for four means are called *quadratic* and *cubic*. If the means show a quadratic trend, they align in a pattern that shows one change of direction. Figure 12-5 shows what I mean.

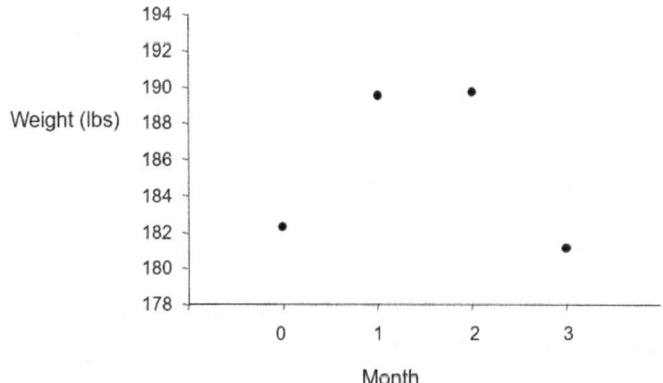

FIGURE 12-5:
A quadratic trend
with four means.

If the means show a cubic trend, they align in a pattern that shows two changes of direction. Figure 12-6 shows what a cubic trend looks like.

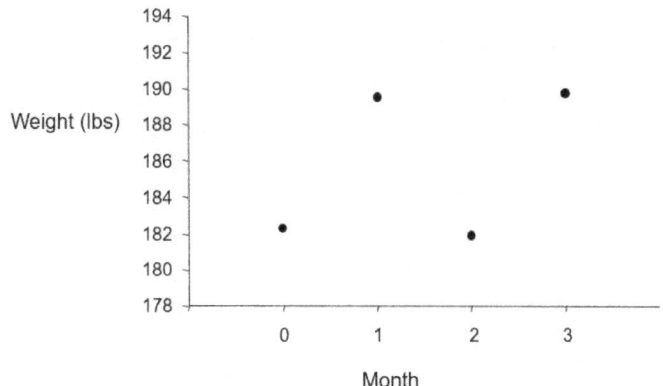

FIGURE 12-6:
A cubic trend with
four means.

We can calculate a Sum of Squares for each component, and the three components add up to the SS_{Linear}

$$SS_{Linear} + SS_{Quadratic} + SS_{Cubic} = SS_{Time}$$

Also:

$$df_{Linear} + df_{Quadratic} + df_{Cubic} = df_{Time}$$

To analyze a trend, you use *comparison coefficients* — those numbers you use in contrasts. You use them in a slightly different way than you did before.

In this section, I describe the theory behind trend analysis. It involves SS, MS, and F. In the next section, I show you how to use the function I created earlier to make it all easier in Python.

The formula for computing a SS for a trend component is

$$SS_{Component} = \frac{N(\sum c\bar{x})^2}{\sum c^2}$$

Resembles the planned comparison, doesn't it?

In this formula, N is the number of people, and c represents the coefficients.

So the idea is to use comparison coefficients to find a sum of squares for linear trend. I abbreviate that as SS_{Linear}.

The comparison coefficients are different for different numbers of samples. For four samples, the linear coefficients are −3, −1, 1, and 3.

TIP

The easiest way to get the coefficients is to look them up in a statistics textbook or on the Internet!

For this example, the SS_{Linear} is

$$SS_{Linear} = \frac{N(\sum c\bar{x})^2}{\sum c^2} = \frac{10[(-3)(192.4)+(-1)(189.5)+(1)(185.8)+(3)(182.4)]^2}{(-3)^2+(-1)^2+(3)^2+(1)^2}$$
$$= 567.845$$

After you calculate SS_{Linear}, you divide it by df_{Linear} to produce MS_{Linear}. This is extremely easy because $df_{Linear} = 1$. Divide MS_{Linear} by MS_{Error}, and you have an F. If that F is higher than the critical value of F with df = 1 and df_{Error} at your α, then weight is decreasing in a linear way over the period of the weight loss program. The F-ratio here is

$$F = \frac{MS_{Linear}}{MS_{Error}} = \frac{567.85}{7.75} = 73.30$$

The critical value for F with 1 and 27 degrees of freedom and $\alpha = .05$ is 4.21. Because the calculated value is larger than the critical value, statisticians would say the data shows a *significant linear component*. This, of course, verifies what you see earlier, in Figure 12-4.

The linear component of SS_{Time} is so large that the other two components are very small. I'll walk you through the computations anyway.

The coefficients for the quadratic component are 1, –1, –1, and 1. So the $SS_{Quadratic}$ is

$$SS_{Quadratic} = \frac{N\left(\sum c\bar{x}\right)^2}{\sum c^2} = \frac{10[(1)(192.4)+(-1)(189.5)+(-1)(185.8)+(1)(182.4)]^2}{(1)^2+(-1)^2+(-1)^2+(1)^2}$$

$$= 0.6$$

The coefficients for the cubic component are –1, 3, –3, and 1. The SS_{Cubic} is

$$SS_{Cubic} = \frac{N\left(\sum c\bar{x}\right)^2}{\sum c^2} = \frac{10[(-1)(192.4)+(3)(189.5)+(-3)(185.8)+(1)(182.4)]^2}{(-1)^2+(3)^2+(-3)^2+(1)^2}$$

$$= 0.6$$

A LITTLE MORE ON TREND

Linear, quadratic, and cubic are as far as you can go with four means. With five means, you can look for those three plus a *quartic component* (three direction changes), and with six, you can try to scope out all the preceding plus a *quintic component* (four direction changes). What do the coefficients look like?

For five means, they're

    Linear: –2, –1, 0, 1, 2

    Quadratic: 2, –1, –2, –1, 2

    Cubic: –1, 2, 0, –2, 1

    Quartic: 1, –4, 6, –4, 1

And for six means, they're

    Linear: –5, –3, –1, 1, 3, 5

    Quadratic: 5, –1, –4, –4, –1, 5

    Cubic: –5, 7, 4, –4, –7, 5

    Quartic: 1, –3, 2, 2, –3, 1

    Quintic: –1, 5, –10, 10, –5, 1

I could go on with more means, coefficients, and exotic component names (hextic? septic?), but enough already. This should hold you for a while.

Rather than complete the final calculations to get the microscopic F-ratios, I'll leave it here.

Trend Analysis in Python

Python provides a variety of ways to analyze trend after a repeated measures ANOVA. Some are a bit complicated, hard to follow, and depend on other ways of computing the ANOVA.

The bottom line, of course, is to calculate an F for each component. So, to keep it simple, I use the t_contrast() function I created earlier in this chapter. Then I square the result to compute the F.

Here it is, short and sweet:

```
linear_component = t_contrast([-3,-1,1,3],'Time','Weight',weight_
    loss_data_long, rm_anova_table)
t-statistic = -8.56
p-value = 1.7782519578340468e-09
```

Remember that this function returns a tuple consisting of t_statistic and p_value, so

```
print(f' F for the linear component =
    {linear_component[0]**2:.2f}')
F for the linear component = 73.30
```

Try this procedure with the components for quadratic and cubic. As you'd expect from Figure 12-4 — the one showing overwhelming linearity — the F values for quadratic and cubic are microscopic (.081 and .078).

IN THIS CHAPTER

» **Working with two variables**

» **Working with replications**

» **Understanding interactions**

» **Mixing variable types**

» **Working with multiple dependent variables**

Chapter **13**

More Complicated Testing

n Chapter 11, I show you how to test hypotheses with two samples. In Chapter 12, I show you how to test hypotheses when you have more than two samples. The common thread in both chapters is one independent variable (also called a *factor*).

Many times, you have to test the effects of more than one factor. In this chapter, I show how to analyze two factors within the same set of data. Several types of situations are possible, and I describe Python functions that deal with each one.

Cracking the Combinations

Imagine that a company has two methods of presenting its training information: One is via a person who presents the information orally, and the other is via a text document. Imagine also that the information is presented in either a humorous way or a technical way. I refer to the first factor as Presentation Method and to the second as Presentation Style.

Combining the two levels of Presentation Method with the two levels of Presentation Style gives four combinations. The company randomly assigns 4 people to each combination, for a total of 16 people. After providing the training, they test the 16 people on their comprehension of the material.

Figure 13-1 shows the combinations, the four comprehension scores within each combination, and summary statistics for the combinations, rows, and columns.

Presentation Style

		Humorous		Technical		
		Spoken and Humorous	57 56 60 64	Spoken and Technical	22 21 29 25	
Presentation Method	Spoken	Mean = 59.25 Variance = 12.92		Mean = 24.25 Variance = 12.92		Mean = 41.75
	Text	Text and Humorous	33 25 28 31	Test and Technical	66 65 71 72	
		Mean = 29.25 Variance = 12.25		Mean = 68.50 Variance = 12.33		Mean = 48.88
		Mean = 44.25		Mean = 46.38		Grand Mean = 44.31

FIGURE 13-1: Combining the levels of Presentation Method with the levels of Presentation Style.

REMEMBER

With each of two levels of one factor combined with each of two levels of the other factor, this kind of study is called a 2 X 2 *factorial* design.

Here are the hypotheses:

$$H_0 : \mu_{\text{Spoken}} = \mu_{\text{Text}}$$
$$H_1 : \text{Not } H_0$$

and

$$H_0 : \mu_{\text{Humorous}} = \mu_{\text{Technical}}$$
$$H_1 : \textit{Not } H_0$$

Because the two presentation methods (Spoken and Text) are in the rows, I refer to Presentation Type as the *row factor*. The two presentation styles (Humorous and Technical) are in the columns, so Presentation Style is the *column factor*.

Interactions

When you have rows and columns of data and you're testing hypotheses about the row factor and the column factor, you have an additional consideration. Namely, you have to be concerned about the row-column combinations. Do the combinations result in peculiar effects?

For the example I present, it's possible that combining Spoken and Text with Humorous and Technical yields an unexpected result. In fact, you can see that in the data in Figure 13-1: For Spoken presentation, the Humorous style produces a higher average than the Technical style. For Text presentation, the Humorous style produces a lower average than the Technical style.

REMEMBER

A situation like this one is called an *interaction*. In formal terms, an interaction occurs when the levels of one factor affect the levels of the other factor differently. The label for the interaction is row factor × column factor, so for this example, that's Method × Type.

The hypotheses for this are

H_0 : Presentation Method does not interact with Presentation Style
H_1 : Not H_0

The analysis

The statistical analysis is, once again, an analysis of variance (ANOVA). As is the case with the ANOVAs I show you earlier, in Chapter 12, it depends on the variances in the data. It's called a *two-factor* ANOVA, or a *two-way* ANOVA.

The first variance is the total variance, labeled MS_T. That's the variance of all 16 scores around their mean (the grand mean), which is 44.81:

$$MS_T = \frac{(57-45.31)^2 + (56-45.31)^2 + \ldots + (72-45.31)^2}{16-1} = \frac{5885.43}{15} = 392.36$$

The denominator tells you that df = 15 for MS_T.

The next variance comes from the row factor. That's MS_{Method}, and it's the variance of the row means around the grand mean:

$$MS_{Method} = \frac{(8)(41.75-45.31)^2 + (8)(48.88-45.31)^2}{2-1} = \frac{203.06}{1} = 203.06$$

The 8 in the equation multiplies each squared deviation because you have to take into account the number of scores that produced each row mean. The df for MS_{Method} is the number of rows − 1, which is 1.

Similarly, the variance for the column factor is

$$MS_{Style} = \frac{(8)(43.25 - 45.31)^2 + (8)(46.38 - 45.31)^2}{2 - 1} = \frac{18.06}{1} = 18.06$$

The df for MS_{Style} is 1 (the number of columns − 1).

Another variance is the pooled estimate based on the variances within the four row-column combinations. It's called the MSWithin, or MSW. (For details on MSw and pooled estimates, see Chapter 12.) For this example,

$$MS_W = \frac{(4-1)(12.92) + (4-1)(12.92) + (4-1)(12.25) + (4-1)(12.33)}{(4-1) + (4-1) + (4-1) + (4-1)}$$

$$= \frac{151.25}{12} = 12.60$$

This one is the error term (the denominator) for each F you calculate. Its denominator tells you that df = 12 for this MS.

The last variance comes from the interaction between the row factor and the column factor. In this example, it's labeled $MS_{Method \, X \, Type}$. You can calculate this in a couple of ways. The easiest way is to take advantage of this general relationship:

$$SS_{Row \, X \, Column} = SS_T - SS_{Row \, Factor} - SS_{Column \, Factor} - SS_W$$

And this one:

$$df_{Row \, X \, Column} = df_T - df_{Row \, Factor} - df_{Column \, Factor} - df_W$$

Another way to calculate this is

$$df_{Row \, X \, Column} = (\text{number of rows - 1})(\text{number of columns - 1})$$

The MS is

$$MS_{Row \, X \, Column} = \frac{SS_{Row \, X \, Column}}{df_{Row \, X \, Column}}$$

For this example,

$$MS_{Method \, X \, Style} = \frac{SS_{Method \, X \, Style}}{df_{Method \, X \, Style}} = \frac{5885.43 - 203.06 - 18.06 - 151.25}{15 - 12 - 1 - 1}$$

$$= \frac{5513.06}{1} = 5513.06$$

To test the hypotheses, you calculate three Fs:

$$F = \frac{MS_{Style}}{MS_W} = \frac{18.06}{12.60} = 1.43$$

$$F = \frac{MS_{Method}}{MS_W} = \frac{203.06}{12.60} = 16.12$$

$$F = \frac{MS_{Method \, X \, Style}}{MS_W} = \frac{5513.06}{12.60} = 437.54$$

For df = 1 and 12, the critical F at α = .05 is 4.75. (You can use $qf()$ to verify). The decision is to reject H_0 for the Presentation Method and the Method X Style interaction and not to reject H_0 for the Presentation Style.

It's possible, of course, to have more than two levels of each factor. It's also possible to have more than two factors. In that case, things (like interactions) become much more complex.

Two-Way ANOVA in Python

I begin by importing the libraries I need:

```
import pandas as pd
import statsmodels.formula.api as smf
from statsmodels.stats.anova import anova_lm
```

Then, as in any analysis, the next step in tackling my Presentation Method/ Presentation Style example is to get the data in shape. In Python, that means getting the data into long format.

Start with a list for the scores in each of the columns in Figure 13-1:

```
humorous = [57,56,60,64,33,25,28,31]
technical = [22,21,29,25,66,65,71,72]
```

To begin the move to long format, I combine them into one long list:

```
score = humorous + technical
```

Now I need a list for the levels of the `style` variable and another for the levels of the `method` variable. The levels have to line up to reflect the row X column combinations in Figure 13-1:

```
style = ['humorous']*8 + ['technical']*8
method = ['spoken']*4 + ['text']*4 + ['spoken']*4 + ['text']*4
```

Then I create the data frame:

```
data = {'score': score,
        'method': method,
        'style': style}
two_way_data_frame = pd.DataFrame(data)
```

And here's the analysis:

```
model = smf.ols('score ~ method * style', data=two_way_data_
    frame).fit()
anova_table = anova_lm(model)
print(anova_table)
```

	df	sum_sq	mean_sq	F	PR(>F)
method	1.0	203.0625	203.062500	16.110744	1.718448e-03
style	1.0	18.0625	18.062500	1.433058	2.543800e-01
method:style	1.0	5513.0625	5513.062500	437.400000	8.272384e-11
Residual	12.0	151.2500	12.604167	NaN	NaN

Again, the F-values and p-values indicate rejection of the null hypothesis for Method and for the Style X Method interaction, but not for Style.

With just two levels of each factor, no post-analysis tests are necessary to explore a significant result.

Visualizing the Two-Way Results

The best way to show the results of a study like the preceding Style X Method study is with a grouped bar plot that shows the means and the standard errors. So I start with

```
import matplotlib.pyplot as plt
```

The foundation for the plot consists of one DataFrame that holds the mean for each combination of levels of the independent variables, and another that holds the standard error of the mean for each combination. Although we need the data in long format for the analysis, we need wide format for the plot, so the means DataFrame we require looks like this:

method	spoken	text
style		
humorous	59.25	29.25
technical	24.25	68.50

and the standard errors DataFrame like this:

method	spoken	text
style		
humorous	1.796988	1.750000
technical	1.796988	1.755942

Here's how to get there. First, I use groupby() to retrieve the means and standard errors. I can group by the combination of independent variables:

```
grouped_means = two_way_data_frame.groupby(['style', 'method'])
    ['score'].mean()
grouped_standard_errors = two_way_data_frame.groupby(['style',
    'method'])['score'].sem()
```

The resulting DataFrames are in long format. It looks like this for the means:

style	method	
humorous	spoken	59.25
	text	29.25
technical	spoken	24.25
	text	68.50

In Chapter 12, I show how to reshape data from wide format to long format. That's called *melting.* The opposite, from long format to wide, is called *unstacking.*

So, to reshape the data into wide format, I use unstack():

```
unstacked_means = grouped_means.unstack()
unstacked_standard_errors = grouped_standard_errors.unstack()
```

The default colors for the bars are orange and blue. Although near and dear to the hearts of native New Yorkers and graduates of the University of Florida, orange and blue do not show up well on a printed page like this one.

So I begin the plot by setting the bar colors to a combination that looks better:

```
colors = ['gray', 'lightgray', 'gray', 'lightgray']
```

The plot() function is

```
unstacked_means.plot(kind='bar', yerr = unstacked_standard_
    errors, capsize = 5,figsize=(10, 6), color= colors,edgecolor
    = 'black')
```

Then I label the axes:

```
plt.xlabel('Style')
plt.ylabel('Mean Score')
```

When I plot the tick marks, I want to ensure that their labels don't rotate to a vertical orientation:

```
plt.xticks(rotation=0)
```

Then I create the legend to reflect the method variable:

```
plt.legend(title='Method')
```

Then I add plt.tight_layout() to keep plot elements from overlapping each other:

```
plt.tight_layout()
```

And I render the plot:

```
plt.show()
```

The result of all this activity is shown in Figure 13-2.

This graph clearly shows the Method X Style interaction. For the humorous presentation, spoken is more effective than text, and it's the reverse for the technical presentation.

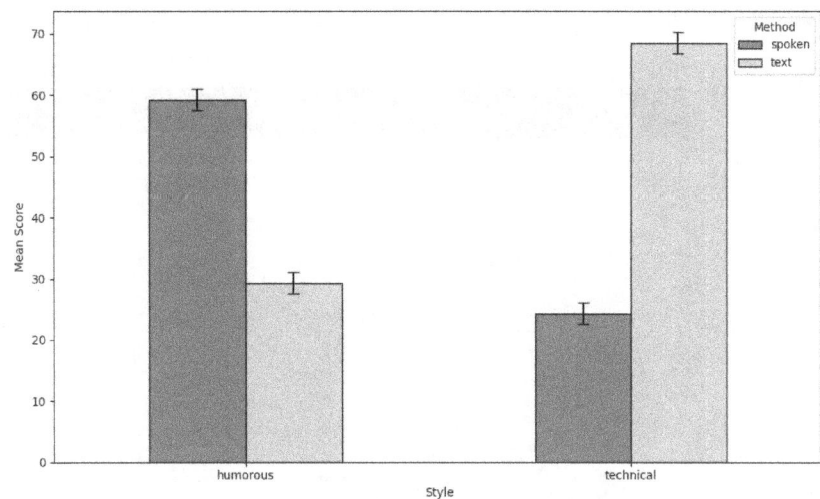

FIGURE 13-2:
Means and
standard
errors of the
presentation
study.

Two Kinds of Variables . . . at Once

What happens when you have a Between Groups variable and a Within Groups variable . . . at the same time? How can that happen?

Very easily. Suppose you want to study the effects of presentation media on the reading speeds of fourth-graders. You randomly assign the fourth-graders (I'll call them *subjects*) to read either books or e-readers. So `"Medium"` is the Between Groups variable.

Let's say you're also interested in the effects of font. So you assign each subject to read each of these fonts: Haettenschweiler, Arial, and Calibri. (I've never seen a document in Haettenschweiler, but it's my favorite font because "Haettenschweiler" is fun to say. Try it. Am I right?) Because each subject reads all the fonts, `"Font"` is the Within Groups variable. For completeness, you have to randomly order the fonts for each subject.

Table 13-1 shows data that might result from a study like this. The dependent variable is the score on a reading comprehension test.

REMEMBER

Because this kind of analysis mixes a Between Groups variable with a Within Groups variable, it's called a *Mixed ANOVA*.

TABLE 13-1

Data for a Study of Presentation Media (Between Groups Variable) and Font (Within Groups Variable)

Medium	Subject	Haettenschweiler	Arial	Calibri
Book	Alice	48	40	38
	Brad	55	43	45
	Chris	46	45	44
	Donna	61	53	53
E-reader	Eddie	43	45	47
	Fran	50	52	54
	Gil	56	57	57
	Harriet	53	53	55

To show you how the analysis works, I present the kind of table that results from a Mixed ANOVA. It's a bit more complete than the output of an ANOVA in R, but bear with me. Table 13-2 shows it to you in a generic way. It's categorized into a set of sources that make up Between Groups variability and a set of sources that make up Within Groups (also known as Repeated Measures) variability.

TABLE 13-2

The ANOVA Table for the Mixed ANOVA

Source	SS	df	MS	F
Between	$SS_{Between}$	$df_{Between}$		
A	SS_A	df_A	SS_A/df_A	$MS_A/MS_{S/A}$
S/A	$SS_{S/A}$	$df_{S/A}$	$SS_{S/A}/df_{S/A}$	
Within	SS_{Within}	df_{Within}		
B	SS_B	df_B	SS_B/df_B	$MS_B/MS_{B \times S/A}$
A X B	$SS_{A \times B}$	$df_{A \times B}$	$SS_{A \times B}/df_{A \times B}$	$MS_{A \times B}/MS_{B \times S/A}$
B X S/A	$SS_{B \times S/A}$	$df_{B \times S/A}$	$SS_{B \times S/A}/df_{B \times S/A}$	
Total	SS_{Total}	df_{Total}		

In the Between category, A is the name of the Between Groups variable. (In the example, that's Medium.) Read "S/A" as "Subjects within A." This just says that the people in one level of A are different from the people in the other levels of A.

In the Within category, B is the name of the Within Groups variable. (In the example, that's Font.) A X B is the interaction of the two variables. B X S/A is something like the B variable interacting with subjects within A. As you can see, anything associated with B falls into the Within Groups category.

The first thing to note is the three F-ratios. The first one tests for differences among the levels of A, the second for differences among the levels of B, and the third for the interaction of the two. Notice also that the denominator for the first F-ratio is different from the denominator for the other two. This happens more and more as ANOVAs increase in complexity.

Next, it's important to be aware of some relationships. At the top level:

$$SS_{Between} + SS_{Within} = SS_{Total}$$
$$df_{Between} + df_{Within} = df_{Total}$$

The Between component breaks down further:

$$SS_A + SS_{S/A} = SS_{Between}$$
$$df_A + df_{S/A} = df_{Between}$$

The Within component breaks down, too:

$$SS_B + SS_{AXB} + SS_{BXS/A} = SS_{Within}$$
$$df_B + df_{AXB} + df_{BXS/A} = df_{Within}$$

It's possible to have more than one Between Groups factor and more than one repeated measure in a study.

REMEMBER

On to the analysis. . . .

Mixed ANOVA in Python

First, I show you how to use the data from Table 13-1 to build a DataFrame in long format. When finished, it looks like this:

```
     Medium  Font                Subject      Score
0    Book    Haettenschweiler    Alice        48
1    Book    Haettenschweiler    Brad         55
2    Book    Haettenschweiler    Chris        46
3    Book    Haettenschweiler    Donna        61
4    Book    Arial               Alice        40
5    Book    Arial               Brad         43
6    Book    Arial               Chris        45
7    Book    Arial               Donna        53
```

8	Book	Calibri	Alice	38
9	Book	Calibri	Brad	45
10	Book	Calibri	Chris	44
11	Book	Calibri	Donna	53
12	E-reader	Haettenschweiler	Eddie	43
13	E-reader	Haettenschweiler	Fran	50
14	E-reader	Haettenschweiler	Gil	56
15	E-reader	Haettenschweiler	Harriet	53
16	E-reader	Arial	Eddie	45
17	E-reader	Arial	Fran	52
18	E-reader	Arial	Gil	57
19	E-reader	Arial	Harriet	53
20	E-reader	Calibri	Eddie	47
21	E-reader	Calibri	Fran	54
22	E-reader	Calibri	Gil	57
23	E-reader	Calibri	Harriet	55

I begin by creating a list for the rightmost column. It's easiest if I start with a list for the Book Scores, another for the E-reader scores, and then combine them:

```
Book_Scores= [48,55,46,61,40,43,45,53,38,45,44,53]
E_Reader_Scores = [43,50,56,53,45,52,57,53,47,54,57,55]
Score= Book_Scores + E_Reader_Scores
```

I do the same for the Subjects:

```
Book_Subjects = ["Alice","Brad","Chris","Donna"]*3
E_Reader_Subjects = ["Eddie","Fran","Gil","Harriet"]*3
Subject= Book_Subjects + E_Reader_Subjects
```

Next, I deal with the Medium:

```
Medium = ["Book"]*12 +["E-reader"]*12
```

And finally, the Font:

```
Font =["Haettenschweiler"] *4 + ["Arial"]*4 + ["Calibri"]*4
Font= Font * 2
```

I combine them all into a dictionary:

```
mixed_data = {'Medium': Medium,'Font': Font, 'Subject':
    Subject,'Score': Score}
```

and turn the dictionary into the DataFrame:

```
mixed_data_frame = pd.DataFrame(mixed_data)
```

Now the DataFrame is ready for the analysis. The method for the analysis is called mixed_anova(). It's in the pingouin library, which I install:

```
!pip install pingouin
```

Next, I import:

```
import pingouin as pg
```

And then I carry out the analysis:

```
mixed_anova_results = pg.mixed_anova(
    dv='Score',
    within='Font',
    between='Medium',
    subject='Subject',
    data=mixed_data_frame
)
```

The results look a little daunting, but the part that concerns us looks pretty consistent with what I show you after previous analyses:

```
print(mixed_anova_results)
     Source        SS         DF1 DF2 MS         F         p-unc
0 Medium       108.37500 1   6   108.37500 1.227080  0.3103
1 Font          40.083333 2   12  20.04166  5.68110   0.01836
2 Interaction 120.25000 2   12  60.125000 17.043307 0.0003


     p-GG-corr  np2       eps     sphericity W-spher   p-spher
0 NaN        0.169789 NaN     NaN        NaN       NaN
1 0.229622   0.4863   0.5483  False      0.1764    0.00549
2 NaN        0.739621 NaN     NaN        NaN       NaN
```

The entries in the upper table show that the Between variable, Medium (Book versus E-reader), made no difference. The results indicate a significant effect of Font and a significant Font X Medium interaction.

For our purposes, don't worry about the lower table.

The entries in the lower table cover corrections to the analysis in case the repeated measures data (Font) don't satisfy an assumption called sphericity. *Sphericity* means that the variances of the pairwise differences among the three fonts are equal.

Visualizing the mixed ANOVA results

As was the case in the two-way ANOVA, I use groupby() to get long format DataFrames of the means and standard errors, and then use unstack() to turn them into the wide format that matplotlib works with.

First, I make sure to import the libraries I need:

```
import matplotlib.pyplot as plt
import pandas as pd
```

Next, I have groupby() do its thing:

```
grouped_means_mixed = mixed_data_frame.groupby(['Medium',
    'Font'])['Score'].mean()
grouped_standard_errors_mixed = mixed_data_frame.
    groupby(['Medium', 'Font'])['Score'].sem()
```

Then I use unstack():

```
unstacked_means_mixed = grouped_means_mixed.unstack()
unstacked_standard_errors_mixed = grouped_standard_errors_
    mixed.unstack()
```

And create the bar plot:

```
unstacked_means_mixed.plot(
    kind='bar',
    yerr=unstacked_standard_errors_mixed,
    capsize=5,
    figsize=(10, 6),
     color=['gray', 'lightgray','white'],
    edgecolor='black'
)
```

I label the axes:

```
plt.xlabel('Medium')
```

```
plt.ylabel('Mean Score')
plt.xticks(rotation=0)
```

base the legend on the Font variable:

```
plt.legend(title='Font')
```

and set up the layout so that plot items don't bump into each other:

```
plt.tight_layout()
```

and finally render the plot:

```
plt.show()
```

The result is shown in Figure 13-3.

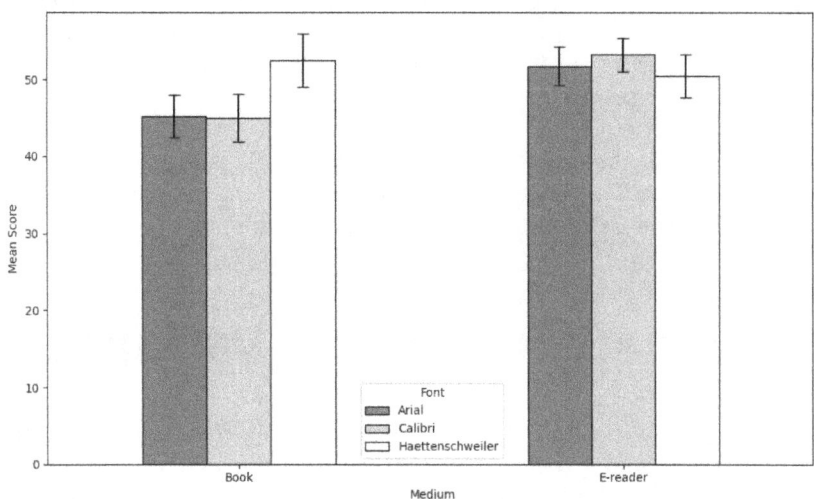

FIGURE 13-3:
Means and
standard errors
for the book-
versus-e-
reader study.

After the Analysis

As I point out in Chapter 12, a significant result in an ANOVA tells you that an effect is lurking somewhere in the data. Post-analysis tests tell you where. Two types of tests are possible: planned or unplanned. Chapter 12 provides the details.

In this example, the Between Groups variable has only two levels. For this reason, if the result is statistically significant, no further test would be necessary. The Within Groups variable, `Font`, is significant. Ordinarily, the test would proceed as described in Chapter 12. In this case, however, the interaction between `Media` and `Font` necessitates a different path.

With the interaction, post-analysis tests can proceed in either (or both) of two ways. You can examine the effects of each level of the `A` variable (the Between Groups variable) on the levels of the `B` variable (the repeated measure), or you can examine the effects of each level of the `B` variable on the levels of the `A` variable. Statisticians refer to these as *simple main effects.*

For this example, the first way examines the means for the three fonts in a book and the means for the three fonts in the e-reader. The second way examines the means for the book versus the mean for the e-reader with Haettenschweiler font, with Arial, and with Calibri.

Statistics texts provide complicated formulas for calculating these analyses. Python makes them easy. To analyze the three fonts in the book, do a repeated measures ANOVA for Subjects 1–4. To analyze the three fonts in the e-reader, do a repeated measures ANOVA for Subjects 5–8.

For the analysis of the book versus the e-reader in the Haettenschweiler font, that's a single-factor ANOVA for the Haettenschweiler data. You'd complete a similar procedure for each of the other fonts.

Multivariate Analysis of Variance

The examples thus far in this chapter involve a dependent variable and more than one independent variable. Is it possible to have more than one dependent variable? Absolutely! That gives you MANOVA — the abbreviation for the title of this section.

When might you encounter this type of situation? Suppose you're thinking of adopting one of three textbooks for a basic science course. You have 12 students and you randomly assign 4 of them to read Book 1, another 4 to read Book 2, and the remaining 4 to read Book 3. You're interested in how each book promotes knowledge in physics, chemistry, and biology, so after the students read the books, they take a test of fundamental knowledge in each of those three sciences.

The independent variable is Book, and the dependent variable is multivariate — it combines Physics score, Chemistry score, and Biology score. Table 13-3 shows the data.

TABLE 13-3 **Data for the Science Textbook MANOVA Study**

Student	Book	Physics	Chemistry	Biology
Art	Book 1	50	66	71
Brenda	Book 1	53	45	56
Cal	Book 1	52	48	65
Dan	Book 1	54	51	68
Eva	Book 2	75	55	88
Frank	Book 2	72	58	85
Greg	Book 2	64	59	79
Hank	Book 2	76	59	82
Iris	Book 3	68	67	55
Jim	Book 3	61	56	59
Kendra	Book 3	62	66	63
Lee	Book 3	64	78	61

The dependent variable for the first student in the Book 1 sample consists of 50, 66, and 71.

What are the hypotheses in a case like this? The null hypothesis has to take all components of the dependent variable into account, so here are the null and the alternative:

$$H_0 : \begin{pmatrix} \mu_{Book1,Phys} \\ \mu_{Book1,Chem} \\ \mu_{Book1,Bio} \end{pmatrix} = \begin{pmatrix} \mu_{Book2,Phys} \\ \mu_{Book2,Chem} \\ \mu_{Book2,Bio} \end{pmatrix} = \begin{pmatrix} \mu_{Book3,Phys} \\ \mu_{Book3,Chem} \\ \mu_{Book3,Bio} \end{pmatrix}$$

$$H_1 : Not\ H_0$$

I don't go into the same depth on MANOVA in this chapter as I do on ANOVA in Chapter 12. I don't discuss SS, MS, and df — that would require knowledge of math (matrix algebra) and other material that's beyond the scope of this chapter. Instead, I dive right in and show you how to get the analysis done.

MANOVA in Python

The DataFrame for the MANOVA looks just like Table 13-3:

```
     Student  Book    Physics   Chemistry   Biology
0    Art      book1   50        66          71
1    Brenda   book1   53        45          56
2    Cal      book1   52        48          65
3    Dan      book1   54        51          68
4    Eva      book2   75        55          88
5    Frank    book2   72        58          85
6    Greg     book2   64        59          79
7    Hank     book2   76        59          82
8    Iris     book3   68        67          55
9    Jim      book3   61        56          59
10   Kendra   book3   62        66          63
11   Lee      book3   64        78          61
```

This is a pandas DataFrame, so, of course:

```
import pandas as pd
```

To create the DataFrame, I begin with lists that represent the columns:

```
student = ['Art', 'Brenda', 'Cal','Dan','Eva', 'Frank','Greg',
    'Hank','Iris','Jim','Kendra','Lee']
book = ['book1']*4 + ['book2']*4 + ['book3']*4
physics = [50,53,52,54,75,72,64,76,68,61,62,64]
chemistry = [66,45,48,51,55,58,59,59,67,56,66,78]
biology = [71,56,65,68,88,85,79,82,55,59,63,61]
```

I turn the lists into a dictionary:

```
textbooks_data = {'Student': student, 'Book': book, 'Physics':
    physics, 'Chemistry': chemistry, 'Biology': biology}
```

And then I turn the dictionary into the DataFrame:

```
textbooks_data_frame = pd.DataFrame(textbooks_data)
```

The tool that performs the MANOVA is called, unsurprisingly, MANOVA, and it lives in statsmodels.multivariate.manova. So:

```
from statsmodels.multivariate.manova import MANOVA
```

To set up the analysis, I create a string for a formula that shows the combination of the three dependent variables depending on Book:

```
formula = 'Physics + Chemistry + Biology ~ Book'
```

Then the analysis is

```
manova = MANOVA.from_formula(formula, data=textbooks_data_frame)
```

TIP

It's possible to do the analysis with just MANOVA() (and without .from_formula), but that makes everything more complicated.

Time to compute the results (the mv.test() method gets that done)

```
manova_results = manova.mv_test()
```

and see what they look like:

```
print(manova_results)
```

```
                          Multivariate linear model
==============================================================================

------------------------------------------------------------------------------
Intercept              Value    Num DF     Den DF     F Value     Pr > F
Wilks' lambda          0.0060   3.0000     7.0000     386.6606    0.0000
Pillai's trace         0.9940   3.0000     7.0000     386.6606    0.0000
Hotelling-
Lawley trace         165.7117   3.0000     7.0000     386.6606    0.0000
Roy's
greatest root        165.7117   3.0000     7.0000     386.6606    0.0000
------------------------------------------------------------------------------

------------------------------------------------------------------------------
Book                   Value    Num DF     Den DF     F Value     Pr > F
------------------------------------------------------------------------------
Wilks' lambda          0.0157   6.0000     14.0000    16.3085     0.000
Pillai's trace         1.7293   6.0000     16.0000    17.0359     0.000
Hotelling-
Lawley trace          15.2783   6.0000     7.7895     17.1302     0.0004
Roy's
greatest root         10.9262   3.0000     8.0000     29.1365     0.0001
==============================================================================
```

Although this looks like nothing you've seen before, it's easy to wade through. First, the upper table, Intercept, doesn't concern us. The lower table, Book, shows the effects of the independent variable on the combination of the dependent variables. Each row shows an exotically named statistic, whose value is converted into an F-value. The high F-values and extremely low probabilities show that we can reject H_0.

If you have to report MANOVA results in a paper, report Pillai's trace. It's the one that statisticians usually rely on because the others depend on some esoteric mathematics.

This example is a MANOVA extension of an ANOVA with just one factor. It's possible to have multiple dependent variables with more complex designs (like the ones I discuss earlier in this chapter).

Visualizing the MANOVA results

The objective of the study is to show how the distribution of Physics, Chemistry, and Biology scores differs from book to book. A separate set of box plots for each book visualizes the differences. Figure 13-4 shows what I'm talking about.

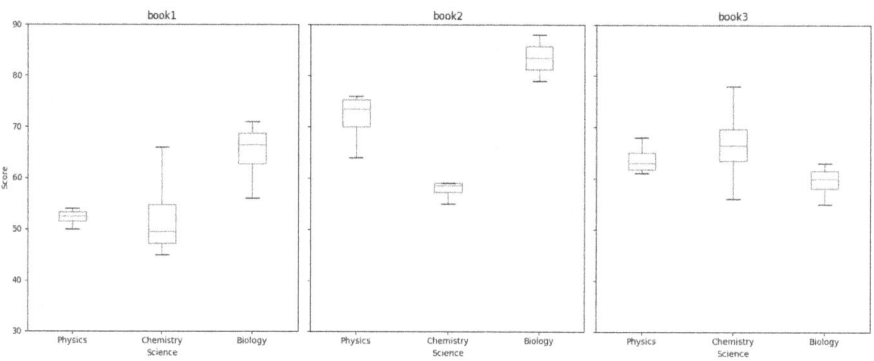

FIGURE 13-4:
Three box plots show the distribution of scores for Physics, Chemistry, and Biology for each book.

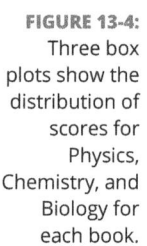

Here's how to create this triad of box plots. Start with the imports:

```
import matplotlib.pyplot as plt
import pandas as pd
```

Next, I need a list of the levels of Book, and how many levels we have (yes, I know this already, but it helps to understand the code):

```
book_types = textbooks_data_frame['Book'].unique()
num_books = len(book_types)
```

Now I create a subplot for each book, which means creating axes for each subplot:

```
fig, axes = plt.subplots(1, num_books, figsize=(5 * num_books,
    6), sharey=True)
```

I use a for loop to iterate through the three books and create a box plot for each one:

```
for i, book in enumerate(book_types):
```

I filter the DataFrame for the current book:

```
book_data = textbooks_data_frame[textbooks_data_
    frame['Book'] == book]
```

Then I select the score columns for the current book's box plot:

```
book_scores = book_data[['Physics', 'Chemistry', 'Biology']]
```

And then I create the box plot (without a grid):

```
book_scores.boxplot(ax=axes[i], grid=False)
```

I set a title for the box plot and label its axes, taking care to label only the y-axis of the first one:

```
axes[i].set_title(book)
axes[i].set_xlabel('Science')
if i == 0: # Only set the y-label for the first plot
    axes[i].set_ylabel('Score')
else:
    axes[i].set_ylabel('')
```

I keep consistent limits for the y-axes:

```
axes[i].set_ylim([30, 90])
```

And that's the end of the for loop.

I make sure the graphical elements don't cramp each other, and I show the plot:

```
plt.tight_layout()
plt.show()
```

The result is shown in Figure 13-4.

After the analysis

When a MANOVA results in rejection of the null hypothesis, one way to proceed is to perform an ANOVA on each component of the dependent variable. The results tell you which components contribute to the significant MANOVA.

After importing what I need for ANOVA, I use a for loop to do all the analyses:

```
from statsmodels.formula.api import ols

for var in ['Physics', 'Chemistry','Biology']:
 anova_results = ols(f'{var} ~ Book', data=textbooks_data_
   frame).fit()
 anova_table = anova_lm(anova_results)
 print(f"ANOVA for {var}:\n", anova_table,"\n")

ANOVA for Physics:
          df    sum_sq       mean_sq     F          PR(>F)
Book      2.0   768.666667   384.333333  27.39802   0.000149
Residual  9.0   126.250000   14.027778   NaN        NaN

ANOVA for Chemistry:
          df    sum_sq       mean_sq     F          PR(>F)
Book      2.0   415.5        207.750000  3.634111   0.069672
Residual  9.0   514.5        57.16666    NaN        NaN

ANOVA for Biology:
          df    sum_sq       mean_sq     F          PR(>F)
Book      2.0   1264.666667  632.333333  27.626214  0.000144
Residual  9.0   206.000000   22.888889   NaN        NaN
```

These analyses show that Physics and Biology contribute to the overall effect, and Chemistry just misses significance.

TECHNICAL STUFF

This separate-ANOVAs procedure doesn't consider the relationships among pairs of components. The relationship is called *correlation*, which I discuss in Chapter 15.

IN THIS CHAPTER

» Summarizing a relationship

» Working with regression

» Taking another look at ANOVA

» Exploring analysis of covariance

» Examining the general linear model

Chapter **14**

Regression: Linear, Multiple, and the General Linear Model

O ne of the main things you do when you work with statistics is make predictions. The idea is to use data from one or more variables to predict the value of another variable. To do this, you have to understand how to summarize relationships among variables as well as how to test hypotheses about those relationships.

In this chapter, I introduce regression, a statistical way to do just that. *Regression* also enables you to use the details of relationships to make predictions. First, I show you how to analyze the relationship between one variable and another. Then I show you how to analyze the relationship between a variable and two others. Finally, I let you in on the connection between regression and ANOVA.

The Plot of Scatter

FarMisht Consulting, Inc., is a consulting firm with a wide range of specialties. It receives numerous applications from people interested in becoming FarMisht consultants. Accordingly, FarMisht Human Resources has to be able to predict which applicants will succeed and which ones will not. They've developed a Performance measure they use to assess their current employees. The scale is 0–100, where 100 indicates top performance.

What's the best prediction for a new applicant? Without knowing anything about an applicant, and knowing only their own employees' Performance scores, the answer is clear: It's the average Performance score among their employees. Regardless of who the applicant is, that's all the Human Resources team can say if its members' knowledge is limited.

With more knowledge about the employees and about the applicants, a more accurate prediction becomes possible. For example, if FarMisht develops an aptitude test and assesses its employees, Human Resources can match up every employee's Performance score with their Aptitude score and see whether the two pieces of data are somehow related. If they are, an applicant can take the FarMisht aptitude test, and Human Resources can use that score (and the relationship between Aptitude and Performance) to help make a prediction.

Figure 14-1 shows the Aptitude-Performance matchup in a graphical way. Because the points are scattered, it's called a *scatterplot.* By convention, the vertical axis (the y-*axis*) represents what you're trying to predict. That's also called the *dependent variable* or the *y-variable.* In this case, that's Performance. Also, by convention, the horizontal axis (the x-*axis*) represents what you're using to make your prediction. That's also called the *independent variable,* or *x-variable.* Here, that's Aptitude.

Each point in the graph represents an individual's Performance and Aptitude. In a scatterplot for a real-life corporation, you'd see many more points than I show here. The general tendency of the set of points seems to be that high Aptitude scores are associated with high Performance scores and that low Aptitude scores are associated with low Performance scores.

I've singled out one of the points. It shows a FarMisht employee with an Aptitude score of 54 and a Performance score of 58. I also show the average Performance score, to give you a sense that knowing the Aptitude–Performance relationship provides an advantage over knowing only the mean.

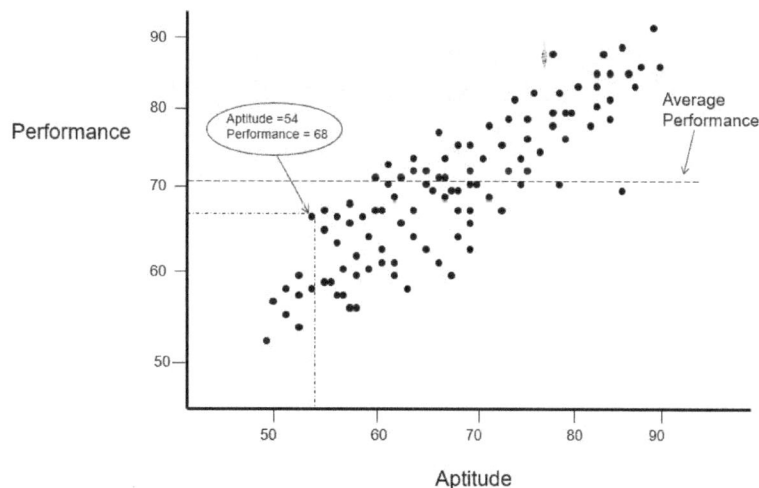

FIGURE 14-1:
Aptitude and
Performance at
FarMisht
Consulting.

How do you make that advantage work for you? You start by summarizing the relationship between Aptitude and Performance. The summary is a line through the points. How and where do you draw the line?

I get to that in a minute. First, I have to tell you about lines in general.

Graphing Lines

In the world of mathematics, a line is a way to picture a relationship between an independent variable *(x)* and a dependent variable *(y)*. In this relationship,

$$y = 4 + 2x$$

if you supply a value for *x*, you can figure out the corresponding value for *y*. The equation says to multiply the *x*-value by 2 and then add 4.

If *x* = 1, for example, *y* = 6. If *x* = 2, *y* = 8. Table 14-1 shows a number of *x*-*y* pairs in this relationship, including the pair in which *x* = 0.

Figure 14-2 shows these pairs as points on a set of *x*-*y* axes, along with a line through the points. Each time I list an *x*-*y* pair in parentheses, the *x-value* is first.

As the figure shows, the points fall neatly onto the line. The line *graphs* the equation *y* = 4 + 2*x*. In fact, whenever you have an equation like this one, where *x* isn't squared or cubed or raised to any power higher than 1, you have what mathematicians call a *linear* equation. (If *x* is raised to a higher power than 1, you connect the points with a curve, not a line.)

TABLE 14-1

x-y Pairs in y = 4 + 2x

x	y
0	4
1	6
2	8
3	10
4	12
5	14
6	16

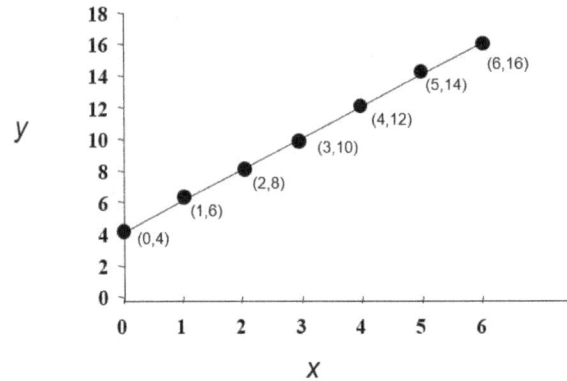

REMEMBER

Here are a couple of points to keep in mind about a line: You can describe a line in terms of how slanted it is and by where it runs into the y-axis.

The how-slanted-it-is part is the slope. The *slope* tells you how much y changes when x changes by one unit. In the line shown in Figure 14-2, when x changes by 1 (from 4 to 5, for example), y changes by 2 (from 12 to 14).

The where-it-runs-into-the-y-axis part is called the *y-intercept* (or sometimes just the *intercept*). That's the value of y when $x = 0$. In Figure 14-2, the y-intercept is 4.

You can see these numbers in the equation. The slope is the number that multiplies x, and the intercept is the number you add to x. In general,

$$y = a + bx$$

where a represents the intercept and b represents the slope.

The slope can be a positive number, a negative number, or 0. In Figure 14-2, the slope is positive. If the slope is negative, the line is slanted in a direction opposite to the one you see in Figure 14-2. A negative slope means that y *decreases* as x increases. If the slope is 0, the line is parallel to the horizontal axis. If the slope is 0, y doesn't change as x changes.

The same applies to the intercept — it can be a positive number, a negative number, or 0. If the intercept is positive, the line cuts off the y-axis *above* the x-axis. If the intercept is negative, the line cuts off the y-axis *below* the x-axis. If the intercept is 0, it intersects with the y-axis and the x-axis at the point called the *origin.*

And now, back to what I was originally talking about.

Regression: What a Line!

I mention earlier that a line is the best way to summarize the relationship in the scatterplot in Figure 14-1. It's possible to draw an infinite number of straight lines through the scatterplot. Which one best summarizes the relationship?

Intuitively, the *best-fitting* line ought to be the one that passes through the maximum number of points and isn't too far away from the points it doesn't pass through. For statisticians, that line has a special property: If you draw that line through the scatterplot, draw distances (in the vertical direction) between the points and the line, and then square those distances and add them up, the sum of the squared distances is a minimum.

Statisticians call this line the *regression line,* and they indicate it as

$$y' = a + bx$$

Each y' (pronounced "y prime") is a point on the line. It represents the best prediction of y for a given value of x.

To figure out exactly where this line is, you calculate its slope and its intercept. For a regression line, the slope and intercept are called *regression coefficients.*

The formulas for the regression coefficients are pretty straightforward. For the slope, the formula is

$$b = \frac{\sum(x - \bar{x})(y - \bar{y})}{\sum(x - \bar{x})^2}$$

The intercept formula is

$$a = \bar{y} - b\bar{x}$$

I illustrate with an example. To keep the numbers manageable and comprehensible, I use a small sample instead of the hundreds (or perhaps thousands) of employees you'd find in a scatterplot for a corporation. Table 14-2 shows a sample of data from 16 FarMisht consultants.

TABLE 14-2

Aptitude Scores and Performance Scores for 16 FarMisht Consultants

Consultant	Aptitude	Performance
1	45	56
2	81	74
3	65	56
4	87	81
5	68	75
6	91	84
7	77	68
8	61	52
9	55	57
10	66	82
11	82	73
12	93	90
13	76	67
14	83	79
15	61	70
16	74	66
Mean	72.81	70.63
Variance	181.63	126.65
Standard deviation	13.48	11.25

For this set of data, the slope of the regression line is

$$b = \frac{\begin{array}{c}(45-72.81)(56-70.63)(81-72.81)(74-70.63)+ \ldots \\ (74-72.81)(66-70.63)\end{array}}{(45-72.81)^2 + (81-72.81)^2 + \ldots (74-72.81)^2}$$

$$= 0.654$$

The intercept is

$$a = \bar{y} - b\bar{x} = 70.63 - 0.654(72.81) = 23.03$$

So the equation of the best-fitting line through these 16 points is

$$y' = 23.03 + 0.654x$$

Or, in terms of Performance and Aptitude, it's

$$Predicted\ Performance = 23.03 + 0.654(Aptitude)$$

The slope and the intercept of a regression line are generically called *regression coefficients*.

REMEMBER

Using regression for forecasting

Based on this sample and this regression line, you can take an applicant's Aptitude score — say, 85 — and predict the applicant's Performance:

$$Predicted\ Performance = 23.03 + 0.654(85) = 78.59$$

Without this regression line, the only prediction is the mean Performance, 70.63.

Variation around the regression line

In Chapter 5, I explain how the mean doesn't tell the whole story about a set of data. You have to show how the scores vary around the mean. For that reason, I introduce the variance and standard deviation.

You have a similar situation here. To form the full picture of the relationship in a scatterplot, you have to show how the scores vary around the regression line. Here, I introduce the residual variance and standard error of estimate, which are analogous to the variance and the standard deviation, respectively.

The *residual variance* is sort of an average of the squared deviations of the observed y-values around the predicted y-values. Each deviation of a data point from a predicted point $(y - y')$ is called a *residual*; hence, the name. The formula is

$$s_{yx}^2 = \frac{\sum(y - y')^2}{N - 2}$$

I say "sort of" because the denominator is $N-2$ rather than N. Telling you the reason for the -2 is beyond the scope of this discussion. As I mention in Chapter 5, the denominator of a variance estimate is *degrees of freedom* (df), and that concept comes in handy in a little while.

The *standard error of estimate* is

$$s_{yx} = \sqrt{s_{yx}^2} = \sqrt{\frac{\sum(y-y')^2}{N-2}}$$

To show you how the residual error and the standard error of estimate play out for the data in the example, here's Table 14-3. This table extends Table 14-2 by showing the predicted Performance score for each given Aptitude score.

TABLE 14-3 **Aptitude Scores, Performance Scores, and Predicted Performance Scores for 16 FarMisht Consultants**

Consultant	Aptitude	Performance	Predicted Performance
1	45	56	52.44
2	81	74	75.98
3	65	56	65.52
4	87	81	79.90
5	68	75	67.48
6	91	84	82.51
7	77	68	73.36
8	61	52	62.90
9	55	57	58.98
10	66	82	66.17
11	82	73	76.63
12	93	90	83.82
13	76	67	72.71
14	83	79	77.28
15	61	70	62.90
16	74	66	71.40
Mean	72.81	70.63	
Variance	181.63	126.65	
Standard deviation	13.48	11.25	

As the table shows, sometimes the predicted Performance score is pretty close, and sometimes it's not.

For these data, the residual variance is

$$s_{yx}^2 = \frac{\sum (y - y')^2}{N - 2} = \frac{(56 - 52.44)^2 + (74 - 75.98)^2 + \ldots + (66 - 71.40)^2}{16 - 2} = \frac{735.65}{14}$$
$$= 52.54$$

The standard error of estimate is

$$s_{yx} = \sqrt{s_{yx}^2} = \sqrt{52.54} = 7.25$$

If the residual variance and the standard error of estimate are small, the regression line is a good fit to the data in the scatterplot. If the residual variance and the standard error of estimate are large, the regression line is a poor fit.

What's "small"? What's "large"? What's a "good" fit?

Keep reading.

Testing hypotheses about regression

The regression equation you're working with:

$$y' = a + bx$$

summarizes a relationship in a scatterplot of a sample. The regression coefficients a and b are sample statistics. You can use these statistics to test hypotheses about population parameters, and that's what you do in this section.

The regression line through the population that produces the sample (like the entire set of FarMisht consultants) is the graph of an equation that consists of parameters rather than statistics. By convention, remember, Greek letters stand for parameters, so the regression equation for the population is

$$y' = \alpha + \beta x + \varepsilon$$

The first two Greek letters on the right are α (alpha) and β (beta) — the equivalents of a and b. What about that last one? It looks a little like the Greek equivalent of e. What's it doing there?

That last term is the Greek letter *epsilon*. It represents "error" in the population. In a way, *error* is an unfortunate term. It's a catchall for "things you don't know or things you have no control over." Error is reflected in the residuals — the deviations from the predictions. The more you understand about what you're measuring, the more you decrease the error.

You can't measure the error in the relationship between Aptitude and Performance, but it's lurking there. Someone might score low on Aptitude, for example, and then go on to have a wonderful consulting career with a higher-than-predicted Performance. On a scatterplot, this person's Aptitude–Performance point looks like an error in prediction. As you find out more about that person, you might discover that they were sick on the day of the Aptitude test, and that explains the "error."

You can test hypotheses about α, β, and ε, and that's what you do in the upcoming subsections.

Testing the fit

You begin with a test of how well the regression line fits the scatterplot. This is a test of ε, the error in the relationship.

The objective is to decide whether the line really does represent a relationship between the variables. It's possible that what looks like a relationship is just due to chance and that the equation of the regression line doesn't mean anything (because the amount of error is overwhelming) — or it's possible that the variables are strongly related.

These possibilities are testable, and you set up hypotheses to test them:

H_0 : No real relationship

H_1 : Not H_0

Although those hypotheses make for nice, light reading, they don't set up a statistical test. To set up the test, you have to consider the variances. To consider the variances, you start with the deviations. Figure 14-3 focuses on one point in a scatterplot and its deviation from the regression line (the residual) and from the mean of the y-variable. It also shows the deviation between the regression line and the mean.

As the figure shows, the distance between the point and the regression line and the distance between the regression line and the mean add up to the distance between the point and the mean:

$$(y - y') + (y' - \bar{y}) = (y - \bar{y})$$

This sets the stage for some other important relationships.

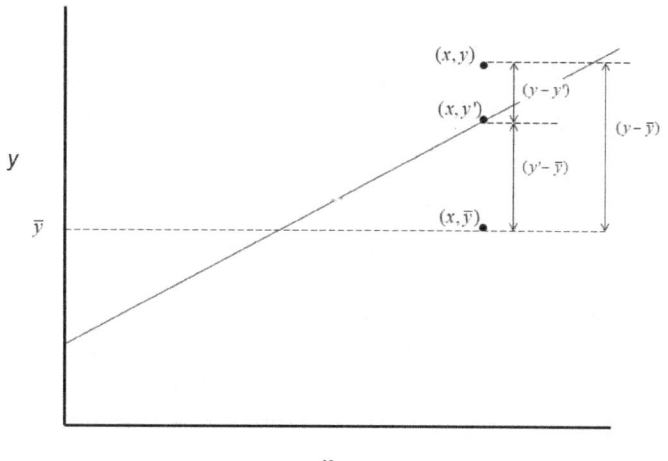

FIGURE 14-3:
The deviations in
a scatterplot.

Start by squaring each deviation. That gives you $(y-y')^2$, $(y'-\bar{y})^2$, and $(y-\bar{y})^2$. If you add up each of the squared deviations, you have

$$\sum(y-y')^2$$

You just saw this one. That's the numerator for the residual variance. It represents the variability around the regression line — the "error" I mention earlier. In the terminology of Chapter 12, the numerator of a variance is called a sum of squares, or SS. So, this is $SS_{Residual}$.

$$\sum(y'-\bar{y})^2$$

This one is new. The deviation $(y'-\bar{y})$ represents the gain in prediction due to using the regression line rather than the mean. The sum reflects this gain and is called $SS_{Regression}$:

$$\sum(y-\bar{y})^2$$

I show you this one in Chapter 5 — although I use x rather than y. That's the numerator of the variance of y. In Chapter 12 terms, it's the numerator of *total variance*. This one is SS_{Total}.

This relationship holds among these three sums:

$$SS_{Residual} + SS_{Regression} = SS_{Total}$$

Each one is associated with a value for degrees of freedom — the denominator of a variance estimate. As I point out in the preceding section, the denominator for $SS_{Residual}$ is $N-2$. The df for SS_{Total} is $N-1$ (see Chapters 5 and 12). As with the SS, the degrees of freedom add up:

$$df_{Residual} + df_{Regression} = df_{Total}$$

This leaves one degree of freedom for Regression.

Where is all this headed, and what does it have to do with hypothesis testing? Well, since you asked, you get variance estimates by dividing SS by df. Each variance estimate is called a *mean-square*, abbreviated MS (again, see Chapter 12):

$$MS_{Regression} = \frac{SS_{Regression}}{df_{Regression}}$$

$$MS_{Residual} = \frac{SS_{Residual}}{df_{Residual}}$$

$$MS_{Total} = \frac{SS_{Total}}{df_{Total}}$$

Now for the hypothesis part. If H_0 is true and what looks like a relationship between x and y is truly no big deal, the piece that represents the gain in prediction because of the regression line ($MS_{Regression}$) should be no greater than the variability around the regression line ($MS_{Residual}$). If H_0 is not true and the gain in prediction is substantial, $MS_{Regression}$ should be much bigger than $MS_{Residual}$.

So the hypotheses are now set up as

$$H_0 : \sigma^2_{Regression} \leq \sigma^2_{Residual}$$
$$H_1 : \sigma^2_{Regression} > \sigma^2_{Residual}$$

These are hypotheses you can test. How? To test a hypothesis about two variances, you use an F test (see Chapter 11). The test statistic here is

$$F = \frac{MS_{Regression}}{MS_{Residual}}$$

To show you how it all works, I apply the formulas to the FarMisht example. The $MS_{Residual}$ is the same as s^2_{yx} from the section "Variation around the regression line," earlier in this chapter, and that value is 18.61. The $MS_{Regression}$ is

$$MS_{Regression} = \frac{(59.64 - 70.63)^2 + (71.40 - 70.63)^2 + \ldots + (66.17 - 70.63)^2}{1} = 1164.1$$

This sets up the F:

$$F = \frac{MS_{Regression}}{MS_{Residual}} = \frac{1164.1}{52.55} = 22.15$$

With 1 and 14 df and α = .05, the critical value of F is 4.60. The calculated F is greater than the critical F, so the decision is to reject H_0. That means the regression line provides a good fit to the data in the sample.

Testing the slope

Another question that arises in linear regression is whether the slope of the regression line is significantly different from zero. If it's not, the mean is just as good a predictor as the regression line.

In this example, the hypotheses for this test are

$$H_0 : \beta \leq 0$$
$$H_1 : \beta > 0$$

It's a directional (one-tailed) test because the Aptitude test is set up for higher Aptitude scores to correspond with higher levels of performance and lower Aptitude scores with lower levels of performance.

The statistical test is t, which I discuss in Chapters 9, 10, and 11 in connection with means. The t-test for the slope is

$$t = \frac{b - \beta}{s_b}$$

with df = $N-2$. The denominator estimates the standard error of the slope. This term sounds more complicated than it is. The formula is

$$s_b = \frac{s_{yx}}{s_x \sqrt{(N-1)}}$$

where s_x is the standard deviation of the x-variable. For the data in the example:

$$s_b = \frac{s_{yx}}{s_x \sqrt{(N-1)}} = \frac{7.25}{(13.48)\sqrt{(16-1)}} = .139$$

$$t = \frac{b - \beta}{s_b} = \frac{.654 - 0}{.139} = 4.71$$

This is greater than the critical value of t for 14 df and α = .05 (2.14), so the decision is to reject H_0.

Testing the intercept

Finally, here's the hypothesis test for the intercept. The hypotheses are

$$H_0 : \alpha = 0$$
$$H_1 : \alpha \neq 0$$

The test, once again, is a t-test. The formula is

$$t = \frac{a - \alpha}{s_a}$$

The denominator is the estimate of the standard error of the intercept. Without going into detail, the formula for s_a is

$$s_a = s_{yx} \sqrt{\left[\frac{1}{N} + \frac{\bar{x}^2}{(N-1)s_x^2} \right]}$$

where s_x is the standard deviation of the x-variable, s_x^2 is the variance of the x-variable, and $\bar{x}^2$ is the squared mean of the x-variable. Applying this formula to the data in the example,

$$s_a = s_{yx} \sqrt{\left[\frac{1}{N} + \frac{\bar{x}^2}{(N-1)s_x^2} \right]} = 10.27$$

the t-test is

$$t = \frac{a - \alpha}{s_a} = \frac{23.03}{10.27} = 2.24$$

With 15 degrees of freedom, and the probability of a Type I error at .05, the critical t is 2.13 for a two-tailed test. (It's a two-tailed test because H_1 is that the intercept doesn't equal 0 — it doesn't specify whether the intercept is greater than 0 or less than 0.) Because the calculated value is greater than the critical value, the decision is to reject H_0.

Linear Regression in Python

It's time to see how Python handles linear regression. I start with the necessary import:

```
import pandas as pd
```

To start the analysis for this example, I create a list for the Aptitude scores and another for the Performance scores:

```
Aptitude = [45, 81, 65, 87, 68, 91, 77, 61, 55, 66, 82, 93, 76,
    83, 61, 74]
Performance = [56, 74, 56, 81, 75, 84, 68, 52, 57, 82, 73, 90,
    67, 79, 70, 66]
```

Then I combine the two vectors into a dictionary

```
FarMisht_data = {'Aptitude':Aptitude, 'Performance':Performance}
```

and create a DataFrame:

```
FarMisht_data_frame = pd.DataFrame(FarMisht_data)
```

The `statsmodels` library supplies the analysis tool:

```
import statsmodels.formula.api as smf
```

Here's how to use the tool:

```
model = smf.ols('Performance ~ Aptitude', data = FarMisht_data_
    frame).fit()
```

I show you code like this in Chapters 12 and 13, and I deferred a detailed explanation until now. Here it is:

> The `ols()` function sets the stage for an *ordinary least squares* model with
> Performance as the dependent variable and Aptitude as the independent variable
> in the DataFrame.

> This means that the objective is to generate the line that minimizes the sum of the
> squared distances between the points in the scatterplot and the points on the line.

> The `fit()` function finds the slope and intercept that make that happen. In other
> words, it "fits" the line to the data.

Now let's examine the details of the fit:

```
print(model.summary())

                    OLS Regression Results
==================================================================
Dep. Variable:      Performance    R-squared:             0.613
Model:                      OLS    Adj. R-squared:        0.585
Method:           Least Squares    F-statistic:           22.15
```

```
Date:                Wed, 21 May 2025  Prob (F-statistic)   0.000337
Time:                     21:30:33     Log-Likelihood:        -53.328
No. Observations:               16     AIC:                     110.7
Df Residuals:                   14     BIC:                     112.2
Df Model:                        1
Covariance Type:          nonrobust
================================================================
                 coef   std err        t    P>|t|    [0.025    0.975]
----------------------------------------------------------------
Intercept     23.0299    10.273    2.242    0.042     0.996    45.064
Aptitude       0.6537     0.139    4.707    0.000     0.356     0.952
================================================================
Omnibus:                      1.112    Durbin-Watson:             2.18
Prob(Omnibus):                0.574    Jarque-Bera (JB):         0.598
Skew:                         0.465    Prob(JB):                 0.742
Kurtosis:                     2.821    Cond. No.                  419.
================================================================
```

The middle part of the table holds the regression coefficients, their standard errors, and their significance tests. The tests indicate that each coefficient is significantly greater than zero.

The upper part of the table shows the F-statistic that tests the model's fit to the data. The high value of the F-statistic and the low associated probability indicate that the model (the regression line, in other words) fits the data well.

We can ignore everything else in the upper part of the table — although I do tell you about R-squared in Chapter 15. For now, I just tell you that it's called the *coefficient of determination* and it measures the association between the dependent variable and the independent variable. A higher value means more association; a lower value means less. Its maximum value is 1.00; its minimum is 0.00. The higher the association, the better the fit of the regression line.

If that's the case, R-squared should be related to F, and it is:

$$F = \frac{R^2}{1 - R^2} \times \frac{df_{\text{Residual}}}{df_{\text{Model}}}$$

We can ignore everything in the lower part of the table.

The coefficients are also in model.params in the fitted model. You can retrieve them if you need them:

```
intercept = model.params['Intercept']
slope = model.params['Aptitude']
print(f"Intercept = {intercept}")
print(f"Slope = {slope}")
Intercept = 23.02986855084771
Slope = 0.6536670413617487
```

I use this technique a bit later when I show you how to visualize a more complicated model.

You can also retrieve F and Prob(F), but in a slightly different way:

```
F= model.fvalue
print('F = ', F)
Prob_F = model.f_pvalue
print('Prob(F) = ', Prob_F)
F =   22.15370680824192
Prob(F) =   0.00033684884649344364
```

I retrieve F and Prob(F) in an upcoming section on analysis of covariance.

Regression and ANOVA

If you go back and reread the subsection where I introduce F as the test for how well the model fits the data, it might dawn on you that the test of fit is really an ANOVA. You might also develop the strong impression that linear regression and ANOVA are the same thing.

If that's what you're thinking — you're right!

If you're also thinking that we can use our model as the basis of an ANOVA — you're right again!

Just to show you, here's the tool that gets it done:

```
from statsmodels.stats.anova import anova_lm
```

I can also reveal that lm stands for *linear model*:

```
anova_table = anova_lm(model)
print(anova_table)
             df       sum_sq       mean_sq           F     PR(>F)
Aptitude   1.0     1164.099      1164.099    22.15370   0.000337
Residual  14.0   735.650708     52.546479         NaN        NaN
```

Making predictions using Python

The value of linear regression is that it gives you the ability to predict, and model.predict() does just that.

Imagine that three FarMisht applicants have Aptitude scores of 85, 62, and 73. What is the prediction for their Performance scores?

First, I create a DataFrame of the applicants' Aptitude scores:

```
applicant_aptitude = pd.DataFrame({'Aptitude': [85, 62, 73]})
```

Then I let model.predict() do its thing:

```
predicted_performance = model.predict(applicant_aptitude)
print(applicant_aptitude)
print("\nPredicted Performance")
print(predicted_performance)
        Aptitude
0             85
1             62
2             73

Predicted Performance
0      78.591567
1      63.557225
2      70.747563
dtype: float64
```

TIP

You can ignore the unsightly dtype: float64 on the last line.

Visualizing the scatterplot and regression line

The seaborn library makes it easy to visualize the scatterplot and its regression line for our example, along with shading that shows the 95% confidence interval around the line.

I start with the imports:

```
import matplotlib.pyplot as plt
import seaborn as sns
import pandas as pd
```

Then I set the size of the figure:

```
plt.figure(figsize=(10, 6))
```

I use the regplot() function in the seaborn library to create the plot:

```
sns.regplot(x='Aptitude', y='Performance', data=FarMisht_data_
    frame, ci=95, color = 'black')
```

The ci argument sets the confidence interval at 95%. I added the color argument to make sure the plot looks good on this page.

I label the axes, add a grid, and show the plot:

```
plt.xlabel('Aptitude')
plt.ylabel('Performance')
plt.grid(True)
plt.show()
```

The result is shown in Figure 14-4.

Plotting the residuals

After a regression analysis, it's a good idea to plot the residuals against the predicted values. If the residuals form a random pattern around a horizontal line at 0, that's evidence in favor of a linear relationship between the independent variable and the dependent variable.

Figure 14-5 shows the residual plot for the example. The pattern of residuals around the line is consistent with a linear model.

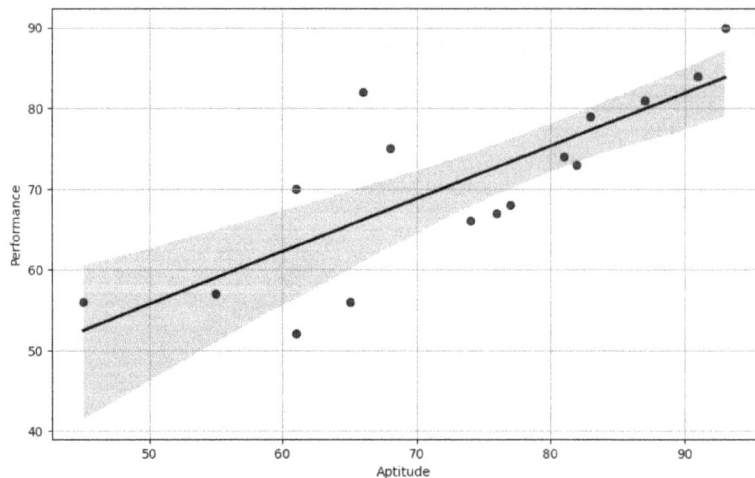

FIGURE 14-4:
Scatterplot
and regression
line for the
16 FarMisht
consultants.

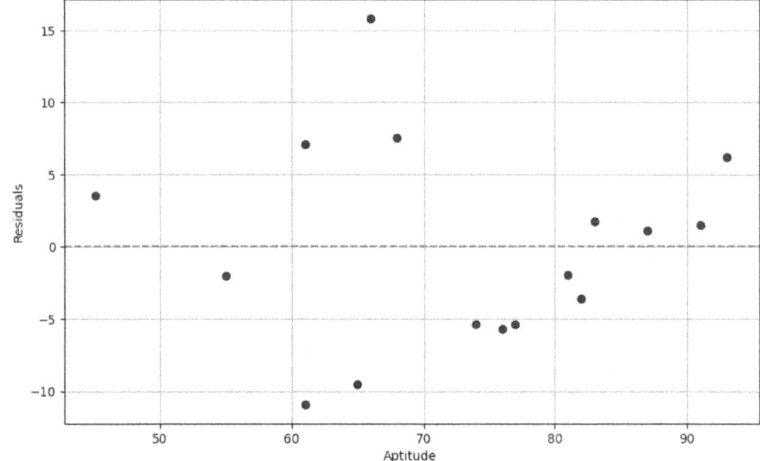

FIGURE 14-5:
Residuals plot for
the FarMisht
example.

The code for Figure 14-5 is based on the `residplot()` function in the seaborn library. First come the imports and the figure size:

```
import matplotlib.pyplot as plt
import seaborn as sns
import pandas as pd
plt.figure(figsize=(10, 6))
```

Here's the seaborn function:

```
sns.residplot(x='Aptitude', y='Performance', data=FarMisht_data_
    frame, color = 'black')
```

I label the axes and add a grid:

```
plt.xlabel('Aptitude')
plt.ylabel('Residuals')
plt.grid(True)
```

I add a dotted line at y = 0

```
plt.axhline(y=0, color='gray', linestyle='--', linewidth=1.5)
```

and show the plot:

```
plt.show()
```

Juggling Many Relationships at Once: Multiple Regression

Linear regression is a useful tool for making predictions. When you know the slope and the intercept of the line that relates two variables, you can take a new x-value and predict a new y-value. In the example you've been working through in this chapter, you take an Aptitude score and predict a Performance score for a FarMisht applicant.

What if you knew more than just the Aptitude score for each applicant? For example, imagine that the FarMisht management team decides that a particular personality type is ideal for their consultants. So they develop the FarMisht Personality Inventory, a 20-point scale in which a higher score indicates greater compatibility with the FarMisht corporate culture and, presumably, predicts better performance. The idea is to use that data along with Aptitude scores to predict performance.

Table 14-4 shows the Aptitude, Performance, and Personality scores for the 16 current consultants. Of course, in a real-life corporation, you might have many more employees in the sample.

When you work with more than one independent variable, you're in the realm of *multiple regression.* As in linear regression, you find regression coefficients. In the case of two independent variables, you're looking for the best-fitting *plane* through a three-dimensional scatterplot. Once again, the term *best-fitting* means that the sum of the squared distances from the data points to the plane is a minimum.

TABLE 14-4

Aptitude, Performance, and Personality Scores for 16 FarMisht Consultants

Consultant	Aptitude	Performance	Personality
1	45	56	9
2	81	74	15
3	65	56	11
4	87	81	15
5	68	75	14
6	91	84	19
7	77	68	12
8	61	52	10
9	55	57	9
10	66	82	14
11	82	73	15
12	93	90	14
13	76	67	16
14	83	79	18
15	61	70	15
16	74	66	12
Mean	72.81	70.63	13.63
Variance	181.63	126.65	8.65
Standard Deviation	13.48	11.25	2.94

Here's the equation of the regression plane:

$$y' = a + b_1 x_1 + b_2 x_2$$

You can test hypotheses about the overall fit and about all three of the regression coefficients.

I don't walk you through all the formulas for finding the coefficients, because that gets *really* complicated. Instead, I go right to the Python analysis.

Here are a few things to bear in mind before I proceed:

» You can have any number of x-variables. (I use two in this example.)

» Expect the coefficient for Aptitude to change from linear regression to multiple regression. Expect the intercept to change, too.

» Expect the standard error of estimate to decrease from linear regression to multiple regression. Because multiple regression uses more information than linear regression, it reduces the error.

Multiple regression in Python

I begin by creating a list for the personality scores in Column 4 of Table 14-4, and then I add the list to the FarMisht DataFrame:

```
Personality = [9, 15, 11, 15, 14, 19, 12, 10, 9, 14, 15, 14,
16, 18, 15, 12]
FarMisht_data_frame['Personality'] = Personality
```

It's time for another ordinary least squares fit, so

```
import statsmodels.formula.api as smf
model = smf.ols('Performance ~ Aptitude + Personality', data =
   FarMisht_data_frame).fit()
```

As you can see, the formula this time shows Performance depending on Aptitude and Personality.

Now, a look at the results:

```
print(model.summary())

                    OLS Regression Results
==============================================================
Dep. Variable:      Performance    R-squared:           0.690
Model:                      OLS    Adj. R-squared:      0.642
Method:           Least Squares    F-statistic:         14.47
Date:         Thu, 22 May 2025    Prob (F-statistic)  0.000494
Time:                 17:46:42    Log-Likelihood:     -51.548
No. Observations:            16    AIC:                 109.1
```

```
Df Residuals:               13    BIC:                    111.4
Df Model:                    2
Covariance Type:     nonrobust
==========================================================================
                  coef   std err        t    P>|t|    [0.025    0.975]
--------------------------------------------------------------------------
Intercept    20.2825     9.659    2.100    0.056    -0.586    41.150
Aptitude      0.3905     0.195    2.003    0.066    -0.031     0.812
Personality   1.6079     0.893    1.800    0.095    -0.322     3.538
==========================================================================
Omnibus:                 1.852    Durbin-Watson:            2.486
Prob(Omnibus):           0.396    Jarque-Bera (JB):         1.094
Skew:                    0.635    Prob(JB):                 0.579
Kurtosis:                2.827    Cond. No                   432.
==========================================================================
```

Once again, the high value of the `F-statistic` and the low value of `Prob(F-statistic)` in the upper part of the table indicate that the linear model fits the data very well.

The linear model, in generic form is

$$Predicted\ Performance = a + b_1(Aptitude) + b_2(Personality)$$

The coefficients (Intercept, Aptitude, and Personality) are in the middle part of the table, so the equation for the model in this example is

$$y' = 20.2825 + 0.3905x_1 + 1.6079x_2$$

Making predictions

Once again, `model.predict()` enables predictions of Performance. This time, I use it with the multiple regression model.

Imagine two applicants: The first has Aptitude and Personality scores of 85 and 14, the second has Aptitude and Personality scores of 62 and 17, the third has Aptitude and Personality scores of 73 and 20. This requires two lists — one for the Aptitude scores and one for the Personality scores — and I turn them into a DataFrame:

```
applicant_aptitude_and_personality = pd.DataFrame({'Aptitude':
    [85, 62, 73],'Personality': [14,17,20]})
```

Then I call on `model.predict()` and print the predictions:

```
predicted_performance = model.
    predict(applicant_aptitude_and_personality)
print(applicant_aptitude_and_personality)
print("\nPredicted Performance")
print(predicted_performance)
        Aptitude        Personality
0             85                 14
1             62                 17
2             73                 20

Predicted Performance
     0        75.987420
     1        71.829236
     2        80.948698
dtype:       float64
```

TIP

Again, you can ignore the unsightly `dtype: float64` on the last line.

Visualizing the 3D scatterplot and regression plane

In this section, I show you how to use `matplotlib` and `numpy` to create the snappy 3D scatterplot in Figure 14-6.

TIP

I put the dashed vertical lines in Figure 14-6 because I think they help the viewer perceive where the points are in the 3-dimensional space.

REMEMBER

When I talk about the multiple regression model, I refer to the independent variables as X_1 and X_2, and to the dependent variable as Y. In the context of plotting, I refer to them as x, y, and z, respectively, to be consistent with `matplotlib`.

I begin with the imports:

```
import matplotlib.pyplot as plt
import numpy as np
```

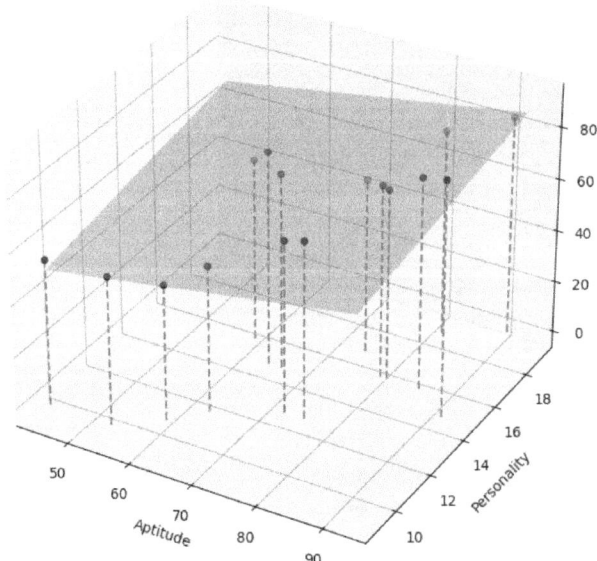

FIGURE 14-6:
Scatterplot for
the FarMisht
multiple
regression
example.

Next, I set up the data so that the subsequent code is easy to read:

```
x=FarMisht_data_frame['Aptitude']
y=FarMisht_data_frame['Personality']
z=FarMisht_data_frame['Performance']
```

Then I create the figure and the 3-dimensional plot:

```
fig = plt.figure(figsize=(10, 8))
ax = fig.add_subplot(projection='3d')
```

Now I add the scatterplot

```
scatter = ax.scatter(x,y,z,c='black', marker='o')
```

and label the axes:

```
ax.set_xlabel('Aptitude')
ax.set_ylabel('Personality')
ax.set_zlabel('Performance')
```

Now I use a for loop to add the dashed vertical lines from the x-y plane to the data points:

```
for i in range(len(x)):
    ax.plot([x[i],x[i]],[y[i], y[i]],[0,z[i]], color='gray',
    linestyle='--')
```

Next, I add the regression plane. I use np.meshgrid() to create a grid of x-y points that ultimately constitute the plane. To set that up, I use linspace() to create 100 evenly spaced points from the minimum value of x (Aptitude) to its maximum value, and 100 evenly spaced points from the minimum value of y (Personality) to its maximum value:

```
x_range = np.linspace(min(x), max(x), 100)
y_range = np.linspace(min(y), max(y), 100)
```

Consider each range to be a 1-dimensional array of 100 evenly spaced points. Then meshgrid() goes to work, creating a 2-dimensional array of 10,000 points:

```
X, Y = np.meshgrid(x_range, y_range)
```

The next step is to use the regression coefficients (that is, the model parameters) to position the 2-dimensional array within the 3-dimensional space:

```
Z = model.params['Intercept'] + model.params['Aptitude'] * X +
    model.params['Personality'] * Y
```

Then I plot the 2-dimensional array

```
ax.plot_surface(X, Y, Z, color='gray', alpha=0.4)
```

and show the whole thing:

```
plt.show()
```

And that's Figure 14-6.

ANOVA: Another Look

Let me revisit a statement I made earlier: Analysis of variance and linear regression *are really the same thing.*

They're both part of what's called the general linear model (GLM). In linear regression, the objective is to predict a value of a dependent variable given a value of an independent variable. In ANOVA, the objective is to decide whether several sample means differ enough from one another to enable you to reject the null hypothesis about levels of the independent variable.

How are they similar? It's easier to see the connection if you rethink ANOVA: Given the data, imagine that the objective is to predict the dependent variable given the level of the independent variable. What would be the best prediction? For any level of the independent variable, that would be the mean of the sample for that level — also known as the *group mean*. This means that deviations from the group mean (the best predicted value) are residuals, and this is why, in a Python ANOVA, the MS_{Error} is called $MS_{Residuals}$.

It goes deeper than that. To show you how, I revisit the ANOVA example from Chapter 12. For convenience, here's Table 12-1 reproduced as Table 14-5.

TABLE 14-5

Data from Three Training Methods (ANOVA Example from Chapter 12)

	Method 1	Method 2	Method 3
	95	83	68
	91	89	75
	89	85	79
	90	89	74
	99	81	75
	88	89	81
	96	90	73
	98	82	77
	95	84	
		80	
Mean	93.44	85.20	75.25
Variance	16.28	14.18	15.64
Standard Deviation	4.03	3.77	3.96

You have to test

$H_0 : \mu_1 = \mu_2 = \mu_3$

$H_1 : $ Not H_0

In Chapter 12, I created a long format method_data_frame.

When I carried out the ANOVA, the result was this:

```
              df       sum_sq      mean_sq          F        PR(>F)
Method      2.0  1402.677778   701.338889  45.823891  6.380978e-09
Residual   24.0   367.322222    15.305093        NaN           NaN
```

How about a linear regression analysis on the data?

```
import statsmodels.formula.api as smf
model = smf.ols('Score ~ Method', data = method_data_frame).fit()
print(model.summary())


                           OLS Regression Results
===============================================================================
Dep. Variable:             Score   R-squared:                       0.792
Model:                       OLS   Adj. R-squared:                  0.775
Method:            Least Squares   F-statistic:                     45.82
Date:          Fri, 23 May 2025   Prob (F-statistic):           6.38e-09
Time:                  21:56:54   Log-Likelihood:                -73.552
No. Observations:            27   AIC:                             153.1
Df Residuals:                24   BIC:                             157.0
Df Model:                     2
Covariance Type:      nonrobust
===============================================================================
                       coef std err        t P>|t|    [0.025   0.975]
-------------------------------------------------------------------------------
Intercept           93.4444   1.304  71.657 0.000    90.753   96.136
Method[T.Method 2]  -8.2444   1.798  -4.587 0.000   -11.954   -4.535
Method[T.Method 3] -18.1944   1.901  -9.571 0.000   -22.118  -14.271
===============================================================================
Omnibus:                   3.685   Durbin-Watson:                   2.195
Prob(Omnibus):             0.158   Jarque-Bera (JB):                1.510
Skew:                     -0.107   Prob(JB):                        0.470
Kurtosis:                  1.862   Cond. No.                        3.75
-------------------------------------------------------------------------------
```

You see a good bit more information than in the ANOVA table, but the upper part of the table shows the same F-ratio as the analysis of variance. Also, the coefficients provide the group means: The intercept (93.444) is the mean of Method 1, the intercept plus the second coefficient (−8.244) is the mean of Method 2 (85.20), and the intercept plus the third coefficient (−18.194) is the mean of Method 3 (75.25). Check the Means in Table 14-1 if you don't believe me.

A bit more on the coefficients: The intercept represents Method 1, which is a baseline against which to compare each of the others. The *t*-value for Method 2 (along with its associated probability, which is much less than .05) shows that Method 2 differs significantly from Method 1. It's the same story for Method 3, which also differs significantly from Method 1.

Here's a question that should be forming in your mind: How can you perform a linear regression when the independent variable (Method) is categorical rather than numerical?

Glad you asked.

REMEMBER

To form a regression analysis with categorical data, Python (and other statistical software packages) recode the levels of a variable like Method into combinations of numeric *dummy variables*. The only values a dummy variable can take are 0 or 1: 0 indicates the *absence* of a categorical value; 1 indicates the *presence* of a categorical value.

For the three levels of Method (Method 1, Method 2, and Method 3), I need two dummy variables. I'll call them D1 and D2. Here are their values:

» For Method 1, D1 = 0 and D2 = 0

» For Method 2, D1 = 1, and D2 = 0

» For Method 3, D1 = 0, and D2 = 1

To illustrate further, here's a DataFrame called method_data_frame_with_ dummies. Ordinarily, I wouldn't show you all 27 rows of a DataFrame, but here I think it's instructive:

	Score	D1	D2
0	95	0	0
1	91	0	0
2	89	0	0
3	90	0	0
4	99	0	0
5	88	0	0
6	96	0	0
7	98	0	0
8	95	0	0
9	83	1	0
10	89	1	0
11	85	1	0
12	89	1	0

13	81	1	0
14	89	1	0
15	90	1	0
16	82	1	0
17	84	1	0
18	80	1	0
19	68	0	1
20	75	0	1
21	79	0	1
22	74	0	1
23	75	0	1
24	81	0	1
25	73	0	1
26	77	0	1

This code snippet

```
model = smf.ols('Score ~ D1 + D2', data = method_data_frame_
    with_dummies).fit()
print(model.summary())
```

yields the same output as the one I just showed you. The only difference is that the coefficients are expressed in terms of the dummy variables:

	coef	std err	t	P>|t|	[0.025	0.975]
Intercep	93.4444	1.304	71.657	0.000	90.753	96.136
D1	-8.2444	1.798	-4.587	0.000	-11.954	-4.535
D2	18.1944	1.901	-9.571	0.000	-22.118	-14.271

TECHNICAL
STUFF

If you'd like to attempt this exercise, here's how to create the dummies DataFrame:

```
method_data_frame_with_dummies = pd.get_dummies(method_data_
    frame, columns=['Method'], drop_first=True, dtype = int)
```

The pd.get_dummies() function creates three dummy variables. The first is unnecessary, so drop.first = True. Also, dtype = int creates 1 and 0 rather than True and False.

I create a set of new column names because the default names aren't helpful:

```
new_col_names = ['Score', 'D1', 'D2']
method_data_frame_with_dummies.columns = new_col_names
```

So dummy variables enable a linear regression model with categorical independent variables. In fact, linear regression with categorical independent variables *is* the analysis of variance.

Analysis of Covariance: The Final Component of the GLM

In this chapter, I show you how linear regression works with a numeric independent (predictor) variable, and with a categorical independent (predictor) variable. Is it possible to have a study with both a numeric predictor variable and a categorical predictor variable?

Absolutely! The analytical tool for this type of study is called the Analysis of Covariance (ANCOVA). It's the third and final component of the general linear model. (Linear regression and ANOVA are the first two.) The easiest way to describe it is with an example and an analysis in Python.

In the `MASS` package, which is an R resource, there is a DataFrame called `anorexia`. This DataFrame contains data for 72 young women randomly assigned to one of three types of treatment for anorexia: `Cont` (a control condition with no therapy), `CBT` (cognitive behavioral therapy), or `FT` (family treatment).

Here's how to turn it into a pandas DataFrame:

```
import statsmodels.api as sm
import pandas as pd
anorexia = sm.datasets.get_rdataset("anorexia", "MASS")
anorexia_data_frame = pd.DataFrame(anorexia.data)
```

Here are the first five rows:

```
print(anorexia_data_frame.head())
       Treat    Prewt    Postwt
0      Cont     80.7      80.2
1      Cont     89.4      80.1
2      Cont     91.8      86.4
3      Cont     74.0      86.3
4      Cont     78.1      76.1
```

Prewt is the weight before treatment, and Postwt is the weight after treatment. What you need, of course, is a variable that indicates the amount of weight gained during treatment. I'll call it WtGain, and here's how to add it to the DataFrame:

```
anorexia_data_frame["WtGain"] = anorexia_data_frame["Postwt"]
    - anorexia_data_frame["Prewt"]
```

Now:

```
print(anorexia_data_frame.head())
      Treat    Prewt    Postwt    WtGain
0     Cont     80.7     80.2      -0.5
1     Cont     89.4     80.1      -9.3
2     Cont     91.8     86.4      -5.4
3     Cont     74.0     86.3      12.3
4     Cont     78.1     76.1      -2.0
```

Figure 14-7 plots the data points for Weight Gain as the dependent variable and Treatment as the independent variable.

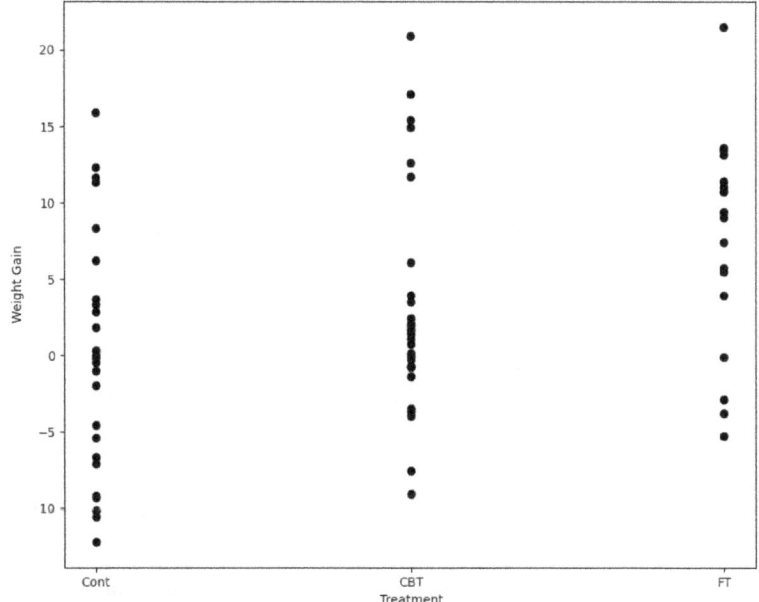

FIGURE 14-7:
Weight Gain
versus Treatment
in the anorexia
DataFrame.

Here's the code for this plot, in case you're curious:

```
import matplotlib.pyplot as pl

# Set the figure size and add the plot
fig = plt.figure(figsize=(10, 8))
ax = fig.add_subplot()

# Create the scatterplot
scatter = ax.scatter(x = "Treat", y = "WtGain",data = anorexia_
    data_frame,c='black', marker='o')

# Label the axes and show the plot
ax.set_xlabel('Treatment')
ax.set_ylabel('Weight Gain')
plt.show()
```

An analysis of variance or a linear regression analysis would be appropriate to test these:

$$H_0 : \mu_{\text{Cont}} = \mu_{\text{CBT}} = \mu_{\text{FT}}$$
$$H_1 : \text{Not } H_0$$

Here's the linear regression model:

```
model = smf.ols('WtGain ~ Treat', data = anorexia_data_
    frame).fit()
```

Rather than show the entire summary, here's the F and its associated probability:

```
F = model.fvalue
print(f'F = {F:.3f}')
Prob_F = model.f_pvalue
print(f'Prob(F) = {Prob_F:.4f}')
F =  5.422
Prob(F) = 0.0065
```

These values indicate that you can reject the null hypothesis.

Let's look at the coefficients. Here's the middle part of the summary (which I didn't print):

	coef	std err	t	P>|t|	[0.025	0.975]
Intercept	3.0069	1.398	2.151	0.035	0.218	5.796
Treat[T.Cont]	-3.4569	2.033	-1.700	0.094	-7.513	0.599
Treat[T.FT]	4.2578	2.300	1.852	0.068	-0.330	8.845

The intercept represents CBT. This is the baseline against which you compare the other treatments. The t-values and associated probabilities (greater than .05) tell you that neither of those levels differs from CBT. The significant F-ratio must result from some other comparisons.

Here's the analysis cast into an ANOVA table:

	df	sum_sq	mean_sq	F	PR(>F)
Treat	2.0	614.6436	307.321833	5.4222	0.006499
Residual	69.0	3910.742444	56.677427	NaN	NaN

I leave it as an exercise for you to create this table.

You can dig a little deeper. Suppose that weight gain depends not only on the type of treatment but also on a person's initial weight (which is called a *covariate*). Taking Prewt into consideration might yield a more accurate picture. Treat is a categorical variable, and Prewt is a numerical variable. Figure 14-8 is a plot showing WtGain depending on Treat and Prewt.

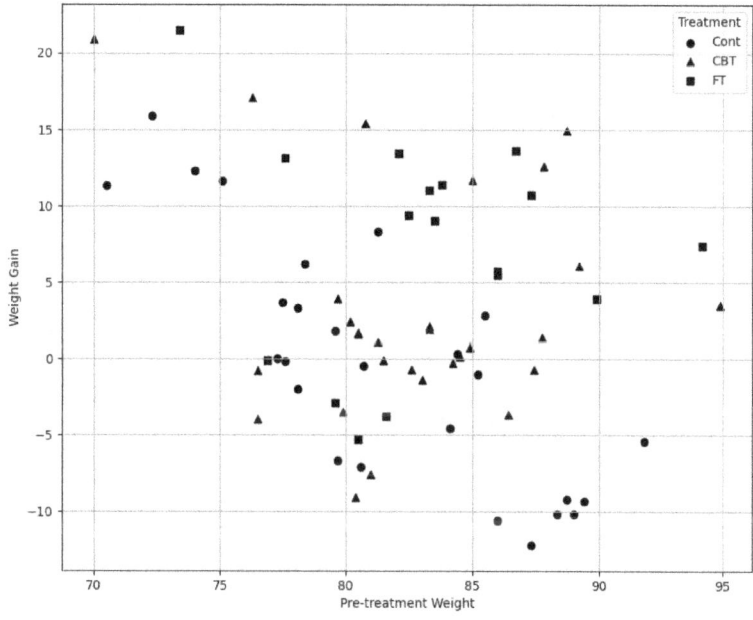

FIGURE 14-8: WtGain versus Treat and Prewt in the anorexia DataFrame.

Here's the code that produced the plot. First, I import `matplotlib`, set up the figure, and add the plot:

```
import matplotlib.pyplot as plt
fig = plt.figure(figsize=(10, 8))
ax = fig.add_subplot()
```

Inside the plot, I want each data point's shape to reflect that data point's treatment (CBT, Cont, or FT), so I first identify the unique treatment names

```
treatments = anorexia_data_frame['Treat'].unique()
```

and then I set the style of the data-point shapes:

```
markers = ['o', '^' ,'s']
```

Now I use a `for` loop to iterate through the data, creating a separate scatterplot for each treatment. Each treatment's data is contained in a subset of the anorexia DataFrame:

```
for i, treatment in enumerate(treatments):
    subset = anorexia_data_frame[anorexia_data_frame['Treat'] ==
    treatment]
    ax.scatter(x=subset['Prewt'], y=subset['WtGain'],
    marker=markers[i], label=treatment, c='black')
```

Then I label the axes, title the legend, set up a grid, and show the plot:

```
ax.set_xlabel('Pre-treatment Weight')
ax.set_ylabel('Weight Gain')
ax.legend(title='Treatment')
plt.grid(True)
plt.show()
```

An ANCOVA uncovers some differences that the ANOVA does not:

```
import statsmodels.formula.api as sm
ancova_model = sm.ols('WtGain ~ Treat + Prewt', data=anorexia_
    data_frame).fit()
print(ancova_model.summary())
```

Rather than show you the whole summary, here's the middle part with the coefficients:

	coef	std err	t	P>|t|	[0.025	0.975]
Intercept	49.7711	13.391	3.717	0.000	23.050	76.492
Treat[T.Cont]	-4.0971	1.893	-2.164	0.034	-7.875	-0.319
Treat[T.FT]	4.5631	2.133	2.139	0.036	0.306	8.820
Prewt	-0.5655	0.161	-3.509	0.001	-0.887	-0.244

This time, the *t*-values show that the difference between CBT and Cont is significant, as is the difference between CBT and FT.

The new F value is larger, too:

```
F = ancova_model.fvalue
print(f'F =  {F:.3f}')
Prob_F = ancova_model.f_pvalue
print(f'Prob(F) = {Prob_F:.4f}')
F =  8.311
Prob(F) = 0.0001
```

So it seems that adding Prewt to the analysis has helped uncover treatment differences. Bottom line: The ANCOVA shows that when evaluating the effect of an anorexia treatment, it's important to also know an individual's pretreatment weight.

But "it seems" is not quite sufficient for statisticians. Can you really and truly be sure that the ANCOVA adds value? To find out, you have to compare the linear regression model with the ANCOVA model. To make the comparison, use the stats.anova_lm() function, which does double duty: In addition to creating an ANOVA table for a model (which is the way you see it used earlier), you can use it to compare models. Here's how:

```
import statsmodels.api as sm
comparison = sm.stats.anova_lm(model,ancova_model)
print(comparison)
   df_resid          ssr  df_diff   ss_diff        F   Pr(>F)
0      69.0  3910.742444      0.0       NaN      NaN      NaN
1      68.0    3311.2626      1.0  599.4798  12.3109   0.0008
```

What do the numbers in the table mean? The ssr indicates the residual sums of squares from each model. They're next to their degrees of freedom in the df_resid column. In the df_diff column, 1 is the difference between the two df_resid. In the ss_diff column, 599.48 is the difference between the two ssr. The *F*-ratio is the result of dividing two mean squares: The mean square for the numerator is 599.48 divided by its df (1), and the mean square for the denominator is 3311.3 divided by its df (68). The high *F*-ratio and low Pr(>F) (probability of a Type 1 error) tell you that adding `Prewt` significantly lowered the residual sum of squares. In English, that means it was a good idea to add `Prewt` to the mix.

TECHNICAL STUFF

Statisticians would say that this analysis statistically controls for the effects of the covariate (`Prewt`).

But Wait — There's More

In an analysis of covariance, it's important to ask whether the relationship between the dependent variable and the numerical predictor variable (the covariate) is the same across the levels of the categorical variable.

In this example, that's the same as asking whether the slope of the regression line between `WtGain` and `Prewt` is the same for the scores in `Cont` as it is for the scores in `CBT` and for the scores in `FT`. If the slopes are the same, that's called *homogeneity of regression*. If not, you have an interaction of `Prewt` and `Treat`, and you have to be careful about how you state your conclusions.

Adding the regression lines to the plot in Figure 14-8 is helpful. To do this, I add this line before the `for` loop that produced Figure 14-8:

```
linestyles = ['-', '--', ':']
```

This renders a different line style for each treatment.

Then I add four lines to the end of the `for` loop. The first one fits a regression line to the subset (`Cont`, `CBT`, or `FT`) that the `for` loop is working on:

```
model_subset = smf.ols('WtGain ~ Prewt', data=subset).fit()
```

The second creates a range of `Prewt` values that lie within the subset's range:

```
prewt_range = pd.DataFrame({'Prewt': [subset['Prewt'].min(),
    subset['Prewt'].max()]})
```

Next, I use the model to predict WtGain values within that range:

```
predicted_wtgain = model_subset.predict(prewt_range)
```

And then I plot the regression line and supply a label for the legend:

```
ax.plot(prewt_range['Prewt'], predicted_wtgain, color='black',
    linestyle=linestyles[i], label=f'{treatment} Regression')
```

It's instructive to see it all together. With the new `linestyles` line and the new `for` loop lines, that part of the code looks like this:

```
linestyles = ['-', '--', ':']

for i, treatment in enumerate(treatments):
    subset = anorexia_data_frame[anorexia_data_frame['Treat'] ==
    treatment]
    ax.scatter(x=subset['Prewt'], y=subset['WtGain'],
    marker=markers[i], label=treatment, c='black')
    model_subset = smf.ols('WtGain ~ Prewt', data=subset).fit()
    prewt_range = pd.DataFrame({'Prewt': [subset['Prewt'].min(),
    subset['Prewt'].max()]})
    predicted_wtgain = model_subset.predict(prewt_range)
    ax.plot(prewt_range['Prewt'], predicted_wtgain, color='black',
    linestyle=linestyles[i], label=f'{treatment} Regression')
```

The result is shown in Figure 14-9.

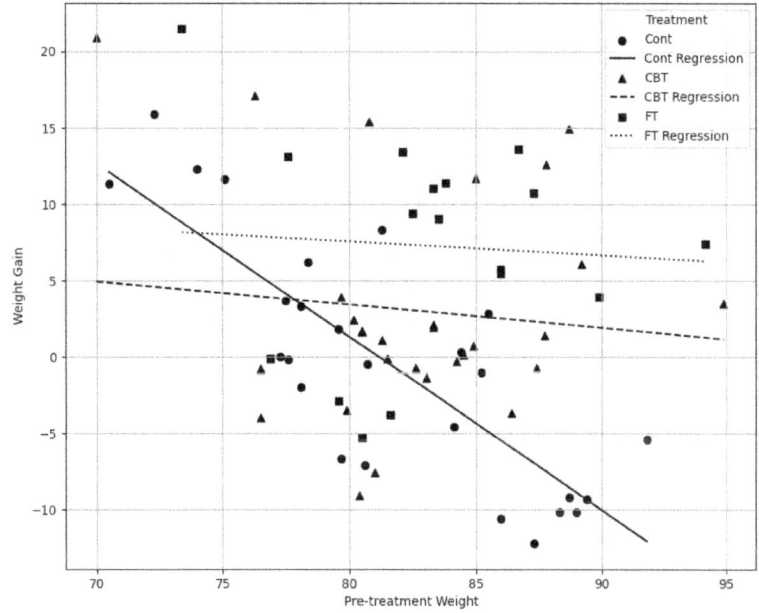

FIGURE 14-9: WtGain versus Treat and Prewt in the anorexia DataFrame, with a regression line for the scores in each level of Treat.

As you can see, the three negatively sloped regression lines are not parallel. The line for CBT parallels the line for FT, but the line for Cont (the control condition) has a much greater negative slope. Assuming that patients in the control group received no treatment, this sounds fairly intuitive: Because they received no treatment, many of these anorexic patients (the heavier ones) continued to lose weight (rather than gain weight), resulting in the highly negative slope for that line.

Apparently, we have a Treat X Prewt interaction. Does analysis bear this out?

To include the interaction in the model, I have to add Treat*Prewt to the formula:

```
ancova_model_with_interaction = smf.ols('WtGain ~ Treat + Prewt
    + Treat*Prewt', data=anorexia_data_frame).fit()
```

```
anova_table = anova_lm(ancova_model_with_interaction)
print(anova_table)
                df        sum_sq       mean_sq           F    PR(>F)
Treat          2.0    614.643667    307.321833    7.129975  0.001572
Prewt          1.0    599.479824    599.479824   13.908144  0.000401
Treat:Prewt    2.0    466.478317    233.239158    5.411231  0.006666
Residual      66.0   2844.784303     43.10279         NaN       NaN
```

Does adding the interaction make a difference?

```
comparison =
    anova_lm(ancova_model,ancova_model_with_interaction)
print(comparison)
     df_resid         ssr  df_diff    ss_diff       F     Pr(>F)
0        68.0  3311.26262      0.0        NaN     NaN        NaN
1        66.0  2844.78430      2.0   466.4783  5.4112   0.006666
```

It sure does! In your conclusions about this study, you have to include the caveat that the relationship between pre-weight and weight-gain is different for the control than it is for the cognitive-behavioral treatment and for the family treatment.

Chapter **15**

Correlation: The Rise and Fall of Relationships

In Chapter 14, I introduce the concept of regression, a tool for summarizing and testing relationships between (and among) variables. In this chapter, I introduce you to the ups and downs of correlation, another tool for looking at relationships. I use the example of employee aptitude and performance from Chapter 14 and show how to think about the data in a slightly different way. The new concepts connect to what I show you in Chapter 14, and you'll see how those connections work. I also show you how to test hypotheses about relationships and how to use Python functions for correlation.

Scatterplots, Again

A *scatterplot* is a graphical way of showing a relationship between two variables. In Chapter 14, I show you a scatterplot of the data for employees at FarMisht Consulting, Inc. I reproduce that scatterplot here as Figure 15-1. Each point represents one employee's score on a measure of Aptitude (on the x-axis) and on a measure of Performance (on the y-axis).

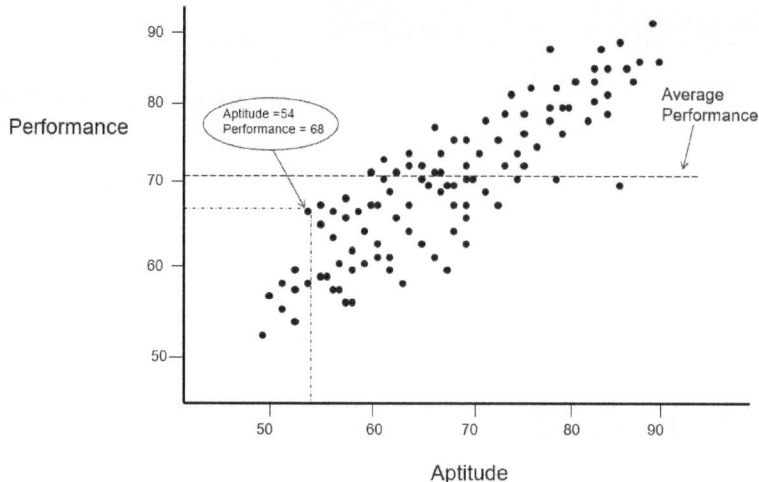

FIGURE 15-1:
Aptitude and
Performance at
FarMisht
Consulting.

Understanding Correlation

In Chapter 14, I refer to Aptitude as the *independent variable* and to Performance as the *dependent variable.* The objective in Chapter 14 is to use Aptitude to predict Performance.

REMEMBER

Although I use scores on one variable to *predict* scores on the other, I do *not* mean that the score on one variable *causes* a score on the other. *Relationship* doesn't necessarily mean *causality.*

Correlation is a statistical way of looking at a relationship. When two things are correlated, it means that they vary together. *Positive* correlation means that high scores on one are associated with high scores on the other, and that low scores on one are associated with low scores on the other. The scatterplot in Figure 15-1 is an example of positive correlation.

Negative correlation, on the other hand, means that high scores on the first thing are associated with *low* scores on the second. Negative correlation also means that low scores on the first are associated with high scores on the second. An example is the correlation between body weight and the time spent on a weight loss program. If the program is effective, the higher the amount of time spent on the program, the lower the body weight. Also, the lower the amount of time spent on the program, the higher the body weight.

Table 15-1, a repeat of Table 14-2 (refer to Chapter 14), shows the data for 16 FarMisht consultants.

TABLE 15-1

Aptitude Scores and Performance Scores for 16 FarMisht Consultants

Consultant	Aptitude	Performance
1	45	56
2	81	74
3	65	56
4	87	81
5	68	75
6	91	84
7	77	68
8	61	52
9	55	57
10	66	82
11	82	73
12	93	90
13	76	67
14	83	79
15	61	70
16	74	66
Mean	72.81	70.63
Variance	181.63	126.65
Standard deviation	13.48	11.25

In keeping with the way I use Aptitude and Performance in Chapter 14, Aptitude is the x-variable and Performance is the y-variable.

The formula for calculating the correlation between the two is

$$r = \frac{\left[\frac{1}{N-1}\right]\sum(x-\bar{x})(y-\bar{y})}{s_x s_y}$$

The term on the left, r, is called the *correlation coefficient*. It's also called *Pearson's product-moment correlation coefficient*, after its creator, Karl Pearson.

The two terms in the denominator on the right are the standard deviation of the x-variable and the standard deviation of the y-variable. The term in the numerator is called the *covariance.* Another way to write this formula is

$$r = \frac{\text{cov}(x,y)}{s_x s_y}$$

The covariance represents x and y varying together. Dividing the covariance by the product of the two standard deviations imposes some limits. The lower limit of the correlation coefficient is –1.00, and the upper limit is +1.00.

A correlation coefficient of –1.00 represents perfect negative correlation (low x-scores associated with high y-scores, and high x-scores associated with low y-scores). A correlation of +1.00 represents perfect positive correlation (low x-scores associated with low y-scores and high x-scores associated with high y-scores). A correlation of 0.00 means that the two variables aren't related.

Applying the formula to the data in Table 15-1,

$$r = \frac{\left[\frac{1}{N-1}\right]\sum(x-\bar{x})(y-\bar{y})}{s_x s_y}$$

$$= \frac{\left[\frac{1}{16-1}\right][(45-72.81)(56-70.63)+ \ldots +(74-72.81)(66-70.83)]}{(13.48)(11.25)} = .783$$

What, exactly, does this number mean? I'm about to tell you.

Correlation and Regression

Figure 15-2 shows the scatterplot of just the 16 employees in Table 15-1 with the line that best fits the points. It's possible to draw an infinite number of lines through these points. Which one is best?

To be the best, a line has to meet a specific standard: If you draw the distances in the vertical direction between the points and the line, square those distances, and then add those squared distances, the best-fitting line is the one that makes the sum of those squared distances as small as possible. This line is called the *regression line.*

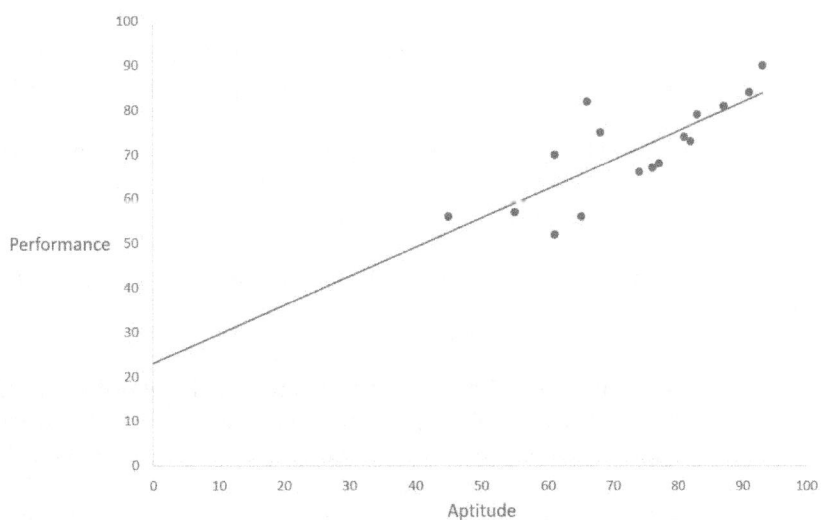

FIGURE 15-2:
Scatterplot of 16 FarMisht consultants, including the regression line.

The regression line's purpose in life is to enable you to make predictions. As I mention in Chapter 14, without a regression line, the best predicted value of the y-variable is the mean of the y's. A regression line takes the x-variable into account and delivers a more precise prediction. Each point on the regression line represents a predicted value for y. In the symbology of regression, each predicted value is a y' ("y-prime")

Why do I tell you all this? Because correlation is closely related to regression. Figure 15-3 focuses on one point in the scatterplot, its distance to the regression line, and its distance to the mean. (This is a repeat of Figure 14-3.)

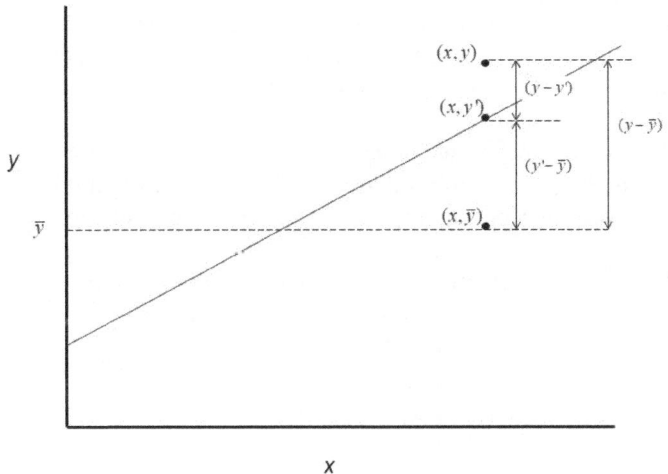

FIGURE 15-3:
One point in the scatterplot and its associated distances.

Notice the three distances laid out in the figure. The distance labeled $(y-y')$ is the difference between the point and the regression line's prediction for where the point should be. (In Chapter 14, I call that a *residual*.) The distance labeled $(y-\bar{y})$ is the difference between the point and the mean of the y's. The distance labeled $(y'-\bar{y})$ is the gain in prediction capability you get from using the regression line to predict the point instead of using the mean to predict the point.

Figure 15-3 shows that the three distances are related like this:

$$(y-y')+(y'-\bar{y})=(y-\bar{y})$$

As I point out in Chapter 14, you can square all the residuals and add them, square all the deviations of the predicted points from the mean and add them, and square all the deviations of the actual points from the mean and add them, too.

It turns out that these sums of squares are related in the same way as the deviations I just showed you:

$$SS_{Residual} + SS_{Regression} = SS_{Total}$$

If $SS_{Regression}$ is large in comparison to $SS_{Residual}$, the relationship between the x-variable and the y-variable is a strong one. It means that, throughout the scatterplot, the variability around the regression line is small.

On the other hand, if $SS_{Regression}$ is small in comparison to $SS_{Residual}$, the relationship between the x-variable and the y-variable is weak. In this case, the variability around the regression line is large throughout the scatterplot.

One way to test $SS_{Regression}$ against $SS_{Residual}$ is to divide each by its degrees of freedom (1 for $SS_{Regression}$ and $N-2$ for $SS_{Residual}$) to form variance estimates (also known as mean-squares, or MS), and then divide one by the other to calculate an F. If $MS_{Regression}$ is significantly larger than $MS_{Residual}$, you have evidence that the x-y relationship is strong. (See Chapter 14 for details.)

Here's the clincher, as far as correlation is concerned: Another way to assess the size of $SS_{Regression}$ is to compare it with SS_{Total}. Divide the first by the second. If the ratio is large, this tells you the x-y relationship is strong.

This ratio has a name. It's called the *coefficient of determination*. Its symbol is r^2. (It appears as R^2 in Chapter 14.) Take the square root of this coefficient and you have . . . the correlation coefficient!

$$r = r^2 = \pm\sqrt{\frac{SS_{Regression}}{SS_{Total}}}$$

The plus-or-minus sign ($\pm$) means that r is either the positive or negative square root, depending on whether the slope of the regression line is positive or negative.

So if you calculate a correlation coefficient and you quickly want to know what its value signifies, just square it. The answer — the *coefficient of determination* — lets you know the proportion of the SS_{Total} that's tied up in the relationship between the x-variable and the y-variable. If it's a large proportion, the correlation coefficient signifies a strong relationship. If it's a small proportion, the correlation coefficient signifies a weak relationship.

In the Aptitude-Performance example, the correlation coefficient is .783. The coefficient of determination is

$$r^2 = (.783)^2 = .613$$

In this sample of 16 consultants, the $SS_{Regression}$ is 61.3 percent of the SS_{Total}. Sounds like a large proportion, but what's large? What's small? Those questions scream out for hypothesis tests.

Testing Hypotheses About Correlation

In this section, I show you how to answer important questions about correlation. Like any other kind of hypothesis testing, the idea is to use sample statistics to make inferences about population parameters. Here, the sample statistic is r, the correlation coefficient. By convention, the population parameter is ρ (rho), the Greek equivalent of r. (Yes, it does look like the letter p, but it really is the Greek equivalent of r.)

Returning once again to the Aptitude-Performance example, you can use the sample r to test hypotheses about the population ρ — the correlation coefficient for all consultants at FarMisht Consulting.

Assuming that you know in advance (before you gather any sample data) that any correlation between Aptitude and Performance should be positive, the hypotheses are

$$H_0 : \rho \leq 0$$
$$H_1 : \rho > 0$$

Set $\alpha = .05$.

The appropriate statistical test is a t-test. The formula is

$$t = \frac{r - \rho}{s_r}$$

This test has $N-2$ df.

For the example, the values in the numerator are set: r is .783 and ρ (in H_0) is 0. What about the denominator? I won't burden you with the details. I'll just tell you that's

$$\sqrt{\frac{1 - r^2}{N - 2}}$$

With a little algebra, the formula for the t-test simplifies to

$$t = \frac{r\sqrt{N - 2}}{\sqrt{1 - r^2}}$$

For the example:

$$t = \frac{r\sqrt{N - 2}}{\sqrt{1 - r^2}} = \frac{.783\sqrt{16 - 2}}{\sqrt{1 - .783^2}} = 4.707$$

With df = 14 and α = .05 (one-tailed), the critical value of t is 1.76. Because the calculated value (4.707) is greater than the critical value, the decision is to reject H_0.

Correlation in Python

In this section, I work with the FarMisht example. The DataFrame, `FarMisht_data_frame`, holds the data points shown over in Table 14-4 (from Chapter 14). I create it just a bit differently than I did in Chapter 14. I begin by importing pandas:

```
import pandas as pd
```

Next, I create a list for each variable:

```
Aptitude = [45, 81, 65, 87, 68, 91, 77, 61, 55, 66, 82, 93, 76,
    83, 61, 74]
Performance = [56, 74, 56, 81, 75, 84, 68, 52, 57, 82, 73, 90,
    67, 79, 70, 66]
```

```
Personality = [9, 15, 11, 15, 14, 19, 12, 10, 9, 14, 15, 14, 16,
    18, 15, 12]
```

Here's the slight difference from Chapter 14. Rather than take one step to create a dictionary and then take another to create the DataFrame, I do it all in one step:

```
FarMisht_data_frame = pd.DataFrame(
    {
        "Aptitude": Aptitude,
        "Performance": Performance,
        "Personality": Personality,
    }
)
```

To compute the correlation coefficient for the relationship between Aptitude and Performance and test it at the same time, I import pearsonr() from scipy.stats:

```
from scipy.stats import pearsonr
```

Then I apply pearsonr() to the parts of the DataFrame I'm interested in:

```
Apt_Performance_Correlation, p_value =
    pearsonr(FarMisht_data_frame['Aptitude'],
    FarMisht_data_frame['Performance'])
print(Apt_Performance_Correlation)
print(p_value)
0.7827927343480359
0.0003368488464934431
```

The low *p*-value indicates a significant correlation between Aptitude and Performance.

Calculating a correlation matrix

To calculate the matrix of all pairwise correlations in the FarMisht DataFrame, I use the corr() function in pandas:

```
FarMisht_matrix = FarMisht_data_frame.corr()
print(FarMisht_matrix)
              Aptitude  Performance  Personality
Aptitude      1.000000  0.782793     0.749930
```

```
Performance   0.782793   1.000000   0.770927
Personality   0.749930   0.770927   1.000000
```

Visualizing a correlation matrix

The seaborn library has a couple of functions that enable you to produce eye-catching visualizations of correlation matrices. First, the imports:

```
import seaborn as sns
import matplotlib.pyplot as plt
```

The first function is pairplot(). In each cell of the main diagonal, it renders a histogram of that cell's variable. In each off-diagonal cell, it renders a scatterplot of the cell's row variable as the dependent variable and its column variable as the independent variable:

```
sns.pairplot(FarMisht_data_frame, kind = "reg")
```

The kind argument specifies a regression line through each scatterplot. (Omit this argument if you just want the scatterplots.)

Then this command

```
plt.show()
```

produces Figure 15-4. The shading around each regression line is the 95% confidence interval (see Chapter 14).

The second function, heatmap(), color-codes each cell. The best way to explain this concept is with an example. This code snippet

```
sns.heatmap(FarMisht_matrix, annot=True)
plt.show()
```

produces Figure 15-5. The annot = True argument prints the correlation coefficients in the cells.

Admittedly, with only three variables and a narrow range of correlations, the heat map isn't exactly informative. Consider it when you have many more variables and a wide range of correlation coefficients.

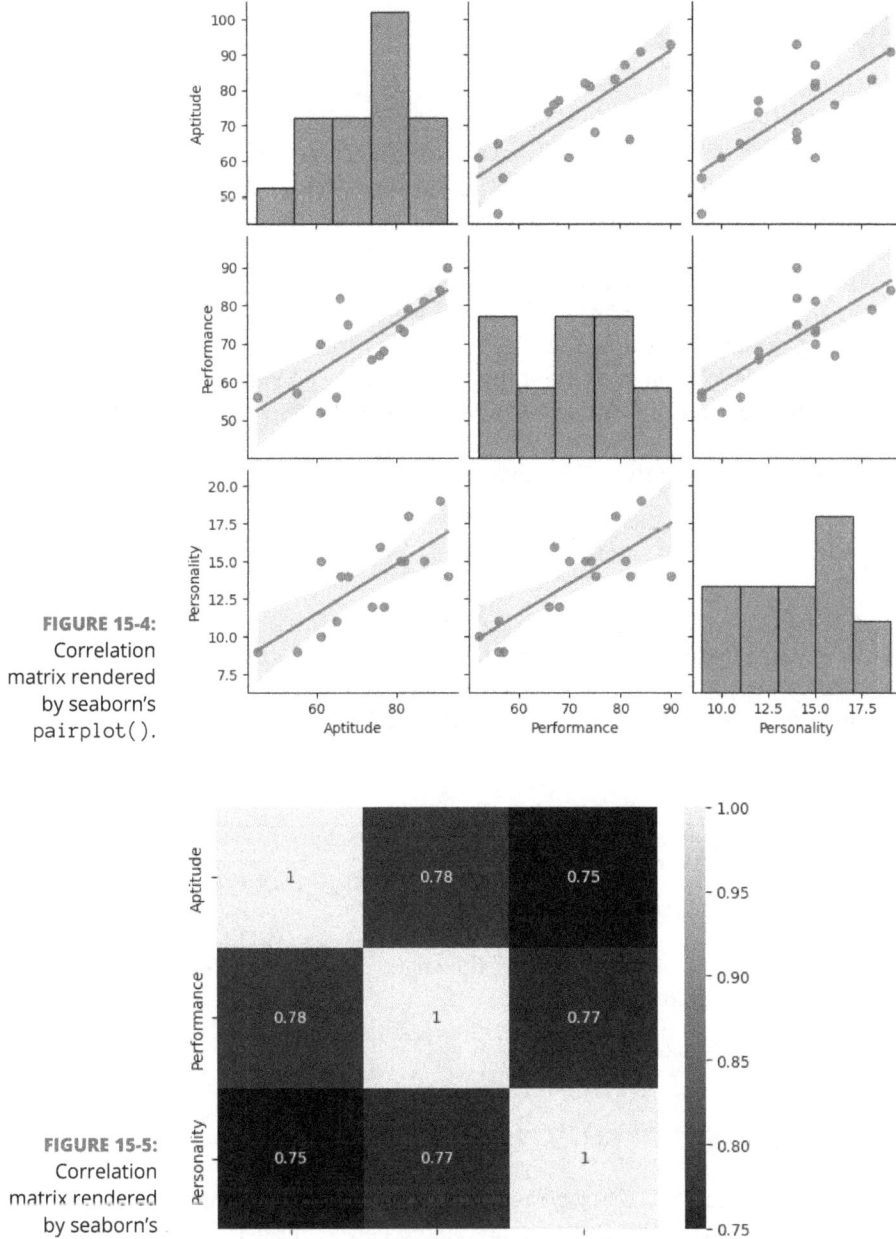

FIGURE 15-4:
Correlation
matrix rendered
by seaborn's
pairplot().

FIGURE 15-5:
Correlation
matrix rendered
by seaborn's
heatmap().

Multiple Correlation

The correlation coefficients in the correlation matrix described in the preceding section combine to produce a *multiple correlation coefficient* — It's a number that summarizes the relationship between the dependent variable — Performance, in this example — and the two independent variables (Aptitude and Personality).

To show you how these correlation coefficients combine, I abbreviate Performance as P, Aptitude as A, and Personality as F (FarMisht Personality Inventory). So r_{PA} is the correlation coefficient for Performance and Aptitude (.7827927), r_{PF} is the correlation coefficient for Performance and Personality (.7709271), and r_{AF} is the correlation coefficient for Aptitude and Personality (.7499305).

Here's the formula that puts them all together:

$$R_{P.AF} = \sqrt{\frac{r_{PA}^2 + r_{PF}^2 - 2r_{PA}r_{PF}r_{AF}}{1 - r_{AF}^2}}$$

The uppercase R on the left indicates that this is a multiple correlation coefficient, as opposed to the lowercase r, which indicates a correlation between two variables. The subscript P.AF means that the multiple correlation is between Performance and the combination of Aptitude and Personality.

For this example,

$$R_{P.AF} = \sqrt{\frac{(.7827927)^2 + (.7709271)^2 - 2(.7827927)(.7709271)(.7499305)}{1 - (.7499305)^2}}$$

$$= .8306841$$

If you square this number, you get the *multiple coefficient of determination*. For this example, that result is

$$R_{P.AF}^2 = (.830641)^2 = .6900361$$

Multiple correlation in Python

The easiest way to calculate a multiple correlation coefficient is to fit a multiple regression model with Performance as the dependent variable and Aptitude and Personality as the independent variables (as in Chapter 14):

```
import statsmodels.formula.api as smf
model = smf.ols('Performance ~ Aptitude + Personality', data =
    FarMisht_data_frame).fit()
```

Rather than print the entire summary, I show you R^2 and calculate R:

```
R_squared = model.rsquared
print(f'Multiple Coefficient of Determination = {R_squared}')

from math import sqrt
R = sqrt(R_squared)
print(f'Multiple Correlation Coefficient = {R}')
```

Adjusting R-squared

In the summary of a fitted model (as in Chapter 14), you see *Adjusted R-squared.* Here it is for the model in the preceding subsection:

```
Adjusted_R_squared = model.rsquared_adj
print(f'Adjusted_R_squared = {Adjusted_R_squared}')
Adjusted_R_squared = 0.6423493510180701
```

Why is it necessary to "adjust" R-squared?

In multiple regression, adding independent variables (like `Personality`) sometimes makes the regression equation less accurate. The multiple coefficient of determination, R-squared, doesn't reflect this. Its denominator is SS_{Total} (for the dependent variable), and that never changes. The numerator can only increase or stay the same. So any decline in accuracy doesn't result in a lower R-squared.

Taking degrees of freedom into account fixes the flaw. Every time you add an independent variable, you change the degrees of freedom, and that makes all the difference. Just so you know, here's the adjustment:

$$Adjusted\ R^2 = 1 - \left(1 - R^2\right)\left[\frac{(N-1)}{(N-k-1)}\right]$$

The k in the denominator is the number of independent variables.

Partial Correlation

Performance and Aptitude are associated with Personality (in the example). Each one's association with Personality might somehow hide the true correlation between them.

What would their correlation be if you could remove that association? Here's another way to ask this: What would be the Performance–Aptitude correlation if you could hold Personality constant?

One way to hold Personality constant is to find the Performance-Aptitude correlation for a sample of consultants who have one Personality score — 17, for example. In a sample like this, the correlation of each variable with Personality is 0. This usually isn't feasible in the real world, however.

Another way is to find the *partial correlation* between Performance and Aptitude. This is a statistical way of removing each variable's association with Personality in your sample. You use the correlation coefficients in the correlation matrix to do this:

$$r_{PA.F} = \frac{r_{PA} - r_{PF}r_{AF}}{\sqrt{1-r_{PF}^2}\sqrt{1-r_{AF}^2}}$$

Once again, P stands for Performance, A for Aptitude, and F for Personality. The subscript *PA.F* means that the correlation is between Performance and Aptitude with each one's correlation with Personality removed — "partialled out," in other words.

For this example,

$$r_{PA.F} = \frac{.7827927 - (.7709271)(.7499305)}{\sqrt{1-(.7709271)^2}\sqrt{1-(.7499305)^2}} = .4857198$$

Partial Correlation in Python

The `pingouin` library provides `partial_corr()`. Here's how to use it.

First, make sure `pingouin` is installed and imported:

```
!pip install pingouin
import pingouin as pg
```

Then it's just a matter of filling in the arguments to `partial_corr()`:

```
partial_correlation = pg.partial_corr(
    data=FarMisht_data_frame,
    x='Performance',
    y='Aptitude',
```

```
        covar='Personality'
)
print(f'The correlation between Performance and Aptitude with
    Personality partialled out: \n {partial_correlation}')
The correlation between Performance and Aptitude with
    Personality partialled out:
                    n           r           CI95%          p-val
pearson       16       0.48572      [-0.04, 0.8]      0.066423
```

In the last line of the output, the first number is the number of consultants, the second number is the correlation between Aptitude and Performance with Personality partialled out, and the parenthesized numbers are the lower and upper bounds of the 95% confidence interval for the partial correlation coefficient.

The final number is the p-value of a statistical test of the partial correlation coefficient. With $\alpha = .05$, we can't conclude that Aptitude is significantly correlated with Performance when we remove each one's correlation with Personality.

Semipartial Correlation

It's possible that the correlation of Personality with just Aptitude is influencing the correlation between Aptitude and Performance.

To test this, I can remove the correlation with Personality from just Aptitude without removing it from Performance. This is called *semipartial correlation*. The formula for this one also uses the correlation coefficients from the correlation matrix:

$$r_{P(A.F)} = \frac{r_{PA} - r_{PF}r_{AF}}{\sqrt{1 - r_{AF}^2}}$$

The subscript $P(A.F)$ means that the correlation is between Performance and Aptitude with Personality partialed out of Aptitude only.

Applying this formula to the example,

$$r_{P(A.F)} = \frac{.7827927 - (.7709271)(.7499305)}{\sqrt{1 - (.7499305)^2}} = .3093663$$

REMEMBER

Some statistics textbooks refer to semipartial correlation as *part correlation*.

Semipartial Correlation in Python

The `pingouin` function `partial_corr()` calculates semipartial correlation, too. The only difference is the specification of the fourth argument. Instead of `covar` (as in partial correlation), it's called `x_covar` to partial out of the x variable or `y_covar` to partial out of the *y*-variable.

In this example, the correlation is between Performance and Aptitude with Personality partialed out of Aptitude only:

```
semipartial_correlation = pg.partial_corr(
    data=FarMisht_data_frame,
    x='Aptitude',
    y='Performance',
    x_covar='Personality' # Control for Personality only on
  Aptitude (x)
)

print(f'The correlation between Performance and Aptitude with
  Personality partialled out of Aptitude only:
  \n{semipartial_correlation}')
The correlation between Performance and Aptitude with
  Personality partialled out of Aptitude only:
               n           r          CI95%        p-val
pearson       16     0.309366   [-0.24, 0.71]   0.261849
```

The first number in the output is the number of consultants, the second is the correlation between Aptitude and Performance with the correlation between Aptitude and Personality removed, and the parenthesized numbers are the lower and upper bounds of the 95% confidence interval for the correlation coefficient.

The rightmost number is the p-value of a statistical test of the semipartial correlation coefficient. With $\alpha = .05$, we can't conclude that Aptitude is significantly correlated with Performance when we remove Aptitude's correlation with Personality.

Chapter **16**

Curvilinear Regression: When Relationships Get Complicated

n Chapters 14 and 15, I describe linear regression and correlation — two concepts that depend on the straight line as the best-fitting summary of a scatterplot.

But a line isn't always the best fit. Processes in a variety of areas, from biology to business, conform more to curves than to lines.

For example, think about when you learned a skill — like tying your shoelaces. When you first tried it, it took quite a while, didn't it? And then whenever you tried again, it took progressively less time for you to finish, right? Until finally, you can tie your shoelaces quickly, but you can't really get any faster — you're now doing it as efficiently as you can.

If you plotted shoelace-tying-time (in seconds) on the y-axis and trials (occasions when you tried to tie your shoes) on the x-axis, the graph might look something like Figure 16-1. A straight line is clearly not the best summary of a plot like this one.

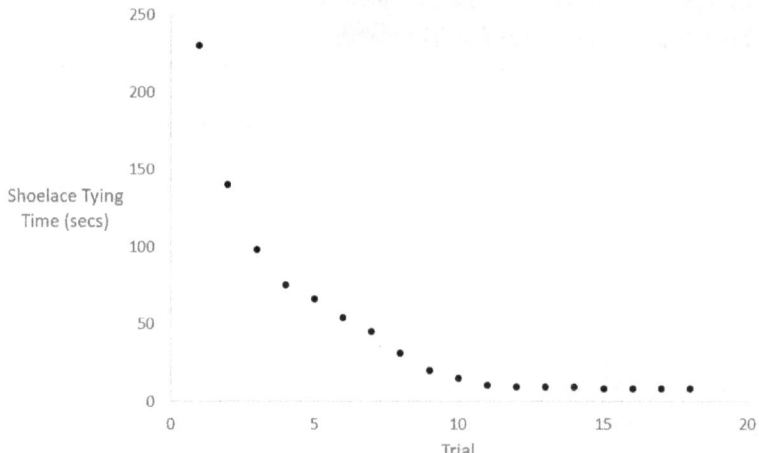

FIGURE 16-1:
Hypothetical plot
of learning a
skill — like tying
your shoelaces.

Shoelace Tying
Time (secs)

Trial

How do you find the best-fitting curve? (Another way to say this: "How do you formulate a model for these data?") I'll be happy to show you, but first I have to tell you about logarithms, and about an important number called *e*.

Why? Because those concepts form the foundation of three kinds of nonlinear regression.

What Is a Logarithm?

Plainly and simply, a logarithm is an *exponent* — a power to which you raise a number. In the equation

$$10^2 = 100$$

2 is an exponent. Does that mean that 2 is also a logarithm? Well . . . yes. In terms of logarithms,

$$\log_{10} 100 = 2$$

That's really just another way of saying $10^2 = 100$. Mathematicians read it as "the logarithm of 100 to the base 10 equals 2." It means that if you want to raise 10 to some power to get 100, that power is 2.

How about 1,000? As you know

$$10^3 = 1000$$

so

$$\log_{10}1000 = 3$$

How about 763? Uh . . . . Hmm . . . . That's like trying to solve

$$10^x = 763$$

What could that answer possibly be? The term 10^2 means 10×10 and that gives you 100; 10^3 means $10 \times 10 \times 10$ and that's 1,000. But 763?

Here's where you have to think outside the dialog box. You have to imagine exponents that aren't whole numbers. I know, I know: How can you multiply a number by itself a fraction at a time? If you could, somehow, the number in that 763 equation would have to be between 2 (which gets you to 100) and 3 (which gets you to 1,000).

In the 16th century, the mathematician John Napier showed how to do it, and logarithms were born. Why did Napier bother with this? One reason is that it was a great help to astronomers. Astronomers have to deal with numbers that are, well, astronomical. Logarithms ease computational strain in a couple of ways. One way is to substitute small numbers for large ones: The logarithm of 1,000,000 is 6, and the logarithm of 100,000,000 is 8. Also, working with logarithms opens up a helpful set of computational shortcuts. Before calculators and computers appeared on the scene, this was a very big deal.

Incidentally,

$$10^{2.882525} = 763$$

which means that

$$\log_{10}763 = 2.882525$$

I just mentioned computational shortcuts that result from logarithms. Here's one: If you want to multiply two numbers, add their logarithms and then find the number whose logarithm is the sum. That last part is called "finding the antilogarithm." Here's a quick example: To multiply 100 by 1,000:

$$\log_{10}(100) + \log_{10}(1000) =$$
$$2 + 3 = 5$$
$$\text{antilog}_{10}(5) = 10^5 = 100,000$$

Here's another computational shortcut: Multiplying the logarithm of a number x by a number b corresponds to raising x to the b power.

Ten, the number that's raised to the exponent, is called the *base*. Because it's also the base of the number system we use every day, and everyone is familiar with it, logarithms of base 10 are called *common logarithms*.

Does that mean you can have other bases? Absolutely. *Any* number (except 0 or 1 or a negative number) can be a base. For example,

$$7.8^2 = 60.84$$

So

$$\log_{7.8} 60.84 = 2$$

In terms of bases, one number is special . . .

What Is e?

Which brings me to *e*, a constant that's all about growth.

Imagine the princely sum of $1 deposited in a bank account. Suppose that the interest rate is 2 percent a year. (Yes, this is just an example!) If it's simple interest, the bank adds $.02 every year, and in 50 years, you have $2.

If it's compound interest, at the end of 50 years, you have $(1 + .02)^{50}$ — which is just a bit more than $2.68, assuming that the bank compounds the interest once a year.

Of course, if the bank compounds interest twice a year, each payment is $.01, and after 50 years, the bank has compounded it 100 times. That gives you $(1 + .01)^{100}$, or just over $2.70. What about compounding it four times a year? After 50 years — 200 compoundings — you have $(1 + .005)^{200}$, which results in the don't-spend-it-all-in-one-place amount of $2.71 and a tiny bit more.

Focusing on "just a bit more" and "a tiny bit more" and taking it to extremes, after 100,000 compoundings, you have $2.718268. After 100 million, you have $2.718282.

If you could get the bank to compound many more times in those 50 years, your sum of money approaches a *limit* — an amount it gets ever so close to but never quite reaches. That limit is *e*.

The way I set up the example, the rule for calculating the amount is

$$\left(1+\left(\frac{1}{x}\right)\right)^x$$

where x represents the number of payments. Two cents is 1/50th of a dollar, and I specified 50 years — 50 payments. Then I specified 2 payments a year (and each year's payments have to add up to 2 percent) so that in 50 years, you have 100 payments of $\frac{1}{100}$th of a dollar, and so on.

To see this concept in action, take Python for a spin. For that to happen, you import numpy and pandas, and then create an array to work on and a DataFrame to hold the results:

```
import numpy as np
import pandas as pd
x =[1,10,50,100,200,500,1000,10000,100000000]
```

I convert this list to a numpy array so that I can perform computations element by element:

```
x_np = np.array(x)
y =(1+(1/x_np))**x_np
df = pd.DataFrame({'x': x, 'y': y})
print(df)
              x           y
0             1    2.000000
1            10    2.593742
2            50    2.691588
3           100    2.704814
4           200    2.711517
5           500    2.715569
6          1000    2.716924
7         10000    2.718146
8     100000000    2.718282
```

So e is associated with growth. Its value is 2.718282 . . . . The ellipsis (the three dots at the end) means that you never quite get to the exact value (like π, the constant that enables you to find the area of a circle).

The number e pops up in all kinds of places. It's in the formula for the normal distribution (along with π; see Chapter 8), and it's in a distribution I discuss in Chapter 18. Many natural phenomena are related to e.

It's so important that scientists, mathematicians, and business analysts use it as a base for logarithms. Logarithms to the base *e* are called *natural* logarithms. In many textbooks, a natural logarithm is abbreviated as *ln.* In Python, it's `np.log()`:

```
import numpy as np
number = 50
natural_log = np.log(number)
print(f"The natural logarithm of {number} is: {natural_log}")
The natural logarithm of 50 is: 3.912023005428146
```

Table 16-1 presents some comparisons (rounded to three decimal places) between common logarithms and natural logarithms.

TABLE 16-1 ## Some Common Logarithms (Log10) and Natural Logarithms (Log)

Number	Log10	Log
e	0.434	1.000
10	1.000	2.303
50	1.699	3.912
100	2.000	4.605
453	2.656	6.116
1000	3.000	6.908

One more thing: In many formulas and equations, it's often necessary to raise *e* to a power. Sometimes the power is a fairly complicated mathematical expression. Because superscripts are usually printed in a small font, it can be a strain to have to constantly read them. To ease the eyestrain, mathematicians have invented a special notation: *exp.* Whenever you see *exp* followed by something in parentheses, it means to raise *e* to the power of whatever's in the parentheses. For example,

$$\exp(1.6) = e^{1.6} = 4.953032$$

In Python,

```
x = 1.6
exponential_value = np.exp(x)
print(f"e to the power of {x} is: {exponential_value}")
e to the power of 1.6 is: 4.953032424395115
```

Applying the np.exp() function with natural logarithms is like finding the anti-log with common logarithms.

Speaking of raising *e*, when executives at Google, Inc., filed its IPO, they said they wanted to raise $2,718,281,828, which is *e* times a billion dollars rounded to the nearest dollar.

And now . . . back to curvilinear regression.

Power Regression

Biologists have studied the interrelationships between the sizes and weights of parts of the body. One fascinating relationship is the relation between body weight and brain weight. One way to study this is to assess the relationship across different species. Intuitively, it seems like heavier animals should have heavier brains — but what's the exact nature of the relationship?

To study the body-weight-brain relationship, I work with the Animals data set, which resides in R's MASS library:

```
import statsmodels.api as sm
import pandas as pd
Animals = sm.datasets.get_rdataset("Animals", "MASS")
```

and then turn the data set into a pandas DataFrame:

```
Animals_df= pd.DataFrame(Animals.data)
```

The first six rows look like this:

```
print(Animals_df.head(6))
                    body        brain
rownames
Mountain beaver     1.35          8.1
Cow               465.00        423.0
Grey wolf          36.33        119.5
Goat               27.66        115.0
Guinea pig          1.04          5.5
Dipliodocus     11700.00         50.0
```

Have you ever seen a diplodocus No? Outside of a natural history museum, no one else has, either. In addition to this dinosaur in row 5, Animals_df has triceratops in Row 15 and brachiosaurus in Row 25. Here, I'll show you:

```
print(Animals_df.iloc[[5,15,25],])
                    body              brain
Diplodocus          11700            50.0
Triceratops          9400            70.0
Brachiosaurus       87000           154.5
```

To confine our work to living species, I create

```
living_animals_df = Animals_df.drop(Animals_df.index[[5,15,25]])
```

which causes those three dinosaurs to vanish from the DataFrame as surely as they have vanished from the face of the earth.

Let's take a look at the data points. First, I set up the plot:

```
import matplotlib.pyplot as plt
plt.figure(figsize=(10, 6))
plt.scatter(x=living_animals_df['body'],
   y=living_animals_df['brain'])
```

Then I label the axes, create a grid, and show the plot:

```
plt.xlabel('Body Weight')
plt.ylabel('Brain Weight')
plt.grid(True)
plt.show()
```

The result is shown in Figure 16-2. Note that the idea is to use body weight to predict brain weight.

Doesn't look much like a linear relationship, does it? In fact, it's not. Relationships in this field often take the form

$$y' = ax^b$$

REMEMBER

Because the independent (predictor) variable x (body weight, in this case) is raised to a power, this type of model is called *power regression*.

In my view, the easiest way to proceed is to leverage what we already know about linear regression from Chapter 14 and apply it here.

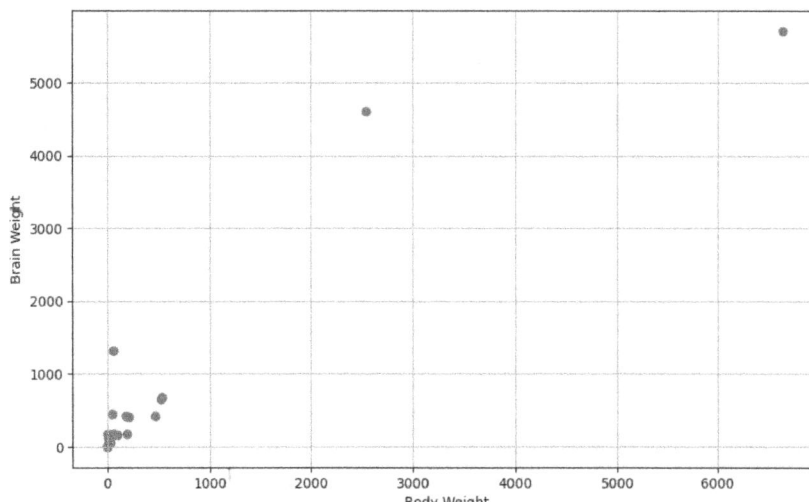

FIGURE 16-2:
The relationship between body weight and brain weight for 25 animal species.

To do this, we have to somehow transform the data so that the relationship between the transformed body weight and the transformed brain weight is linear.

And this is why I told you about logarithms.

You can linearize the scatterplot by working with the logarithm of the body weight and the logarithm of the brain weight. Here's some code to do just that:

```
log_body = np.log(living_animals_df['body'])
log_brain = np.log(living_animals_df['brain'])
```

Now the code to plot the transformed data points is

```
import matplotlib.pyplot as plt
import numpy as np
plt.figure(figsize=(10, 6))

log_body = np.log(living_animals_df['body'])
log_brain = np.log(living_animals_df['brain'])

plt.scatter(x=log_body, y=log_brain)

plt.xlabel('Log Body Weight')
plt.ylabel('Log Brain Weight')
plt.grid(True)
plt.show()
```

The plot is shown in Figure 16-3.

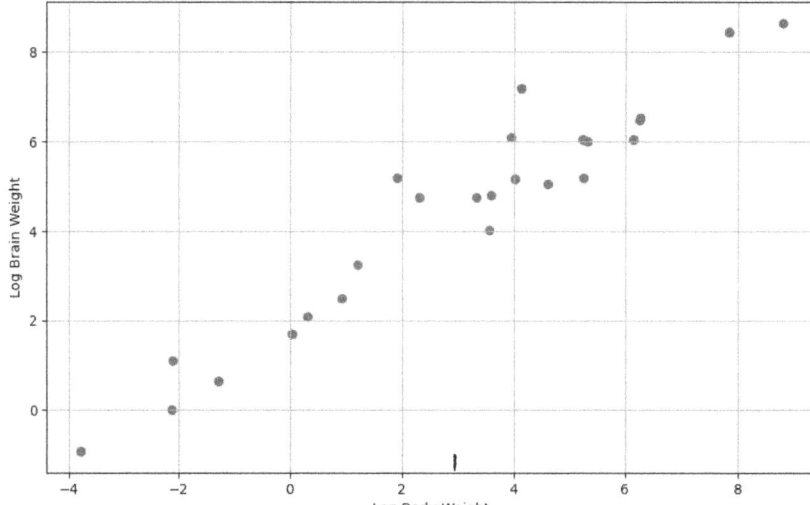

FIGURE 16-3:
The relationship
between the log
of body weight
and the log of
brain weight for
25 animal species.

This plot seems to be tailor-made for a regression line. My preferred function for this is in the seaborn library, so

```
import seaborn as sns
```

The seaborn regression line function requires a DataFrame:

```
import pandas as pd
```

and the DataFrame is

```
log_df = pd.DataFrame({'log_body': log_body, 'log_brain':
    log_brain})
```

To plot the regression line

```
sns.regplot(x='log_body', y='log_brain', data=log_df)
```

All the code to plot the data points and the regression line is

```
import matplotlib.pyplot as plt
import seaborn as sns
import numpy as np
import pandas as pd

plt.figure(figsize=(10, 6))
```

```
log_body = np.log(living_animals_df['body'])
log_brain = np.log(living_animals_df['brain'])
plt.scatter(x=log_body, y=log_brain)

log_df = pd.DataFrame({'log_body': log_body, 'log_brain':
    log_brain})
sns.regplot(x='log_body', y='log_brain', data=log_df)

plt.xlabel('Log Body Weight')
plt.ylabel('Log Brain Weight')
plt.grid(True)
plt.show()
```

Figure 16-4 shows the regression line complete with the shaded 95% confidence interval (see Chapter 14).

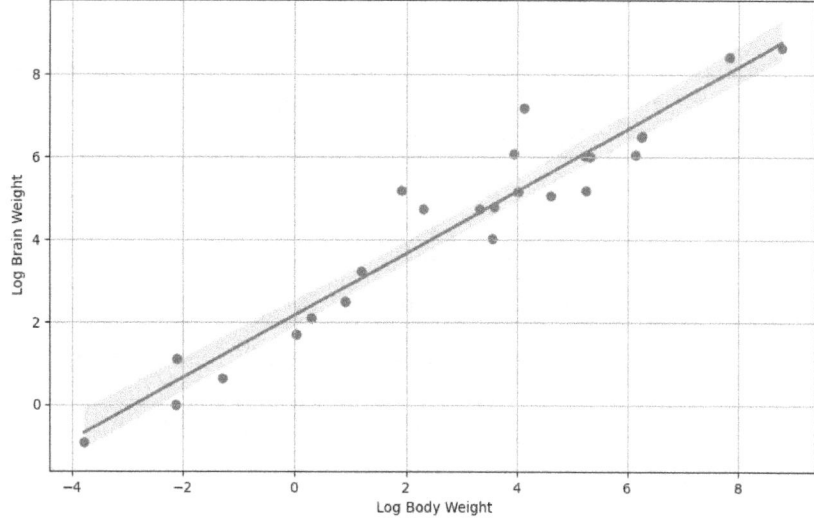

FIGURE 16-4: The relationship between the log of body weight and the log of brain weight for 25 animal species, with a regression line.

The tight confidence interval around the regression line suggests that the model fits the data quite well.

Does analysis bear this out?

```
model = smf.ols('np.log(brain) ~ np.log(body)', data = living_
    animals_df).fit()
print(f'F = {model.fvalue}')
print(f'p = {model.f_pvalue}')
```

```
F = 270.73876647386305
p = 3.242750054132664e-14
```

It sure does!

How about the coefficients?

```
Intercept = model.params.iloc[0]
Slope = model.params.iloc[1]
print(f'Intercept = {Intercept}')
print(f'Slope = {Slope}')
Intercept = 2.1504120915636116
Slope = 0.752260712638005
```

The coefficients tell you that, in logarithmic form, the regression equation is

$$\log(y') = \log(a + bx)$$
$$\log(\text{brainweight}') = \log(2.15041 + (.75226 \times \text{bodyweight}))$$

For the power regression equation, you have to take the antilog of both sides. As I mention earlier, when you're working with natural logarithms, that's the same as applying the exp() function:

$$\exp(\log(y')) = \exp(\log(a + bx))$$
$$y' = \exp(a)x^b$$
$$\text{brainweight}' = \exp(2.15041) \times \text{bodyweight}^{.75226}$$
$$\text{brainweight}' = 8.588397 \times \text{bodyweight}^{.75226}$$

All this is in keeping with what I say earlier in this chapter:

» Adding the logarithms of numbers corresponds to multiplying the numbers.

» Multiplying the logarithm of x by b corresponds to raising x to the b power.

Here's how to calculate the antilog of the intercept:

```
antilog_intercept = np.exp(Intercept)
print(f'Antilog of Intercept = {antilog_intercept}')
Antilog of Intercept = 8.588396873936306
```

You can plot the power regression equation as a curve in the original plot. To the code that produced Figure 16-2, add these lines:

```
x_power_fit = np.linspace(living_animals_df['body'].min(),
    living_animals_df['body'].max(), 100)
```

```
y_power_fit = antilog_intercept * x_power_fit ** Slope
plt.plot(x_power_fit, y_power_fit)
```

The first line creates 100 equally spaced points on the *x*-variable, the second applies the power regression equation to predict a *y*-value for each of those 100 points, and the third adds the resulting curve to the plot, which now looks like Figure 16-5.

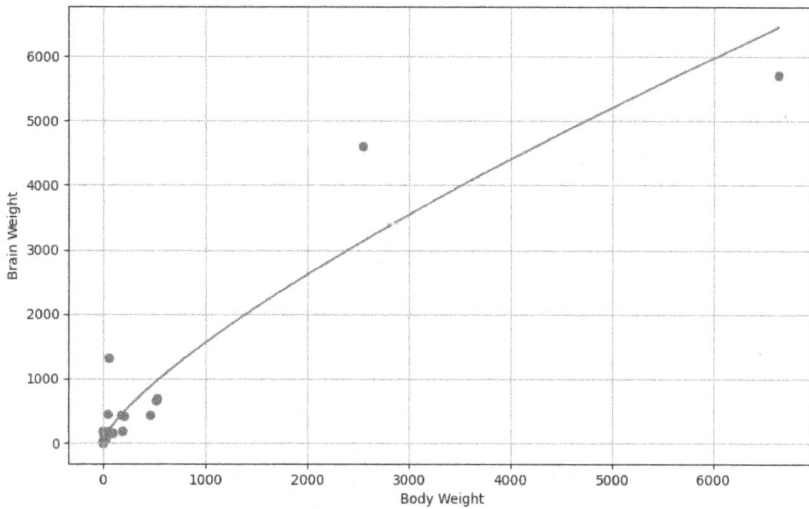

FIGURE 16-5: Original plot of brain weights and body weights of 25 species, with the power regression curve.

Exponential Regression

As I mention earlier, *e* figures into processes in a variety of areas. Some of those processes, like compound interest, involve growth. Others involve decay.

Here's an example. If you've ever poured a glass of beer and let it stand, you might have noticed that the head gets smaller and smaller (it *decays,* in other words) as time passes. You haven't done that? Okay. Go ahead and pour a tall, cool one and watch it for six minutes. I'll wait.

. . . And we're back. Was I right? Notice that I didn't ask you to measure the height of the head as it decayed. Physicist Arnd Leike did that for us for three brands of beer.

He measured head-height every 15 seconds from 0 to 120 seconds after pouring the beer, and then every 30 seconds from 150 seconds to 240 seconds, and, finally, at 300 seconds and 360 seconds. (In the true spirit of science, he then drank the beer.) Here I use Python to generate those intervals as a list:

```
seconds_after_pour = np.array(list(range(0, 121, 15)) +
    list(range(150, 241, 30)) + [300, 360])
```

And here are the head heights that Arnd measured for one of the brands of beer:

```
head_cm = [17, 16.1, 14.9, 14, 13.2, 12.5, 11.9, 11.2, 10.7,
    9.7, 8.9, 8.3, 7.5, 6.3, 5.2]
```

I combine the two lists into a DataFrame:

```
beer_df = pd.DataFrame({'seconds_after_pour': seconds_after_
    pour, 'head_cm': head_cm})
```

Let's see what the plot looks like. This code

```
import matplotlib.pyplot as plt
import numpy as np
plt.figure(figsize=(10, 6))
plt.scatter(x=beer_df['seconds_after_pour'],
    y=beer_df['head_cm'])
plt.xlabel('Seconds After Pour')
plt.ylabel('Beer Head Height (cm)')
plt.grid(True)
plt.show()
```

produces Figure 16-6.

This one is crying out (in its beer?) for a curvilinear model, isn't it?

One way to linearize the plot (so that you can use smf.ols() to create a model) is to work with the log of the y-variable. To visualize the transformed plot, along with the regression line, here's the code:

```
import matplotlib.pyplot as plt
import numpy as np
import pandas as pd
import seaborn as sns

plt.figure(figsize=(10, 6))
```

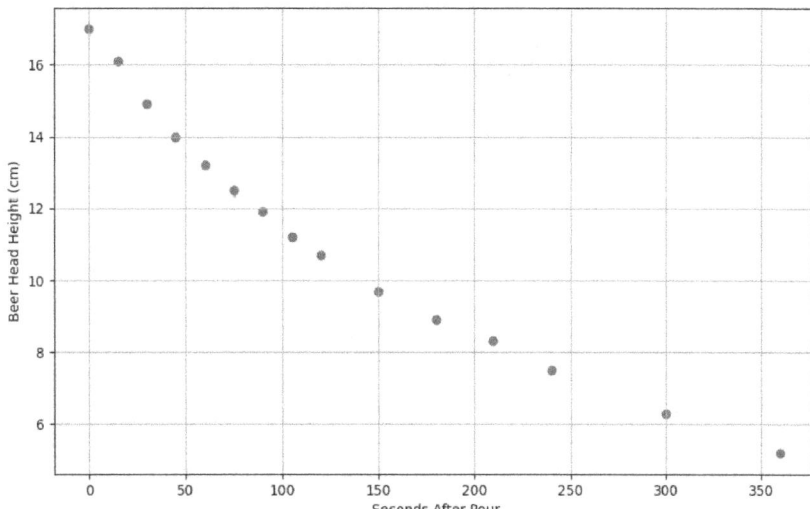

FIGURE 16-6:
How beer
head-height
(head.cm)
decays over time.

Next, I plot the data points with the logarithm of the y-variable:

```
plt.scatter(x=beer_df['seconds_after_pour'], y=np.
    log(beer_df['head_cm']))
```

Then I use `sns.regplot` (a seaborn function) to plot the regression line:

```
sns.regplot(x=beer_df['seconds_after_pour'], y=np.log(beer_
    df['head_cm']), data=beer_df)
```

Finally, I label the axes, set a grid, and show the plot:

```
plt.xlabel('Seconds After Pour')
plt.ylabel('Log(Beer Head Height (cm))')
plt.grid(True)
plt.show()
```

The code produces Figure 16-7.

As you can see, we have another tight 95% confidence interval, which is consistent with the analysis:

```
import statsmodels.formula.api as smf
model = smf.ols('np.log(head_cm) ~ seconds_after_pour', data =
    beer_df).fit()
print(f'F = {model.fvalue}')
print(f'p = {model.f_pvalue}')
```

```
F = 2373.4478110051223
p = 4.1965904467907543e-16
```

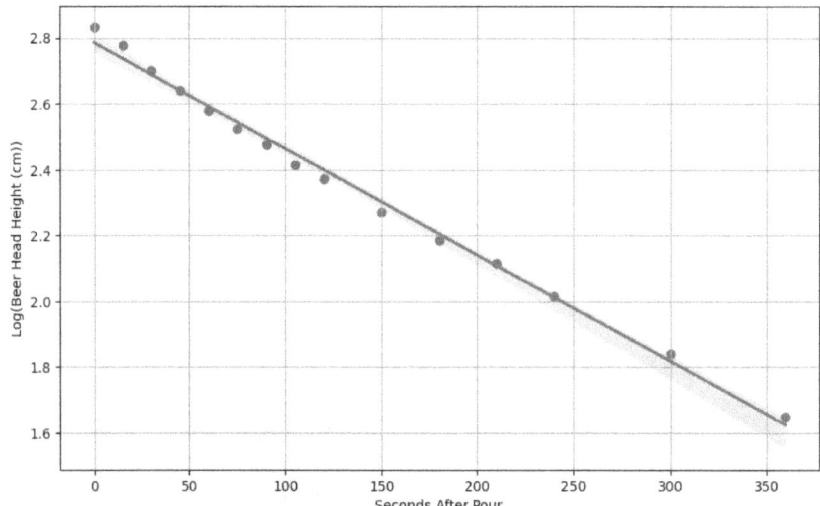

FIGURE 16-7:
How log
(head.cm)
decays over time,
including the
regression line.

The F and p-value show that this model is a phenomenally great fit. In fact, Arnd did all this to show his students how an exponential process works. [If you want to see his data for the other two brands, check out Leike, A. (2002), "Demonstration of the exponential decay law using beer froth," *European Journal of Physics*, 23(1), 21–26.]

Here are the coefficients:

```
Intercept = model.params.iloc[0]
Slope = model.params.iloc[1]
print(f'Intercept = {Intercept}')
print(f'Slope = {Slope}')
Intercept = 2.7854072450442833
Slope = -0.003222965740750936
```

According to the coefficients, the regression equation in logarithmic form is

$$\log(y') = a + bx$$
$$\log(\text{head.cm'}) = 2.785 + ((-.003223) \times \text{seconds\_after\_pour})$$

For the exponential regression equation, you take the exponential of both sides — in other words, you apply the exp() function:

$$\exp(\log(y')) = \exp(a+bx)$$
$$y' = \exp(a)e^{bx}$$
$$\text{head.cm}' = \exp(2.785) \times e^{-.003223 \times \text{seconds\_after\_pour}}$$
$$\text{head.cm}' = 16.20642 \times e^{-.003223 \times \text{seconds\_after\_pour}}$$

Just to verify,

```
print(np.exp(Intercept))
16.206416515851597
```

Analogous to what you did in the preceding section, you can plot the exponential regression equation as a curve in the original scatterplot. You just have to add 3 lines of code to the snippet that created Figure 16-6:

```
x_exponential_fit = np.linspace(beer_df[min], beer_df[max], 100)
y_exponential_fit = np.exp(Intercept)*np.
    exp(Slope*x_exponential_fit)
plt.plot(x_exponential_fit, y_exponential_fit)
```

The first creates 100 evenly spaced points between the minimum value of Seconds After Pour and the maximum value of Seconds After Pour.

The second is the Python equivalent of

$$\text{head.cm}' = \exp(2.785) \times e^{-.003223 \times \text{seconds\_after\_pour}}$$

and predicts a y-value for each of the 100 x-values.

The third plots the 100 xy pairs.

The whole snippet is now

```
import matplotlib.pyplot as plt
import numpy as np

plt.figure(figsize=(10, 6))
plt.scatter(x=beer_df['seconds_after_pour'],
    y=beer_df['head_cm'])

x_exponential_fit = np.linspace(beer_df[min], beer_df[max], 100)
y_exponential_fit = np.exp(Intercept)*np.
    exp(Slope*x_exponential_fit)
plt.plot(x_exponential_fit, y_exponential_fit)

plt.xlabel('Seconds After Pour')
```

```
plt.ylabel('Beer Head Height (cm)')
plt.grid(True)
plt.show()
```

and renders Figure 16-8.

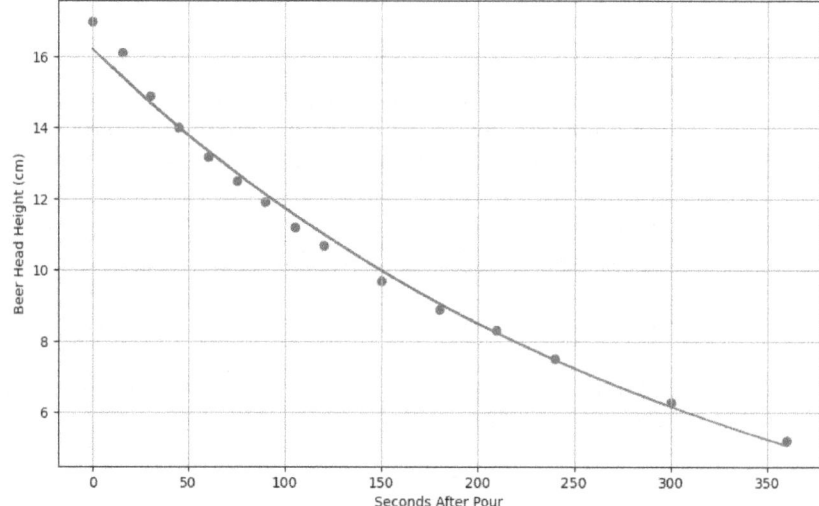

FIGURE 16-8:
The decay of
head.cm over
time, with the
exponential
regression curve.

Logarithmic Regression

In the two preceding sections, I explain how power regression analysis works with the log of the *x*-variable and the log of the *y*-variable, and how exponential regression analysis works with the log of just the *y*-variable. As you might imagine, one more analytic possibility is available to you: working with just the log of the *x*-variable. The equation of the model looks like this:

$$y' = a + b\log(x)$$

Because the logarithm is applied to the predictor variable, this is called *logarithmic regression*.

Here's an example that uses the Cars93 DataFrame in the MASS package, which is an R resource. To retrieve the data,

```
import statsmodels.api as sm
Cars93 = sm.datasets.get_rdataset("Cars93", "MASS")
Cars93_df= pd.DataFrame(Cars93.data)
```

This DataFrame, featured prominently in Chapter 3, holds data on a number of variables for 93 cars in the model year 1993. Here, I focus on the relationship between Horsepower (the *x*-variable) and MPG.highway (the *y*-variable).

REMEMBER

The dot in MPG.highway signifies more than a variable name in Python. This format gums up the analysis. Accordingly, I change it to the more Python-friendly MPG_Highway:

```
Cars93_df.rename(columns={'MPG.highway': 'MPG_Highway'},
    inplace=True)
```

This is the code to create the scatterplot in Figure 16-9:

```
import matplotlib.pyplot as plt
plt.figure(figsize=(10, 6))
plt.scatter(x=Cars93_df['Horsepower'],
    y=Cars93_df['MPG_Highway'])
plt.xlabel('Horsepower')
plt.ylabel('MPG Highway')
plt.grid(True)
plt.show()
```

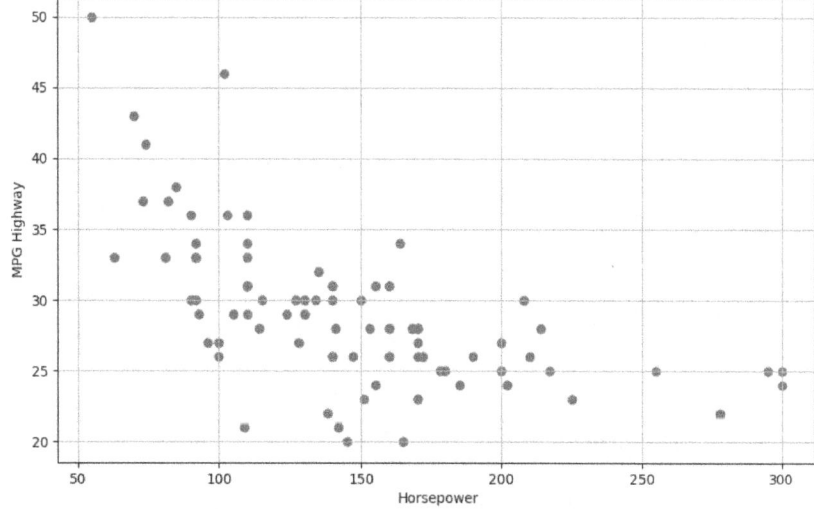

FIGURE 16-9:
MPG Highway
and Horsepower
in the Cars93
DataFrame.

For this example, linearize the plot by taking the log of Horsepower. In the plot, include the regression line, and here's how to draw it:

```
import matplotlib.pyplot as plt
import numpy as np
import seaborn as sns
plt.figure(figsize=(10, 6))
plt.scatter(x=np.log(Cars93_df['Horsepower']),
    y=Cars93_df['MPG_Highway'])
sns.regplot(x=np.log(Cars93_df['Horsepower']),
    y=Cars93_df['MPG_Highway'], data=Cars93_df)
plt.xlabel('Log(Horsepower)')
plt.ylabel('MPG Highway')
plt.grid(True)
plt.show()
```

Figure 16-10 shows the result.

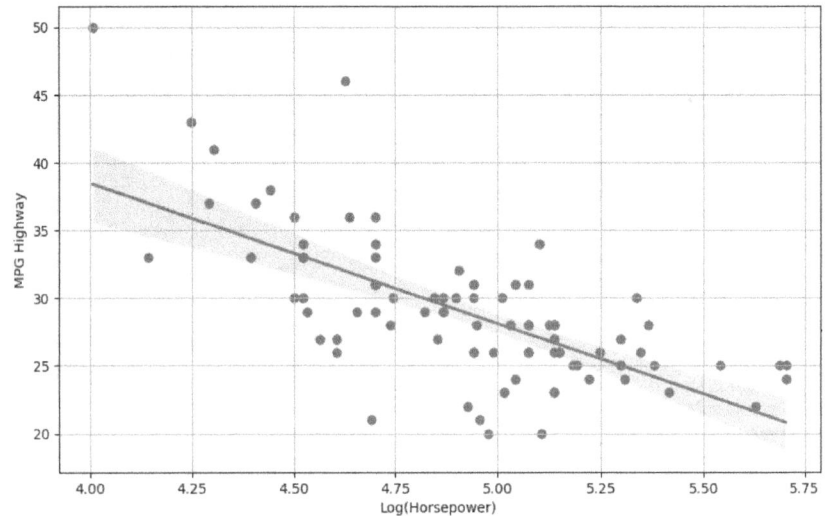

FIGURE 16-10: MPG_Highway and Log(Horsepower) in Cars93, along with the regression line.

The analysis is

```
import statsmodels.formula.api as smf
import numpy as np
model = smf.ols('MPG_Highway ~ np.log(Horsepower)',data =
    Cars93_df).fit()
```

```
print(f'F = {model.fvalue}')
print(f'p = {model.f_pvalue}')
F = 85.52989167492478
p = 9.547557422435498e-15
```

The high F and low p once again indicate an excellent fit.

The coefficients are

```
Intercept = model.params.iloc[0]
Slope = model.params.iloc[1]
print(f'Intercept = {Intercept}')
print(f'Slope = {Slope}')
Intercept = 80.00348496656164
Slope = -10.379241936142638
```

From the coefficients, the regression equation is

$$\text{MPG.highway'} = 80.03 - 10.379\log(\text{Horsepower})$$

As in the preceding sections, I plot the regression curve in the original plot:

```
import matplotlib.pyplot as plt

plt.figure(figsize=(10, 6))
plt.scatter(x=Cars93_df['Horsepower'],
    y=Cars93_df['MPG_Highway'])

x_log_fit = np.linspace(Cars93_df['Horsepower'].min(), Cars93_
    df['Horsepower'].max(), 100)
y_log_fit = Intercept + Slope * np.log(x_log_fit)
plt.plot(x_log_fit, y_log_fit)

plt.xlabel('Horsepower')
plt.ylabel('MPG Highway')
plt.grid(True)
plt.show()
```

Figure 16-11 shows the plot with the regression curve.

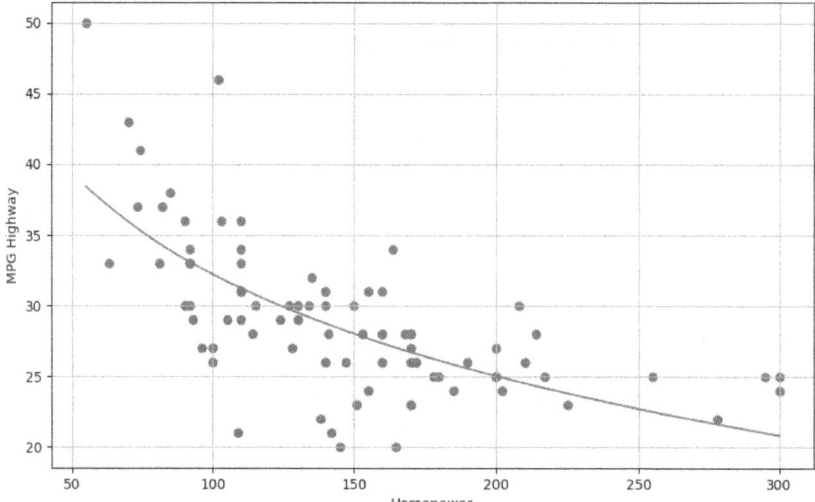

Polynomial Regression: A Higher Power

In all the types of regression I describe earlier in this chapter, the model is a line or a curve that doesn't change direction. It's possible, however, to create a model that incorporates a direction-change. This is the province of *polynomial regression.*

I touch on direction-change in Chapter 12, in the context of trend analysis. To model one change of direction, the regression equation has to have an x-term raised to the second power:

$$y' = a + b_1 x + b_2 x^2$$

To model two changes of direction, the regression equation has to have an x-term raised to the third power:

$$y' = a + b_1 x + b_2 x^2 + b_3 x^3$$

and so forth.

I illustrate polynomial regression with another DataFrame from the MASS package. It's called Boston:

```
import statsmodels.api as sm
Boston = sm.datasets.get_rdataset("Boston", "MASS")
Boston_df= pd.DataFrame(Boston.data)
```

It holds data on housing values in the Boston suburbs. Among its variables are rm (the number of rooms in a dwelling) and medv (the median value of the dwelling). I focus on those two variables in this example, with rm as the predictor variable.

Begin by creating the scatterplot and regression line:

```
import matplotlib.pyplot as plt
import seaborn as sns

plt.figure(figsize=(10, 6))
plt.scatter(x=Boston_df['rm'],y=Boston_df['medv'])
sns.regplot(x=Boston_df['rm'],y=Boston_df['medv'])

plt.xlabel('Rooms')
plt.ylabel('Median Value')
plt.grid(True)
plt.show()
```

Figure 16-12 shows what this code produces.

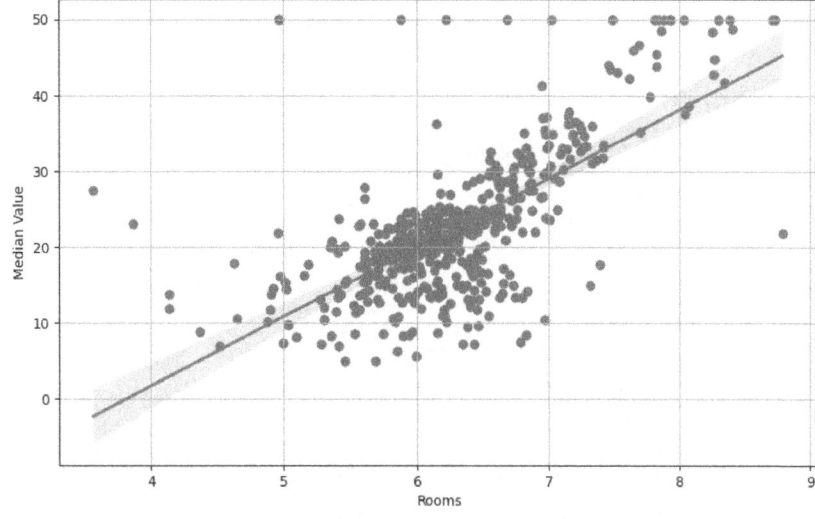

FIGURE 16-12: Scatterplot of median value (medv) versus rooms (rm) in the Boston DataFrame, with the regression line.

The linear regression model (I call it model1) is

```
import statsmodels.formula.api as smf

model1 = smf.ols('medv ~rm',data = Boston_df).fit()
```

```
print(f'F = {model1.fvalue}')
print(f'p = {model1.f_pvalue}')
print(f'R-squared = {model1.rsquared}')
print(f'Intercept = {model1.params[0]}')
print(f'Slope= {model1.params[1]}')
F = 471.84673987638644
p = 2.4872288710081537e-74
R-squared = 0.483525455991334
Intercept = -34.67062077643859
Slope= 9.10210898118031
```

The *F* and *p*-value show that this is a good fit. R-squared tells you that about 48 percent of the SS_{Total} for medv is tied up in the relationship between rm and medv. (Check out Chapter 15 if that last sentence sounds unfamiliar.)

The coefficients tell you that the linear model is

$$medv' = -34.671 + 9.102rm$$

But perhaps a model with a change of direction provides a better fit. To set this up in Python, I create a new variable rm2 — which is just rm squared:

```
rm2 = np.square(Boston_df['rm'])
```

I have to make this variable part of Boston_df:

```
Boston_df['rm2'] = rm2
```

and treat the analysis as a multiple regression with two predictor variables.

So, the code for the new model — I call it model2 — is

```
import statsmodels.formula.api as smf
import numpy as np

rm2 = np.square(Boston_df['rm'])
Boston_df['rm2'] = rm2
model2 = smf.ols('medv ~ rm + rm2',data = Boston_df).fit()
```

```
print(f'F = {model2.fvalue}')
print(f'p = {model2.f_pvalue}')
print(f'R^2 = {model2.rsquared}')
F = 305.44038640799505
p = 1.4602032629346517e-87
R^2 = 0.5484256373971057
```

Looks like a better fit than the linear model. This time, R-squared tells you that almost 55 percent of the SS_{Total} for medv is due to the relationship between medv and the combination of rm and rm^2.

What about the coefficients?

```
Intercept = model2.params.iloc[0]
rm_Coefficent = model2.params.iloc[1]
rm2_Coefficent = model2.params.iloc[2]
print(f'Intercept = {Intercept}')
print(f'rm_Coefficient = {rm_Coefficent}')
print(f'rm2_Coefficient = {rm2_Coefficent}')
Intercept = 66.05884748479394
rm_Coefficient = -22.643262374243577
rm2_Coefficient = 2.470123844033259
```

The coefficients indicate that the polynomial regression equation is

$$medv' = 66.0588 - 22.6433 * rm + 2.4701 * rm^2$$

Is it worth the effort to add rm^2 to the model? To find out, I use stats.anova_lm() to compare the linear model (model1) with the polynomial model (model2) — a technique I show you in Chapter 14.

```
import statsmodels.api as sm
comparison = sm.stats.anova_lm(model1,model2)
print(comparison)
   df_resid          ssr df_diff      ss_diff          F        Pr(>F)
0     504.0 22061.879196     0.0          NaN        NaN           NaN
1     503.0 19289.583875     1.0 2772.295321  72.291064  2.128924e-16
```

The high F-ratio (72.291) and extremely low Pr(>F) indicate that adding rm^2 is a good idea — at a cost of just 1 df (the df_diff).

Here's the code for the scatterplot, along with the curve for the polynomial model:

```
import matplotlib.pyplot as plt
plt.figure(figsize=(10, 6))
plt.scatter(x=Boston_df['rm'],y=Boston_df['medv'])
```

To plot the curve, I create 100 evenly spaced points on the *x*-variable from the minimum value to the maximum value, and then I use the model2 coefficients to calculate a value for each of the 100 x values:

```
x_polynomial_fit = np.linspace(Boston_df['rm'].min(), Boston_
    df['rm'].max(),100)
y_polynomial_fit = Intercept + rm_Coefficent * x_polynomial_fit
    + rm2_Coefficent * x_polynomial_fit**2
```

Then I plot the curve, label the axes, set the grid, and show the plot:

```
plt.plot(x_polynomial_fit, y_polynomial_fit)
plt.xlabel('Rooms')
plt.ylabel('Median Value')
plt.grid(True)
plt.show()
```

The code renders Figure 16-13.

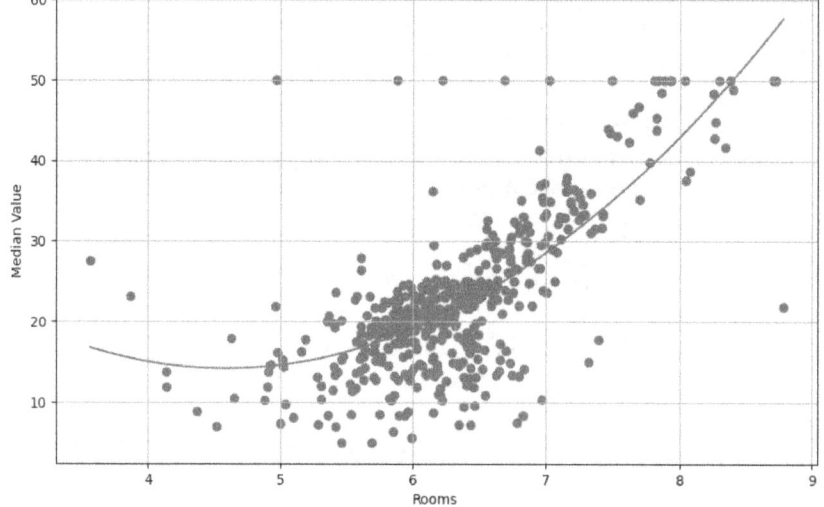

FIGURE 16-13: Scatterplot of median value (medv) versus rooms (rm) in the Boston DataFrame, with the polynomial regression curve.

The curve in the figure shows a slight downward trend in the dwelling's value as rooms increase from fewer than 4 to about 4.5, and then the curve trends more sharply upward.

Which Model Should You Use?

I present a variety of regression models in this chapter. Deciding on the one that's right for your data isn't necessarily straightforward. One superficial answer might be to try each one and see which one yields the highest F and R-squared.

The operative word in that last sentence is *superficial.* The choice of model should depend on your knowledge of the domain from which the data comes and the processes in that domain that produce the data. Which regression type allows you to formulate a theory about what might be happening in the data?

For instance, in the Boston example, the polynomial model showed that dwelling-value *decreases* slightly as the number of rooms *increases* at the low end, and then value steadily *increases* as the number of rooms increases. The linear model couldn't discern a trend like that. Why would that trend occur? Can you come up with a theory? Does the theory make sense?

I'll leave you with an exercise. Remember the shoelace-tying example at the beginning of this chapter? All I gave you was Figure 16-1, but here are the numbers:

```
import numpy as np
trials = [np.arange(1,19,1)]
time_sec = [230, 140, 98, 75, 66, 54, 45, 31, 20, 15,
10, 9, 9, 9, 8, 8, 8, 8]
```

What model can *you* come up with? And how does it help you explain the data?

4

Working with Probability

Work with random variables.

Understand counting rules.

Work with conditional probability.

Visualize probability distributions.

Model and simulate.

Learn logistic regression.

IN THIS CHAPTER

» **Defining probability**

» **Working with probability**

» **Dealing with random variables and their distributions**

» **Focusing on the binomial distribution**

» **Learning probability-related Python functions**

Chapter **17**

Introducing Probability

Probability is the basis of hypothesis testing and inferential statistics, so I use this concept throughout the book. (Seems like a fine time to introduce it!)

Most of the time, I represent probability as the proportion of area under part of a distribution. For example, the probability of a Type I error (also known as α) is the area in a tail of the standard normal distribution or in a tail of the t distribution.

It's time to examine probability in greater detail, including random variables, permutations, and combinations. First, I show you some fundamentals and applications of probability, and then I focus on a couple of specific probability distributions and also tell you about some probability-related Python functions.

What Is Probability?

Most people have an intuitive idea of probability. Toss a fair coin, and you have a 50–50 chance that it comes up heads. Toss a fair die (one of a pair of dice), and you have a 1-in-6 chance that it comes up displaying a 2.

If you wanted to be more formal in your definition, you'd most likely say something about all the possible things that could happen and the proportion of those things you care about. Two things can happen when you toss a coin, and if you care about only one of them (heads), the probability of that event happening is one out of two. Six things can happen when you toss a die, and if you care about only one of them (tossing a 2), the probability of that event happening is one out of six.

Experiments, trials, events, and sample spaces

Statisticians and others who work with probability refer to a process like tossing a coin or throwing a die as an *experiment*. Each time you go through the process, that's a *trial*.

This might not fit your personal definition of an experiment (or of a trial, for that matter), but for a statistician, an *experiment* is any process that produces one of at least two distinct results (like heads or tails).

Here's another piece of the definition of an experiment: You can't predict the result with certainty. Each distinct result is called an *elementary outcome*. Put a bunch of elementary outcomes together and you have an *event*. For example, with a die, the elementary outcomes 2, 4, and 6 make up the event "even number."

Put together all the possible elementary outcomes, and you have yourself a *sample space*. The numbers 1, 2, 3, 4, 5, and 6 make up the sample space for a die. Heads and tails make up the sample space for a coin.

Sample spaces and probability

How do events, outcomes, and sample spaces play into probability? If each elementary outcome in a sample space is equally likely, the probability of an event is

$$\text{pr}(\text{Event}) = \frac{\text{Number of Elementary Outcomes in the Event}}{\text{Number of Elementary Outcomes in the Sample Space}}$$

So the probability of tossing a die and rolling an even number is

$$\text{pr}(\text{Even Number}) = \frac{\text{Number of Even} - \text{Numbered Elementary Outcomes}}{\text{Number of Possible Outcomes of a Die}}$$

$$= \frac{3}{6} = .5$$

If the elementary outcomes are not equally likely, you find the probability of an event in a different way. First, you have to have some way to assign a probability to each one. Then you add up the probabilities of the elementary outcomes that make up the event.

A couple of points to bear in mind about outcome probabilities:

>> Each probability has to be between 0 and 1.

>> All the probabilities of elementary outcomes in a sample space have to add up to 1.00.

How do you assign those probabilities? Sometimes you have advance information — such as knowing that a coin is biased toward coming up heads 60 percent of the time. Sometimes you just have to think through the situation to figure out the probability of an outcome.

Here's a quick example of thinking through the situation. Suppose a die is biased so that the probability of an outcome is proportional to the numerical label of the outcome: A 6 comes up six times as often as a 1, a 5 comes up five times as often as a 1, and so on. What is the probability of each outcome? All the probabilities have to add up to 1.00, and all the numbers on a die add up to 21 (1 + 2 + 3 + 4 + 5 + 6 = 21), so the probabilities are: pr(1) = 1/21, pr(2) = 2/21, . . ., pr(6) = 6/21.

Compound Events

Some rules for dealing with compound events help you "think through." A *compound event* consists of more than one event. It's possible to combine events by either *union* or *intersection* (or both).

Union and intersection

With a fair die, what's the probability of rolling a 1 or a 4? Mathematicians have a symbol for *or*. It's called *union*, and it looks like this: ∪. Using this symbol, the probability of a 1 or a 4 is pr(1 ∪ 4).

In approaching this kind of probability, it's helpful to keep track of the elementary outcomes. One elementary outcome is in each event, so the event "1 or 4" has two elementary outcomes. With a sample space of six outcomes, the probability is 2/6, or 1/3. Another way to calculate this is

$$pr(1 \cup 4) = pr(1) + pr(4) = \frac{1}{6} + \frac{1}{6} = \frac{2}{6} = \frac{1}{3}$$

Here's a slightly more involved one: What's the probability of rolling a number between 1 and 3 or a number between 2 and 4?

Just adding the elementary outcomes in each event won't get it done this time. Three outcomes are in the event "between 1 and 3," and three are in the event "between 2 and 4." The probability can't be 3 + 3 divided by the six outcomes in the sample space, because that's 1.00, leaving nothing for $pr(5)$ and $pr(6)$. For the same reason, you can't just add the probabilities.

The challenge arises in the overlap of the two events. The elementary outcomes in "between 1 and 3" are 1, 2, and 3. The elementary outcomes in "between 2 and 4" are 2, 3, and 4. Two outcomes overlap: 2 and 3. To avoid counting them twice, the trick is to subtract them from the total.

A couple of clarifications will make life easier as I proceed. I abbreviate "between 1 and 3" as A and "between 2 and 4" as B. Also, I use the mathematical symbol for *overlap*. The symbol is ∩, and it's called *intersection*.

Using the symbols, the probability of "between 1 and 3" or "between 2 and 4" is

$$pr(A \cup B) = \frac{\text{Number of Outcomes in A} + \text{Number of Outcomes in B} - \text{Number of Outcomes in } (A \cap B)}{\text{Number of Outcomes in the Sample Space}}$$

$$pr(A \cup B) = \frac{3 + 3 - 2}{6} = \frac{4}{6} = \frac{2}{3}$$

You can also work with the probabilities:

$$pr(A \cup B) = \frac{3}{6} + \frac{3}{6} - \frac{2}{6} = \frac{4}{6} = \frac{2}{3}$$

The general formula is

$$pr(A \cup B) = pr(A) + pr(B) - pr(A \cap B)$$

Why was it okay to just add the probabilities together in the earlier example? Because $pr(1 \cap 4)$ is 0: It's impossible to roll a 1 and a 4 in the same roll of a die. Whenever $pr(A \cap B) = 0$, A and B are said to be *mutually exclusive*.

Intersection again

Imagine throwing a coin and rolling a die at the same time. These two experiments are *independent* because the result of one has no influence on the result of the other.

What's the probability of getting heads and a 4? You use the intersection symbol and write this as $pr(\text{heads} \cap 4)$:

$$pr(\text{Heads} \cap 4) = \frac{\text{Number of Elementary Outcomes in Heads } \cap 4}{\text{Number of Elementary Outcomes in the Sample Space}}$$

Start with the sample space. Table 17-1 lists all the elementary outcomes.

TABLE 17-1

The Elementary Outcomes in the Sample Space for Throwing a Coin and Rolling a Die

Heads, 1	Tails, 1
Heads, 2	Tails, 2
Heads, 3	Tails, 3
Heads, 4	Tails, 4
Heads, 5	Tails, 5
Heads, 6	Tails, 6

As the table shows, 12 outcomes are possible. How many outcomes are in the event "heads and 4"? Just one. So:

$$pr(\text{Heads} \cap 4) = \frac{\text{Number of Elementary Outcomes in Heads } \cap 4}{\text{Number of Elementary Outcomes in the Sample Space}} = \frac{1}{12}$$

You can also work with the probabilities:

$$pr(\text{Heads} \cap 4) = pr(\text{Heads}) \times pr(4) = \frac{1}{12}$$

In general, if A and B are independent,

$$pr(A \cap B) = pr(A) \times pr(B)$$

Conditional Probability

In some circumstances, you narrow the sample space. Suppose that I roll a die and tell you the result is greater than 2. What's the probability that it's a 5?

Ordinarily, the probability of a 5 would be 1/6. In this case, however, the sample space isn't 1, 2, 3, 4, 5, and 6. When you know the result is greater than 2, the sample space becomes 3, 4, 5, and 6. The probability of a 5 is now 1/4.

This is an example of *conditional probability*. It's conditional because I've given a condition — the roll resulted in a number greater than 2. The notation for this is

$$pr(5 \mid \text{Greater than 2})$$

The vertical line (|) is shorthand for the word *given*, and you read that notation as "the probability of a 5 given greater than 2."

Working with the probabilities

In general, if you have two events A and B,

$$pr(A \mid B) = \frac{pr(A \cap B)}{pr(B)}$$

as long as $pr(B)$ isn't zero.

For the intersection in the numerator on the right, this is *not* a case where you just multiply probabilities together. In fact, if you could do that, you wouldn't have a conditional probability, because that would mean A and B are independent. If they're independent, one event can't be conditional on the other.

You have to think through the probability of the intersection. In a die, how many outcomes are in the event "5 ∩ Greater than 2"? Just one, so $pr(5 \cap \text{Greater than 2})$ is 1/6, and

$$pr(5 \mid \text{Greater than 2}) = \frac{pr(5 \cap \text{Greater than 2})}{pr(\text{Greater than 2})} = \frac{\frac{1}{6}}{\frac{4}{6}} = \frac{1}{4}$$

The foundation of hypothesis testing

All the hypothesis testing I discuss in previous chapters involves conditional probability. When you calculate a sample statistic, compute a statistical test, and then compare the test statistic against a critical value, you're looking for a conditional probability. Specifically, you're trying to find

$$pr(\text{obtained test statistic or a more extreme value} \mid H_0 \text{ is true})$$

If that conditional probability is low (less than .05 in all the examples I show you in hypothesis-testing chapters), you reject H_0.

Large Sample Spaces

When dealing with probability, it's important to understand the sample space. In the examples I've shown you so far in this chapter, the sample spaces are small. With a coin or a die, it's easy to list all the elementary outcomes.

The world, of course, isn't that simple. In fact, even the probability problems that live in statistics textbooks aren't that simple. Most of the time, sample spaces are large, and it's less than convenient to list every elementary outcome.

Take, for example, rolling a die twice. How many elementary outcomes are in the sample space consisting of both tosses? You can sit down and list them, but it's better to reason it out: Six possibilities for the first toss, and each of those six can pair up with six possibilities on the second. So the sample space has $6 \times 6 = 36$ possible elementary outcomes.

This is similar to the coin-and-die sample space in Table 17-1, where the sample space consists of $2 \times 6 = 12$ elementary outcomes. With 12 outcomes, it was easy to list them all in a table. With 36 outcomes, it starts to become, well, dicey. (Sorry.)

Events often require some thought, too. What's the probability of rolling a die twice and totaling 5? You have to count the number of ways the two tosses can total 5 and then divide by the number of elementary outcomes in the sample space (36). You total a 5 by rolling any of these pairs: 1 and 4, 2 and 3, 3 and 2, or 4 and 1. That totals four ways, and they don't overlap (excuse me — *intersect*), so

$$\text{pr}(5) = \frac{\text{Number of Ways of Rolling a 5}}{\text{Number of Possible Outcomes of Two Tosses}} = \frac{4}{36} = .11$$

Listing all the elementary outcomes for the sample space is often a nightmare. Fortunately, shortcuts are available, as I show in the upcoming subsections. Because each shortcut quickly helps you count a number of items, another name for a shortcut is a *counting rule.*

Believe it or not, I just slipped one counting rule past you. A couple of paragraphs ago, I say that, in two rolls of a die, you have a sample space of $6 \times 6 = 36$ possible outcomes. This is the *product rule.* If N_1 outcomes are possible on the first trial of an experiment and N_2 outcomes are possible on the second trial, the number of possible outcomes is N_1N_2. Each possible outcome on the first trial can associate with all possible outcomes on the second. What about three trials? That's $N_1N_2N_3$.

Now for a couple more counting rules.

Permutations

Suppose you have to arrange five objects into a sequence. How many ways can you do that? For the first position in the sequence, you have five choices. After you make that choice, you have four choices for the second position. Then you have three choices for the third, two for the fourth, and one for the fifth. The number of ways is $(5)(4)(3)(2)(1) = 120$.

In general, the number of sequences of N objects is $N(N-1)(N-2) \ldots (2)(1)$. This kind of computation occurs fairly frequently in the probability world, and it has its own notation: $N!$ You don't read this by screaming out "N" in a loud voice. Instead, it's "N factorial." By definition, $1! = 1$, and $0! = 1$.

Now for the good stuff. If you have to order the 26 letters of the alphabet, the number of possible sequences is 26!, a huge number. But suppose the task is to create 5-letter sequences so that no letter repeats in the sequence. How many ways can you do that? You have 26 choices for the first letter, 25 for the second, 24 for the third, 23 for the fourth, 22 for the fifth, and that's it. So that's $(26)(25)(24)(23)(22)$. Here's how that product is related to 26!:

$$\frac{26!}{21!}$$

Each sequence is called a *permutation*. In general, if you take permutations of N things r at a time, the notation is $_NP_r$ (the P stands for *permutation*). The formula is

$$_NP_r = \frac{N!}{(N-r)!}$$

Just for completeness, here's another wrinkle. Suppose that I allow repetitions in these sequences of 5. That is, aabbc is a permissible sequence. In that case, the number of sequences is $26 \times 26 \times 26 \times 26 \times 26$, or, as mathematicians would say, "26 raised to the fifth power." Or, as mathematicians would write, "26^5."

Combinations

In the preceding example, these sequences are different from one another: *abcde, adbce, dbcae,* and on and on and on. In fact, you could come up with $5! = 120$ of these different sequences just for the letters *a, b, c, d,* and *e*.

Suppose I add the restriction that one of these sequences is no different from another, and all I'm concerned about is having sets of five nonrepeating letters in no particular order. Each set is called a *combination*. For this example, the number of combinations is the number of permutations divided by 5!:

$$\frac{26!}{5!(21!)}$$

In general, the notation for combinations of N things taken r at a time is ${}_NC_r$ (the C stands for *combination*). The formula is

$$_NC_r = \frac{N!}{r!(N-r)!}$$

Python Functions for Counting Rules

In Python, functions for counting rules live in the math module. Here's factorial() in action:

```
import math
factorial = math.factorial(5)
print(factorial)
120
```

You can calculate all the factorials in an np array:

```
import numpy as np
numbers = [2,3,4,5,6]
numbers_array = np.array(numbers)
factorials = np.array([math.factorial(int(x)) for x in
    numbers_array])
print(factorials)
[  2   6  24 120 720]
```

Next, permutations. That's perm():

```
number_of_permutations=math.perm(26,5)
print(number_of_permutations)
7893600
```

The function for combinations is comb():

```
number_of_combinations = math.comb(26,5)
print(number_of_combinations)
65780
```

To generate itemized combinations and permutations, the relevant functions are in `itertools`:

```
from itertools import combinations, permutations

Beatles = ['John', 'Paul', 'George', 'Ringo']
for b in combinations(Beatles,2):
   print(b)
('John', 'Paul')
('John', 'George')
('John', 'Ringo')
('Paul', 'George')
('Paul', 'Ringo')
('George', 'Ringo')

for b in permutations(Beatles,2):
   print(b)
('John', 'Paul')
('John', 'George')
('John', 'Ringo')
('Paul', 'John')
('Paul', 'George')
('Paul', 'Ringo')
('George', 'John')
('George', 'Paul')
('George', 'Ringo')
('Ringo', 'John')
('Ringo', 'Paul')
('Ringo', 'George')
```

Random Variables: Discrete and Continuous

Let me go back to tosses of a fair die, where six elementary outcomes are possible. If I use x to refer to the result of a toss, x can be any whole number from 1 to 6. Because x can take on a set of values, it's a variable. Because x's possible values correspond to the elementary outcomes of an experiment (meaning you can't predict its values with absolute certainty), x is called a *random variable*.

Random variables come in two varieties. One variety is *discrete*, of which die-tossing is a good example. A discrete random variable can only take on what mathematicians like to call a *countable* number of values — like the numbers 1 through 6. Values between the whole numbers 1 through 6 (like 1.25 and 3.1416) are impossible for a random variable that corresponds to the outcomes of die tosses.

The other kind of random variable is continuous. A *continuous* random variable can take on an infinite number of values. Temperature is an example. Depending on the precision of a thermometer, having temperatures like 34.516 degrees is possible.

Probability Distributions and Density Functions

Back to die-rolling again. Each value of the random variable x (1–6, remember) has a probability. If the die is fair, each probability is 1/6. Pair each value of a discrete random variable like x with its probability, and you have a *probability distribution*.

Probability distributions are easy enough to represent in graphs. Figure 17-1 shows the probability distribution for x.

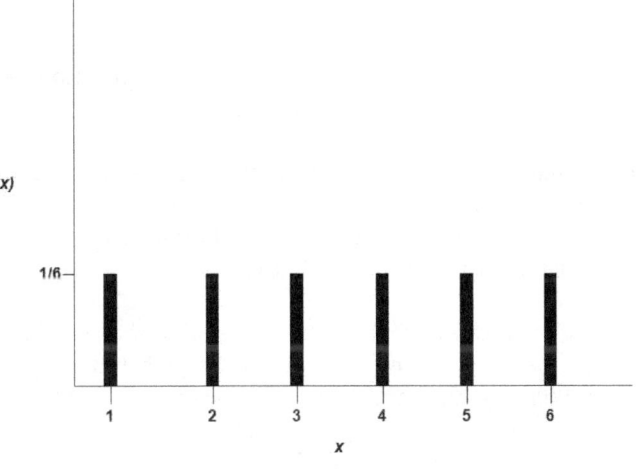

A random variable has a mean, a variance, and a standard deviation. Calculating these parameters is pretty straightforward. In the random-variable world, the mean is called the *expected value*, and the expected value of random variable *x* is abbreviated as *E(x)*. Here's how you calculate it:

$$E(x) = \sum x(pr(x))$$

For the probability distribution in Figure 17-1, that's

$$E(x) = \sum x(pr(x)) = (1)\left(\frac{1}{6}\right) + (2)\left(\frac{1}{6}\right) + (3)\left(\frac{1}{6}\right) + (4)\left(\frac{1}{6}\right) + (5)\left(\frac{1}{6}\right) + (6)\left(\frac{1}{6}\right)$$
$$= 3.5$$

The variance of a random variable is often abbreviated as *V(x)*, and the formula is

$$V(x) = \sum x^2(pr(x)) - [E(x)]^2$$

Working with the probability distribution in Figure 17-1 once again:

$$V(x) = (1^2)\left(\frac{1}{6}\right) + (2^2)\left(\frac{1}{6}\right) + (3^2)\left(\frac{1}{6}\right) + (4^2)\left(\frac{1}{6}\right) + (5^2)\left(\frac{1}{6}\right) + (6^2)\left(\frac{1}{6}\right) - [3.5]^2$$
$$= 2.917$$

The standard deviation is the square root of the variance, which in this case is 1.708.

For continuous random variables, things get a little trickier. You can't pair a value with a probability because you can't really pin down a value. Instead, you associate a continuous random variable with a mathematical rule (an equation) that generates *probability density,* and the distribution is called a *probability density function.* To calculate the mean and variance of a continuous random variable, you need calculus.

In Chapter 8, I show you a probability density function — the standard normal distribution. I reproduce it here as Figure 17-2.

In the figure, *f(x)* represents the probability density. Because probability density can involve some heavyweight mathematical concepts, I don't go into it. As I mention in Chapter 8, think of probability density as something that turns the area under the curve into probability.

Although you can't speak of the probability of a specific value of a continuous random variable, you can work with the probability of an interval. To find the probability that the random variable takes on a value within an interval, you find the proportion of the total area under the curve that's inside that interval. Figure 17-2 shows this concept. The probability that *x* is between 0 and 1α is .3413.

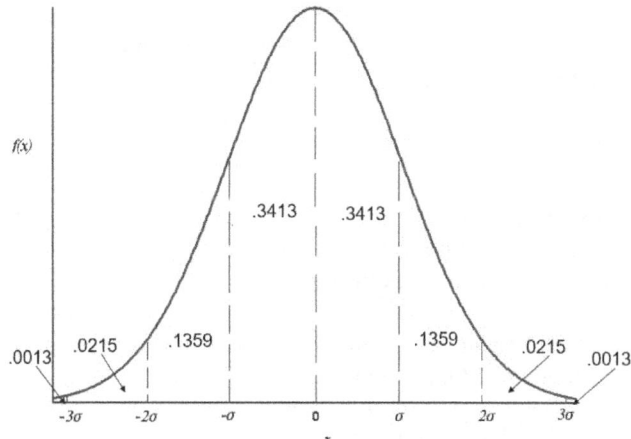

FIGURE 17-2:
The standard normal distribution: a probability density function.

For the rest of this chapter, I deal just with discrete random variables. A specific one is up next.

The Binomial Distribution

Imagine an experiment that has these five characteristics:

>> The experiment consists of *N* identical trials.

    A trial could be the toss of a die or the toss of a coin.

>> Each trial results in one of two elementary outcomes.

    It's standard to call one outcome a success and the other a failure. For die-tossing, a success might be a toss that comes up 3, in which case a failure is any other outcome.

>> The probability of a success remains the same from trial to trial.

    Again, it's standard to use p to represent the probability of a success and to use 1–p (or q) to represent the probability of a failure.

>> The trials are independent.

>> The discrete random variable x is the number of successes in the N trials.

This type of experiment is called a *binomial experiment.* The probability distribution for *x* follows this rule:

$$pr(x) = \frac{N!}{x!(N-x)!} p^x (1-p)^{N-x}$$

On the extreme right, $p^x(1-p)^{N-x}$ is the probability of one combination of *x* successes in *N* trials. The term to its immediate left is $_NC_x$, the number of possible combinations of *x* successes in *N* trials.

This is called the *binomial distribution.* You use it to find probabilities like the probability that you roll four 3s in ten tosses of a die:

$$pr(4) = \frac{10!}{4!(6!)} \left(\frac{1}{6}\right)^4 \left(\frac{5}{6}\right)^6 = .054$$

The *negative binomial distribution* is closely related. In this distribution, the random variable is the number of trials before the *x*th success. For example, you use the negative binomial to find the probability of five tosses that result in anything but a 3 before the fourth time you roll a 3.

For this to happen, in the eight tosses before the fourth 3, you have to roll five non-3s and three successes (tosses when a 3 comes up). Then the next toss results in a 3. The probability of a combination of four successes and five failures is $p^4(1-p)^5$. The number of ways you can have a combination of five failures and four-to-one successes is $_{5+4-1}C_{4-1}$. So the probability is

$$pr(5 \text{ failures before the 4th success}) = \frac{(5+4-1)!}{(4-1)!(5!)} \left(\frac{1}{6}\right)^4 \left(\frac{5}{6}\right)^5 = .017$$

In general, the negative binomial distribution (sometimes called the *Pascal distribution*) is

$$pr(f \text{ failures before the } x\text{th success}) = \frac{(f+x-1)!}{(x-1)!(f!)} p^x (1-p)^f$$

The Binomial and Negative Binomial in Python

Python's functions for the binomial distribution and the negative binomial distribution are in `scipy.stats`. They're members of the `rv_discrete` class (see Chapter 8).

For both distributions, I work with die tosses so that *p* (the probability of a success) = 1/6.

Binomial distribution

Analogous to the probability density function for a continuous random variable, a discrete random variable has a *probability mass function* (pmf). The probability mass function gives the probability that the variable has an exact value. My objective is to use Python to plot the probability mass function for the number of successes in ten tosses of a fair die. The final result would look like Figure 17-3.

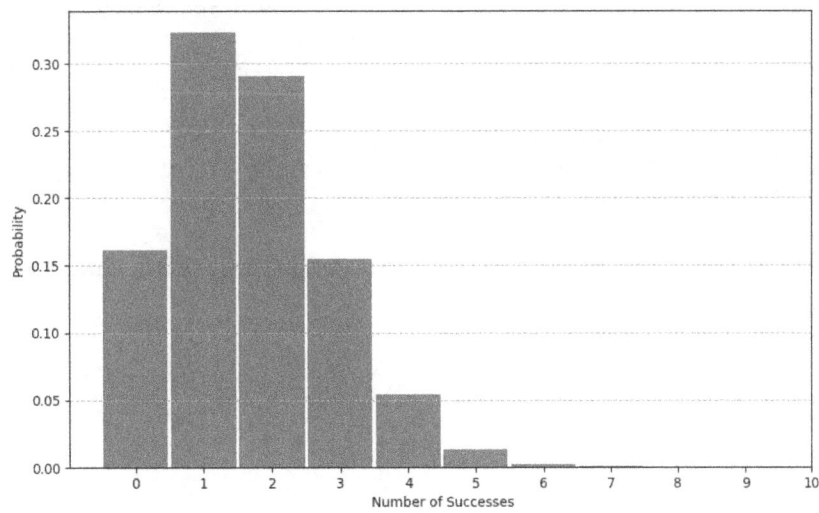

FIGURE 17-3:
Binomial distribution of the number of successes in ten tosses of a fair die.

I begin with the necessary imports:

```
import scipy.stats as stats
import numpy as np
import matplotlib.pyplot as plt
```

Next, I set the number of trials and the probability of a success:

```
n_trials = 10
p_success = 1/6
```

Then I use stats.binom() to create a binomial distribution object.

```
binomial_dist = stats.binom(n=n_trials, p=p_success)
```

TIP

If the phrase "create an object" sounds strange, go back and read Chapter 8.

Here's the code for creating Figure 17-3. First, I set the dimensions of the plot:

```
plt.figure(figsize=(10, 6))
```

Then I use a for loop to have `binomial_dist.pmf()` calculate the probability of each possible number of successes:

```
plt.bar(range(n_trials), [binomial_dist.pmf(i) for i in range
    (n_trials)], width = .95, color='gray')
```

Finally, I deal with the axes, create a grid, and show the plot:

```
plt.xlabel('Number of Successes')
plt.ylabel('Probability')
plt.xticks(successes)
plt.grid(axis='y', linestyle='--')
plt.show()
```

I can also plot the cumulative distribution for the number of successes. The plot will look like Figure 17-4.

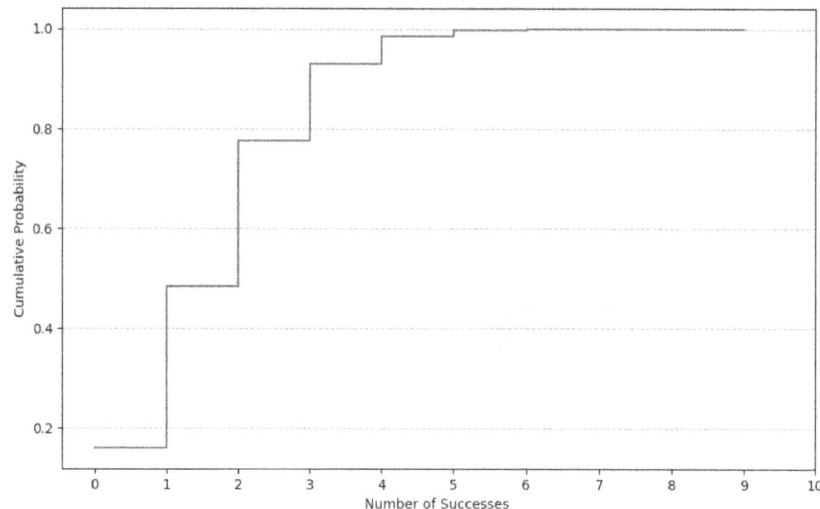

FIGURE 17-4:
Cumulative distribution of the number of successes in ten tosses of a fair die.

The code involves a couple of changes from the preceding snippet. The command with the for loop changes to

```
plt.plot(range(n_trials), [binomial_dist.cdf(i) for i in
    range(n_trials)], drawstyle='steps-post' )
```

In this for loop, I use `binomial_dist.cdf()` to plot the cumulative density function. The `drawstyle = 'steps-post'` argument renders the stepwise effect in Figure 17-4.

Here's the code snippet for Figure 17-4, with the name of the *y*-axis changed to `'Cumulative Probability'`.

```
plt.figure(figsize=(10, 6))
plt.plot(range(n_trials), [binomial_dist.cdf(i) for i in
    range(n_trials)], drawstyle='steps-post' )
plt.xlabel('Number of Successes')
plt.ylabel('Cumulative Probability')
plt.xticks(successes)
plt.grid(axis='y', linestyle='--')
plt.show()
```

In addition to `pmf()` and `cdf()`, `scipy.stats` provides `rvs()`, which allows you to randomly select numbers from the binomial distribution:

```
sample_size = 5
random_sample = binomial_dist.rvs(size=sample_size)
print(f"{sample_size} randomly selected numbers:
    {random_sample}")
5 randomly selected numbers: [2 2 3 1 4]
```

Negative binomial distribution

To set up a negative binomial distribution, I use `stats.nbinom()`:

```
num_successes = 4
p_success_neg_bin = 1/6
negative_binomial_dist = stats.nbinom(n=num_successes,
    p=p_success_neg_bin)
```

I set `num_successes = 4` because of the example I'm working with.

REMEMBER Once again, `pmf()` provides probability mass function, `cdf()` gives you the cumulative distribution function, and `rvs()` produces random numbers.

The example I show you earlier involves the number of failures before the fourth success of a die roll. That case was the probability of five failures before the fourth success, and I use `pmf()` to calculate that probability:

```
num_failures = 5
prob_failures = negative_binomial_dist.pmf(num_failures)
print(f"Probability of a success = {p_success_neg_bin:.2f}")
print(f'Probability of {num_failures} failures before the
    {num_successes}th success = {prob_failures:.4f}')
Probability of a success = 0.17
Probability of 5 failures before the 4th success = 0.0174
```

If I want to know the probability of five or fewer failures before the fourth success, I use `cdf()`:

```
num_failures = 5
cum_prob_failures = negative_binomial_dist.cdf(num_failures)
print(f"Probability of a success = {p_success_neg_bin:.2f}")
print(f"Probability of {num_failures} or fewer failures before
    the {num_successes}th success = {cum_prob_failures:.4f}")
Probability of a success = 0.17
Probability of 5 or fewer failures before the 4th
    success = 0.0480
```

And to sample five random numbers from the negative binomial with four successes and $p = 1/6$:

```
sample_size = 5
random_sample = negative_binomial_dist.rvs(size=sample_size)
print(f"Probability of a success = {p_success_neg_bin:.2f}")
print(f"{sample_size} randomly selected numbers:
    {random_sample}")
Probability of a success = 0.17
5 randomly selected numbers: [27 17 13  9  5]
```

Hypothesis Testing with the Binomial Distribution

Hypothesis tests sometimes involve the binomial distribution. Typically, you have some idea about the probability of a success, and you put that idea into a null hypothesis. Then you perform N trials and record the number of successes.

Finally, you compute the probability of getting that many successes or a more extreme amount if your H$_0$ is true. If the probability is low, reject H$_0$.

When you test in this way, you're using sample statistics to make an inference about a population parameter. Here, that parameter is the probability of a success in the population of trials. By convention, Greek letters represent parameters. Statisticians use π (pi), the Greek equivalent of p, to stand for the probability of a success in the population.

Continuing with the die-rolling example, suppose you have a die and you want to test whether it's fair. You suspect that if it's not, it's biased toward 3. Define a roll that results in 3 as a success. You roll it ten times. Five rolls are successes. Casting all this into hypothesis-testing terms:

$H_0 : \pi \leq 1/6$
$H_1 : \pi > 1/6$

As I usually do, I set $\alpha = .05$.

To test these hypotheses, you have to find the probability of getting at least five successes in ten rolls with $p = 1/6$. That probability is $pr(5)+pr(6)+pr(7)+pr(8)+pr(9)+pr(10)$.

If the total is less than .05, reject H$_0$.

Once upon a time, that would have been a lot of calculating. With Python, not so much. The scipy.stats function binomtest() does all the work. Here's its format:

```
stats.binomtest(successes, trials, pr(success),
    alternative = ' ')
```

The first three arguments are straightforward: The possible values for the fourth argument are 'two-sided', 'greater', or 'less'.

For our example,

```
test_result - stats binomtest(5, 10, 1/6, alternative='greater')
```

The result is stored in test_result.pvalue, so

```
print(f'{test_result.pvalue:.3f}')
0.015
```

The p-value (0.015) is much less than .05, and that tells me to reject the null hypothesis.

If you've been following the discussion, you know that another way to calculate that p-value is the sum of the probabilities of 5 ... 10 successes:

```
success_range = np.arange(5,11,1)
success_range_probability = np.sum(binomial_dist.
   pmf(success_range))
print(f'{success_range_probability:.3f}')
0.015
```

Any way you slice it, the decision is to reject the null hypothesis.

More on Hypothesis Testing: Python versus Tradition

When both $N \pi \geq 5$ (number of trials × the hypothesized probability of a success) and $N(1 - \pi) \geq 5$ (number of trials × the hypothesized probability of a failure), the binomial distribution approximates the standard normal distribution. In those cases, statistics textbooks typically tell you to use the statistics of the normal distribution to answer questions about the binomial distribution. For the sake of tradition, let's carry that through and then compare with `binom.test()`.

Those statistics involve z-scores, which means you have to know the mean and the standard deviation of the binomial. Fortunately, they're easy to compute. If N is the number of trials and π is the probability of a success, the mean is

$$\mu = N\pi$$

the variance is

$$\sigma^2 = N\pi(1-\pi)$$

and the standard deviation is

$$\sigma = \sqrt{N\pi(1-\pi)}$$

When you test a hypothesis, you're making an inference about π, and you have to start with an estimate. You run N trials and get x successes. The estimate is

$$P = \frac{x}{N}$$

To create a z-score, you need one more piece of information: the standard error of P. This sounds harder than it is, because this standard error is just

$$\sigma_P = \sqrt{\frac{\pi(1-\pi)}{N}}$$

Now you're ready for a hypothesis test.

Here's an example. The CEO of FarKlempt Robotics, Inc., believes that 50 percent of FarKlempt robots are purchased for home use. A sample of 1,000 FarKlempt customers indicates that 550 of them use their robots at home. Is this significantly different from what the FarKlempt CEO believes? The hypotheses:

$$H_0 : \pi = .50$$
$$H_1 : \pi \neq .50$$

I set $\alpha = .05$.

$N\pi = 500$, and $N(1 - \pi) = 500$, so the normal approximation is appropriate.

First, calculate P:

$$P = \frac{x}{N} = \frac{550}{1000} = .55$$

Now create a z-score:

$$z = \frac{P - \pi}{\sqrt{\frac{\pi(1-\pi)}{N}}} = \frac{.55 - .50}{\sqrt{\frac{(.50)(1-.50)}{1000}}} = \frac{.05}{\sqrt{\frac{.25}{1000}}} = 3.162$$

With $\alpha = .05$, is 3.162 a large enough z-score to reject H_0?

```
from scipy.stats import norm
standard_normal = norm()
two_tail_probability = 2*standard_normal.sf(3.162)
print(f'{two_tail_probability}')
0.0015668956434215261
```

This is much less than .05, so the decision is to reject H_0.

With a little thought, you can see why statisticians recommended this procedure back in the day. To compute the exact probability, you have to calculate the probability of at least 550 successes in 1,000 trials. That would be $pr(550) + pr(551) + \ldots + pr(1000)$, so an approximation based on a well-known distribution was most welcome — particularly in statistics textbooks.

But now

```
result = stats.binomtest(550,1000,.5,alternative="two-sided")
print(f'{result.pvalue}')
0.0017305360849763115
```

Voilà! The `binomtest()` method calculates the exact probability in the blink of an eye. As you can see, the exact probability (0.001731) differs slightly from the normally approximated p-value, but the conclusion (reject H_0) is the same.

Chapter **18**

Introducing Modeling

A *model* is something you know and can work with that helps you understand something you know little about. A model is supposed to mimic, in some way, the thing it's modeling. A globe, for example, is a model of the Earth. A street map is a model of a neighborhood. A blueprint is a model of a building.

Researchers use models to help them understand natural processes and phenomena. Business analysts use models to help them understand business processes. The models these people use might include concepts from mathematics and statistics — concepts so well-known that they can shed light on the unknown. The idea is to create a model that consists of concepts you understand, put the model through its paces, and see whether the results look like real-world results.

In this chapter, I discuss modeling. My goal is to show how you can harness Python to help you understand processes in your world.

Modeling a Distribution

In one approach to modeling, you gather data and group them into a distribution. Next, you try to figure out a process that results in that kind of a distribution. Restate that process in statistical terms so that it can generate a distribution and then see how well the generated distribution matches up with the real one. This "process you figure out and restate in statistical terms" is the model.

If the distribution you generate matches up well with the real data, does this mean your model is "right"? Does it mean that the process you guessed is the process that produces the data?

Unfortunately, no. The logic doesn't work that way. You can show that a model is wrong, but you can't prove that it's right.

Plunging into the Poisson distribution

In this section, I walk you through an example of modeling with the Poisson distribution, which seems to characterize an array of processes in the real world. By "characterize a process," I mean that a distribution of real-world data looks a lot like a Poisson distribution. When this happens, it's possible that the kind of process that produces a Poisson distribution is also responsible for producing the data.

What is that process? Start with a random variable x that tracks the number of occurrences of a specific event in an interval. An interval can be a sample of 1,000 universal joints, and the specific event is "defective joint." Poisson distributions are also appropriate for events occurring in intervals of time, and the event can be something like "arrival at a toll booth."

With "defining the process" out of the way, I outline the conditions for a *Poisson process* and use both defective joints and toll booth arrivals to illustrate:

>> **The number of occurrences of the event in two non-overlapping intervals are independent.**

The number of defective joints in one sample is independent of the number of defective joints in another. The number of arrivals at a tollbooth during one hour is independent of the number of arrivals during another.

>> **The probability of an occurrence of the event is proportional to the size of the interval.**

The chance that you'll find a defective joint is larger in a sample of 10,000 than it is in a sample of 1,000. The chance of an arrival at a tollbooth is greater for one hour than it is for a half-hour.

>> **The probability of more than one occurrence of the event in a small interval is 0 or close to 0.**

In a sample of 1,000 universal joints, you have an extremely low probability of finding two defective ones right next to one another. At any time, two vehicles don't arrive at a toll booth simultaneously.

The formula for the Poisson distribution is

$$pr(x) = \frac{\mu^x e^{-\mu}}{x!}$$

In this equation, μ represents the average number of occurrences of the event in the interval you're looking at, and e is the constant 2.781828 (followed by infinitely more decimal places).

Modeling with the Poisson distribution

Time to use the Poisson distribution in a model. At the FarBlonJet Corporation, web designers track the number of hits per hour on the intranet home page. They monitor the page for 200 consecutive hours and group the data, as listed in Table 18-1.

TABLE 18-1

Hits Per Hour on the FarBlonJet Intranet Home Page

Hits per Hour	Observed Hours	Hits per Hour X Observed Hours
0	10	0
1	30	30
2	44	88
3	44	132
4	36	144
5	18	90
6	10	60
7	8	56
Total	200	600

The first column shows the variable Hits per Hour. The second column, Observed Hours, shows the number of hours in which each value of hits per hour occurred. In the 200 hours observed, 10 of those hours went by with no hits, 30 hours had one hit, 44 had two hits, and so on. These data lead the web designers to use a Poisson distribution to model hits per hour. Here's another way to say this: They believe that a Poisson process produces the number of hits per hour on the web page.

Multiplying the first column by the second column results in the third column. Summing the third column shows that in the 200 observed hours, the intranet page received 600 hits. So the average number of hits per hour is 3.00.

Applying the Poisson distribution to this example,

$$pr(x) = \frac{\mu^x e^{-\mu}}{x!} = \frac{3^x e^{-3}}{x!}$$

Figure 18-1 shows the probability mass function for the Poisson distribution with $\mu = 3$.

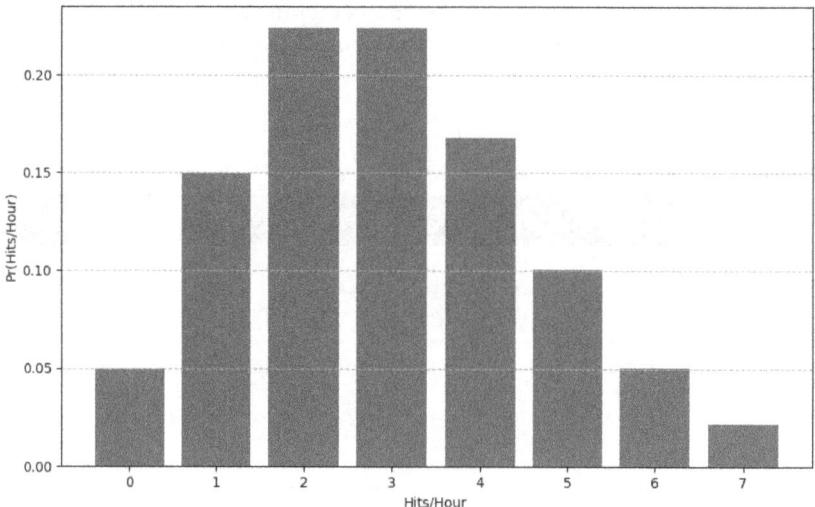

FIGURE 18-1:
The Poisson distribution with $\mu = 3$.

How did I plot this figure? I'll be happy to tell you, but first:

In Python, the Poisson distribution lives in `scipy.stats`:

```
from scipy.stats import poisson
```

A discrete random variable, `poisson` is a member of the `rv_discrete` class. To create a Poisson object with $\mu = 3$,

```
poisson_dist = poisson(3)
```

And now for the plot. I get the ball rolling by importing `matplotlib` and setting the dimensions of the plot:

```
import matplotlib.pyplot as plt
plt.figure(figsize=(10, 6))
```

Next, I add list comprehension(see Chapter 2). The for loop uses poisson_dist.
pmf() to calculate the probability for every x-value in the range and plt.bar()
plots the resulting bars.

```
plt.bar(range(8), [poisson_dist.pmf(i) for i in range(8)])
```

I create a grid, label the axes, and show the plot:

```
plt.grid(axis='y', linestyle='--')
plt.xlabel('Hits/Hour')
plt.ylabel('Pr(Hits/Hour)')
plt.show()
```

And there you have it.

For this model, I use the Poisson distribution to predict the distribution of
hits per hour.

First, the Poisson probabilities:

```
predicted_probs = [poisson_dist.pmf(i) for i in range(8)]
```

Then I multiply each probability by 200 (the total number of observed hits) to
predict hits per hour:

```
predicted_hits_per_hour = [(prob * 200) for prob in
    predicted_probs]
for i in range(len(predicted_hits_per_hour)):
 print(f"{predicted_hits_per_hour[i]:.4f}")
9.9574
29.8722
44.8084
44.8084
33.6063
20.1638
10.0819
4.3208
```

How close are the predicted values to the data?

Let's take a look at the data. From Table 18-1, that's

```
observed_hits_per_hour = [10,30,44,44,36,18,10,8]
```

Figure 18-2 shows the observations and the predictions side by side.

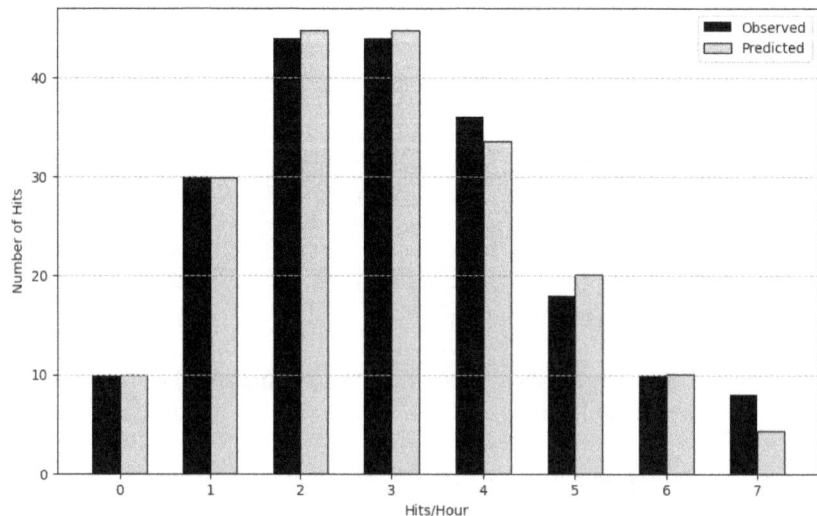

This is called a grouped bar plot.

REMEMBER   Here's the code:

```
import numpy as np
import matplotlib.pyplot as plt
```

I define the numbers that go on the x-axis:

```
x_numbers = range(len(observed_hits_per_hour))
```

Then I set the width of the bars (feel free to experiment):

```
bar_width = 0.30
```

Next, I position the bars for the observations (on the left in each pair)

```
observed = np.arange(len(observed_hits_per_hour))
```

and the bars for the predictions (on the right in each pair):

```
predicted = observed + bar_width
```

I set the dimensions for the plot:

```
plt.figure(figsize=(10, 6))
```

Then I create the bars for the observed values

```
plt.bar(observed, observed_hits_per_hour, bar_width,
    label='Observed', color = 'black')
```

and for the predicted values:

```
plt.bar(predicted, predicted_hits_per_hour, bar_width,
    label='Predicted', color = 'lightgray',edgecolor = 'black')
```

I make sure the x-axis tick marks are in the centers of the bar-pairs:

```
plt.xticks(observed + bar_width / 2, x_numbers)
```

I finish by labeling the axes, creating a legend and a grid, and showing the plot:

```
plt.xlabel('Hits/Hour')
plt.ylabel('Number of Hits')
plt.legend()
plt.grid(axis='y', linestyle='--')
plt.show()
```

In Figure 18-2, the observed and the predicted look pretty close, don't they?

Testing the model's fit

Well, "looking pretty close" isn't sufficient for a statistician — a statistical test is a necessity. As is the case with all statistical tests, this one starts with a null hypothesis and an alternative hypothesis. Here they are:

H_0 : The distribution of observed hits per hour follows a Poisson distribution.
H_1 : Not H_0

The appropriate statistical test involves an extension of the binomial distribution. It's called the *multinomial* distribution — *multi* because it encompasses more categories than just success and failure. This is a difficult distribution to work with.

Fortunately, pioneering statistician Karl Pearson (the inventor of the correlation coefficient) noticed that χ^2 (chi-square), a distribution I show you in Chapter 10, approximates the multinomial. Originally intended for one-sample hypothesis tests about variances, χ^2 has become much better known for applications like the one I'm about to show you.

Pearson's big idea was this: If you want to know how well a hypothesized distribution (like the Poisson) fits a sample (like the observed hours), use the distribution to generate a hypothesized sample (your predicted hours, for instance), and work with this formula:

$$\chi^2 = \sum \frac{(\text{Observed} - \text{Predicted})^2}{\text{Predicted}}$$

Usually, the formula is written with *Expected* rather than *Predicted*, and both Observed and Expected are abbreviated. The usual form of this formula is

$$\chi^2 = \sum \frac{(O - E)^2}{E}$$

For this example,

$$\chi^2 = \sum \frac{(O - E)^2}{E} = \frac{(10 - 9.9574)^2}{9.9574} + \frac{(30 - 29.8722)^2}{29.8722} + \cdots + \frac{(8 - 4.3208)^2}{4.3208}$$

To calculate that value and thus test the hypotheses, I use `chisquare()`, which lives in `scipy.stats`. (I introduce it in Chapter 10.)

```
import numpy as np
from scipy.stats import chisquare
```

Now I set up the test:

```
chi2_test = chisquare(np.array(observed_hits_per_hour),
    np.array(predicted_hits_per_hour), ddof=1, sum_check=False)
```

The first two arguments, of course, are the arrays that represent the observed values and the predictions.

The third argument (`ddof`) stands for "delta degrees of freedom" and allows me to adjust the degrees of freedom as necessary. The default value is 0, and the default degrees of freedom is the number of possible values −1 (8−1 = 7, in this case). I have to subtract an additional degree of freedom, however, because I used $\mu = 3$ to calculate the predictions. That's why I set `ddot` = 1. The degrees of freedom for this test is 8−1−1 = 6.

The fourth argument, `sum_check=False`, requires some explanation. One of the requirements of the chi-square test is that the sum of the predictions equals the sum of the observed values. When fitting a Poisson distribution, though, that doesn't always happen. You're working with products that involve decimals, and discrepancies between totals typically occur. So that last argument tells `chisquare()` not to check for equal sums.

The `chisquare()` function returns `statistic` and `pvalue`, so

```
print(f'Chi-Square = {chi2_test.statistic:.4f}')
print(f'Probability of a Chi-Square this high or higher =
   {chi2_test.pvalue:.4f}')
Chi-Square = 3.5661
Probability of a Chi-Square this high or higher = 0.7352
```

If α = .05, the returned probability (.7352) tells me to not reject H_0 — meaning you can't reject the hypothesis that the observed data come from a Poisson distribution.

This is one of those infrequent times when it's beneficial to *not* reject H_0 — if you want to make the case that a Poisson process is producing the data. A low value of χ^2 indicates a close match between the data and the Poisson predictions. If the probability had been just a little greater than .05, not rejecting H_0 would look suspicious. The high probability, however, makes it reasonable to not reject H_0 — and to think that a Poisson process might account for the data.

Playing ball with a model

Baseball is a game that generates huge amounts of statistics — and many people study these statistics closely. The Society for American Baseball Research (SABR) has sprung from the efforts of a band of dedicated fan-statisticians (fantasticians?) who delve into the statistical nooks and crannies of the great American pastime. They call their work *sabermetrics*. (I made up *fantasticians*. They call themselves *sabermetricians*.)

The reason I mention this is that sabermetrics supplies a nice example of modeling. It's based on the obvious idea that, during a game, a baseball team's objective is to score runs and to keep its opponent from scoring runs. The better a team does at both tasks, the more games it wins. Bill James, who gave sabermetrics its name and is its leading exponent, discovered a neat relationship between the number of runs a team scores, the number of runs the team allows, and its winning percentage. He calls it the *Pythagorean percentage*:

$$\text{Pythagorean Percentage} = \frac{(\text{Runs Scored})^2}{(\text{Runs Scored})^2 + (\text{Runs Allowed})^2}$$

The squares in the expression reminded James of the Pythagorean theorem, hence the name *Pythagorean percentage.* Think of it as a model for predicting games won. (This is James' original formula, and I use it throughout. Over the years, sabermetricians have found that 1.83 is more accurate than 2.)

Calculate this percentage and multiply it by the number of games a team plays. Then compare the answer to the team's wins. How well does the model predict the number of games each team won during the 2024 season?

To find out, I found all the relevant data (number of games won and lost, runs scored, and runs allowed) for every American League (AL) team in 2024. I put the data into an Excel spreadsheet on my local hard drive. Then I have to upload the spreadsheet into Colab and use the spreadsheet to create a DataFrame.

I do this by clicking the File icon with the up arrow in Colab's left panel. Figure 18-3 shows the icon — it's the leftmost one.

FIGURE 18-3:
The Upload icon
(it's the File icon
with the up
arrow) in Colab's
left panel, and
the uploaded
spreadsheet.

That enables me to navigate to the spreadsheet on my hard drive. I select the spreadsheet and it uploads to Colab, as the AL_2024.xlsx icon shows.

REMEMBER

When you upload a file to Colab, you upload it to session storage — meaning that when the session ends, the upload goes away. When you restart the session, you have to upload the file again.

I right-click on the AL_2024.xlsx icon and choose Copy Path from the menu that appears. (See Figure 18-4.) This, unsurprisingly, copies the path of the file after it's uploaded into Colab. I can then paste the path into the Python code.

The code that creates the DataFrame AL_2024 from the spreadsheet is:

```
import pandas as pd
AL_2024 = pd.read_excel('/content/AL_2024.xlsx')
```

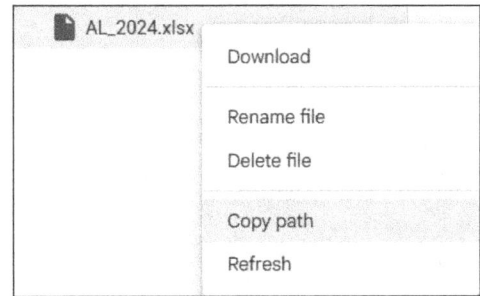

FIGURE 18-4:
Copying the
path of the
uploaded file.

The quoted file path in parentheses is the one I just copied via Copy Path.

```
print(AL_2024)
       Team    Won    Lost    Runs_Scored    Runs_Allowed
0       NYY     94      68            815             668
1       CLE     92      69            708              62
2       BAL     91      71            786             699
3       HOU     88      73            740             649
4       KAN     86      76            735             644
5       DET     86      76            682             642
6       SEA     85      77            676             607
7       MIN     82      80            742             735
8       BOS     81      81            751             747
9        TB     80      82            604             663
10      TEX     78      84            683             738
11      TOR     74      88            671             743
12      OAK     69      93            643             764
13      LAA     63      99            635             797
14      CHW     41     121            507             813
```

Next, I calculate each team's Pythagorean percentage and use it to predict each team's number of wins:

```
AL_2024['Pythagorean'] = AL_2024['Runs_Scored'] ** 2 /
    (AL_2024['Runs_Scored'] ** 2 + AL_2024['Runs_Allowed'] ** 2)
AL_2024['Predicted Wins'] = AL_2024['Pythagorean'] *
    (AL_2024['Won'] + AL_2024['Lost'])
print(AL_2024[['Team', 'Won', 'Predicted_Wins', 'Pythagorean']])

       Team    Won    Predicted_Wins    Pythagorean
0       NYY     94          96.901749       0.598159
1       CLE     92          90.994530       0.565183
2       BAL     91          90.458445       0.558385
3       HOU     88          91.002796       0.565235
```

4	KAN	86	91.644004	0.565704
5	DET	86	85.889797	0.530184
6	SEA	85	89.687267	0.553625
7	MIN	82	81.767755	0.504739
8	BOS	81	81.432574	0.502670
9	TB	80	73.472519	0.453534
10	TEX	78	74.739147	0.461353
11	TOR	74	72.772393	0.449212
12	OAK	69	67.170510	0.414633
13	LAA	63	62.904768	0.388301
14	CHW	41	45.360699	0.280004

Now I use `chisquare()` to see how well the model fits the data:

```
AL_chi2_test = chisquare(AL_2024['Won'], AL_2024['Predicted_
    Wins'], sum_check=False)
```

I didn't use the `Won` data to estimate any parameters, like a mean or a variance, and then apply those parameters to calculate predicted wins. Instead, the predictions came from other data — `Runs_Scored` and `Runs_Allowed`. For this reason, the degrees of freedom = 15−1 = 14, and no adjustments (via `ddof`) are necessary:

```
print(f'Chi-Square = {AL_chi2_test.statistic:.4f}')
print(f'Probability of a Chi-Square this high or higher =
    {AL_chi2_test.pvalue:.4f}')
Chi-Square = 2.0081
Probability of a Chi-Square this high or higher = 0.9999
```

The very high Probability tells you that, with 14 degrees of freedom, the model fits the data extremely well.

If you're a baseball fan (as I am), it's fun to match up `Won` with `Predicted_Wins` for each team. This gives you an idea of which teams overperformed and which ones underperformed, given how many runs they scored and how many they allowed. First, I create a column for the predicted wins rounded to the nearest whole number,

```
AL_2024['Predicted'] = round(AL_2024['Predicted_Wins'])
```

and another column for `Won` − `Predicted`:

```
AL_2024['Difference'] = AL_2024['Won'] − AL_2024['Predicted']
print(AL_2024[['Team','Won', 'Predicted', 'Difference']])
```

	Team	Won	Predicted	Difference
0	NYY	94	97.0	-3.0
1	CLE	92	91.0	1.0
2	BAL	91	90.0	1.0
3	HOU	88	91.0	-3.0
4	KAN	86	92.0	-6.0
5	DET	86	86.0	0.0
6	SEA	85	90.0	-5.0
7	MIN	82	82.0	0.0
8	BOS	81	81.0	0.0
9	TB	80	73.0	7.0
10	TEX	78	75.0	3.0
11	TOR	74	73.0	1.0
12	OAK	69	67.0	2.0
13	LAA	63	63.0	0.0
14	CHW	41	15.0	-4.0

The Difference column shows that TB (the Tampa Bay Rays) outperformed their prediction by seven games — and that was the biggest overperformance in the American League in 2024.

Surprisingly, the winningest team — the NYY (New York Yankees, my personal favorite) — *underperformed* their prediction by three games. They more than made up for it, however, by going on to win the American League Championship Series. (What's that you say? The 2024 World Series? That shall not appear in this book. Ever.)

A Simulating Discussion

Another approach to modeling is to simulate a process. The idea is to define as much as you can about what a process does and then somehow use numbers to represent that process and carry it out. It's a useful way to find out what a process does in case other methods of analysis are overly complex.

Taking a chance: The Monte Carlo method

Many processes contain an element of randomness. You just can't predict the outcome with certainty. To simulate this type of process, you have to have some way of simulating the randomness. Simulation methods that incorporate randomness are called *Monte Carlo* simulations. The name comes from the city in Monaco whose main attraction is gambling casinos.

In the next few sections, I show you a couple of examples. These examples aren't so complex that you can't analyze them. I use them for just that reason: You can check the results against analysis.

Loading the dice

In Chapter 17, in the section on sample spaces and probability, I talk about a *die* (one member of a pair of dice) that's biased to come up according to the numbers on its faces: A 6 is six times as likely as a 1, a 5 is five times as likely, and so on. On any toss, the probability of rolling a number *n* is *n*/21.

Suppose you have a pair of dice loaded this way. What would the outcomes of 2,000 tosses of these dice look like? What would be the average of those 2,000 tosses? What would be the variance and the standard deviation? You can use Python to set up Monte Carlo simulations and answer these questions.

I begin by writing a function to calculate the probability of each possible outcome. Before I develop the function, I'll trace the reasoning for you. For each outcome (2–12), I have to have all the ways of producing the outcome. For example, to roll a 4, I can have a 1 on the first die and a 3 on the second, 2 on the first die and 2 on the second, or 3 on the first and 1 on the second. The probability (I call it *loaded_pr*) of a 4, then, is

$$loaded\_pr(4) = \left(\frac{1}{21} \times \frac{3}{21}\right) + \left(\frac{2}{21} \times \frac{2}{21}\right) + \left(\frac{3}{21} \times \frac{1}{21}\right) = \frac{(1 \times 3) + (2 \times 2) + (3 \times 1)}{21^2}$$
$$= .02267574$$

Rather than enumerate all possibilities for each outcome and then calculate the probability, I create a function called `loaded_pr()` to do the work. I want it to work like this:

```
loaded_probability_of_four = loaded_pr(4)
print(loaded_probability_of_four)
0.022675736961451247
```

First, I define the function, and write a doc string:

```
def loaded_pr(x):
    '''
    Calculates the probability of a pair of loaded dice having
        a sum of x.
    On each die, a value's probability is proportional to its value --
        e.g., pr(1) = 1/21, pr(2) = 2/21, etc.
```

```
arg: a number between 2 and 12, inclusive
return: a probability between 0 and 1

'''
```

Next, I want to stop the whole thing and print a warning if *x* is less than 2 or greater than 12:

```
if x < 2 or x > 12:
  warning("x must be between 2 and 12, inclusive")
```

Then I set a variable called `first` that tracks the value of the first die, depending on the value of *x*. If *x* is less than 7, I set `die_1` to 1.

```
if x < 7:
  die_1 = 1
  step = 1
```

The step variable serves double-duty: It denotes the step size in the upcoming for loop, and it helps set the stop value in the `for` loop.

If *x* is 7 or more, I set `die_1` to 6 (the maximum value of a roll of one die) and step to –1 — again, to denote the step size in the upcoming `for` loop and to help set the stop value in the `for` loop. It's –1 because the start value is greater than the stop value in this case:

```
else:
  die_1 = 6
  step = -1
```

I'll want to keep track of the sum for the numerator (as in the equation I just showed you), so I start the sum at 0:

```
sum = 0
```

Next, I set the value of the second die, which is of course:

```
die_2 = x - die_1
```

And now the business end — the `for` loop that does the calculations:

```
for die_1 in range(die_1, die_2 + step, step):
  die_2 = x - die_1
  sum = sum + (die_1 * die_2)
```

Finally, the `return` value:

```
return sum / 21**2
```

Here it is all together:

```python
def loaded_pr(x):
    '''
    Calculates the probability of a pair of loaded dice having
      a sum of x.
    On each individual die, a value's probability is proportional
      to its value --
    e.g., pr(1) = 1/21, pr(2) = 2/21, etc.

    arg: a number between 2 and 12, inclusive
    return: a probability between 0 and 1

    '''
    if x < 2 or x > 12:
        warning("x must be between 2 and 12, inclusive")
    if x < 7:
        die_1 = 1
        step = 1
    else:
        die_1 = 6
        step = -1
    sum = 0
    die_2 = x - die_1
    for die_1 in range(die_1, die_2 + step, step):
        die_2 = x - die_1
        sum = sum + (die_1 * die_2)
    return sum / 21**2
```

Next, I create the range of possible outcomes of rolling a pair of dice:

```python
import numpy as np
outcomes = np.arange(2,13)
print(outcomes)
[ 2  3  4  5  6  7  8  9 10 11 12]
```

Then I use my newly minted function to compute the probability of each outcome:

```python
loaded_probabilities = [loaded_pr(x) for x in outcomes]
for prob in loaded_probabilities:
```

```
   print(f'{prob:.3f}')
0.002
0.009
0.023
0.045
0.079
0.127
0.159
0.172
0.166
0.136
0.082
```

I rounded off the probabilities so that they look good on the page.

At this point, I put the outcomes and the probabilities together to create a discrete random variable distribution. I want it to be a member of the rv_discrete class, as is the case for the binomial distribution and the Poisson, so:

```
import numpy as np
from scipy.stats import rv_discrete
loaded_dist = rv_discrete(values=(outcomes,
    loaded_probabilities))
```

TIP

Think of the loaded_dist object I just created as the distribution of the discrete random variable outcomes.

The loaded_dist object inherits all the methods of the rv_discrete class. One of those methods, rvs(), generates random numbers and thus performs the random sampling.

REMEMBER

Randomization functions in Python (or in any other language) are *pseudorandom:* They start from a seed number and work from there. If you set the seed, you can determine the course of the randomization. If you don't set the seed, the randomization takes off on its own each time you run it.

So I start by setting a seed:

```
np.random.seed(2352632)
```

REMEMBER

This isn't necessary, but if you want to reproduce my results, start with that function and that seed number. If you don't, your results won't look exactly like mine (which is not necessarily a bad thing).

Now I draw 10,000 random samples from `loaded_dist`:

```
samples = loaded_dist.rvs(size=10000)
```

What are the statistics for these simulated rolls of the dice? I use the `mean()`, `var()`, and `std()` methods to calculate them:

```
mean_samples = samples.mean()
print(f'mean = {mean_samples:.4f}')
variance_samples = samples.var()
print(f'variance = {variance_samples:.4f}')
standard_deviation_samples = samples.std()
print(f'standard deviation = {standard_deviation_samples:.4f}')
mean = 8.6357
variance = 4.4596
standard deviation = 2.1118
```

How do these values match up with the parameters of the random variable (`loaded_dist`)? This is what I meant earlier by "check the results against analysis." In Chapter 17, I show how to calculate the expected value (the mean), the variance, and the standard deviation for a discrete random variable.

The expected value is

$$E(x) = \sum x(pr(x))$$

The variance is

$$V(x) = \sum x^2(pr(x)) - [E(x)]^2$$

The standard deviation is, of course

$$Std(x) = \sqrt{V(x)} = \sqrt{\sum x^2(pr(x)) - [E(x)]^2}$$

I use the `mean()`, `var()`, and `std()` methods to compute these parameters of `loaded_dist`:

```
expected_value = loaded_dist.mean()
print(f'expected value = {expected_value:.4f}')
distribution_variance = loaded_dist.var()
print(f'variance = {distribution_variance:.4f}')
distribution_standard_deviation = loaded_dist.std()
print(f'standard deviation =
    {distribution_standard_deviation:.4f}')
expected value = 8.6667
```

```
variance = 4.4444
standard deviation = 2.1082
```

Table 18-2 shows that the results from the simulation match up closely with the parameters of the random variable. You might try repeating the simulation with lots more simulated tosses — 50,000, perhaps. Will increased tosses pull the simulation statistics closer to the distribution parameters?

TABLE 18-2   **Statistics from the Loaded-Dice-Tossing Simulation and the Parameters of the Discrete Distribution**

	Simulation Statistic	Distribution Parameter
Mean	8.6357	8.6667
Variance	4.4596	4.4444
Standard Deviation	2.1118	2.1082

Simulating the central limit theorem

This might surprise you, but statisticians often use simulations to make determinations about some of their statistics. They do this when mathematical analysis becomes quite difficult.

For example, some statistical tests depend on normally distributed populations. If the populations aren't normal, what happens to those tests? Do they still do what they're supposed to? To answer that question, statisticians might create non-normally distributed populations of numbers, simulate experiments with them, and apply the statistical tests to the simulated results.

In this section, I use simulation to examine an important statistical item: the central limit theorem. In Chapter 9, I introduce this theorem in connection with the sampling distribution of the mean. In fact, I simulate sampling from a population with only three possible values to show you that even with a small sample size, the sampling distribution starts to look normally distributed.

Here, I set up a normally distributed population and draw 10,000 samples of 25 scores each. I calculate the mean of each sample and then set up a distribution of those 10,000 means. The idea is to see how that distribution's statistics match up with the central limit theorem's predictions.

The population for this example has the parameters of the population of scores on the IQ test, a distribution I use for examples in several chapters. It's a normal distribution with μ = 100 and σ = 15. According to the central limit theorem, the mean of the distribution of means (the sampling distribution of the mean) should be 100, and the standard deviation (the standard error of the mean) should be 3 — the population standard deviation (15) divided by the square root of the sample size (5). The central limit theorem also predicts that the sampling distribution of the mean is normally distributed.

To get started, I set up the population of IQ scores and the sample size:

```
from scipy.stats import norm
import numpy as np
IQ_dist = norm(100, 15)
sample_size =25
```

I'm going to randomly sample 25 numbers from IQ_dist, calculate the mean, add the mean to a list called sampling_distribution, and go through the process a total of 10,000 times. First, I initialize the sampling distribution:

```
sampling_distribution = []
```

Then I set up the for loop that does the sampling, calculates the mean, appends the mean to the sampling distribution, and iterates 10,000 times:

```
for sample_count in range(1, 10001):
 np.random.seed(sample_count)
 #sample_mean = np.mean(np.random.normal(100, 15, sample_size))
 sample_mean = np.mean(IQ_dist.rvs(size=sample_size))
 sampling_distribution = np.append(sampling_distribution,
   sample_mean)
```

REMEMBER

The np.random_seed(sample_count) statement is optional. Use it if you want to duplicate my results.

How about the statistics of the sampling distribution?

```
print(f'mean of the sampling distribution = {np.mean
  (sampling_distribution):.4f}')
print(f'standard error of the mean = {np.
  std(sampling_distribution):.4f}')
mean of the sampling distribution = 100.0112
standard error of the mean = 2.9964
```

Pretty close to the predicted values!

TIP

Be sure to reset `sampling_distribution` to `[]` before each time you run the `for` loop.

Figure 18-5 shows that the sampling distribution looks very much like a normal distribution.

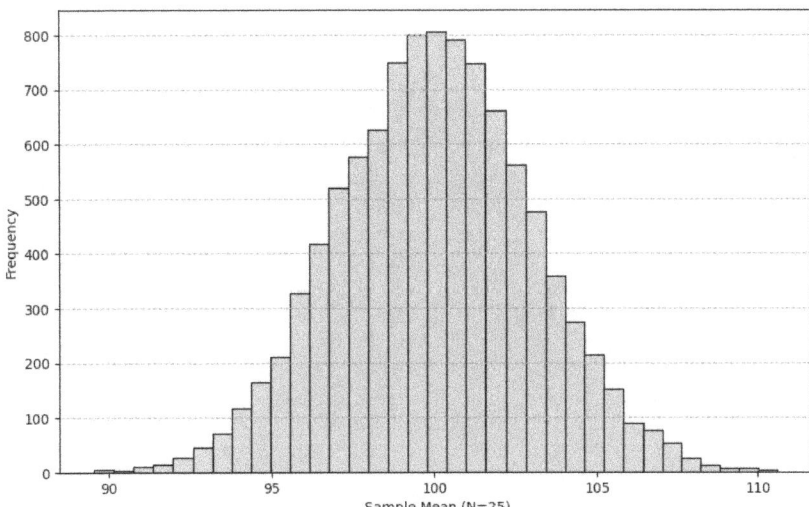

FIGURE 18-5: Sampling distribution of the mean (N = 25) based on 10,000 samples from a normal distribution with μ = 100 and σ = 15.

I leave most of the coding for this histogram as an exercise for you. This line sets up the histogram:

```
plt.hist(sampling_distribution, bins=35, color='lightgray',
    edgecolor='black')
```

The `bins` argument defines the number of intervals of equal width in which to divide the set of 10,000 sample means. The height of each bin — its value on the y-axis — shows how many sample means are in that bin. I picked 35 as the number of bins because I liked the way the resulting histogram looked. Feel free to try other values and see how they affect the histogram.

Chapter **19**

Probability Meets Regression: Logistic Regression

I n this chapter, I explore a type of regression that's different from any regression analysis I discuss in Chapters 14 and 16. The regression I talk about there involves a continuous dependent variable whose value you predict from a continuous independent variable (or from a set of independent variables). You make that prediction on the basis of data on each independent variable.

In this new and different type of regression, the dependent variable is the probability of a "success" of a binary event — like, say, if a person decides to buy a product (success) or not (failure) after spending some time looking at an ad for the product. "Time spent looking at the ad" is the independent variable.

The goal is to estimate the probability of buying the product based on how much time the person looks at the ad. The dependent variable is continuous, but based on what you've learned about probability, you know it has a minimum value of 0 and a maximum value of 1.

This is called *logistic regression*.

As in all regression analyses, you start with data. Table 19-1 shows data for 24 people. The first column shows the time (in seconds) each person spent looking at the ad, and the second shows the outcome — whether they bought the product (1) or didn't (0).

TABLE 19-1

Time (in Seconds) Spent Looking at an Ad and Outcome (1 = Bought the Product, 0 = Did Not Buy the Product)

Seconds	Outcome
10	0
12	0
15	0
17	0
22	0
23	0
23	1
24	1
25	0
28	1
30	0
33	1
35	0
36	0
38	1
40	0
42	0
45	1
47	1
50	1
52	1
53	1
55	1
60	1

Because the only possible values for the dependent variable are 0 and 1, the scatterplot is unlike any you've seen. Figure 19-1 shows the scatterplot.

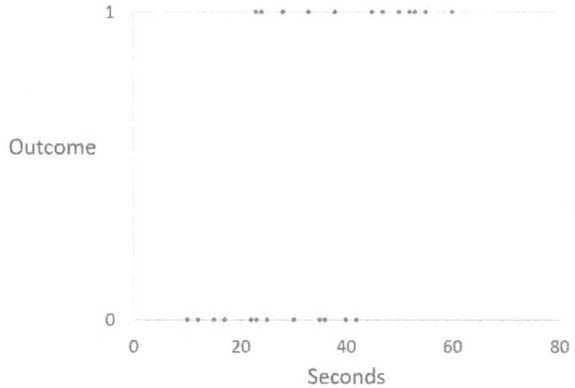

FIGURE 19-1:
The scatterplot for the data in Table 19-1.

What would a graph of a logistic regression model look like? Intuitively, you might think it looks something like Figure 19-2, and you'd be right.

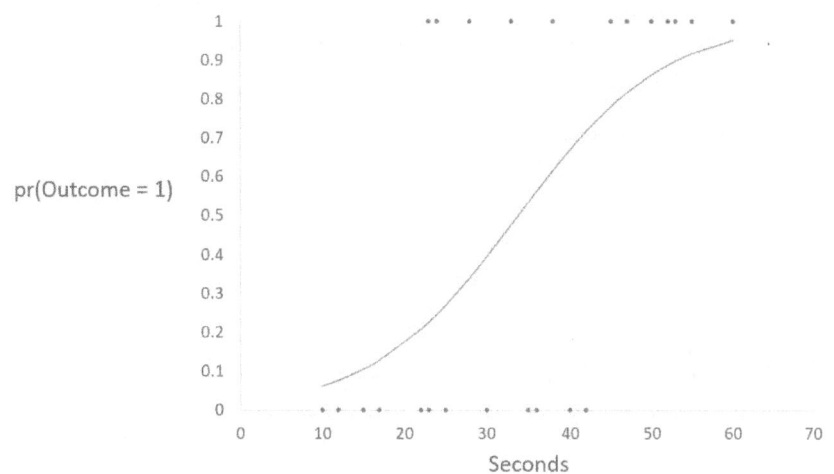

FIGURE 19-2:
Logistic regression model for the data in Table 19-1.

The function (that curved line) in Figure 19-2 is the solution to this equation:

$$\hat{p} = \frac{e^{(a+b*Seconds)}}{1+e^{(a+b*Seconds)}}$$

If you don't know what e represents, read the sections in Chapter 16 describing what a logarithm is and what e is.

TIP

So logistic regression is all about finding values for *a* and *b* that result in the function that best fits the data. In linear regression, the idea is to find the best-fitting line that minimizes the sum of the squared residuals. By contrast, logistic regression finds the best fit by using an algorithm called Maximum Likelihood method repeatedly on the data to converge on the values for the regression coefficients.

I don't discuss the nuts and bolts of how the Maximum Likelihood method works. What I do show you is how to do a logistic regression analysis in Python.

Getting the Data

I begin by building a DataFrame for the data in Table 19-1. I import the library that will create the DataFrame:

```
import pandas as pd
```

Then I set up a list for each variable:

```
seconds = [10,12,15,17,22,23,23,24,25,28,30,33,35,36,38,40,42,
   45,47,50,52,53,55,60]
outcome = [0,0,0,0,0,0,1,1,0,1,0,1,0,0,1,0,0,1,1,1,1,1,1,1]
```

And then pandas does its thing:

```
ad_frame = pd.DataFrame({'seconds': seconds,
   'outcome': outcome})
```

Doing the Analysis

The analysis is based on a statsmodels function called logit(), and it's easy to do:

```
import statsmodels.formula.api as smf
logistic_model = smf.logit('outcome ~ seconds',
   data=ad_frame).fit()
```

For a look at the results, I print the `summary()`:

```
print(logistic_model.summary())

                         Logit Regression Results
==================================================================
Dep.Variable:            outcome  No. Observations:            24
Model:                     Logit  Df Residuals:                22
Method:                      MLE  Df Model:                     1
Date:          Sat, 14 Jun 2025  Pseudo R-squ.:           0.2909
Time:                  12:03:35  Log-Likelihood:         -11.796
converged:                 True  LL-Null:                -16.636
Covariance Type:      nonrobust  LLR p-value:           0.001863
==================================================================
                coef    std err       z    P>|z|   [0.025  0.975]
------------------------------------------------------------------
Intercept    -3.8298      1.610  -2.379    0.017   -6.985  -0.675
seconds       0.1135      0.046   2.484    0.013    0.024   0.203
==================================================================
```

The highlights are the two regression coefficients. The intercept coefficient (-3.82891) and the seconds coefficient (0.11345) tell you that the logistic regression equation for this data set is

$$\hat{p} = \frac{e^{-3.82891+0.11345*Seconds}}{1+e^{-3.82891+0.11345*Seconds}}$$

Each coefficient divided by its standard error results in its z-score. As the listing shows, each z-score has a probability less than .05, so you'd conclude that each z-score is significantly different from 0 — and that each coefficient plays an important role in predicting the probabilities.

How well does the model fit the data? Let's examine some of the terms on the right side of the upper part of the summary. `Log-Likelihood` and `LL-Null` involve some fancy mathematics, so rather than look at them directly, I use them to calculate a couple of statistics that are a bit easier to understand.

Multiply `Log-Likelihood` by -2 and you have *residual deviance*:

```
residual_deviance = -2 * logistic_model.llf
print(residual_deviance)
23.591001270158753
```

Multiply LL-Null by −2, and you have *null deviance*:

```
null_deviance = -2 * logistic_model.llnull
print(null_deviance)
33.27106466687737
```

Deviance is something like variance. In linear regression, variance represents deviation from the mean of the dependent variable or from the regression line. In logistic regression, deviance means deviation from a perfect model that predicts the data points exactly.

In practice, this so-called perfect model doesn't exist, nor should you want it to. To exactly predict every data point, it would have to have as many parameters as data points — and that's useless. Statisticians refer to such a model as *saturated.*

Residual deviance is the deviance of the logistic regression model from the saturated model. It's the deviance that the logistic regression model leaves unaccounted for.

Now imagine a model that only uses the intercept (and nothing else) to make predictions. Null deviance is the deviance of that model from the saturated model.

To help you understand all this, Figure 19-3 shows the logistic regression model, the null model, and the saturated model for the data in this example. (For the coding details, see the next section.)

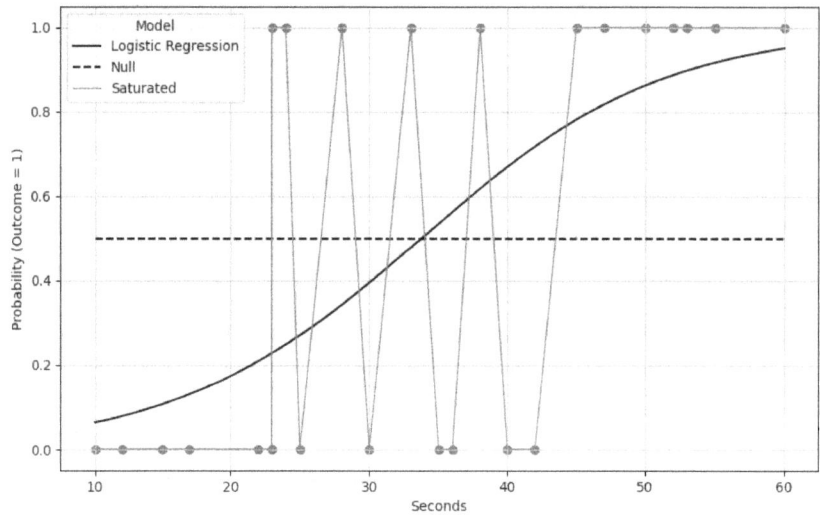

FIGURE 19-3:
The logistic regression model, null model, and saturated model for the data in ad_frame.

You can draw some analogies with variance in linear regression. Null deviance is reminiscent of SS_{Total} in linear regression. Residual deviance is like $SS_{Residual}$ in linear regression — as I say earlier, it reflects how much the model *doesn't* account for. Ideally, you want to see a large difference between the two. That difference is analogous to $SS_{Regression}$ in linear regression — the SS that shows how much the model *does* account for. (See Chapter 14 and Chapter 15.)

Remember, $SS_{Regression} = SS_{Total} - SS_{Residual}$. In logistic regression, the difference between null deviance and residual deviance is analogous to $SS_{Regression}$. It's called *drop in deviance.*

```
drop_in_deviance = null_deviance - residual_deviance
print(drop_in_deviance)
9.68006339671862
```

In linear regression, remember — or go back and look — you calculate R^2 (an indicator of fit) by dividing the $SS_{Regression}$ by the SS_{Total}. Nobel laureate Daniel McFadden pointed out that you can calculate a pseudo R-squared for logistic regression by dividing the drop in deviance by the null deviance:

```
pseudo_r_squared = drop_in_deviance / null_deviance
print(f'{pseudo_r_squared:.4f}')
0.2909
```

It means that the logistic model is an improvement over the null model. By how much? By 29.09% of the maximum possible improvement that the saturated model would provide.

By the way, take another look at the model summary: You'll find this statistic on the right side of the upper part. And now you know what it means.

How do you make sense of the size of the drop in deviance? Is a statistical test available?

Absolutely.

In Chapter 10, I discuss the chi-square distribution as a way of testing hypotheses about variances. (I discuss chi-square again in Chapter 18 in a different context.) It turns out (for reasons too technical to go into) that you can treat the drop in deviance as a value in a chi-square distribution with degrees of freedom equal to the number of predictor variables in the model. If the distribution yields a low probability (less than .05) of a drop in deviance at least as large as the one you observe, you can conclude that the drop in deviance is significant — large enough to indicate that the model fits the data well and is a good predictor, in other words.

The expected value of a chi-square distribution is its degrees of freedom. In this case, df = 1 (because you have one predictor, Seconds). The drop in deviance is 9.680063, so the question becomes "How probable is a value at least as high as 9.68003 in a chi-square distribution whose expected value is 1?"

Short answer: Not very.

Long answer:

```
from scipy.stats import chi2
p_value = chi2.sf(drop_in_deviance, 1)
print(f'{p_value:.6f}')
0.001863
```

You'll find this one in the model summary, too. It's hiding out under the name LLr p-value. And now you know what this statistic means.

Bottom line: That very low probability means it's unlikely that the value of the drop in deviance is due to chance, and the logistic model provides a significantly better fit to the data over the null model.

REMEMBER

Logistic regression is a powerful and increasingly popular tool. To acquaint you with its basics, I've just scratched the surface with this simple example.

Coding the models

I include this section in case you're wondering how to create Figure 19-3.

I begin with the imports:

```
import numpy as np
import matplotlib.pyplot as plt
```

Next, I create the dimensions of the plot:

```
plt.figure(figsize=(10, 6))
```

Then I plot the data points:

```
plt.scatter(ad_frame['seconds'], ad_frame['outcome'])
```

On to the logistic regression curve. I create a range of 100 evenly spaced x values, starting from the minimum value of seconds and ending at the maximum value of seconds:

```
x_range = np.linspace(ad_frame['seconds'].min(), ad_
    frame['seconds'].max(), 100)
```

Then I use `predict()` to calculate the logistic regression probability for each of those 100 x values:

```
logistic_fit = logistic_model.predict({'seconds': x_range})

plt.plot(x_range, logistic_fit, color = 'black', label='Logistic
    Regression', linewidth = 1.5)
```

The value of the `label` argument for this model (and the others) is what appears in the legend to denote that model. I make `linewidth` a bit bigger for the logistic regression model to make it stand out from the others.

If I end the plotting here and skip to `plt.xlabel()`, `plt.ylabel()`, and `plt.show()`, the result would look much like Figure 19-2.

Instead, I add the predicted probabilities for the null model — which is just the average of the outcomes:

```
null_model_fit = [ad_frame['outcome'].mean()] * len(x_range)
```

And then I plot the average as a dashed line across the x range:

```
plt.plot(x_range, null_model_fit, color = 'black',
    linestyle='--', label='Null')
```

Finally, I visualize the saturated model by adding lines that connect the data points:

```
plt.plot(ad_frame['seconds'], ad_frame['outcome'],
    label='Saturated', color = 'gray', linestyle='-', linewidth=1)
```

I finish up by adding the grid, the legend with a title, and labels for the axes, and then showing the plot:

```
plt.grid(True, color - "lightgray")
plt.legend(title = 'Model')
plt.xlabel('Seconds')
plt.ylabel('Probability(Outcome = 1)')
plt.show()
```

Enjoy!

5
The Part of Tens

IN THIS PART . . .

Examine similarities and differences between Python and R.

Harness R graphics capabilities in Python.

Explore online resources for learning Python.

Chapter **20**

Ten Tips for R Veterans

D esigned by and for statisticians (and as a tool for teaching statistical concepts), R has an impressive array of statistical analysis tools. Many people use these tools, which, as the author of several books on the subject, I'm thrilled about.

If you're one of those R aficionados and you need a bit of help transitioning to Python, this chapter is for you. I offer words of advice that might help you make the leap.

Python Libraries Are (Somewhat) Different from R Libraries

As is the case with R, Python's libraries contain functionality that augments the base language. And library() in R is something like import in Python.

The difference lies in the syntax. In R, once library() does its thing, you just go ahead and call its functions. In Python, however, once you import a library, you have to somehow note the library in the function call. That might take some time to get used to.

The next two sections show what I mean.

Python's Statistics Functions Live in Libraries

Important statistical functions are baked into base R. It's straightforward to call them and use them.

Using statistical functions in Python requires a few extras. As I mention in the preceding section, you first have to import a library. For example:

```
import statistics
my_data = [3,4,5,6]
```

Then, to calculate a statistic, you first specify the name of the library, followed by a dot, and then specify the name of the statistical function — or, more properly, statistical method:

```
average = statistics.mean(my_data)
```

In Python, Distributions Also Live in Libraries

Like statistical functions, probability density functions (like the normal distribution) and probability mass functions (like the binomial) are baked into base R. And in Python, like statistical functions, they live in a library — specifically, scipy.stats. Here, for example, is how to create a normal distribution with mean = 100 and standard deviation = 15:

```
import scipy.stats as stats
my_normal_distribution = stats.norm(100,15)
```

To eliminate the need for stats. in front of norm(), you can be more specific about what you import:

```
from scipy.stats import norm
my_normal_distribution = norm(100,15)
```

To operate on the distribution, you'd start with the name of the distribution, followed by a dot, and then add the name of the appropriate method:

```
mu = my_normal_distribution.mean()
```

Dot Notation in Python Is Important

As the preceding sections show, in Python, you use dot notation to access the methods of an object (like the normal distribution I created).

In R, dots don't have that kind of status. For example, in R, you can name a variable `my.variable`.

Don't even think of doing that in Python. The proper format is `my_variable`.

Also, it's a good idea (no matter what language you code in) to use meaningful names for variables. That way, human readers can better understand the code you write.

And speaking of dot notation . . . .

Dot in Python is Much Like $ in R

As R honchos know, in R, you access a data frame column like this:

```
data_frame_name$column_name
```

In Python, you access a Pandas DataFrame column like this:

```
DataFrame_name.column_name
```

But "much like" doesn't mean "exactly like." As I point out in the preceding section, you use dot notation to access a method as well as an attribute. The $ doesn't serve that function in R.

Two Important Libraries: NumPy and Pandas

NumPy (pronounced "numb-pie") stands for *Num*erical *Py*thon. As its name suggests, NumPy is intended for numerical computing — which, of course, is indispensable for statistical analysis. Its simple syntax and collection of functions make it easy to perform complex calculations.

Pandas is a library for data manipulation and analysis. The name comes from *pan*el *dat*a — data sets that consist of multiple observations over time for a group of individuals (a panel). The name also evokes Python data analysis. Among its many capabilities, you use pandas to create DataFrames.

Here's an example of using the two libraries to create a DataFrame:

```
import numpy as np
import pandas as pd
year = np.array([2023,2024,2025])
sales = np.array([700,800,900])
my_df = pd.DataFrame(data={'Year':year,'Sales':sales})
print(my_df)
        Year     Sales
0       2023       700
1       2024       800
2       2025       900
```

What's the story on those curly braces in the my_df statement?

Glad you asked . . . .

Use the Dictionary

The curly braces in the preceding example denote a *dictionary*. This is a Python structure that stores data in key-value pairs. In the example, I create a dictionary for the data argument in pd.DataFrame().

The dictionary consists of the key 'Year' paired with the values in the array year, and the key 'Sales' paired with the values in the array sales.

Creating DataFrames is one of the many applications of this useful structure. You'll find others as you journey through Python.

Learn the statsmodels Library

For R veterans, this is a must. The statsmodels library provides a gateway to well-known R data sets. Here's how it's done:

```
import statsmodels.api as sm
```

Then use `get_rdataset()`. In this example, I get the `Cars93` data set from the MASS package:

```
cars_93 = sm.datasets.get_rdataset("Cars93", "MASS")
```

Finally,

```
cars_93_data = cars_93.data
```

Is `cars_93_data` a DataFrame?

```
import pandas as pd
isinstance(cars_93_data, pd.DataFrame)
True
```

Yes, it is!

Incidentally, if you want to read the documentation for the data set, run

```
help(cars_93)
```

Another reason to familiarize yourself with the `statsmodels` library is that it enables you to use R-like syntax to formulate models in Python, as I do in Chapters 12–14, 16, and 19.

Here's an example from Chapter 14 using the already defined DataFrame called `FarMisht_data_frame`.

```
import statsmodels.formula.api as smf
model = smf.ols('Performance ~ Aptitude', data = FarMisht_data_
    frame).fit()
```

Where Are the Vectors?

The vector is at the foundation of R but is not part of Python. The nearest Python equivalent is a NumPy array. For example,

```
import numpy as np
my_list = [17,18,19,20,21]
my_array = np.array(my_list)
```

You can also use a list (like `my_list`) as a stand-in for a vector, if the list contains only numbers.

A Python Grammar of Graphics

If you're well-versed in R, you've almost certainly worked with `ggplot2`. As R's library for creating sophisticated graphics, it's based on the "grammar of graphics," created by Leland Wilkinson and implemented in R by Hadley Wickham.

Wilkinson's idea is that all graphs have common underlying common components — data, a coordinate system, statistical transformations (like frequency counts), and objects within the graph (like dots, lines, and bars). He proposed a grammar — a set of rules — for combining these components to produce graphs. The `ggplot2` library embodies these concepts.

Although I focus on `MatPlotLib`, and to a lesser extent on `seaborn`, the grammar of graphics approach is available in Python, and it works exactly like the `ggplot2` you remember from R. It lives in a library called `plotnine`, which is preinstalled in Colab.

Just to keep everything in the R family, I use plotnine on the R-based DataFrame from earlier in this chapter (`cars_93_data`). From the data, I create a scatterplot that shows each car's city MPG versus its horsepower. The kicker is that each point in the graph is a number — the number of cylinders in the car's engine. Figure 20-1 shows what I mean (including the rotary engine for one of the cars).

First, the import:

```
from plotnine import *
```

The wildcard character (*) indicates that I import everything in this library.

And now the plot:

```
ggplot(cars_93_data,aes(x='Horsepower',y='MPG.city',
    label = 'Cylinders'))+ geom_text()
```

It's exactly as in R, and that's all there is to it. The `aes()` function (it's called the "aesthetic") maps columns from the data to x, y, and the label. The `+ geom_text` adds the data labels (the cylinders) as a layer on the graph.

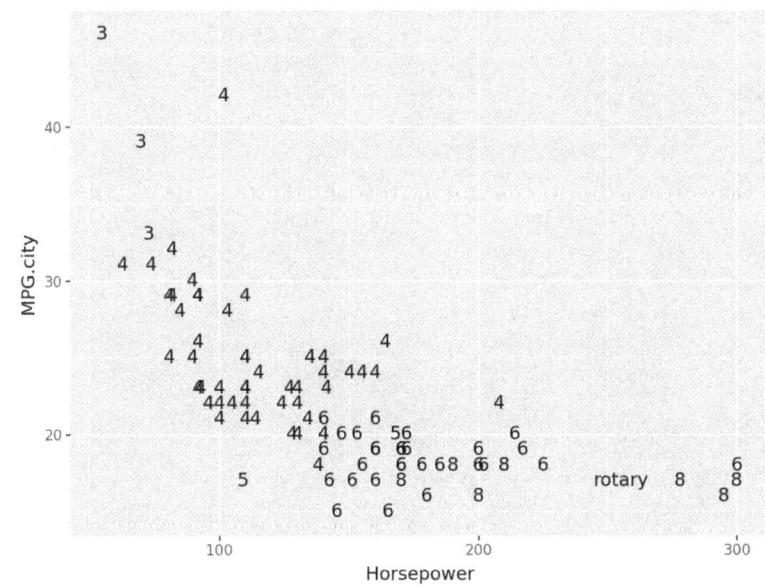

FIGURE 20-1:
MPG.city versus
Horsepower for
the cars in
Cars93 — each
data point is the
car's number of
cylinders.

If you've worked with R, the code will look familiar. (The graph will, too, if you've read the timeless classic *Statistical Analysis with R For Dummies*, written by me and published by Wiley.)

REMEMBER

If you want to use Python to work on `cars_93_data`, be sure to change column-names that have dots like `MPG.city` to `MPG_city`.

Chapter **21**

Ten Valuable Python Resources

P ython has a large, vibrant community. Pythonistas, it seems, enjoy supporting and nurturing others. This chapter points you to some of the many helpful resources the Python community has created.

Python.org

This is the Python community's ultimate welcome wagon. In addition to immediately making you feel right at home in the Python world, it's a gigantic one-stop shop. You'll find downloads, documentation, community news, jobs info, and more.

Python Library Websites

Each major library's website provides a wealth of knowledge about how to use that library. Looking for information about numpy, scipy, and matplotlib? Check out https://numpy.org/, https://scipy.org/, and https://matplotlib.org/. As for pandas, it has a slightly different URL: https://pandas.pydata.org/.

(It turns out that the website for `seaborn` is similar — `https://seaborn.pydata.org/`.) For `statsmodels`, it's `www.statsmodels.org/stable/index.html`.

W3 Schools

Located at `www.w3schools.com/`, W3 Schools presents tutorials on Python and all other major programming languages. You'll also find helpful tutorials on `numpy` and `pandas`.

Pythonbooks

Looking for a book on Python? Visit `https://pythonbooks.org/`. Updated monthly, this list of books covers all aspects of the language. Some of the books show how to apply Python to areas like biology, finance, and engineering. Are you on a budget? You can set a filter to look for free books.

The Python Papers

If you want to stay current on developments within Python, perusing *The Python Papers* is a great way to do it. Located at `https://www.pythonpapers.com/`, this reader-supported newsletter is the brainchild of Python powerhouse Mike Driscoll. Each edition features articles by Mike on a variety of Python-related topics, from website construction to image manipulation and much, much more.

Python for Everybody

This website (`https://www.py4e.com/`) is designed to help you learn Python. It's a growing set of free materials that constitute a free, global online course complete with a grade book, autograded assignments, and discussion forums. And, how can you not want to enroll in a course whose creator, Charles "Dr. Chuck" Severance, drives a racecar in a series called "24 Hours of Lemons"?

KDNuggets

If you learned statistical analysis as a foundation for data science, machine learning, and AI, KDNuggets is for you. (KD stands for Knowledge Discovery.) You'll find, in addition to the aforementioned topics, blog posts on natural language processing, computer vision, and more. To access all this, and data sets too, visit www.kdnuggets.com/.

Geeks for Geeks

This website is loaded with tutorials on Python and associated subjects, like machine learning and data science. Want to brush up on computer science fundamentals? Learn about data structures and algorithms? You'll find all that and more at www.geeksforgeeks.org/.

Real Python

Under the direction of Dan Bader and his leadership team, Real Python (https://realpython.com/) has become a prime go-to site for learning Python. This website offers tutorials, podcasts, courses, quizzes, and entire learning plans. Much of the content is free, and a paid subscription unlocks everything.

The Zen of Python

This is a set of 19 aphorisms to guide you through your Python journey. I won't summarize any further. Instead, it's more, well, zen to show you how to access them. Just type and run

```
import this
```

Then let it all sink in so that you become one with the Python universe . . . .

Index

A

adjusted R-squared, 285
alpha, 138
alternative hypothesis, 15, 138, 159–160
analysis of covariance (ANCOVA), 264–270
analysis of variance (ANOVA), 186, 187–192, 192, 213, 226, 259–264
  contrasts in Python, 195–197
  mixed ANOVA in Python, 221–224
  planned comparisons after, 192–195
  regression and, 249–250
  repeated measures, 199–206
  two-way ANOVA in Python, 215–216
  unplanned comparisons after, 197–199
  visualization, 190–192
  visualizing mixed ANOVA results, 224–225
annotate( ) method, 157
anorexia, 264
a posteriori tests, 198
append( ) method, 34
a priori tests, 193
Aptitude-Performance matchup, 234
arange( ) function, 111
argument, 26
array( ) method, 36
array, creating, 35–36
asymptotic curve, 108
average. *See* mean (average)

B

bar graph, 50–52
bar plot, 224
baseball, 349
bell curve, 105–108
best-fitting line, 237
best-fitting plane, 253
beta, 138
Between Groups variable, 219 220, 226
binomial_dist.pmf( ), 334
binomial distribution, 331–332, 333–335
  hypothesis testing with, 336–338
  negative binomial distribution, 332, 335–336
binomial experiment, 332
binomtest( ) function, 337, 338, 340
bins, 101, 129
bins argument, 50, 361
Boolean, 29
Boston DataFrame, 310–311, 314
box-and-whiskers plot, 56–58
built-in statistical functions, 43

C

Cars93 DataFrame, 47, 48, 49, 63, 71, 81, 87, 93, 101, 306
cdf( ) method, 113, 114, 148, 155, 335, 336
cells, 20–22

center, finding, 61
  mean (average), 61–63
  mean in Python, 63–69
  median, 69–70
  median in Python, 70–71
  mode, 71–72
  mode in Python, 72
central limit theorem, 125, 134, 166
  predictions of, 130–131
  simulations of, 127–129, 359–361
central moment, 95
chi distribution, 109
chisquare( ) function, 349, 352
chi-square distributions, 151, 153
  expected value of, 370
  visualizing, 156–157
  working with, 155–156
chi_square_values, 155
cloud, computing in, 18
Code cell, 21
coefficient of determination, 248, 278, 279
coin-tossing, probability of, 13, 14,
    15, 319–320
Colab, 18–20
Colab environment, exploring, 20
  cells, 20–22
  Gemini, 24–26
  left panel, 22–23
  Menu bar, 23–24
color, 178
column factor, 212
  variance for, 214
comb( ), 327
combinations, 326–327
comment, 39
common logarithms, 292

comparison coefficients, 207
compound events, 321
  intersection, 322–323
  union and intersection, 321–322
conditional probability, 14, 323
  hypothesis testing, foundation of, 324
  working with probabilities, 324
conditional statements, 40–41
confidence interval, 133, 134, 251, 282,
    287, 288, 299, 303
confidence_interval_95, 133
confidence limits, 131–132
  finding, for a mean, 132–134
continuous random variables,
    109, 328–329
continuous variables, 58–60
contrasts, 193
corr( ) function, 281
correlation, 232, 275. *See also* curvilinear
    regression; regression; scatterplots
  hypothesis testing about, 279–280
  multiple correlation, 284–285
  partial correlation, 285–286
  partial correlation in Python, 286–287
  in Python, 280–283
  and regression, 276–279
  semipartial correlation, 287
  semipartial correlation in Python, 288
  understanding, 274–276
correlation coefficient, 275, 279
correlation matrix
  calculating, 281–282
  visualizing, 282–283
counting rule, 325
  Python functions for, 327–328
crosstab( ) method, 103
cubic component, coefficients for, 209

cubic trend, 207
cumulative density
  calculating, 113–114
  percentiles and, 114–115
curvilinear regression, 289
  choice of model, 315
  e, the constant, 292–295
  exponential regression, 301–306
  logarithm, 290–292
  logarithmic regression, 306–310
  polynomial regression, 310–314
  power regression, 295–301

D

data
  getting, 47–48
  types of, 12–13
data exploration, 65–66
`dataframe()` method, 37
DataFrame, 35, 36–37, 103–104, 189, 191, 217, 223, 228, 231, 366, 378
data visualization, 47. *See also* graphics
`ddof`, 78
degrees of freedom (df), 135, 146, 166, 176, 183, 185, 240
delta degrees of freedom, 348
density functions, probability distributions and, 329–331
density plot, 98
dependent variable, 11–12, 219, 234
`describe()` function, 103
descriptive statistics, 10, 93
  DataFrame, 103–104
  frequency, tuning in, 100–103
  `len()` function, 93–94

maximum and minimum values, 94
`moment()` function, 96
moments, 95–100
deviating from average, 73
  conditions, 80–81
  standard deviation, 79–80
  standard deviation in Python, 80
  variance, 74–77
  variance in Python, 78–79
dice, loading, 354–359
dice-rolling, probability, 13, 319–320, 329, 337
dictionary, 29, 33, 378
discrete random variables, 109, 130, 328–329
distribution, modeling, 341
  applications, playing ball with a model, 349–353
  Poisson distribution, 342–343
  Poisson distribution, modeling with, 343–347
  testing the model's fit, 347–349
distributions in Python libraries, 376
docstring, 144, 165
dot in Python vs. $ in R, 377
dot notation in Python, 377
drop in deviance, 369
dummy variables, 262

E

e, the constant, 292–295
`elif` statement, 41
`else` statement, 41
ending index, 31
epsilon, 241

equal_var, 168

error, types of, 16

errorbar() method, 205

error term, ANOVA, 186, 201

estimation, 123

  central limit theorem, 125–131

  confidence limits, 131–134

  sampling distributions, 124–125

  t-distribution, 134–136

events, 320

exp() function, 300, 304

expected value, 130, 358

  of chi-square distributions, 370

experiments, 320

exponential regression, 301–306

F

f.cdf(), 176

f.pdf(), 176, 177

f.ppf(), 176

f.rvs(), 176

factor, ANOVA, 186

Fahrenheit scale of temperature, 12

FarBlonJet Corporation, 132, 134, 343

FarKlempt Robotics, Inc., 147, 151, 167, 173, 339

FarMisht Consulting, Inc., 234

FarMisht_data_frame, 280

FarMisht Personality Inventory, 253

f distribution, 109

F-distributions, 173–174, 186

  in conjunction with *t*-test, 176

  visualizing, 178–179

  working with, 176–177

Fibonacci numbers, 33

figsize, 50

File icon, 23

File menu, 24

first raw moment, 95

Fisher, Ronald, 173

fit() function, 247

float() function, 34

floating-point (float) number, 28

Folder icon, 22, 23

Font (ANOVA factor), 226

forecasting, regression for, 239

for loop, 39, 40, 42, 119, 155, 334–335, 345, 360

fourth central moment, 95

F-ratio, 173, 186, 221, 261, 269

frequency, tuning in, 100

  nominal variables, 101

  numerical and nominal together, 102–103

  numerical variables, 101–102

F-statistic, 248

f-string, 27, 30, 119

F-test, 173, 186, 198. *See also t*-test/t-testing; *z*-test

F-testing for two samples in Python, 175–176

function, user-defined, 42–44

F-value, 230, 304, 312

G

Geeks for Geeks, 385

Gemini, 24–26

general linear model (GLM), 259, 264–270

geometric mean, 68

get_rdataset(), 379

ggplot2 library, 380

GitHub, 17

gmean( ), 68

Google Colaboratory. *See* Colab

graphics, 47

  bar graph, 50–52

  box-and-whiskers plot, 56–58

  continuous variables, 58–60

  data, getting, 47–48

  histogram, 49–50

  pie graph, 53–54

  Python grammar of, 380–381

  scatter plot, 55–56

graphing regression lines, 235–237

groupby( ), 191, 217, 224

group mean, 260

H

harmonic mean, 68–69

heatmap( ), 282

heights_series.var( ), 78

held constant from pair to pair, 160–161

help( ) function, 44

hinges, 57

histogram, 49–50

Horsepower_USA data, 96

Human Resources, 234

Humorous style, 213

hypothesis testing, 14

  with binomial distribution, 336–338

  correlation, about, 279–280

  error, types of, 16

  foundation of, 324

  null and alternative hypotheses, 15

  Python versus tradition, 338–340

hypothesis testing, one-sample, 137

  chi-square distributions, 155–157

  and errors, 137–139

  sampling distributions, 139–141

  t-distribution, 146–150

  t-testing in Python, 147–148

  variance test, 150–152

  variance test in Python, 152–154

  z-score in hypothesis test, 141–143

  z-testing in Python, 144–146

hypothesis testing, two-sample, 159

  building hypotheses, 159–160

  F-distributions, visualizing, 178–179

  F-distributions, working with, 176–177

  paired samples, 171–172

  paired sample *t*-testing in
    Python, 172–173

  sampling distributions, 160–166

  testing two variances, 173–176

  t-testing, 166–168

  t-testing in Python, 168–171

hypothesis testing in regression, 241

  fit, 242–245

  intercept, 246

  slope, 245

I

if statement, 39, 41

import statement, 50

indentation, 39

independent variable, 11–12, 234

inferential statistics, 10, 14

  error, types of, 16

  null and alternative hypotheses, 15

insert() method, 34
int() function, 34
integer (int), 28
interaction, 213
intersection, 322–323
  union and, 321–322
interval data, 12
IQ_dist, 110
IQ score, 88
iterables, 42
itertools, 328

J

James, Bill, 349–350
Jupyter Notebook, 18

K

KDNuggets, 385
Kelvin scale of temperature, 12
kurtosis, 96, 99–100

L

label argument, 371
left panel, 22–23
len() function, 31, 34, 93–94
leptokurtic, 99
level (factor in ANOVA), 187
libraries
  installing, 37–38
  Python's statistics functions in, 376
libraries, Python, 34
  array, creating, 35–36
  DataFrame, creating, 36–37
  library, installing, 37–38

linear regression, 246, 253
  making predictions using
    Python, 250–253
  regression and ANOVA,
    249–250
linestyle, 178
linewidth, 371
linspace(), 58, 59, 110
list, 29, 31
list comprehension, 41–42, 119
LL–Null, 367
loaded_pr(), 354
logarithm, 290–292
logarithmic regression,
  306–310
logistic regression, 363
  analysis, 366–371
  coding the models, 370–371
  getting the data, 366
logit(), 366
Log–Likelihood, 367
long format, 188
looping, 38–40
lower confidence limit, calculating, 133

M

MANOVA, 228, 229
MASS package, 47, 264, 310
matplotlib library, 49, 110, 111, 129, 149,
  156, 169, 170, 178, 224, 268, 344, 380
maximum and minimum values, 94
Maximum Likelihood method, 366
McFadden, Daniel, 369
mean(), 358
mean (average), 61–63, 107

mean in Python, 63
  conditions, 63–65
  data exploration, 65–66
  geometric mean, 68
  harmonic mean, 68–69
  outliers, 67
mean-square, 183–184, 244
Media (ANOVA factor), 226
median, 57, 69–70
  in Python, 70–71
melting, 203, 217
Menu bar, 23–24
meshgrid( ), 259
method, 109
method argument, 90
method variable, 216
Mixed ANOVA, 219–220
  in Python, 221–224
mixed_anova( ), 223
mode, 71–72
  in Python, 72
model.params, 248
model.predict( ), 250, 256, 257
modeling, 341
  applications, playing ball with a
    model, 349–353
  central limit theorem,
    simulating, 359–361
  loading the dice, 354–359
  Monte Carlo method, 353–354
  Poisson distribution, 342–343
  Poisson distribution, modeling
    with, 343–347
  simulation, 353–361
  testing model's fit, 347–349
modulo operator, 39

moment( ) function, 96, 97, 100
moments, 95
  kurtosis, 96, 99–100
  skewness, 96–99
Monte Carlo simulations, 353–354
Move to Panel icon, 25
MSWithin (MSW), 214
multinomial distribution, 347
multiple correlation, 284
  adjusting R-squared, 285
  in Python, 284–285
multiple correlation coefficient, 284
multiple regression, 253
  predictions, making, 256–257
  in Python, 255–256
  visualizing the 3D scatterplot and
    regression plane, 257–259
multivariate analysis of variance
  (MANOVA), 226
  post-analysis, 232
  in Python, 228–230
  visualizing MANOVA results, 230–231
mutually exclusive events, 322
mv_test( ) method, 229

N

Napier, John, 291
negative binomial distribution,
  332, 335–336
negative correlation, 274
New Notebook button, 18, 19
nominal data, 12
nominal variables, 101
norm.interval( ) method, 133
norm.ppf( ) method, 142

norm.sf() method, 145

normal density function in Python, 110

normal distribution, 105. *See also* Poisson distribution; sampling distributions

  bell curve, 105–108

  cumulative density, calculating, 113–114

  parameters of, 107–108

  percentiles and cumulative density, 114–115

  plotting, 110–113

  in Python, 109

  random sampling, 115

  standard normal distribution, 116–120

normalize argument, 102

np.arange(), 111

np.exp() function, 295

np.meshgrid(), 259

np.random.seed(), 115

np.random_seed(sample_count), 360

np.var(), 153

np.var(heights), 78

np array, 327

null hypothesis, 15, 138, 159

numerical and nominal together, 102–103

numerical variables, 101–102

numeric dummy variables, 262

numpy library, 35, 110, 377–378

  arrays, 293

  functions, 78

  methods, 58, 78, 80

numpy quantile() function, 91

O

ols() function, 247

one-tailed hypothesis test, 142, 143

one-tailed *p*-value, 145

one-tailed test, 160

Open Notebook dialog box, 18, 19

ordinal data, 12

outliers, 67

P

paired samples, 171–172

paired sample *t*-testing in Python, 172–173

pairplot(), 282

pandas cut() method, 103

pandas describe() method, 103

pandas library, 35, 377–378

  DataFrame, 64, 81, 103, 202, 228, 295

  function, 78, 80, 280, 366

parameters, 10

partial_corr(), 286, 288

partial correlation, 285–286

  in Python, 286–287

Pascal distribution. *See* negative binomial distribution

pd.DataFrame(), 189

pd.get_dummies() function, 263

pdf() method, 110–111, 148, 155

Pearson, Karl, 275, 348

pearsonr(), 281

Pearson's product-moment correlation coefficient, 275

Pencil icon, 22

percentile() method, 90

percentiles, 90–91

  and cumulative density, 114–115

percent point function, 114

perm(), 327

permutations, 326

Person variance, 204

pie graph, 53–54

pingouin function, 38, 223, 286, 288

pip command, 38

planned comparisons, 193

platykurtic, 99

playing cards, probability of drawing a diamond in, 13

plot() function, 218

plotnine, 380

plt, 49

plt.boxplot(), 191

plt.fill_between(), 112

plt.plot(), 111

plt.show(), 371

plt.tight_layout(), 218

plt.vlines(), 119

plt.xlabel(), 371

plt.xticks(), 111

plt.ylabel(), 371

pmf(), 335, 336

Poisson distribution, 342–345. *See also* normal distribution; sampling distributions

formula for, 343

modeling with, 343–347

polynomial regression, 310–314

pooling, 167

population, 123

samples and, 10–11

population mean, 132

population standard deviation, 79

population variance

estimate of, 135, 146

formula for calculating, 76

positive correlation, 274

post-ANOVA *t*-tests, 193

post hoc tests, 198

power regression, 295–301

ppf() method, 114, 148, 155

predict(), 371

predictions, making, using Python, 250

residuals, plotting, 251–253

scatterplot and regression line, visualizing, 251

Presentation Method, 211, 212

Presentation Style, 211, 212

print() function, 26, 27, 34, 65, 71

printing, 26–28

probability, 13–14, 319

binomial distribution, 331–335

combinations, 326–327

compound events, 321–323

conditional probability, 323–324

events, 320

experiments, 320

formula for, 13

hypothesis testing, Python versus tradition, 338–340

hypothesis testing with binomial distribution, 336–338

negative binomial distribution, 335–336

permutations, 326

Python functions for counting rules, 327–328

random variables, 328–329

sample spaces, 320–321, 325–327

trials, 320

working with, 324

probability density, 107, 330

probability density function, 107, 330

probability distributions and density functions, 329–331

probability mass function (pmf), 333

product rule, 325

pseudorandom numbers, 115

pseudo R-squared, 369

p-value, 152, 153, 154, 168, 173, 175. 281, 304, 312, 337–338

p_value, 210

Pythagorean percentage, 349–350, 351

Pythagorean theorem, 350

Python, 17, 26

  array, creating, 35–36

  binomial and negative binomial in, 332–336

  cells, 20–22

  Colab, 18–20

  Colab environment, exploring, 20–26

  conditional statements, 40–41

  correlation in, 280–283

  DataFrame, creating, 36–37

  dictionaries, 33

  dot notation in, 377

  for everybody, 384

  F-testing for two samples in, 175–176

  function, user-defined, 42–44

  functions, 34

  Gemini, 24–26

  left panel, 22–23

  libraries, 34–38

  library, installing, 37–38

  linear regression in, 246–253

  list comprehension, 41–42

  lists, 31

  looping, 38–40

  mean in, 63–69

  median in, 70–71

  mixed ANOVA in, 221–224

  mode in, 72

  multiple correlation in, 284–285

  multiple regression in, 255–256

  multivariate analysis of variance (MANOVA) in, 228–230

  normal density function in, 110

  normal distributions in, 109

  paired sample *t*-testing in, 172–173

  partial correlation in, 286–287

  printing, 26–28

  ranking in, 89

  repeated measures ANOVA in, 202–205

  semipartial correlation in, 288

  sets, 32–33

  standard deviation in, 80

  standard normal distribution in, 117

  strings, 32

  trend analysis in, 210

  t-testing for one sample in, 147–148

  t-testing for two samples in, 168–171

  tuples, 32

  two-way ANOVA in, 215–216

  variable names, 28

  variable types, 28–30

  variance in, 78–79

  variance test in, 152–154

  vectors in, 379–380

  versus tradition, 338–340

  z-scores in, 86–87

  z-testing for one sample in, 144–146

  z-testing for two samples in, 164–166

Python.org, 383

pythonbooks.org, 384

Python functions

  for counting rules, 327–328

  working with, 34

Python grammar of graphics, 380–381
Python libraries, 34
  array, creating, 35–36
  DataFrame, creating, 36–37
  distributions in, 376
  library, installing, 37–38
  vs. R libraries, 375
  websites, 383–384
The Python Papers, 384
Python resources, 383
  Geeks for Geeks, 385
  KDNuggets, 385
  Python.org, 383
  pythonbooks, 384
  Python for everybody, 384
  Python Library Websites, 383–384
  Real Python, 385
  The Python Papers, 384
  W3 Schools, 384
  zen of Python, 385
Python's statistics functions in libraries, 376

Q

quadratic component, coefficients for, 209
quadratic trend, 207

R

`random.choices()` function, 129
randomization, 115, 357
random sampling, 115
random variables, 328–329
random variates, 115
`rankdata()` function, 89–90

ranking, 89
  percentiles, 90–91
  in Python, 89
  tied scores, 89–90
raw moment, 95
Real Python, 385
Reconnect, 24
`regplot()` function, 251
regression, 233. *See also* curvilinear regression; linear regression; logistic regression; multiple regression
  Analysis of Covariance (ANCOVA), 264–270,
  ANOVA, 259–264
  correlation and, 276–279
  for forecasting, 239
  general linear model (GLM), 264–270
  graphing lines, 235–237
  scatterplot, 234–235
regression, hypothesis testing in, 241
  fit, 242–245
  intercept, 246
  slope, 245
regression, logistic, 363
  analysis, 366–371
  coding the models, 370–371
  getting the data, 366
regression coefficients, 237
regression line, 237, 251, 276–277
  variation around, 239–241
regression plane, equation of, 254
Remember icon, 4
repeated measures ANOVA, 199
  Python implementation, 202–205
  visualization, 205–206
  working with, 200–202

Residual, 204

residual deviance, 367–369

residual error, 240

residual variance, 239

return statement, 43

reverse = True argument, 150

R libraries, Python libraries vs., 375

rng() method, 148

rotation, 52

row-column combinations, 213, 214

row factor, 212

R-squared, adjusting, 285

Runtime, 24

Runtime menu, 23

rv_continuous, 109

rv_discrete class, 109, 332, 357

rvs() method, 115, 155, 335, 357

S

sabermetrics, 349

sample_means list, 129

samples, 123

  and populations, 10–11

sample spaces, 320, 325

  combinations, 326–327

  permutations, 326

  and probability, 320–321

sample standard deviation, 80

sample variance, 77

sampling distributions, 124–125, 134, 160. *See also* normal distribution; Poisson distribution

  central limit theorem, applying, 161–162

  of the difference between means, 160

  hypothesis tests and, 139–141

  of the mean, 124

standard deviation of, 162

  z-testing, 163–164

  z-testing for two samples in Python, 164–166

sampling with replacement, 128

SAT scores, 88

scatterplots, 55–56, 234–235, 237, 251

Scheffé, Henry, 198

Scheffé's test, 198

scipy, 68

scipy.stats library, 109, 188

  function, 147, 148, 168, 172, 281, 332, 337, 348

  methods, 155

scipy library, 67

scipy stats.mode() function, 72

Score ~ Method, 190

seaborn library, 251, 252, 282, 298

second central moment, 95, 96

second raw moment, 95

seed, 115

semipartial correlation, 287

  in Python, 288

sets, 29, 32–33

sf() method, 148

simple main effects, 226

simulation, 353

  central limit theorem, simulating, 359–361

  loading the dice, 354–359

  Monte Carlo method, 353–354

single-factor ANOVA, 186

skewed to the left, 96

skewed to the right, 96

skewness, 96–99

slicing, 31

smf.ols(), 302

Society for American Baseball Research (SABR), 349

sort() method, 70

sort argument, 102

sphericity, 224

squared deviations, average of, 74–77

squaring a deviation, 75

standalone functions, 34

standard deviation, 79, 107, 116, 131, 358
  of a population, 79
  in Python, 80
  sample, 80
  of sampling distribution, 162

standard error, 124
  of the difference between means, 162, 165
  of estimate, 240
  estimated, 134
  of the mean, 124, 132

standard normal distribution, 116, 133
  plotting, 117–120
  in Python, 117

standards, meeting, 83
  ranking, 89–91
  ranking in Python, 89
  z-scores, 84–86
  z-scores in Python, 86–87

standard score, 84, 85, 89. See also z-score

Stanford-Binet score, 116

starting index, 31

statistical significance, 142

statistics, 10. See also descriptive statistics; inferential statistics
  alternative hypothesis, 15

data, types of, 12–13

dependent variables, 11–12

error, types of, 16

independent variables, 11–12

null hypothesis, 15

probability, 13–14

samples and populations, 10–11

statistics functions of Python in libraries, 376

stats.anova_lm() function, 269

stats.binom(), 333

stats.mode(), 72

stats.nbinom(), 335

stats.zcore() function, 87

statsmodels.multivariate.manova, 228

statsmodels library, 188, 189, 204, 247, 366, 378–379

std(), 80, 358

string, 27, 29, 32

sum of squares, 183, 207

T

t.cdf(), 148

t_contrast() function, 210

t.interval(), 135–136

t.pdf(), 148

t.rvs(), 148

t distribution, 109

t-distribution, 134–136, 153

t-distribution for one-sample hypothesis testing, 146–147
  visualizing, 149–150
  working with, 148

Technical Stuff icon, 4

Technical style, 213

testing more than two samples, 181
  ANOVA, 192–199
  ANOVA in Python, 187–192
  meaningful relationships, 187
  problem, 182–183
  repeated measures ANOVA,
    199–205
  solution, 183–187
  trend analysis, 206–210
  trend analysis in Python, 210
testing two variances, 173
  F-distribution in conjunction with
    t-test, 176
  F-testing in Python, 175–176
testing with more than one factor, 211
  analysis, 213–215
  cracking the combinations, 211–215
  interactions, 213
  mixed ANOVA in Python, 221–224
  multivariate analysis of variance
    (MANOVA), 226–232
  post-analysis tests, 225–226
  two-way ANOVA in Python, 215–216
  visualizing mixed ANOVA results, 224–225
  visualizing two-way results, 216–219
test statistic, 173–174
  formula for, 146
  z-score as, 141–143
text cell, 21, 22
third central moment, 95, 96
third raw moment, 95
tick marks, 111
tied scores, 89–90
tilde (~), 190
Tip icon, 4

tradition, Python versus, 338–340
trend analysis, 206–210
  in Python, 210
trials, 320
trim_mean( ), 67
T-score, 88
t_statistic, 210
t-test/t-testing, 166, 174, 182–183, 185,
    193, 282. See also F-test; z-test
  F-distribution in conjunction with, 176
  for one-sample hypothesis testing in
    Python, 147–148
  population variance, estimating, 166–168
ttest_1samp( ), 147
t-test for two samples in Python, 168
  bar graphs, 169–170
  boxplots, 170–171
ttest_ind( ), 168
tuples, 29, 32
t-value, 262, 269
2 X 2 factorial design, 212
two-factor ANOVA, 213
two_sample_z_test( ) function, 166
two-tailed hypothesis test, 142, 143
two-tailed p-value, 145, 168, 173
two-tailed test, 160
two-way ANOVA, 213
  in Python, 215–216
Type I errors, 16, 138
Type II errors, 16, 138

U

union and intersection, 321–322
unplanned comparisons, 198

unstack( ), 217, 224
unstacking, 217
upper confidence limit, calculating, 133

V

values_counts( ) function, 101, 102
van Rossum, Guido, 17
var( ) function, 78–79, 81, 358
variable names, 28
variables, 11–12, 28
Variables tab, 29, 30
variable types, 28–30
variance, 74–77, 358
  for column factor, 214
  in Python, 78–79
  sample variance, 77
variance test, 150–152
  in Python, 152–154
variation, 73
vectors in Python, 379–380
virtual machine (VM), 38
visualization, data. *See* graphics

W

W3 Schools, 384
Warning icon, 4
while loop, 40
Wickham, Hadley, 380
wide format, 188
Wilkinson, Leland, 380

Within Groups variable, 219–221, 226
within-subjects analysis, 205
working with Python functions, 34

X

xticks, 52
x-variable. *See* independent variable

Y

y-variable. *See* dependent variable

Z

zen of Python, 385
zero-based indexing, 31
zip( ) function, 155, 189
zscore( ), 86
z-score, 84, 88, 116, 133, 143, 145, 163, 338, 339, 367
z-score in one-sample hypothesis testing, 141–143
  characteristics of, 84–85
  examples (Bonds versus Bambino), 85–86
  exam scores, 86
  in Python, 86–87
z-statistic, 165–166
z_test( ), 144
z-test, 163–164. *See also* F-test; t-test/t-testing
  for one sample in Python, 144–146
  for two samples in Python, 164–166

About the Author

Joseph Schmuller, PhD, is a veteran of academia and corporate information technology. His books on computing include the three editions of *Teach Yourself UML in 24 Hours* (SAMS), the five editions of *Statistical Analysis with Excel For Dummies*, both editions of *Statistical Analysis with R For Dummies*, and *R All-in-One For Dummies* (all from Wiley). His books have been translated into ten languages, and his LinkedIn Learning courses have been taken by more than 100,000 learners worldwide.

Joseph is a former member of the American Statistical Association, and he has taught statistics at the undergraduate and graduate levels. He holds a BS degree from Brooklyn College, an MA from the University of Missouri-Kansas City, and a PhD from the University of Wisconsin, all in psychology. He and his family live in Jacksonville, Florida, where he works on the AI Automation Development Team at Availity.

Dedication

For Katherine Marie — the love of my life, the girl of my dreams, and my constant inspiration.

Author's Acknowledgments

I've always felt that writing a *For Dummies* book is one of the most fun things an author can do, and this book is no exception. I get to write in a friendly, conversational way, and then I add some humor, and above all, do my best to educate readers.

The Wiley editorial team continues to be at the top of its game. Acquisitions editor Steve Hayes, with the expert assistance of Hanna Sytsma, started it all off and got the band back together. Project editor Paul Levesque did his usual marvelous job of tightening up my writing and, at the same time, coordinated everything that goes into a book like this one. He makes it look easy, and I know it's not. Copyeditor Becky Whitney's wordwise wisdom and editorial skill make it easier to read the words I write. Technical editor Guy Hart-Davis oversaw all things technical and did his usual world-class job of ensuring that the code is correct. Any errors that remain are under the ownership and sole proprietorship of the author.

Guy, by the way, is an accomplished author in his own right (check out his books sometime), and I'm fortunate to have him on the team.

My thanks to David Fugate of Launchbooks.com for representing me in this effort. More than an agent, David is a dear friend.

I could never have written this book without the mentors in college and graduate school who helped shape my statistical knowledge: Mitch Grossberg (Brooklyn College); the late Al Hillix, Jerry Sheridan, the late Mort Goldman, and the late Larry Simkins (University of Missouri-Kansas City); and Cliff Gillman and the late John Theios (University of Wisconsin-Madison). I hope this book is an appropriate testament to my mentors who have passed on.

I dedicate this book to my beloved Katherine. As always, I thank her for her love, inspiration, and support.

Publisher's Acknowledgments

Acquisitions Editor: Steve Hayes

Senior Project Editor: Paul Levesque

Copy Editor: Becky Whitney

Technical Editor: Guy Hart-Davis

Managing Editor: Sofia Malik

Production Editor: Magesh Elangovan

Cover Image: © Phongphan/Shutterstock

12 301